Health Informatics
(formerly Computers in Health Care)

Kathryn J. Hannah Marion J. Ball
Series Editors

Health Informatics Series
(formerly Computers in Health Care)

Series Editors
Kathryn J. Hannah Marion J. Ball

Dental Informatics
Integrating Technology into the Dental Environment
L.M. Abbey and J. Zimmerman

Health Informatics Series
Evaluating the Organizational Impact of Health Care Information Systems,
Second Edition
J.G. Anderson and C.E. Aydin

Ethics and Information Technology
A Case-Based Approach to a Health Care System in Transition
J.G. Anderson and K.W. Goodman

Aspects of the Computer-Based Patient Record
M.J. Ball and M.F. Collen

Performance Improvement Through Information Management
Health Care's Bridge to Success
M.J. Ball and J.V. Douglas

Strategies and Technologies for Healthcare Information
Theory into Practice
M.J. Ball, J.V. Douglas, and D.E. Garets

Nursing Informatics
Where Caring and Technology Meet, Third Edition
M.J. Ball, K.J. Hannah, S.K. Newbold, and J.V. Douglas

Healthcare Information Management Systems
A Practical Guide, Second Edition
M.J. Ball, D.W. Simborg, J.W. Albright, and J.V. Douglas

Healthcare Information Management Systems
Cases, Strategies, and Solutions, Third Edition
M.J. Ball, C.A. Weaver, and J.M. Kiel

Clinical Decision Support Systems
Theory and Practice
E.S. Berner

Strategy and Architecture of Health Care Information Systems
M.K. Bourke

Information Networks for Community Health
P.F. Brennan, S.J. Schneider, and E. Tornquist

Informatics for the Clinical Laboratory
A Practical Guide For the Pathologist
D.F. Cowan

(continued after index)

Ursula Hübner   Marc A. Elmhorst
Editors

eBusiness
in Healthcare

From eProcurement
to Supply Chain Management

With Forewords by Dimitris Karagiannis
and Nancy LeMaster

 Springer

Ursula Hübner, PhD
Professor of Health Informatics
    and Quantitative Methods
University of Applied Sciences
Osnabrück, Germany
and
Faculty Associate
The Johns Hopkins University
School of Nursing
Baltimore, MD 21205 USA

Marc A. Elmhorst
trinovis GmbH
Hannover, Germany

Series Editors:
Kathryn J. Hannah, PhD, RN
Adjunct Professor, Department of
    Community Health Science
Faculty of Medicine
The University of Calgary
Calgary, Alberta T2N 4N1, Canada

Marion J. Ball, Ed.D.
Professor Emerita, School of Nursing
Joint Appointment
Health Sciences Informatics
School of Medicine
Johns Hopkins University
and
Fellow, Center for Healthcare Management
IBM Research
Baltimore, MD 21210 USA

British Library Cataloguing in Publication Data

eBusiness in Healthcare. - (Health informatics)
    1. Medical supplies - Purchasing - Data processing
    2. Hospital purchasing - Data processing
    3. Electronic commerce
    I. Hubner, Ursula II. Elmhorst, Marc 362.1'1'0687

Library of Congress Control Number: 2007929731

ISBN 978-1-84628-878-4   e-ISBN 978-1-84628-879-1

Printed on acid-free paper.

9 8 7 6 5 4 3 2 1

Springer Science + Business Media
springer.com

This book is dedicated to all pioneers of eBusiness in healthcare, both on the side of the healthcare providers, and of the suppliers. Their vision, and the time and resources they invested, not only leads to the implementation of modern supply chains, but also contributes to better patient care.

Foreword

An interchange of solution patterns between different industry sectors such as insurance, banking, and telecommunication has always been quite common. Many solution patterns such as different management approaches, document management, process optimization—or outsourcing as a current example—have successfully been copied and adapted. In my personal experience, this was—and partly is—not the case in healthcare. I vividly remember my own workshops in hospitals at the end of the 1990s where the discussion of (business-) process optimization was met with great skepticism. The healthcare sector is undeniably very specific; just think about aspects such as patients instead of customers, different form of financings, non-profit organizations, etc. Insofar it was possibly on my own account that my workshops in hospitals in the 1990s have not been especially successful.

I have been looking forward to this book, written by experienced practitioners and academics, because it ventures to apply the concepts of "eBusiness" and "Supply Chain Management" to the area of healthcare management, where up to now these terms are not (yet) common practice.

The term "eBusiness," originally coined by IBM, has made quite a history since then. Up to the disillusionment taking place after the turn of the millennium, undreamed-of business opportunities were connected to it. Today it is undisputed that the Internet and its deriving technologies have changed our way of living and working fundamentally. Thus the visions formulated at the end of the 1990s are now step-by-step becoming reality. The definition and application of eBusiness in healthcare is the central theme of this book. However, the authors do not stop at describing already existing eBusiness technologies but also discuss potentials that still lie ahead.

Furthermore, the concept of "Supply Chain Management" strikes attention when reading the title, as indeed intended by the authors. The orientation toward the patient's welfare as the highest priority of every organization in healthcare inevitably leads to the commitment to constantly modernize existing treatment methods and structures. Enhanced by concrete case-studies, the book outlines very practically how the concept of "Supply Chain Management"—originating from the production area—can be applied in healthcare in order to reduce costs and improve processes while quality standards are always maintained.

This book is equally suited to practitioners in healthcare management and to students in this field. I especially like its international orientation. I am confident that all readers across the world will benefit from this book. I will certainly use it in my lectures in various different study programmes.

Dimitris Karagiannis
University of Vienna
Austria

Foreword

In the future, healthcare providers will be unable to achieve their mission of providing high-quality patient care while being good stewards of their community's resources without becoming experts at managing their supply chain. Ensuring consistent, high-quality outcomes means ensuring each patient receives the right product, at the right place, at the right time and at the right cost.

The growing cost of new technology coupled with the aging population means the healthcare industry can't afford to be wasteful. It must develop processes to provide front-line care-givers (physicians and nurses) with the "right" information to make informed decisions. The book provides direction and concrete examples of the strategies that organizations can implement to become experts in supply-chain management. Hopefully, everyone within the industry will continue to collaborate and innovate so that in the future we can insure our supply chain is streamlined and efficient and our focus is on the patient.

Nancy LeMaster
Vice President, Supply Chain Operations, for BJC HealthCare
St. Louis, Missouri
USA

Series Preface

This series is directed to healthcare professionals who are leading the transformation of health care by using information and knowledge to advance the quality of patient care. Launched in 1988 as *Computers in Health Care*, the series offers a broad range of titles: some are addressed to specific professions such as nursing, medicine, and health administration; others to special areas of practice such as trauma and radiology. Still other books in the series focus on interdisciplinary issues, such as the computer-based patient record, electronic health records, and networked healthcare systems.

Renamed *Health Informatics* in 1998 to reflect the rapid evolution in the discipline now known as health informatics, the series continues to add titles that contribute to the evolution of the field. In the series, eminent experts, serving as editors or authors, offer their accounts of innovation in health informatics. Increasingly, these accounts go beyond hardware and software to address the role of information in influencing the transformation of healthcare delivery systems around the world. The series also increasingly focuses on "peopleware" and the organizational, behavioral, and societal changes that accompany the diffusion of information technology in health services environments.

These changes will shape health services in the new millennium. By making full and creative use of the technology to tame data and to transform information, health informatics will foster the development of the knowledge age in health care. As coeditors, we pledge to support our professional colleagues and the series readers as they share the advances in the emerging and exciting field of health informatics.

Kathryn J. Hannah
Marion J. Ball

Acknowledgments

This book is based on the accumulated results and experience of three successive research and development projects, the first of which started almost ten years ago. It was initiated by Johannes Mönter, one of the German pioneers of eBusiness in healthcare, who combines the understanding of revolutionizing supply chain processes in healthcare with the sense of utilizing modern technology. To him we owe the first and continuing opportunity to test solutions practically and conduct research in this field. More application sites were to follow – in particular the University Hospital Göttingen (UKG) and the Medizinische Hochschule Hannover (MHH) - which also provided excellent realistic conditions for answering the research questions and which were extremely helpful when supporting our students and research assistants in collecting the necessary data. We especially thank Detlef Bruer (UKG) and Peter Bernhardi (MHH).

In the very first project, we had to learn right from the beginning that eBusiness in healthcare does not only concern the supply chain managers, but also at least to the same extent the clinicians, in particular the nurses. Gerold Kammeyer, nursing manager at Diepholz District Hospital, and Werner Sander, CEO at Diepholz, made us understand the relevance of up-to-date supply chain data for patient care, as well as for managing the healthcare enterprise.

We also wish to thank our colleagues who contributed to this book by providing excellent chapters. We thank them too for their patience in answering the many emails we sent – some across many hundreds of miles, others just next door.

This book would not have been possible without the extremely kind and reassuring help of Hannah Wilson and Grant Weston at Springer, London, who managed the project marvelously.

The critical discussions and good comments made by the Osnabrück students who read the manuscript in the "Process Management" seminar definitely deserve acknowledgment. Their keen interest in the topic was a great source of motivation to finish the book.

There are many people who contributed to the technical making of the book. We particularly thank Björn Sellemann, Daniel Flemming, and Erling Henze at the University of Applied Sciences Osnabrück for producing figures and tables and for managing the different versions of the digital documents.

Finally, we thank our families who with great patience put up with many "lost" weekends and monosyllable conversations at breakfast while the book was being written.

Ursula Hübner
Marc A. Elmhorst

Road Map

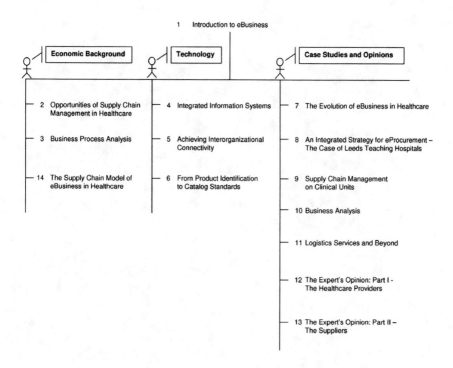

1   Introduction to eBusiness

Economic Background

Technology

Case Studies and Opinions

2   Opportunities of Supply Chain Management in Healthcare

3   Business Process Analysis

14   The Supply Chain Model of eBusiness in Healthcare

4   Integrated Information Systems

5   Achieving Interorganizational Connectivity

6   From Product Identification to Catalog Standards

7   The Evolution of eBusiness in Healthcare

8   An Integrated Strategy for eProcurement – The Case of Leeds Teaching Hospitals

9   Supply Chain Management on Clinical Units

10   Business Analysis

11   Logistics Services and Beyond

12   The Expert's Opinion: Part I - The Healthcare Providers

13   The Expert's Opinion: Part II – The Suppliers

Contents

Part I Elements of eBusiness

Part II Technical Background

Part III   Applications and Experiences

Part IV   Outlook

Contributors

Frank Brüggemann, MD
Gesellschaft für Standardprozesse
im Gesundheitswesen mbH
Hannover, Germany

Karen M. Conway, BA
Corporate Communications
GHX, LLC Westminster, CO, USA

Marc A. Elmhorst
trinovis GmbH
Hannover, Germany

Ursula Hübner, PhD
Faculty of Business Management and Social Sciences
University of Applied Sciences Osnabrück
The Johns Hopkins University School of Nursing Baltimore, MD, USA
Osnabrück, Germany

Volker Gehrnlich, Dipl. Hdl., MBA h.c.
Faculty of Business Management and Social Sciences
University of Applied Sciences Osnabrück
Osnabrück, Germany

Stefan Junginger, PhD
BOC Information Technologies Consulting GmbH
Berlin, Germany

Eva Kabel, Dipl.-BW (BA)
BOC Information Technolgies Consulting GmbH
Berlin, Germany

Keith E. Lilley, BA (Hons), MBA, MCIPS
The University of York
York, UK

Richard A. Perrin, BA, MBA
AdvanTech, Inc.
Annapolis, MD, USA

Michael Schüller, PhD
Faculty of Business Management and Social Sciences
University of Applied Sciences
Osnabrück, Germany

Martin Staemmler, PhD
School of Electrical Engineering and Computer Science
Medical Informatics
University of Applied Sciences
Stralsund, Germany

Gina M. Szymanski, MS, RN
Department of Oncology
The Sidney Kimmel Comprehensive Cancer Center
The Johns Hopkins Hospital
Baltimore, MD, USA

Barbara L. Van de Castle, MSN, RN, APN, BC, OCN
Department of Oncology
The Sidney Kimmel Comprehensive
Cancer Center
The Johns Hopkins Hospital Baltimore, MD, USA

Readers

Alan Hogg, MA (principal reader), University of Applied Sciences Osnabrück, Germany
Abigail Joseph-Magwood, BA (Hons), Postgrad Dipl., University of Applied Sciences Osnabrück, Germany

List of Abbreviations

A

ABAP	Advanced Business Application Programming
ABC	Acitivity Based Costing
ADT	Admission, Discharge, Transfer
AHSC	American Hospital Supply Company
AIDC	Automatic Identification and Data Capture
ANSI	American National Standards Institute
API	Application Programming Interface
AS	Application Server
ASCII	American Standard Code for Information Interchange
ASP	Application Service Provider
ASTM	American Society for Testing and Materials
ATC/DDD	Anatomical Therapeutic Chemical / Defined Daily Dose Classification

B

B2B	Business to Business
B2C	Business to Consumer
BAPI	Business Application Programming Interface
BC	Business Connector
BFI	Business Function Identifier
BME	Federal Association for Materials Management, Purchasing and Logistics (Germany)
BNP	Business Networking Platform
BO	Business Object Type
BPA	Business Process Analysis
BPEL	Business Process Execution Language
BPM	Business Process modeling
BPML	Business Process modeling Language
BPMN	Business Process modeling Notation
BPSS	Business Process Specification Schema

C

C2B	Consumer to Business
CAP	College of American Pathologists

CC	Core Component
CEN	European Committee for Standardisation
CEO	Chief Executive Officer
CHeS	Coalition for Healthcare eStandards
CIO	Chief Information Officer
CIS	Clinical Information System
COINS	Controlling Information System
CORBA	Common Object Request Broker Architecture
CPA	Collaborative Partner Agreement
CPFR	Collaborative Planning, Forecasting and Replenishment
CPH	Collaborative Procurement Hub
CPP	Collaboration Protocol Profile
CPS	Clinical Product Specialist
CSD	Central Supply Department
CT	Computer Tomography
CTQs	Critical to Quality Objectives
CU	Currency Units
CVA	Clinical Value Added
CVAC	Clinical Product Value Analysis Commitee
cXML	Commercial XML

D

DBMS	Database Management System
DCOM	Distributed Component Object Model
DESADV	Despatch Advice or International Advance Ship Notice
DFSS	Design For Six Sigma
DICOM	Digital Imaging Communication in Medicine
DMADV	Define Measure Analyse Design Verify
DMAIC	Define Measure Analyse Improve Control
D-MIM	Domain Message Information Model
DPMO	Defects per Million Opportunities
DRG	Diagnosis Related Groups
DSO	Days Sales Outstanding
DURG	Drug Utilization Research Group

E

EAI	Enterprise Application Integration
EAN	International Article Number (formerly: European Article Number)
EANCOM	European Article Number Communication
ebMSG	ebXML Messaging Service
ebREQ	ebXML Reqirements
ebRIM	ebXML Registry Information Model Specification
ebRS	ebXML Registry Services Specifications
ebTA	ebXML Technical Architecture
ebXML	Electronic Business XML
ECCC	Electronic Commerce Council of Canada
ECCMA	Electronic Commerce Code Management Association
ECHR	Efficient Consumer Healthcare Response
ECR	Efficient Consumer Response

ECRI	formerly the Emergency Care Research Institute
EDI	Electronic Data Interchange
EDIFACT	Electronic Data Interchange for Administration, Commerce and Transport
EDIFICE	Electronic Data Interchange Forum for Companies Interested in Computing and Electronics
EGAR	European Generic Article Register
EHR	Electronic Health Record
EPC	Event-driven Process Chain
EPR	Electronic Patient Record
ERP	Enterprise Resource Planning
ESA	Enterprise Service Architecture

F

FDA	Food and Drug Administration
FI	Financial Information System
FTP	File Transfer Protocol

G

GMDN	Global Medical Device Nomenclature
GDTI	Global Document Type Identifier
GHX	Global Healthcare Exchange
GIAI	Global Individual Asset Identifier
GLN	Global Location Number
GPDS	Global Production and Development System
GPI Classification System	German Proprietary Standard for Medical-Surgical Supplies and Medical Technical Devices
GPO	Group Purchasing Organization
GRAI	Global Returnable Asset Identifier
GSCF	Global Supply Chain Forum
GSG	Gesellschaft für Standardprozesse im Gesundheitswesen
GSRN	Global Service Relation Number
GTIN	Global Trade Item Number
GUI	Graphical User Interface

H

HIBC	Health Industry Bar Code
HIBCC	Health Industry Business Communication Council
HIMSS	Healthcare Information and Management System Society
HIPAA	Health Insurance Portability and Accountability Act
HIS_h	Health Information System used in Hospital
HL7	Health Level Seven
HMO	Health Maintenance Organization
HR	Human Resources
HTTP	Hypertext Transfer Protocol
HTTPS	Hypertext Transfer Protocol Secure
HUG	Healthcare User Group

I

ICD	International Classification of Diseases and Related Health Problems
ICT	Information and Communication Technology
ICU	Intensive Care Unit
ID	Identification Number
IDN	Integrated Delivery Network
IDOC	Intermediate Document
IEC	International Electrotechnical Commission
IHE	Integrating the Healthcare Enterprise
INN	International Non-proprietary Name
IOM	Institute of Medicine (Washington DC, USA)
IOS	Inter-organizational Information System
IP	Internet Protocol
ISBN	International Standard Book Number
ISO	International Organization for Standardization
IT	Information Technology

J

J2EE	Java to Enterprise Edition
JAN	Japanese Article Number
Java EE	Java Platform Enterprise Edition
JIT	Just in Time

K

KLE	Klinik Logistik Eppendorf GmbH
KMS	Knowledge Management System

L

LAN	Local Area Network
LIC	Labeller Identification Code
LIS	Laboratory Information System
LSP	Logistic Service Provider

M

MDC	Material Distribution Center
MHH	Medizinische Hochschule Hannover
MM	Materials Management
MMIS	Materials Management Information System
MOM	Message Oriented Middleware
MRI	Magnetic Resonance Imaging
MRO	Maintenance, Repair and Operations

N

NCPDP	National Council for Prescription Drug Programs
NDC	National Drug Code
NHRIC	National Health Related Item Code
NHS	National Health Service

O

OASIS	Organization for the Advancement of Structured Information Standards
OCI	Open Catalog Interface

ODETTE	Organization for Data Exchange by Tele Transmission in Europe
OECD	Organization for Economic Cooperation and Development
OLAP	Online-Analytical-Processing
OR	Operating Room
OTC	Over the Counter
OU	Organizational Unit

P

PACS	Picture Archiving and Communication System
PASA	NHS Purchasing and Supply Agency
PCN	Labeller Product or Catalogue Code
PICC	Peripherally Inserted Central Line Catheter
PIP	Partner Interface Process
PO	Purchase Order
POAs	Purchase Order Acknowledgement
POES	Physician Order Entry System

Q

R

R&D	Research and Development
RFC	Remote Function Call
RFID	Radio Frequency Identification
RIM	Reference Information Model
RIS	Radiological Information System
RMI	Remote Method Invocation
R-MIM	Refined Message Information Model
ROI	Return of Investment
RPC	Remote Procedure Call

S

SCM	Supply Chain Management
SCOR	Supply Chain Operation Reference-model
SKU	Stock Keeping Unit
SLA	Service Level Agreement
SME	Small and Medium-sized Enterprise
SMTP	Simple Mail Transfer Protocol
SNOMED	Systematized Nomenclature of Medicine
SOA	Service-Oriented Architecture
SOAP	Simple Object Access Protocol
SOC	Standards of Care
SQL	Structured Query Language
SRM	Supplier-Relationship Management
SSCC	Serial Shipping Container Code

T

TCP	Transmission Control Protocol

U

UBL	Universal Business Language
UCC	Uniform Code Council

UDDI	Universal Description, Discovery and Integration
UKE	University Hospital Hamburg-Eppendorf
UMDNS	Universal Medical Device Nomenclature System
UML	Unified Modeling Language
UN/CEFACT	United Nations Centre for Trade Facilitation and Electronic Business
UN/EDIFACT	United Nations Electronic Data Interchange For Administration, Commerce and Transport
UNSPSC	United Nations Standard Products and Services Code
UNDP	United Nations Development Programme
UPN	Universal Product Number
URL	Uniform Resource Locator

V

VAD	Vascular Access Device
VAN	Value Added Network
VMI	Vendor Managed Inventory

W

WFMS	Workflow Management System
WGKT	German Scientific Association for Technology in Hospitals
WHO	World Health Organization
WSDL	Web Service Description Language
WTO	World Trade Organization

X

xCBL	XML Common Business Language
XML	Extensible Markup Language
XPDL	XML Process Definition Language

Y

Z

Other

3LGM^2	Three-Layer Graph-based Meta Model

Trademarks

ABAP is a trademark of SAP AG.

ADONIS is a registered trademark of BOC GmbH

ARIS is a registered trademark of IDS Scheer AG.

ASTM is a registered trademark of The American Society for Testing and Materials.

Baxter is a registered trademark of Baxter International Inc.

BMEcat is a trademark of BME - Bundesverband Materialwirtschaft, Einkauf und Logistik e.V.

BAPI is a registered trademark of SAP AG.

Citrix MetaFrame is a registered mark of Citrix Systems Inc.

CORBA is a registered trademark of the Object Management Group.

Corporate Modeler is a registered trademark of Casewise.

DICOM is a registered trademark of National Electrical Manufacturers Association (NEMA).

Forrester is a registered trademark of Forrester Research Inc.

Gartner is a registered trademark of Gartner Inc.

GHX is a trademark and AllSource is a registered trademark of Global Healthcare Exchange, LLC.

HIBCC is the registered service mark of the Health Industry Business Communications Council.

HL7 is a registered trademark of Health Level Seven (HL7)

HTTP and XML are registered trademarks of the W3 Consortium.

Java is a registered trademark of SUN Microsystems, Inc.

JD Edwards and PeopleSoft are registered trademarks of Oracle Corporation and/or its affiliates.

Microsoft Excel, Microsoft PowerPoint, Microsoft Word and Microsoft Visio are registered trademarks of Microsoft Corporation.

Omnicell and Omni Rx One–Cell are trademarks of Omnicell Inc.

Oracle is a registered trademark of Oracle Corporation.

PAR Excellence is a registered trademark of PAR Excellence Systems Inc.

PIP is a registered trademark of RosettaNet.

ProVision is a product of Proforma Corporation.

PunchOut is a registered trademark of Ariba, Inc.

Pyxis® is a registered trademark of Cardinal Health, Inc.

SAP IS-H is a registered trademark of SAP AG.

SAP NetWeaver is a registered trademark of SAP AG.

SAP R/3 is a registered trademark of SAP AG.

SCOR is a registered trademark of the Supply Chain Council.

Six Sigma is a registered trademark of Motorola Inc.

SNOMED, SNOMED CT and SNOMED RT are registered trademarks of the College of American Pathologists.

UML is a registered trademark of the Object Management Group.
UNSPSC is a registered trademark of UNDP.
WebSphere is a registered trademark of IBM Corporation.
WebLogic is a registered trademark of BEA Systems, Inc.

Part I
Elements of eBusiness

1
Introduction to eBusiness

Ursula Hübner

Executive Summary

General Remarks

When speaking about eBusiness as applied to the healthcare market, two questions arise immediately. First, what is eBusiness? Second, why is eBusiness in healthcare different from eBusiness in other industries? In this chapter, we shall give an overview of the foundations of eBusiness, explain the importance of eBusiness within the healthcare domain, and describe the peculiarities of the healthcare market. This chapter acts as a framework for the topics in the following chapters, and describes the context of the economic and business issues, the technologies, and their applications which will be further elaborated in those chapters.

It is the goal of this book to raise the awareness of, and interest in, electronically mediated business processes in healthcare in a large audience of managers, clinicians, pharmacists, scientists, and students. Within the arena of eBusiness in healthcare, we focus on purchasing and selling online as the most advanced application. Here we shall consider both the perspective of the healthcare providers and that of the suppliers, showing the interdependencies between the two and developing concepts for a new synergistic cooperation. By taking an international approach to the topic, our aim is to demonstrate the many similarities of eBusiness problems and their solutions among the different countries and to permit analysis of the differences that are often defined by the national healthcare systems and their rules. Case studies from healthcare institutions and suppliers in the United States, the United Kingdom, and Germany will illustrate the achievements, barriers, and future plans, thus enabling newcomers to learn from previous experiences. This book explicitly addresses clinicians by demonstrating the interconnection between patient care processes and management issues at the level of medical supplies. It makes a plea for a multidisciplinary effort, so that the right product is procured for the right patient, at the right time.

As a rather new discipline, eBusiness in healthcare needs further scientific backing. Against this background, this book will not only provide answers, but will also raise questions for future research. Managing change and innovation, and establishing the critical mass for eBusiness in healthcare is a major undertaking. The aim of this book is to support this process.

eBusiness – An Introduction

eBusiness is not simply the electronic version of conducting business. It does not merely apply new technology to old structures and processes. eBusiness enables a variety of new types of relationships between customers and suppliers from closely interwoven relationships in supply chains to loose, transient relationships mediated by electronic marketplaces. Building upon existing definitions, we understand eBusiness as a global concept that includes all internal and external business processes of an organization that aim at facilitating business by connecting the business partners and that integrate and synchronize the necessary electronic media. Benefit arises from eBusiness in terms of reduced costs for operating in the market (transaction costs), in particular reduced process costs, and improved knowledge sharing.

Within eBusiness, eCommerce is dedicated to electronic trading with its classic business-to-business (B2B) and business-to-consumer (B2C) relationships. Among the many different technical and organizational approaches for connecting the business partners, electronic marketplaces play an important role. They are either forums–understood in its literal meaning–for presenting goods and negotiating prices, or they act as technical hubs for providing connectivity and applications.

In either case, the underlying technology goes far beyond simple email exchange via the Internet. Workflow-oriented systems with well-defined interfaces that support standards and provide secure data exchange are a prerequisite for exploiting the benefit of eBusiness.

To date, after the initial economic turbulence, eBusiness is a well-established and growing part of the economy in many countries. Online trading among firms (B2B) holds the greatest share of eCommerce, both in terms of financial volume and number of firms active in the field. B2C–though better known by the public– is only successful in certain sectors (e.g., tourism and some subsectors within the retail trade) and comprises a smaller volume than B2B. The larger a company is, and the higher its level of information and communication technology (ICT) use is, the more active it is in eBusiness. Company size and the level of ICT are not independent of each other, however. Larger companies have typically more ICT, which hints at the strong overall impact of ICT on eBusiness. The same holds true for countries: eBusiness flourishes in countries with an excellent technical infrastructure but also with a supportive political, social, and economic environment.

eBusiness in Healthcare

eBusiness has become a fact of life in all sectors, including healthcare. Statistics trying to reflect these activities and trying to compare healthcare with other sectors, however, fail to achieve their aim. This is because healthcare is different from other industries in many respects and its market is exactly defined by these peculiarities.

Supporting electronic processes in healthcare has a long tradition, as in telemedicine, for example. eHealth is the term most commonly in use today and it embraces all aspects of providing connectivity for care, contents, and commerce in healthcare. eBusiness in healthcare is the subset within eHealth that covers the commerce domain. We therefore define all electronically supported processes of healthcare providers originating from business management, and all processes of suppliers and manufacturers in healthcare, as eBusiness in healthcare. In accordance with the customs of the healthcare market, we speak of eProcurement (online purchasing) when describing the healthcare providers' side and of eCommerce (online selling) when referring to the suppliers' side.

The healthcare market–in particular, the medical supplies market–is highly specific, and electronic media that support online purchasing and selling must be built to account for these circumstances. Procuring medical supplies, including drugs, medical-surgical products, medical devices and other products that either stay with the patient or are directly used in the patient care process requires detailed product and process knowledge. This is also true for so-called "simple commodities." In no other sector than in healthcare are products also purchased by the process owners–i.e., the clinicians and the pharmacists. Technical and organizational procedures in eBusiness in healthcare must therefore take the knowledge factor into account when automating the supply chain.

There are only a few other industries besides healthcare in which poor outcomes have such tremendous consequences, including death. This strongly influences the customers' behavior. Healthcare providers must operate in a quality driven way (also in terms of product quality) because their customers, the patients, base their decisions on quality rather than on price. The costs of care, however, including the costs of medical supplies, are an important factor for staying in business and play a major role in today's healthcare politics. Reduced process costs on the healthcare providers' side as well as the suppliers' side are therefore a major driving force and motivation for adopting eBusiness procedures by both parties. Unlike in other industries, prices of goods such as medical supplies are not negotiated online. This is why the classic exchange model of electronic marketplaces has never been accepted in healthcare and why reducing prices is achieved by volume bundling rather than auctions.

eBusiness in healthcare is special because healthcare is special and it needs the combined endeavours of its stakeholders to gain momentum.

The Foundations of eBusiness

Business in a Networked World

There is more to eBusiness than purchasing or selling via the Internet, and its results extend beyond simple process automation. Switching from a paper-based paradigm to an electronic paradigm always combines unknown opportunities with the necessity of re-engineering major structures and processes within an organization. eBusiness, in particular, allows thinking in terms of new and altered business relationships and networked cooperation between customers and suppliers. Not only can customers and suppliers get into contact more directly with each other (disintermediation), but also new types of organizations such as electronic marketplaces come into existence (reintermediation), offering catalogs, auctions, and exchanges. Old confines of enterprises break down to give way to virtual enterprises. Many of these strategies are inspired by technology, namely the Internet with its potential for enabling improved searching and transmitting of information. After the early years of eBusiness, which were characterized by wildly exaggerated promises and the eventual crash of many "dot-com" businesses, the surviving firms have consolidated and electronic business has both become pervasive in many traditional companies and has had an impact on their bottom lines. Empirical evidence indicates that eBusiness initiatives lead to improved economic performance in terms of a higher gross margin and bigger revenue per employee [1]. From the perspective of economic theory [2, 3], web-enabled technologies shape the nature of conducting business by influencing cost and resources structures–in particular, by

  (i) decreasing transaction costs, or costs associated with operating in the market–in particular, information-processing transaction costs (Transaction Cost Theory)
 (ii) improving knowledge sharing among business partners (Network Theory)
(iii) causing greater information transparency of some internal resources, forcing the firm to rethink its strategy and to redefine its core resources (Resource-based View)

Furthermore, the eBusiness literature recognizes the opportunity of allowing access to a market share not confined by geographical constraints, thus enhancing the overall scalability of the business approach [2].

There are many definitions of eBusiness. Most of the recent definitions agree on a global understanding of the term, emphasize the use of electronic media irrespective of their particular nature (Internet, classic EDI, webEDI, and others) and pursue the idea of business networks [4]. Based on a summary of existing definitions, eBusiness will be understood here as a concept that orchestrates all electronic means for conducting business, including all internal and external business processes of an organization that are aimed at networking business partners and their customers.

In eBusiness jargon, the relationships between different types of business partners such as business organizations (B), consumers (C), and government agencies (G) are typically denoted by <business partner>2<business partner>, and expressions like B2B or B2C have become commonly accepted. The set of combinations between possible business partners is often visualized in a matrix as shown in Table 1-1.

Not only are there different business approaches, products, and services behind these acronyms but also different technological requirements. Whereas B2B needs integrated enterprise resource planning (ERP) systems for fully exploiting the potentials of eBusiness, B2C solutions can be set up employing online shops with interactive web pages for interfacing with the customers.

TABLE 1-1. Customer/supplier matrix in eBusiness, including examples.

| | | Customer/Buyer/Recipient | | |
		Consumer/Citizen	Business	Government
Supplier/ Provider	Consumer/ Citizen	C2C electronic auctions (Ebay.com)	C2B selling used car to dealer	C2G online filing of tax forms
	Business	B2C selling books online (Amazon.com)	B2B electronic supply chain in automotive industry (Covisint.com)	B2G online filing of tax forms
	Government	G2C reservation service for federal parks (recreation.gov)	G2B call for bids (e-vergabe.bund.de)	G2G disaster management (disasterhelp.gov)

As reflected in recent publications [10], it has become common to distinguish eCommerce from eBusiness as a subset of the latter that focuses on the selling of products and services with the help of electronic means. In the context of eCommerce, one of the most powerful solutions is eProcurement. It embraces all business-to-business transactions focusing on online purchasing, and describes business activities from the buying side rather than the selling side. Systems bringing together multiple buyers and sellers are known as electronic marketplaces. In the early days of eBusiness, electronic marketplaces were regarded as a means mainly for coordinating multiple open, on-the-spot trading opportunities. As a consequence of marketplace type relationships, close bonds established between firms fell apart in favor of loose, arm's length types of cooperation governed by the market [5]. As eBusiness grew more mature, the picture of electronic marketplaces became more differentiated and today there are many different ways of classifying electronic marketplaces [6, 7]. Markus and Christiaanse [3] distinguish between transaction (negotiations, exchanges and auctions) and collaboration marketplaces (information and knowledge sharing for planning and forecasting), depending on the type of processes they support. Whereas transaction marketplaces tend to serve processes ranging from attracting information and negotiating to performing transactions, collaboration marketplaces tend rather to support fulfilling orders and rendering services.

The different types of marketplaces have different effects on the relationships among firms. Although some types of marketplaces cause the destruction of matured relationships, others help to tighten those same types of relationships by interleaving the business processes. Attempts to create strong, long-lasting links constitute the concept of supply chains which, though closely related to eBusiness, regard technology as only one of the building blocks of an overall strategy for dissolving boundaries between enterprises. In fact, supply chains existed before web-enabled technologies emerged. Through the high degree of connectivity enabled by open networks and the use of standards, however, supply chains now permit an even better and unrestricted flow of information between the enterprises involved, thus enabling forecasting and advanced planning based on information from the downstream section of the supply chain. Collaborative planning in manufacturing and replenishing vendor-managed inventories are good examples of processes that benefit from undistorted real-time information on the current demand for goods.

Adopting new technology is a proven method of transforming organizations. As a catalyst for formal, systematic, and structured approaches, information technology fosters the implementation of well-defined methods, clear rules for decision-making, lean processes, consistent data, coherent planning, and rigorous analysis of all information available for achieving the best possible outcome. Intraorganizational transformations, at the level of process and information management in particular, must precede the external changes. Only then can the benefit of eBusiness be unfolded.

The Role of Process and Information Management

Not only in eBusiness do modern approaches to conducting business refer to processes rather than functions, and strive towards streamlining internal and external processes with the goal of becoming more suitable for satisfying customer needs. Information and communication technology (ICT) has become both a tool and an enabler for re-engineering processes and for achieving a smooth flow of information. As eBusiness is unthinkable without suitable processes, the adoption of eBusiness approaches indeed often goes hand-in-hand with business process re-engineering.

ICT is still regarded as a competitive advantage of companies despite recent statements challenging this fact [8]. It was argued that ICT has become commonplace in firms and no longer permits any differentiation between them. Although the use of ICT is very widespread, ICT does not always mean ICT. Adequate ICT infrastructure is one of the key prerequisites for implementing eBusiness. As a result, research into the readiness of companies for eBusiness includes indicators such as the use of ERP systems, narrowband and broadband access to the Internet, and a presence on the web for predicting the amount and type of eBusiness activities such as selling or buying online. Whereas access to the Internet in companies from industrialized countries is high [9, 10], the use of sophisticated information systems, such as ERP systems and supply chain management (SCM) systems, has not yet reached the level of penetration necessary for completely replacing paper-based trading with electronic trading.

The "eBusiness w@tch" survey conducted in 2005 [10] in the European Union shows that only 28% of all companies in the EU 7 countries (UK, GE, IT, FR, SP, CZ, and PL) use ERP systems, only 19% use specific ICT solutions to support procurement processes, and only 15% use SCM systems. The figures demonstrate that sophisticated business ICT and its use are not commonplace and still merit our attention and interest.

What is the Status Quo of eBusiness?

There are many salient examples of eBusiness that illustrate the existence of online business in our daily life (see Table 1-1). It is much harder, however, to trace the degree (and therefore the success) of electronic business transactions in statistical data [11]. As a result, figures must be handled with care, especially when it comes to comparing data. Nonetheless, general trends have become obvious over the last few years since the so-called Internet hype.

First, B2B scenarios outnumber B2C applications, not only in absolute terms but also in the proportion of overall business. In the United States, B2B accounts for 90% of all online transaction volume and the percentage of electronic wholesale trade exceeds that of electronic retail trade by almost 10 times [12]. In Canada, only 75% of the total amount of eCommerce in private firms can be attributed to business transactions between firms [13]. In the European Union (EU), more than 50% of the firms purchase online, with variations depending on sector. Because eProcurement is a major use case of B2B, the data reflect the prevalence of B2B. In contrast, only 17% accept online orders (B2C) [10].

This might seem surprising at first glance. With its roots in EDI-enabled transactions, however, B2B looks back on a much longer history than B2C. Eighty-five percent of eCommerce sales in commercial wholesale trade are still EDI-based [14].

Second, there is a big variation between distribution channels as to whether electronic means are employed for buying and selling. In the United States, mail orders and electronic shopping, where about one third of the sales is based on electronic transactions (see Figure 1-1), have a top ranking. Within this channel, "books and magazines" are number one, closely followed by "office equipment and supplies" and "electronics and appliances." [14]

Third, company size has a strong influence on purchasing and selling online with larger companies being more active in all types of eBusiness [9, 10]. One of the underlying factors is ICT infrastructure. As larger companies tend to be better equipped with sophisticated information systems and to be better connected, they have a sounder basis for conducting electronic business.

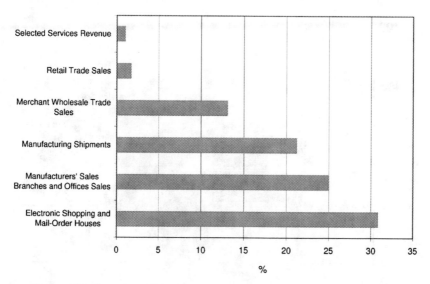

FIGURE 1-1. Percentage of eCommerce value of total value in the United States [14].

Fourth, there is also a considerable variation between business sectors. According to the eBusiness Index [10], IT services, the automotive industry, and pharmaceutical companies come off well (first three places). The differences between the sectors can again be explained by differences in the ICT infrastructure of the firms: the better the ICT infrastructure, the more eBusiness activities take place (see Figure 1-2).

Fifth, online buying and selling is a growing market. Although there are variations in the rate of increase among sectors, eBusiness activities are gaining more and more ground. This holds true for B2B as well as for B2C. Retail eCommerce sales, although still below 5%, have been climbing steadily since 1999 [15]. In specific markets, B2C may gain momentum, as developments from tourism such as online reservation of hotel rooms and flight tickets suggest [10, 12].

Sixth, eBusiness flourishes in countries that provide a supportive environment in terms of technological, social, political, and business issues. On the macroeconomic level, eReadiness is a country's ability to promote and support all facets of the digital economy, including eBusiness and ICT services [16]. eReadiness is expressed as a composite value which aggregates quantitative and qualitative measures of the digital performance of nations. Among other indicators, broadband infrastructure and Internet security, as well as education and training in ICT, contribute to it. Figure 1-3 shows the 2006 results of selected countries among the top 30 of 65 countries.

Seventh, as digital information streams between businesses are becoming more integrated, the importance of eBusiness standards is becoming paramount [17]. EDI used to be the standard choice in communication between limited numbers of well-defined business partners. This has changed dramatically with the advent of the Internet. Not only is there a need for standardized business transaction protocols, but also for standardized catalog formats and classification systems for products and services. New XML-based transaction standards are emerging and competing for market share. All the same, there is a need for a unified approach. In view of this, the United Nations (UN/CEFACT Forum)

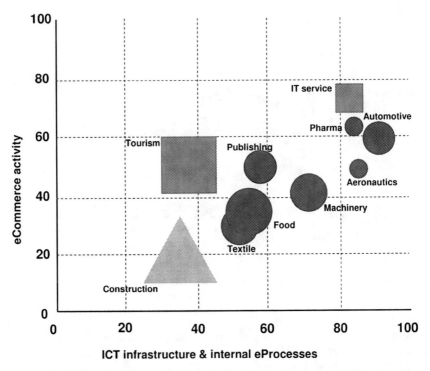

FIGURE 1-2. eCommerce activity vs. IT infrastructure and internal e-processes in different sectors for EU 7 countries [10] (circle = manufacturing, triangle = construction, square = services).

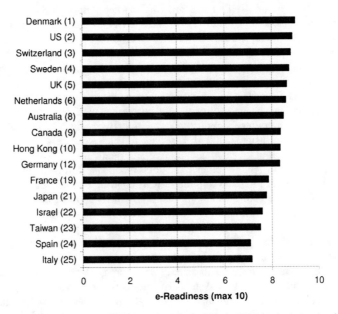

FIGURE 1-3. eReadiness coefficient of selected countries in 2006 (ranks in brackets) [16].

has started developing ebXML, with the goal of providing a global cross-sector solution that should finally replace the variety of other standards [17]. On the level of product and services classification systems, the UNSPSC promises an extendable all-product approach. It remains to be seen which of the different measures will eventually succeed. It is clear, however, that the absence of widely accepted standards causes a threat to the diffusion of eBusiness.

In summary, eBusiness is becoming a well-established and growing part of the economy in many countries. By far the biggest contribution originates from B2B trans-actions within business networks such as supply chains. eBusiness activities and ICT infrastructure are not only closely associated at national levels but also at corporate levels, where the use of broadband networks and sophisticated business information systems (ERP and SCM systems) that integrate standards, pays off.

eBusiness in Healthcare – Simply a New Word in the Jungle of Terms?

Some Definitions

eBusiness, which supports all (business) processes of an enterprise by providing an electronic means of accomplishing those processes, is a generic approach independent of the application sector. In principle, the term could therefore be used for all electronically supported processes in any type of healthcare enterprise–from healthcare providers to manufacturers in the healthcare industry. This understanding of eBusiness in healthcare, however, is very uncommon, as there are other terms such as *telemedicine* that explicitly stand for electronic communication processes between healthcare providers and between healthcare providers and patients. A more comprehensive term than telemedicine is *health(care) telematics*, which embraces all types of communication processes and includes all health professionals rather than just a single profession. *Telematics* is a technology-oriented term emphasizing the convergence of **tele**communications and infor**matics**. In conjunction with healthcare, it describes the technological driving forces behind healthcare. With the advanced use of the Internet, the term *eHealth* emerged as one of the many neologisms with the "e" prefix. It bears a certain resemblance to eBusiness. Its definitions range from *healthcare industry's component of business over the internet* to *e-Health is the process of providing healthcare via electronic means*, referring either to business or to patient care only [18]. One of the most widely accepted definitions [19], however, goes further and positions eHealth in *the inter-section between medical informatics, public health and business*. We will not redefine eHealth in this book, but rather will join forces with the authors who have a broad understanding of the term and for whom eHealth is an umbrella under which all healthcare-related processes and their electronic support gather. It is worth mentioning that eHealth is the first term in the healthcare domain that explicitly relates to business subjects and that therefore opens the mind to the business layer within the healthcare complex.

So what is business in healthcare? First of all, the meaning of business is independent of the purpose of the business: there are profit and non-profit business models, in general and also in healthcare. When talking about business, we primarily refer to business processes within an organization and between organizations.

Second, what is usually understood by *business processes* depends on the type of the healthcare enterprise or organization because business processes describe the core business of the enterprise. From the perspective of the healthcare providers, patient care constitutes the core business, in case of teaching hospitals also education and training, and research and development. In order to distinguish eBusiness in healthcare from eHealth we will subsume only management related issues of patient care, education and training and research and development by eBusiness in healthcare. This comprises all management functions and processes, such as accounting and finance, controlling, purchasing, logistics (including materials management), marketing, asset and facility management, and human resource management. From the suppliers' perspective, all their processes belong to the business domain including production and production planning in the case of the manufacturing industry. Finally, from the payers' perspective all business processes using electronic resources belong to eBusiness in healthcare.

Fourth, individuals can also have business relations with healthcare or wellness enterprises. In this role, they act as customers or consumers. Typical examples of this type of relationship are filling a prescription at a pharmacy or booking sessions with a masseur.

Nearly every type of business process or business relationship in healthcare can be supported by electronic means. As in the case of eBusiness in general, a distinction between the different customers, buyers, or recipients and the suppliers or providers gives a good insight into the various stakeholders and their interactions. It needs to be supplemented, however, by the healthcare providers, the payers (insurance companies, health maintenance organizations, sickness funds, government programs, national health service, etc.), and some specifications.

Assuming that eHealth covers all electronic interactions in the healthcare arena, *eBusiness in healthcare* is a subset of this, and is therefore understood in a much narrower sense than eBusiness in general. We therefore define electronically supported processes originating from the business management domain as eBusiness in healthcare.

Here the flow of clinical information between healthcare providers themselves, and between individuals and healthcare providers in the context of admission, treatment/care, discharge, and transfer of patients is explicitly excluded from what we mean by eBusiness in healthcare. As expanded on in Chapter 2, these processes are called the primary activities of the healthcare value chain, whereas the processes we refer to as eBusiness processes in healthcare are called support activities. Support and primary activities are not independent of each other, but rather are interlinked and cross-influence each other as is shown in Chapters 9 and 10.

In principle, any of the cells in Table 1-2 can be labeled eBusiness in healthcare, as long as the above definition holds true. Some of the cells already contain more or less established cases of use, while others contain piloted or still experimental applications. As this field is highly innovative, and new business models are being established, it is expected that new scenarios will emerge in the future and will fill many, if not all, matrix cells.

Among the more established cases of use are all bidirectional and multidirectional communication processes of healthcare providers with suppliers of products and services (H2B/B2H), as well as between the suppliers themselves (B2B) and healthcare providers themselves (H2H) who cooperate under one business scheme. An example of H2B/B2H is the online purchasing and selling of medical supplies. Further scenarios of a similar maturity are interactions between healthcare providers and the payers (H2P/P2H) in accordance with the Health Insurance Portability and Accountability Act (HIPAA) transaction standard in the United States [20] or with §301 Social Code Book (SGB) V in Germany. The diffusion of the Internet in private households strengthens individuals

TABLE 1-2. Customer/supplier matrix of eBusiness in healthcare.

| | | Customer/Buyer/Recipient | | | | |
		Consumer/ Citizen/ Patient	Business	Government (in general)	Payers	Healthcare Provider
Supplier/ Provider	Consumer/ Citizen/ Patient	C2C	C2B mail-ordering patient appliances	C2G	C2P general inquiries	C2H online pharmacy
	Business	B2C mail-ordering patient appliances	B2B supply chain	B2G	B2P	B2H supply chain
	Government (in general)	G2C information	G2B about	G2G new	G2P regulations	G2H and acts
	Payers	P2C reimbursements	P2B	P2G	P2P reimburse- ments	P2H claim management
	Healthcare provider	H2C marketing	H2B supply chain	H2G	H2P claim management	H2H marketing

in their roles as consumers exchanging business information electronically with either type of healthcare enterprise or organization. One of the most widely discussed examples is the Internet or online pharmacy [21].

In conclusion, we define eBusiness in healthcare as the combination of all electronically supported processes aiming at the exchange of business information in healthcare between one or more customers/buyers/recipients and their suppliers/providers (Table 1-1). Figure 1-4 summarises the relationship between eHealth, eBusiness, and eBusiness in healthcare. eBusiness in healthcare is an integral part of eHealth and applies methods and tools of eBusiness to the healthcare market, paying tribute to its peculiarity.

Within the realm of eBusiness in healthcare, procurement (H2B) and sales cases of use (B2H and B2B) have become established over the last few years and illustrate the principles of eBusiness very well. This corresponds to similar developments in eBusiness generally, where eProcurement is one of the best known and best explored applications of eBusiness.

In contrast to other business sectors, however, eCommerce in healthcare is a term only used by the manufacturers but not widely in use among healthcare providers. We therefore refrain from using eCommerce as an overall framework, as it is not suitable for uniting the perspectives of the industry and the healthcare providers. Instead, we shall follow the conventions of this market and shall speak of eCommerce when describing the suppliers' side, and use eProcurement when referring to the healthcare providers' side.

Procuring and Providing Medical Supplies

Among the products procured by the healthcare providers, medical supplies play an extremely important role because they are the ones that are essential for the care process–the primary process with any healthcare provider. The term *medical supplies*

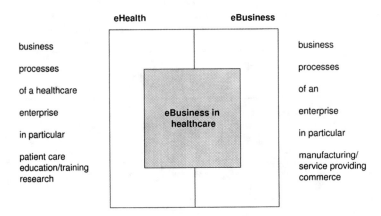

FIGURE 1-4. Relationship between eBusiness and eHealth.

describes a heterogeneous class of goods and comprises a series of quite different types of items. A rough distinction is often made between prescription drugs and medical-surgical commodities, instruments, and devices. Some statistics [e.g., OECD] classify medical supplies into nondurable goods such as prescribed medicines and durable goods such as appliances. Some examples from the spectrum of medical supplies are given in Table 1-3, which exemplifies the diversity of the items and possible schemes for classifying them.

In hospitals, the costs of supplies amount to one third of all costs incurred. Medical supplies account for approximately half of these costs. Figure 1-5 shows the data for U.S. hospitals. In other countries like the United Kingdom and Germany, this ratio is quite similar, despite differences in healthcare system financing.

Generally, expenses are aggregated on the level of institutions, by their cost centers, and by the type of the expense. These methods, however, prove insufficient for analyzing the true cause of expenses. Patient classification systems such as DRG systems, in combination with patient-costing data, serve to further break down cost data and, in particular, to relate the costs to a clinical case. This approach shows that the two thirds/one third ratio for human resources and supplies is not true for every clinical case and that there are diagnosis-related groups with a higher proportion of supplies, particularly of medical supplies, such as all groups involving patients needing implants. Patients suffering from cardiac problems and requiring a pacemaker or a defibrillator, for example, belong to diagnosis-related groups with 50% or more of all costs for medical supplies only. Other examples include patients requiring special antibiotic drugs or chemotherapy. These examples illustrate not only the important contribution of pharmaceuticals but also of specialized devices for treating patients and helping them to become healthy again or survive the disease much longer with a higher quality of life.

Buying and selling these products clearly differs from the buying and selling of other products in the healthcare area. In contrast to other supplies such as food, medical supplies are used in healthcare only and are closely connected with the primary processes in healthcare (i.e., patient care processes). Due to the complex nature of the product itself, or of the process the product is involved in, purchasing and selling these products require greater knowledge about the product than about any other goods in healthcare on

1. Introduction to eBusiness 15

TABLE 1-3. Medical supplies – examples, classification system NHS eClass [22].

Code		Node Name (Example)	Code	Item Name (Example)
D		**Pharmaceuticals Blood Products Medical Gases**		
	DN	Vaccines	DNA	*Vaccines*
	DP	X-ray Contrast Media	DPR	*MRI*
			DPW	*X-ray Contrast media*
	DX	Blood Products	DXA	*Blood Factors*
			DXB	*Human Albumin*
	DY	Medical Gases	DYK	*Medical Liquid Oxygen*
			DYR	*Medical Nitric Oxide*
E		**Dressings**		
	EA	Orthopaedic Casting Materials	EAF	*Casting tapes Moisture cured*
			EAJ	*Synthetic Resin Bandages heat cured*
			EAK	*Polyurethane Foam Based*
	EB	Compression Bandages	EBA	*One way stretch compression Bandages*
F		**Medical & Surgical Equipment**		
	FB	Medical & Surgical Equipment	FBA	*Laryngoscopes*
			FBB	*Medial Lasers*
			FBE	*Endoscopic Equipment*
			FBH	*Defibrillators*
	FQ	Medical Prostheses	FQD	*Pacemakers*
			FQE	*Implantable Cardiac Defribrillators*
			FQF	*Arterial Grafts*
			FQP	*Joint Replacement Hips*
	FX	Medical & Surgical Consumables	FXB	*Catheters*
			FXC	*Stents*
			FXD	*Balloons PTCA Balloons*
G		**Patients Appliances**		
	GF	Audiology	GFB	*Adult Hearing Aids & Accessories*
	GW	Wheelchairs Spares & Accessories	GWB	*Wheelchairs*
H		**Chemicals & Reagents**		
	HW	Stains Indicators & Tracers	HWB	*Stains Indicators & Tracers*
			HWM	*Radioactive Indicators & Tracers*
	HX	Laboratory Chemicals Gases & Reagents	HXB	
			HXM	*Chemicals & Reagents Gases for Laboratory Industrial Use*

both ends. Most of the items are not self-explanatory, not even those that are regarded as rather simple commodities. This is why clinicians and pharmacists who have the necessary background are not only involved but actually do the purchasing.

Relevant product knowledge either originates from the personal experience of the clinician or pharmacist, from their own studies, or from the results of clinical trials that

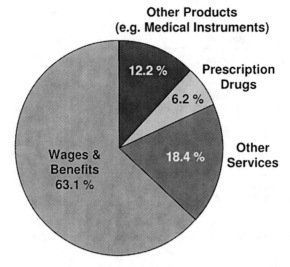

FIGURE 1-5. Percent of Hospital Costs by Type of Expense in the United States [23].

are mandatory for prescription drugs. These studies need to demonstrate the effects, side effects, and the potential harm of the drug or the complex medical device for patients as part of the approval process of national agencies such as the FDA in the United States. There is also a need, however, for objective, well-founded information beyond what is legally necessary that can help in the choice of safe, useful, and innovative products. Evidence-based purchasing, as is being established in the English NHS [24], illustrates a systematic approach towards fact-based decision-making in procurement–in particular, of non-pharmaceutical medical products.

Technical innovation driven by the competition between manufacturers and by research and development (R&D) activities is a core characteristic of medical supplies. Many companies in this sector have dedicated R&D departments and make substantial investments in the development of new products. Consequently, the product life cycle of technical products can be quite short with new products with new features replacing older ones regularly. The knowledge and the innovation factor have clear repercussions on procuring and providing these items, often calling directly for electronic solutions. Keeping catalogs up to date and distributing them are good examples of such a challenge that can often only be coped with by employing electronic means.

Why is eBusiness in Healthcare Different from Other Industries?

It would therefore be too easy to adopt the position that healthcare should fall back on the eBusiness strategies already established in other sectors, such as the automotive industry, and should imitate their methods and implement their tools to solve its problems. This approach would neither pay tribute to the overall goals of healthcare nor to the data, information, and knowledge relevant to healthcare, nor to the role of healthcare professionals and the idiosyncrasies of the healthcare market. What applies generally to eBusiness in healthcare is particularly true for eProcurement and eCommerce scenarios in healthcare, because specific constraints influence the market and determine the behavior of the customers and the suppliers.

Healthcare is Driven by Quality

The primary goals of healthcare are to promote health, to provide public health and prevent diseases, to cure illness, and to care for people with chronic diseases and health-related problems (see the OECD system of health accounts for a comprehensive definition). All other goals are inferior and are meant only to serve the overall goal of helping patients. Quality issues, therefore, have top priority over other aspects of providing healthcare. Reduced costs at the expense of lower levels of quality might be acceptable under certain circumstances in other sectors, but not in healthcare. This applies to the quality of services as well as to the quality of materials, because customers in healthcare (patients) choose a product (the service of the healthcare provider) because it is good, not because it is cheap.

When human life is at stake, the utmost efforts must be undertaken to help and to avoid harm, irrespective of the costs. This conviction adds a dimension to healthcare unknown in other sectors. Cost does play a role, however. Healthcare operates within a certain financial framework and rising costs are a major concern in all Western healthcare systems. An imbalanced approach favoring cost over quality issues, however, would not be accepted by healthcare professionals who are responsible for their patients and for the outcome of the process. Furthermore, low-cost products and services do not automatically lead to cost savings in the long run, and what looks like a bargain at the beginning may end up causing high losses. The risk of costs incurred for rectifying the short-term and long-term consequences of low services and materials quality, therefore, must be considered whenever a decision is made on the basis of price comparisons. Purchasing materials of unknown quality from changing suppliers would not be a suitable procurement scenario in healthcare and would therefore prevent purchasing in certain types of transaction-oriented electronic marketplaces.

Healthcare has Both an International and a National Dimension

Healthcare in the sense of a collective name that aims at uniting different entities such as healthcare professionals, scientists, manufacturers, healthcare systems, and patients has both an international and a national dimension depending on the actor's background. Whereas healthcare professionals and biomedical scientists are organized at the international level, and whereas manufacturers operate globally, healthcare systems are traditionally confined to an individual country or jurisdiction. Contributions to the body of knowledge in biomedicine and in all other healthcare disciplines come from laboratories all over the world, and the scientific exchange between research groups of different countries has a long tradition. Medline, the electronic database of the U.S. National Library of Medicine, is a living example of multiplying and distributing knowledge of all healthcare areas for the benefit of an international community. Manufacturers (in particular, pharmaceutical companies, but also many firms producing medical devices and medical-surgical products) are international in outlook and maintain a worldwide sales network. Large manufacturers frequently conduct their R&D activities in plants located all over the world. In contrast to knowledge and products in the healthcare domain, the financing schemes of healthcare services differ from country to country, with some of them being entirely tax-based while others are insurance-based or privately funded. The percentage of public healthcare expenditures also varies between countries. In the

United States, this is one of the lowest at 44%, while in the United Kingdom and Germany the percentages are among the highest at 83% and 78%, respectively [25]. Differences in the sources of funding, together with differences in healthcare regulations, lead to an understanding of healthcare systems as nationally unique structures with seemingly very little in common. There are several resulting consequences, including country-specific procurement procedures and the use of dedicated administrative and management computer systems in each country. At first glance, this seems justified: aren't the centralized structures defined by the National Health Service (NHS) in the United Kingdom different from the decentralized organization of healthcare provision in Germany? And, aren't healthcare systems where healthcare is free for all citizens, such as in the United Kingdom, different from those where the people have to pay? Obviously there must be an impact on the healthcare market, including the medical supplies market, in terms of marketing strategies, revenues, and forces for product innovation. On the other hand, we shall describe the commonalities and investigate whether different procedures for solving similar problems are useful and effective. After all, healthcare systems are meant to solve problems and to help the people with diseases and other health-related problems that are similar all over the globe, irrespective of where the people live. There is also another fact to be considered. Some differences in healthcare systems vanish with the implementation of similar methods such as diagnosis related groups (DRG) systems. Finally, the adoption of globally available ERP systems in hospitals and other large healthcare institutions, and the availability of global electronic transaction platforms transform the way of acting and thinking in procurement situations.

This mixture of worldwide free flow of scientific knowledge among healthcare providers on the one hand, and country-specific (partly) regulated markets on the other hand, is one of the major characteristics of healthcare and has a strong impact also on buying and selling medical products electronically.

It is still an open question whether globally or locally oriented marketplaces and transaction platforms are preferred by the manufacturers and the customers.

Healthcare is Highly Specific

Like other domains, healthcare is characterized by its data, information, knowledge, and methods. Unlike most other sectors, however, these are highly specific and are rarely used outside the healthcare industry. This high degree of specialization is reflected by the high standard in education and training of physicians, pharmacists, nurses, and other healthcare professionals and has direct repercussions on the systems to be employed in healthcare. Simply customizing standard software is seldom sufficient for meeting user requirements. General materials management software implemented in hospital pharmacies, for example, does not reflect the specific processes and the terminology of pharmacists. The database structure often has to be modified to account for the different properties of healthcare objects. In addition, systems without the integration of proper nomenclatures, terminologies, or classifications (in particular, for medical supplies) have little value in eBusiness scenarios in healthcare. Consequently, standard eProcurement systems and horizontal marketplaces are ruled out for use in the context of medical supplies.

Procurement of Medical Supplies Requires Good Product Knowledge

Highly innovative medical devices and pharmaceutical products have complex features and their practical use with patients needs a sound know-how of the product's therapeutic effects, as explained above. The necessary knowledge can only be acquired in clinical settings and assumes a thorough understanding of the medical conditions under which the product is most suitable. This is the reason why many physicians order rather complex medical devices directly instead of going through the purchasing department of a hospital. Similarly, pharmaceutical products are purchased by the hospital pharmacy in most cases. Not just complex products can cause problems. Even the purchasing of consumables or one-way products to be applied to the patient or to be used directly by the healthcare professionals requires their input about desirable product features. However, if individual healthcare professionals regularly order a variety of products and in low quantities, the positive effects of high volume purchasing on the purchase price are impossible to secure.

This illustrates the dilemma of purchasing medical supplies: channeling all orders through the purchasing department, standardizing the product portfolio, and group purchasing counteract the adverse effects of individual orders by achieving significant volume levels. This may, however, be at the price of reduced influence of the clinicians on the choice of the products. There is no doubt that healthcare professionals such as physicians, nurses, and therapists need to participate in strategic measures in the procurement of medical supplies (i.e., selecting products and suppliers, defining product substitutes and quality parameters, controlling product quality and supplier performance). Growing awareness of the need to establish joint product committees in healthcare institutions reflects the notion that only the combined efforts of clinicians and the purchasing departments will lead to an optimization of product selection.

Electronic procurement will primarily automate the operational processes, but it will, almost in real time, provide the data necessary for continuous quality monitoring and essential for strategic measures as decided by the joint product committee.

Good product knowledge on the part of the clinicians is an asset for all healthcare institutions and extremely valuable for the manufacturers. Collaborative marketplaces lend themselves to knowledge sharing between customers and suppliers, and may therefore allow clinicians and manufacturers to collaborate in product design and conduct clinical product evaluation studies.

Price Negotiations Take Place Outside Cyberspace

It is the basic concept of transaction-oriented electronic marketplaces to provide a platform for exchanges and auctions with electronically mediated price negotiations. Suppliers refuse to participate in this type of marketplace in both healthcare and other industries due to the fear of price erosion. Product prices, therefore, are negotiated offline between suppliers and healthcare institutions in the context of overall contract negotiations, including the minimum purchase volume for a given time period and, if necessary, the service level for devices and trade discounts. This more systematic approach has replaced many of the spot purchases of small product amounts. In the event that a healthcare institution contracts with a group purchasing organization (GPO) or any other type of intermediary to gain price advantages as a result of volume bundling, price issues are dealt with entirely offline. In fact, existing electronic marketplaces in healthcare do not truly deserve the name *marketplace*, because they act more like electronic hubs facilitating order management both for healthcare institutions and suppliers.

Any business model or technical solution for the enabling of electronically mediated business processes in healthcare must take these peculiarities into account to become successful.

eBusiness in Healthcare and Medical Informatics – A New Relationship

Over the last few years, eHealth has become a predominant topic in health and medical informatics, intriguing many researchers in the area. The commerce issue within eHealth, however, has been largely neglected by this field. It seemed that at the core, health and medical informatics focused on patient care topics, leaving business issues (in particular, questions related to reducing costs) to other scientific domains. With the advent of DRG-based financing of hospitals in a growing number of countries, it has become evident, however, that quality and costs are only two sides of the same coin and that health information systems, (in particular, those in hospitals (HIS_h)) must be capable of converting data derived from patient care-oriented processes into data used for managing the enterprise. Instruments aiming at cost reduction without compromising quality, such as clinical pathways, allow both perspectives to converge. The integration of clinical pathways into health information systems in hospitals (HIS_h) in fact reflects this new demand for steering clinical processes both by means of quality and cost issues, and for providing data from clinical processes for management purposes. These data not only include information on clinical processes and associated human resources, but also on the consumption of materials.

What appears to be a one-way flow of information from patient care to management, eventually benefiting only the management, is really working in both directions. Well-organized data on the resources of the healthcare enterprise, such as human resources, materials, and facilities, help patient care to be better informed and to be able to fulfill its tasks properly. If materials management, for example, stores product charge numbers electronically, the recall of faulty products can be managed more simply and potential harm to patients can be avoided. Structured product information using standard terminologies and classification systems assists clinicians in finding and comparing similar products and choosing the best ones for their patients.

Information is the cement between the world of management and the world of patient care, and medical informatics can provide the necessary methods and tools to make the right piece of information available at the right location and time and at the right level of abstraction.

In this new role, medical informatics has adopted approaches originating from economics, business management, and applied computer science, including business process analysis, simulation, reengineering and controlling, and has widened its methods store towards an interdisciplinary and multiprofessional perspective in healthcare. Due to its familiarity with both clinical information and healthcare professionals, medical informatics is bound to shape eBusiness in healthcare and adapt the eBusiness strategies to the peculiarities of the healthcare market.

Goal of the Book

Focus on eProcurement and eCommerce

This book provides a comprehensive overview of eBusiness in healthcare for practitioners and academics interested in business and management topics in healthcare. It focuses on eProcurement and eCommerce applications as the most advanced scenarios of eBusiness in healthcare, and pinpoints their conceptual framework and major components.

The management of supply chains and of internal and external business processes supported by modern information and communication technologies constitutes the main concept for networked thinking and for conducting business between enterprises–also in healthcare. The book expands on the fundamentals of eBusiness in two further chapters, by explaining how supply chain management (Chapter 2) and business process management (Chapter 3) are defined, what experience in other industrial sectors exists, and how this knowledge can be transferred to the healthcare sector. This rather broad perspective of supply chain management and business process analysis is focused on specific eProcurement and eCommerce scenarios in healthcare corresponding with different purchasing and logistics concepts (Chapters 7 to 11).

It is the underlying idea of the book to process technological requirements for eBusiness so that nonexperts gain an understanding of the relevant components, their relationships, and the functional implications of different solutions. To this end, a group of chapters (Chapters 4 to 6) is dedicated to eBusiness technologies and standards as the basis for conducting business electronically. These chapters will also, however, make the case for why technology is not simply a necessary tool but a strong vehicle for shaping a new business reality by offering new and yet unknown functionality and workflows.

Already, after only a few years of eBusiness in healthcare, we are witnessing an impact on clinical and management issues (Chapters 9 and 10) because data and information that were previously hidden in piles of paper became searchable, available, and transparent. This may positively influence patient care in particular patient safety and management decisions on steering the enterprise. The book, therefore, also explicitly addresses clinicians and managers who are not primarily involved in the daily business of purchasing and materials management but who make fundamental decisions on medical supplies and other products and who will find the data provided by eBusiness systems essential for their own work. Over the last few years the eBusiness approach has gained ground and today we are in the position of being able to report on many good examples of how eProcurement and eCommerce work in reality–including great achievements but also the learning experiences of working through unavoidable errors. Users–on both the side of the healthcare enterprises and on the side of the manufacturers–give accounts of their initial expectations and their experiences and provide an appraisal of the current situation and the future (Chapters 12 and 13).

The insight gained is summarized in the Supply Chain Model of eBusiness in Healthcare (Chapter 14). With the knowledge that predicting the future is a tricky business, we will nevertheless try to outline possible future developments and the opportunities that extend beyond mere process automation and demonstrate the multidisciplinary nature of eBusiness.

The book aims to cover these different aspects of eBusiness and to provide background information, as well as specific details for managers, clinicians, pharmacists, computer engineers, and all professionals working in the healthcare industry.

Widen the Perspective Through an International Approach

In the past, questions of purchasing, materials management, and logistics in healthcare were dealt with on a national level within the confines of the country's healthcare system. As shown above, however, a large number of manufacturers operate globally, offering the same products worldwide. Clinical knowledge, including process and product knowledge, is also being exchanged among members of an international scientific community. Hence, it seems justified to question the discussions that are held solely at national levels, along with their inherent limitations.

It is for this reason that the book chooses an international approach. Concepts, solutions, and case studies from the United States, the United Kingdom, and Germany are presented to show differences and similarities between the approaches. The three countries reflect different types of markets for medical supplies, illustrating specific procurement procedures in healthcare institutions. Whereas GPO's and integrated delivery networks (IDN's), representing large numbers of customers, play a key role and contribute to market consolidation in the United States, German hospitals are only recently becoming aware of the powers of group purchasing. The German market is therefore still rather fragmented. In the United Kingdom, the NHS had been pursuing a centralized approach to procurement at national levels through its National Purchasing and Supply Agency. Due to a low level of contract compliance on the part of the hospital trusts (see Chapter 12), however, the theoretical power of volume bundling at a national level did not materialize. Like Germany, the U.K. market also displays fragmentation characteristics.

Looking at electronic trading under these different basic conditions will give insight into various eBusiness models, and into their strengths and flaws, and will permit learning from each other.

Enable Learning by Case Studies

Learning through examples of best practice and benchmarks with other organizations are well-known procedures in business management for managing change and moving toward greater excellence. The idea of learning from others, of incorporating their strategies, of avoiding their mistakes, and benefiting from their achievements underlies the case studies in this book, in which decision-making processes, expectations, individual solutions, outcomes, and plans for the future are described.

eBusiness depends on a critical mass of customers and suppliers to become successful and develop its potential. Similar to communication media, the number of participants determines the acceptance of the new medium. Although there is a growing number of healthcare enterprises purchasing online, and an increasing number of suppliers selling online, the critical mass has not yet been reached in all countries. Technical barriers, resistance within the organization, and a fear of making the wrong decision keep hospitals from trading via the Internet. With only a small community of potential customers accessible, however, many suppliers attach a low priority to eCommerce issues. This vicious circle can only be broken by trusting the new technology and by learning from its early users.

In this context, the use of basic eCommerce technology is not a competitive advantage, and cooperation among suppliers is more desirable than competition so that the critical mass can be established. Suppliers are therefore also invited to learn from each other.

Get Clinicians Involved

eBusiness in healthcare institutions is multidisciplinary and requires the involvement of clinicians. This is why the book explicitly addresses readers with a medical or a nursing background. eBusiness in healthcare demands a highly structured, systematic, and transparent procedure in procurement. It marks the decision to move away from on-the-spot and unsystematic purchases carried out by many busy clerks. It also signals an end to ward staff communicating with suppliers about orders, shipments, and returns. Many of these types of processes will be performed entirely or partly by machines. In an effort to enable the work to be automated, however, essential preparations need to take place. Preferred products and their suppliers must be selected and such lists must be compiled and regularly updated. This is work only clinicians can perform because they are the ones with the greatest product knowledge. When it comes to establishing contacts with suppliers for the negotiation of prices and terms and conditions, experts from the purchasing department can get involved. It requires the combined endeavors of clinicians and managers to finalize contracts that consider quality and cost issues and allow the flexibility needed for adapting to new circumstances such as new products and new pricing schemes.

Chapter 9 is specifically dedicated to the clinical aspects of eProcurement. Furthermore, the impact of online purchasing on patient care is a theme that runs through the entire book. Some of the contributors to this book have a clinical background as physicians, nurses, or other healthcare professionals and are familiar with the clinical domain and its requirements. Their chapters also reflect clinical concerns within technologically oriented and management-oriented topics.

Create New Synergies Between Healthcare Providers and Manufacturers

eBusiness is not only multidisciplinary in terms of involving different professions within healthcare enterprises, but it also bridges gaps between the healthcare providers and the suppliers. In this book, eBusiness in healthcare is described from the point of view of the procurement side (eProcurement) and the sales side (eCommerce), not only because business transactions are two-sided (at least), but also to open up opportunities for setting up discussions that lead to new partnerships and new types of business relationships. With the advent of electronic media, markets have become more global and transparent, allowing open and transient partnerships and increasing the chance of finding new partners (both customers and suppliers). At the same time, electronic media support the flow of information between business partners in an unprecedented way, enabling close coordination and cooperation. In principle, electronic media can be employed for any type of information exchange, be it information concerning business transactions, information to support joint product development, or information in the context of product evaluation. All this is to be subsumed under eBusiness because it serves to optimize the customer–supplier relationship, which is a function of the three factors of product quality, product price, and innovation potential (see Figure 1-6).

There are no limitations whatsoever regarding the availability and the purpose of the electronic media. Limitations, instead, originate from a lack of understanding of each other's needs. This book will contribute to an ongoing dialog between healthcare providers and suppliers for the purposes of building modern, electronically supported partnerships, because national cost containment programs require strategic and creative business thinking on both sides.

Stimulate Scientific Work to Enable Innovation

eBusiness is still in its infancy–this is particularly true for healthcare. At best, the partners are striving for optimization and automation of their processes in the hope that a clear increase in the electronic business volume will happen in the near future. Currently most

degree of innovation

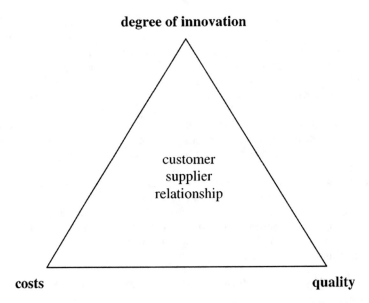

customer
supplier
relationship

costs   **quality**

FIGURE 1-6. Product characteristics defining the customer-supplier relationship.

of the business is still conducted outside cyberspace. Under these circumstances, it is essential to continuously monitor the empirical basis of eBusiness–also in healthcare–to predict the developments and to describe their impact.

How soon will we be able to drop the "e" in eBusiness because electronic media have become commonplace [4]? Is process automation the only benefit of electronic transactions? What impact does eBusiness exert on the magic triangle of product costs, product quality, and potential for innovation? Will the trend towards more mergers of electronic marketplaces in healthcare continue, and will it lead to one big provider of eBusiness connectivity per country or across the globe? Are technological standards able to counteract monopolistic structures by ensuring the necessary interoperability in a plethora of systems? What other areas besides B2B between healthcare providers and suppliers will emerge in healthcare?

These are only a few of a series of unanswered questions. This book will try to answer some of these questions by providing facts. Instead of drawing a complete picture of eBusiness in healthcare, however, we aim to describe its cornerstones so that new questions can be raised, new hypotheses can be developed, and further research can be initiated. eBusiness in healthcare needs a stronger scientific basis for systematically exploiting its own full potential, for predicting and planning future scenarios, and for building bridges to other current developments in eHealth. As a truly interdisciplinary field, it ought to attract researchers not only from economic sciences but also from the healthcare sciences–in particular, from medical and health informatics.

To enable innovative business processes in healthcare, the concerted action of scientists and practitioners thinking ahead, and of organizations daring to invest and to implement is required. It is the goal of this book to help the stakeholders understand the issues and mechanisms of such a concerted action to establish eBusiness in healthcare.

References

[1] Shin, N. (2004) An empirical investigation of the economic payoffs of e-business and CRM innovations. *International Journal of Electronic Business.* **2**, 351–365.

[2] Young, L. W. and R. B. Johnston. (2003) The role of the Internet in business-to-business network transformations: a novel case and theoretical analysis. *Information Systems and e-Business Management.* **1**, 73–91.

[3] Markus, M. L. and E. Christiaanse. (2003) Adoption and impact of collaboration electronic marketplaces. *Information Systems and e-Business Management.* **1**, 139–155.

[4] Jelassi, T. and A. Enders. (2005) *Strategies for E-business: Creating Value through Electronic and Mobile Commerce.* Edinburgh: Pearson Education.

[5] Ho, D. C. K., K. F. Au, and E. Newton. (2003) The impact of e-procurement on the supply chain structure. *International Journal of Electronic Business.* **1**, 383–395.

[6] Chang, H., R. F. Easley, and M. J. Shaw. (2003) A comparative study of exchange and aggregation models in the B2B e-marketplace. *Information Systems and e-Business Management.* **1**, 213–228.

[7] White, A. and E. Daniel. (2004) Electronic marketplaces: an empirical study in the UK health care sector. *International Journal of Electronic Business.* **2**, 603–624.

[8] European Commission, Directorate General for Enterprise (2004) *The European e-Business Report 2004 edition.* Bonn: empirica. Available from: <http://www.ebusiness-watch.org/resources/documents/eBusiness-Report-2004.pdf> [Accessed 01 September 2006].

[9] Electronic Commerce Branch (2005) *Statistics on the digital economy.* Ottawa. Available from: <http://e-com.ic.gc.ca/epic/internet/inecic-ceac.nsf/en/h_gv00005e.html> [Accessed 24 July 2005].

[10] European Commission, Directorate General for Enterprise and Industry (2005) *The European e-Business Report 2005 edition.* Bonn: empirica. Available from: <http://www.ebusiness-watch.org/resources/documents/eBusiness-Report-2005.pdf> [Accessed 01 September 2006].

[11] Tehan, R. (2002) *E-commerce Statistics: Explanation and Sources.* Damascus: Penny Hill. Available from: Thurgood Marshall Law Library <http://www.law.umaryland.edu/marshall/crsreports/crsdocuments/RL31293_06042003.pdf#search=%22E-Commerce%20Statistics%3A%20Explanation%20and%20Sources%22> [Accessed 01 September 2006].

[12] United States Government Printing Office (2005) *Economic Report of the President.* Washington. Available from: <http://www.gpoaccess.gov/eop/2005/2005_erp.pdf> [Accessed 25 July 2005].

[13] Statistics Canada (2005) *The Daily: Electronic commerce and technology 2004.* Ottawa. Available from: <http://www.statcan.ca/Daily/English/050420/d050420b.htm> [Accessed 01 September 2006].

[14] U.S. Census Bureau (2005) *E-Stats: Measuring the Electronic Economy.* Washington. Available from: <http://www.census.gov/eos/www/ebusiness614.htm> [Accessed 01 September 2006].

[15] U.S. Census Bureau (2006) *Quarterly Retail E-commerce Sales.* Washington. Available from: < http://www.census.gov/mrts/www/ecomm.html> [Accessed 1 November 2006].

[16] Economist Intelligence Unit (2006) *The 2006 e-Readiness rankings.* London. Available from: <http://www-935.ibm.com/services/de/bcs/pdf/2006/e_readiness_rankings.pdf> [Accessed 1 November 2006].

[17] CEN/ISSS eBusiness Standards Focus Group (2003) *CEN/ISSS report and recommendations on key eBusiness standards issues 2003-2005*. Brussels. Available from: <http://www.cenorm.be/ cenorm/ businessdomains/ businessdomains/ isss/ activity/reportfinal.pdf> [Accessed 25 July 2005].

[18] Oh H., C. Rizo, M. Enkin and A. Jadad. (2005) What is eHealth?: a systematic review of published definitions. *World hospitals and health services: the official journal of the International Hospital Federation*. **41**, 32–40.

[19] Eysenbach, G. (2001) What is e-health? *Journal of Medical Internet Research*. **3**, e20.

[20] Waymack, P. M. (2005) Harnessing the power of e-commerce to reduce denials. *Healthcare Financial Management*. **59**, 40–43.

[21] Cook, D. P., J. L. Joseph and R. S. Morton. (2004) Quality drivers for e-pharmaceuticals system management: a theoretical framework. *International Journal of Electronic Business*. **2**, 174–192.

[22] NHS Purchasing and Supply Agency *NHS-eClass – eProcurement*. Available from: http://www.pasa.doh.gov.uk/eprocurement/product_coding/ [Accessed 1 November 2006]

[23] American Hospital Association (2005) Chapter 6: The economic contribution of hospitals. *Slide Presentation*. personal communication 23 Sept 2005.

[24] NHS Purchasing and Supply Agency *Centre for Evidence-based Purchasing*. Available from: http://www.pasa.nhs.uk/evaluation/ [Accessed 1 November 2006]

[25] OECD *A System of Health Accounts*. Paris. Available from: Office for National Statistics <http://www.statistics.gov.uk/healthaccounts/system.asp#providers> [Accessed 25 July 2005].

2
Opportunities of Supply Chain Management in Healthcare

VOLKER GEHMLICH

Executive Summary

The challenge of this chapter is to find evidence of whether supply chain management could be applied as a management technique in the healthcare sector–one of the largest and fastest growing sectors in the world. Primarily secondary sources were analyzed to define the scope of research, the models of reference, and examples from other industries to test their usefulness for the sector in question. This had to be interpreted in the light of a changing environment, initiated by two key drivers: globalization and the advancement of information and communication technologies, embedded in different and changing governance systems. Globalization has turned purchasing into global sourcing, and one major opportunity to get a competitive edge appears to be the Internet.

The supply chain was identified as a means to equate supply and demand. Innumerable flows between suppliers and customers, upstream and downstream, have to be considered to strike the balance. It became obvious that the following article could not cover all these various streams and strands and therefore we had to limit their focus on the manufacturer of pharmaceutical and medical-surgical products and devices on the one hand and first-tier customers in particular hospitals, on the other. In this chapter, however, these borders are removed from time to time to allow for an indication of wider perspectives.

The value chain was selected as a starting point, as it permitted the integration of the support activities in the analysis, going beyond a consideration of the primary activities of a supply chain only. This was felt necessary, because state-of-the art thinking looks at the whole, and not even at one enterprise alone but at networks of business organizations that are linked by supplier-customer relationships. To this extent, it could be demonstrated that outsourcing, as one example, might be advantageous at the level of primary activities and also as it relates to support activities, disclosing opportunities of sharing infrastructure, for example.

The first part of the chapter pinpoints that a new way of thinking is crucial. This new way has probably been dominant in the health sector in theory, but not implemented to the same extent–similar to traditional industries, with an orientation towards outcomes rather than focusing on input factors. This approach is underlined by samples taken from industry. These samples highlight the criteria and elements of efficient and effective supply and value chains–critical success factors that are tested later on in a healthcare environment. Achieved results prove that such models have existed in healthcare or will be introduced on the basis of developments that are already recognized. In fact, all key terms identified in the examples can be linked to the value chain of organizations in the healthcare sector. These visions and ideas are detailed as "lessons learned."

Of particular interest are those cases that seem to stretch the present borders in the relationship between suppliers and customers. It has become evident that the old formula of "make or buy" is hardly of any relevance today. Transformational outsourcing is catching on as it rearranges traditional links. The organization itself also changes its core business and orientates itself much more according to its core competencies.

Here and there, this chapter also hints at similarities to progressions in the public sector. These advancements, however, cannot be fully considered for obvious reasons: focus and space. At the end of the chapter, we indicate how the processes are triggered. Similarities with any other sector are obvious, as ICT changes the rule of the game everywhere.

Introduction

Supply chains have always existed. Managing from a supply chain perspective, however, is relatively new. In healthcare, supply chain management (SCM), like many other areas of management, has not really been a focus of discussion, although it has in other areas of the service industry in general. According to Steven Bliss, who chairs a National Health Service (NHS) working group of the Chartered Institute of Management Accountants in the United Kingdom, the issue is a general one: "The key test is whether techniques that work in industry should not work in the public sector and the NHS. I see no reason why not." [1] Robert Bruce underlines in his article [1] that the NHS "is in many ways in the same position as any private sector organisation," and, as a service industry, is based on delivery with limited resources (money) and the dominant cost driver (people). In other words, as in any business sector, "productivity, getting better value out of capital and getting better value in areas such as drugs" [1] are the key issues. The following article tries to test the ground: could healthcare management benefit from SCM?

Background

Lessons learned from many events in history highlight the indispensability of a functioning supply chain. Many problems evolved because of an imperfect delivery of vital goods and services in time; many sustainable market entries or penetrations failed as resources and competencies were not available when needed. On the other hand, new forms of conflicts evolved because of new logistical means (e.g., the steam engine), and new markets came into reach because of new transport facilities (airplane, cooling systems). The issue of striking the right balance between the security of supply and the satisfaction of needs at a specified time, and bridging the distance between supply and demand in and on time is of key importance, and general solutions cannot be offered yet. This dilemma has been demonstrated again recently by labor disputes in several industries. Examples of this were the case of British Airways versus Gate Gourmet, which resulted in British Airways personnel going on strike and flights being cancelled, and when textiles from China could not be picked up because of new quotas in the European Union [2].

As for some years, most markets (in particular, those of consumer goods) have been characterized by very stiff competition, leaving the suppliers hardly any chance to influence the market price. Businesses had to go backwards in their supply chain to find out where money could be saved to increase their margin or achieve a margin at all. The former *make or buy* decisions that had either led to a deep vertical supply chain or a focus on long-standing supplier relationships had been transformed–not the least influenced by Ignacio Lopez while working for General Motors and Volkswagen in the 1980s and 1990s. Outsourcing became one of those fads that were expected to solve the problem forever. In the past years, however, more and more experts have warned organizations not to thoughtlessly outsource parts of their business to other companies and extend supply chains to anywhere in the world guided by costs only without considering the potential risks involved. "You can't outsource your risk, your brand or your problems," Graham Stevens from PA Consulting stated in an interview with the Financial Times, qualifying this attitude as "out of mind, out of sight outsourcing." [3]

The introductory examples, however, demonstrate that the interdependence between processes and partners of a supply chain has not been eased. In fact, a new form has even evolved: a cross-dependence. Personnel of an organization may go on strike although they are not directly affected by a labor dispute, or market forces might be changed on short notice on the basis of political decisions in other areas. Of course, there is no difference between pursuing a real outsourcing such as buying business functions that used to be carried out in the company itself (British Airways example), and shifting the supply chain in geographical terms (e.g., the textile industry). The waves of such eruptions are not just felt within a local, regional, or national area–they have, in fact, a global impact.

Benetton ran into problems because of their marketing campaigns designed by outsourced agencies. Starbucks was accused of to buying coffee from farmers that exploited children. Nike suffered for similar reasons, although the enterprises themselves had no direct influence on these situations, as they often purchased from intermediaries. Oil crises have not always been caused by cutbacks in oil production. Sometimes they have been caused by a blockage of trucks that are unable to leave refineries, or by political decisions to stop delivering products to certain countries. Thus, the risks are not only logistical (oil), but also political (Iraq), ethical, and reputable (e.g. in case of the business organizations Benetton, Starbucks, Nike) [2].

The globalization of markets and competition has driven supply chains to become global, too. After the Iron Curtain fell in 1989, the opportunity for a real global economy evolved. This globalization has affected both the market situation as well as the process of an ever-increasing business interrelationship between regions and throughout the whole world [3]. Theodore Levitt characterized this some years ago: "Different cultural preferences, national tastes and standards, and business institutions are vestiges of the past [...] The world's needs and desires have been irrevocably homogenised. This makes the multinational corporation obsolete and the global corporation absolute[...] Instead of adapting to superficial and even entrenched differences within and between nations, the global corporation will seek sensibly to force suitable standardised products and practices on the entire globe." [4, 5]

It seems that for the time being, healthcare has not been affected. The first signs, however, indicate future changes: DocMorris, a Dutch healthcare group, has just received legal permission to open a pharmacy in Germany where, by tradition, pharmacies have not been allowed to run chain stores.[1]

Globalization has turned purchasing into global sourcing, and in the 2004–2005 Annual Best Practices Reader Survey, global sourcing is already listed among the top five most important activities [6]. Risks in global sourcing are related to delays and hold-ups in transportation, different negotiation cultures, language or cultural misunderstandings, and the sheer distances involved, making it difficult to know more about the supplier and any ethical stances as outlined above [7]. Yip [8] identified the striving for sourcing efficiencies as one element of cost globalization, and thus as one of the four key drivers of globalization: market globalization, cost globalization, globalization of competition, and globalization of government policies. These, in turn, require global strategies independent of the size of the company: "In short, it is virtually impossible to seriously compete in today's business, domestically or globally, by confining buying to solely domestic sources." ([9], p.130) Furthermore, since the events of September 11, 2001, more issues have to be respected–especially security and new compliance requirements. Logistics, documentation, and regulations had to be re-worked. The latter is also an example of the globalization of government policies, as many more security checks on trading have been approved–most of the time on multilateral agreements. The role of governments has just been highlighted again by the failure of the WTO (World Trade Organization) to conclude the Doha Round.[2]

As a consequence, business organizations are driven into the web of a global supply chain that consists of trading partners that range from the supplier's supplier to the customer's customer. "In every industry, to gain a competitive advantage, companies attempt to develop a global network that will outperform rival networks." ([9], p. 136)

A major opportunity to form a competitive edge appears to be the Internet, which has dramatically changed markets and competition. It has created a new globally interconnected world and a global economy, independent of whether business organizations are small or huge and where they are located. Global eBusiness strategically uses information and communication technologies (ICT) to reshuffle supply chains, to communicate with partners, and to support multiple markets anywhere in the world. Global eBusiness is critical in managing the global supply chain. According to several authors, it is one business area which might benefit the most from the use of ICT. "Companies that know how to leverage global eBusiness strategies into Internet-enabled global supply chain management systems no longer see themselves as standing alone or out of touch. Instead, these savvy companies focus on their role as part of a supply chain, with a web of integrated links to customers, suppliers, and other business partners. This approach requires a shift in focus from an internal or product perspective to a pure customer-centric, business partner-oriented mind-set'." ([9], p. 104) The Financial Times [2] qualifies it as an unchained malady: Globalization - Standardization - Customizing - Outsourcing. In this way, business is becoming ever more exposed to supplier problems.

---

[1] A lawsuit was filed against DocMorris and a regional administrative court stopped the company from continuing their business until the federal court made a final decision. Meanwhile DocMorris changed the business strategy and has become partner of German pharmacies. The organization intends to increase its partnerships in the near future.

[2] The Doha (Qatar) round of WTO negotiations began in 2001 and talks were suspended on July 27, 2006. The agenda focused on fairer trade rules for developing countries–in particular, in agricultural and manufacturing markets.

The healthcare industry, one of the largest and fastest-growing sectors in the world, is very much influenced in most countries–if not managed–by governments. As outlined above, globalization and the growth of the Internet have changed at least some rules of the game, and this does not exclude the healthcare sector. The term eBusiness has been introduced to describe all electronically managed business processes that can be seen from an organization's internal perspective (supply chain management) or from an external perspective (eMarkets, eHubs, eCommerce) [10]. eBusiness, therefore, is the "conduct of business on the Internet, not only buying and selling but also servicing customers and collaborating with business partners." [11]. In this chapter, eBusiness comprises all forms, including eCommerce and eProcurement.

Methodology

This chapter is primarily based on secondary research and its objective is to give an overview of the issues related to supply chain management, shedding some light on the healthcare industry as well. Textbooks supply traditional viewpoints, publications of chief executive officers (CEOs) and quotations from managers of global enterprise add an authentic flavor, supported by case studies to highlight state-of-the-art thinking in terms of supply chains and their management. Research in university development and examples of the service industry should demonstrate that the insights gained are valid for the healthcare sector as well, perhaps even more so now that ICT has changed some of the traditional equations.

Scope of Supply Chain Management (SCM)

Definition and Models

The Value Chain

A simple approach to the complex issues of a supply chain may be by systematically examining all activities performed by an organization and how they interact. The model of a value chain, outlined by Porter [12], is useful in revealing sources of competitive advantage by identifying drivers of cost and sources of differentiation. Looking at the primary and secondary activities to create a margin, as Porter sees them, facilitates the selection of those activities that might be bought, outsourced, or brought in by cooperating with other organizations to pursue exactly what is required: inbound materials, raw materials inventories (both considered inbound logistics by Porter), manufacturing (called operations by Porter), finished goods inventories, and distribution within a single organization (considered outbound logistics by Porter). Porter adds the services and also underlines that the primary activities of an organization have to be supported by secondary activities (firm infrastructure, human resource management, technology development, and procurement) to make the supply chain manageable (see Figure 2-1).

If this was applied to the service sector, e.g. education (Figure 2-2), and adapting the technical terms respectively, the following value chain would emerge [12, 13][3]:

If a hospital was used as an example for the healthcare sector, the value chain in Figure 2-3 could be imagined (keeping the elements of a manufacturing organization as reference).

---

[3] For better reference Porter's structure is left and the education elements are included.

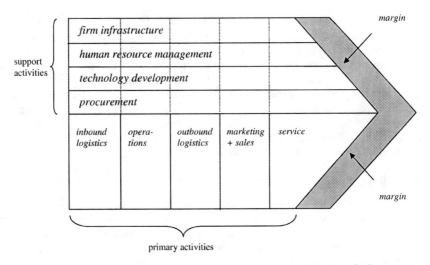

FIGURE 2-1. Value chain for a manufacturing organization (based on [12]).

This indicates that basically healthcare sector value chains can also be identified. If that is the case, the knowledge and understanding gained by our insight into the manufacturing industry might also be transferable to the healthcare sector. Porter, for example, highlights the interdependence of primary and secondary activities and stresses the need to coordinate them in terms of timing. This also appears obvious in a hospital: if a patient has to be treated, the correct technology has to be available to provide the appropriate treatment and care. Linkages exist between activities within an organization as well as between companies and their individual value chains, such as suppliers or buyers. In the case of a hospital, a network of value chains of partners could be realized, as shown in Figure 2-4.

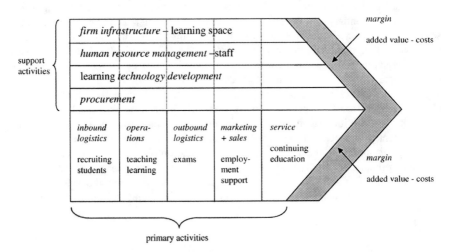

FIGURE 2-2. Value chain for a learning organization.

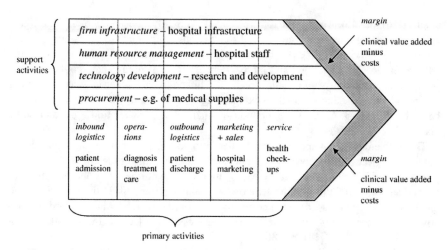

FIGURE 2-3. Value chain for a hospital.

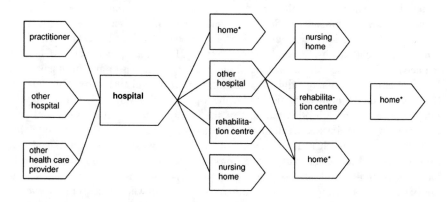

Legend: * If required patient care is supported by home health care technology for monitoring the patient.

FIGURE 2-4. Value chain network of a hospital (simplified model).

The Supply Chain

Other authors consider these activities from where they begin (origin) to where they end (consumption). Johnson/Scholes/Whittington ([14], p. 459) stress the idea of supply and distribution chains. Some hold the view that SCM has its base in the management of relationships between corporate functions as well as between companies [15]. This highlights the view of networks, that all operations that are "linked together so as to provide goods and services through to the end customers." In large organizations, there can be many hundreds of strands or linked operations passing through the primary operation. The strands that allow the ongoing flow of goods and services through this network along individual channels or strands are more commonly referred to as supply chains ([16], p. 445), which have to be managed via SCM. Johnson/Scholes/Whittington call this a "set of interorganizational links and relationships that are necessary to create a product or service." ([14], p. 616) Because this will normally require infrastructure, human resources, technology, and more, it appears that a supply chain could be interpreted as a network of value chains potentially linked to each other in a vertical and/or horizontal way, as demonstrated above (see Figure 2-4). As the introductory examples have shown (British Airways, textile industry), lateral or cross-relationships can also be disclosed.

The problem does not appear to be the definition of the term but instead indicates the potential neglect of the impact of such networks as Merck had to learn: "[...] Merck's problems derive from its reluctance to do small deals with the biotechnology industry to take advantage of the wealth of innovation taking place outside the company. Too much faith has been placed on the company's own scientists[...] About a third of sales now [note: after having introduced a new business policy] come from products that were in-licensed[...]" ([14], p. 486).

Considering supply chain networks, it should be acknowledged that the integration of centers exists for any of the partners in a network. This is clearly stipulated by the Council of Logistics Management (2003), which defines supply chain management as being "[...] implemented by integrating corporate functions using business processes within and across companies." Sometimes, however, SCM is seen as a synonym for logistics [17], operations management [18], procurement [19], or a combination of the three [20], as outlined by Lambert and colleagues [21]. In their paper, Lambert stresses the network idea–a network consisting of business organizations or also of independent business units, comprising original suppliers as well as end-customers. One goal of SCM has to be the implementation of business processes of various functions and the integration of them with other partners of the supply chain. To this extent, business processes form the links between members of a supply chain. According to the Global Supply Chain Forum, SCM is "the integration of key business processes from end user through original suppliers that provides products, services, and information that add value for customers and other stakeholders." [22]. They state that the scope of SCM is not fixed at all. Generally speaking, it comprises all areas in which it helps to achieve the strategic objectives of a business organization. In contrast to this broad interpretation, the framework of the Supply Chain Operations Reference-model (SCOR) is smaller in scope as it "focuses on transactional efficiency rather than relationships with customers and suppliers." ([21], p. 33).

Hammer is quoted as stating [23] that it is in the integration of business processes across firms in the supply chain where the real "gold" can be found [24]. Market-driven business organizations have to implement cross-functional business processes [25]. This is substantiated by Slack ([16], p. 446) who pinpoints "that these benefits centre on three key objectives of SCM: satisfying end customers, doing so efficiently, and responding to change in an agile manner." On the other hand, because of these interdependencies of the chain, a purchase by a customer may have multiple impacts, or even an accelerating effect (bullwhip effect [26]), similar to the Forrester Effect ([7], p. 444). In their research, Lee and colleagues found out that "distorted information from one end of a supply chain to the other can lead to tremendous inefficiencies[...]" realizing that "[...] the variableness of an upstream site is always greater than those of the downstream site." ([26], pp. 93–94) This highlights that correct information is

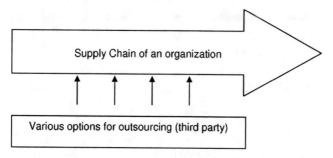

FIGURE 2-5. Simplified model of a supply chain with potential third party involvement (based on [47]).

of key importance in SCM. The Efficient Consumer Response (ECR)[4] is one of the ICT-supported ways to avoid potential drawbacks.

A supply chain with outsourcing options is a simplified model of such a web (see Figure 2-5). If, for example, information management is outsourced, this includes the respective infrastructure as well–i.e., a value chain of an organization where primary and support activities can potentially be outsourced.

An example of a third party could be a logistics provider, a marketing agency, an IT unit, or a human resource organization. This basic supply chain is not different in the healthcare industry. Outsourcing options therefore exist (e.g., the transportation of goods, warehouse management, laundry, or information management, to name but a few).

Each of the third parties involved could act as a center for several providers–for example, by an agreement that one (e.g., logistics supplier) acts on behalf of a group of other logistics providers, as shown in Figure 2-6.

Again, there is no indication that such a model could not be applied in the healthcare sector. Chapter 11 will provide examples of different approaches of third and fourth party providers in healthcare.

This outline of the scope of SCM has clearly revealed that it is still a developing and changing area and will even be more so because of the ICT evolutions shown later on in this chapter.

Operations and SCM

From the perspective of a single operation in the chain (known as the focal operation), SCM can be seen as managing the operations that form its supply side and those that form its demand side as shown in Figure 2-7.

It is obvious that SCM has to balance customer requirements and operations resources through a coordinated delivery of products and services from the supply chain, for which time is required to supply the quantity and quality of products and services demanded. Through the purchasing function, the operation and its suppliers are brought together as indicated in Figure 2-8.

---

[4] The basic idea of ECR is to be well informed about consumers' reactions and wishes and react accordingly: all parts of the supply chain must be integrated and directed towards the needs of the consumer. This can be achieved with an adequate information technology along the supply chain ([16], p.447).

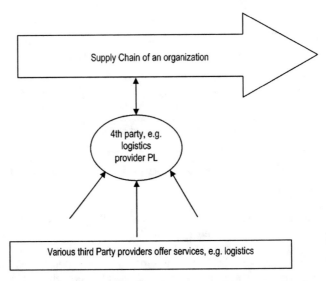

FIGURE 2-6. Establishment of a center to coordinate other third party suppliers (based on [47]).

For healthcare, a simplified supply chain could be made up by the elements in Figure 2-9, stressing both the physical flow and the flow of information, realizing that without correct information the whole process would become distorted (e.g., the bullwhip-effect outlined above).

In Figure 2-9, the business organization is a manufacturer of medical supplies (e.g., a pharmaceutical enterprise) that develops a new drug for which it needs chemical substances and commodities. The company gets those from a first-tier supplier who might have bought them directly from the producer (second-tier supplier). After acquiring all necessary raw materials and producing the medicine according to their research formula, the pharmaceutical organization offers the drug on the market and markets it. The product may be purchased by a hospital because it is required for its patients (end consumers). The product may also be bought by a pharmacy because

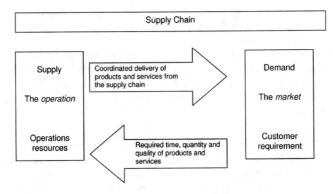

FIGURE 2-7. Scope of a supply chain (based on [16]).

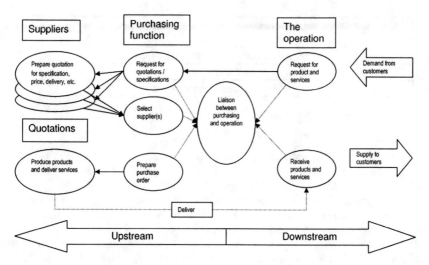

FIGURE 2-8. Balancing supply and demand (based on [16]).

a general practitioner has prescribed it to a patient for treatment and that patient has ordered it at the local pharmacy. Hospitals, wholesalers, and pharmacies (not included in the diagram) may buy the product and store it in case of need. Where hospitals and pharmacies are linked directly to the consumer, wholesalers are not. They sell medical products to hospitals or pharmacies, and there are many more links possible. This example, however, should help clarify the interaction of the key players and the respective physical and information flows, as well as the whole potential scope of a supply chain in the healthcare sector.

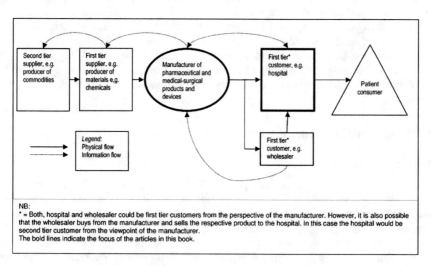

FIGURE 2-9. Simplified model of a supply chain in secondary care.

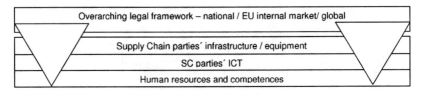

FIGURE 2-10. Support activities.

In integrating the support activities (see Porter's value chain model), a healthcare industry approach would have to consider the legal framework in addition to the supply chain parties' resources, as shown in Figure 2-10.

The support activities seem to become the center of attention (again). The Financial Times recently issued a special report on "Shared Services" [27], highlighting that "shared services, whereby support functions common to multiple units within an organisation are consolidated in a single provider, are a growing trend for companies and public sector bodies looking to cut costs and improve efficiencies." ([28], p. 2). In a contribution to this report, Mark Vernon stresses that if an organization has decided to share services, "it is essential that employees, suppliers and partners develop a cohesive relationship[...]." ([29], p. 10). Obviously, this proposal goes much beyond present practices according to which hospitals, surgeons, and so forth share infrastructure or outsourced services such as invoicing. In the United Kingdom, the NHS set up shared services as a separate business organization in 2003, offering "automated invoicing services to NHS hospitals." ([30], p. 6) Today, this company also runs payroll and procurement services. Presently, it appears, they themselves have discussed outsourcing some of their activities to India to decrease their own costs.

This section should conclude by looking at the situation in Japan as an example of where SCM has been introduced in a specific way. In Japan, SCM is utilized by the Keiretsu network which, in fact, is a "supplier network," in which a large manufacturer might give financial support to the integrated suppliers through loans, or even cross ownership, interlocking directorates, long-term business relationships, and social ties. Keiretsu members are expected to commit to providing excellent service, technical expertise, and quality improvements to the manufacturer. In return, the manufacturer assures the coalition partners of long-term continuity of demand. ([31], p. 112) A potential problem is – as experienced by many organizations – that the companies rely very much on each other and may lose their innovativeness as their need to compete decreases.

Changes in the Supply Chain

Changes Due to ICT

The past years have shown that the speed of changes has increased. There is no reason to believe that this will be different in the future. As all changes more or less affect the supply directly or indirectly, business organizations are advised to take into account potential variations as they design their strategy [32].

Today, most of the changes are closely linked to the development of the Internet. What began with businesses confirming purchase orders and ensuring payments to suppliers continued with fundamental changes in purchasing behavior as much more information became available for potential buyers ([7], p. 453). The Web became well-known in 1994, but it took some years (1998–2000) to be developed and widely deployed ([33], p. 35). Reasons for this delay were lack of security and a corresponding lack of trust [34]. Web browsers provided organizations with a much faster way to look for alternative suppliers. In the past, this was seen as a time-consuming and therefore expensive exercise and as a result, long-standing relationships were preferred and actively developed.

The economies of scale in purchasing also changed. Today, it has become much easier for potential buyers, in particular those requiring low quantities, to form joint purchasing agreements with other organizations in similar situations (as long as this does not fall foul on competition law[5]). The group may be linked into the purchasing companies' own information systems. Such an approach has been adopted, for example, by many of the large automotive, engineering, and petrochemical companies. There is, however, a drawback: the effort to reduce costs may clash with the intent of forming a network of reliable suppliers ([7], p. 454).

A New Way of Thinking

All the models outlined so far are, by and large, traditional, 3 Party examples.[6] These models are *input-oriented*–that is, value is added by the various business processes. At the end, it is hoped that the target is achieved–i.e., the delivery of a product or service is made in time to a market participant. The new models, in particular the *4-Parties* model, stress a different approach. The focus is on the outcome, and subsequently all decisions affecting the processes of all partners and their strategic moves are taken care of.

Today the understanding of a supply chain goes much beyond a "one-line, step-by-step forward model" as it was described earlier on. Is it still adequate to look through an "input" lens when designing a supply chain? Is it not the "output" or even "outcome" lens which is much more important? To turn Porter's model of the value chain upside down, the definition of the competitive advantage (outcome) should be made first, before decisions on how to achieve it (input) are made. This result-oriented approach may be much more obvious in the health or learning sectors: the patient's health status has to be improved and the student has to increase knowledge, skills, and competences. The question is not which primary and secondary activities have to be performed first, but how they have to be defined based on the results that must be achieved. The outcome orientation in the healthcare sector can be demonstrated in the following diagram (see Figure 2-11):

The outcome approach begins with the stakeholders of a healthcare system, their interests, and their objectives. Stakeholders are the society as such, but also the various groups and individuals, such as families, friends, employers, manufacturers of medical supplies, health insurance companies, and the government. Based on interest and power, these stakeholders could be put into a matrix to identify those being interested and having the power to establish a "care environment." The stakeholders are interested in a system in which patients receive better than adequate treatment. The question, therefore,

---

[5] In most of the countries in the world cartels, such purchasing agreements are forbidden. According to EU Law, however, the di minimis rule might be applicable–i.e., such cooperation might be allowed if the effect on trade between Member States is negligible (Steiner 1991, pp. 16).

[6] This expression is preferred to 3 PL, as the latter gives the impression that it can work with the logistics function only – the same refers to the 4 PL examples.

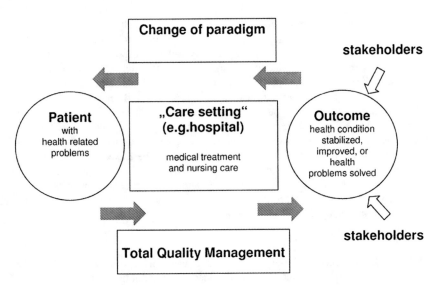

FIGURE 2-11. Outcome-oriented perspective of patient care.

is where and how a patient can be treated or cared for in the best possible manner. The process "care and treatment" begins with the admission of a patient, often initiated by a practitioner. A patient is sent, for example, to a hospital where practitioners hope medical treatment will achieve a targeted outcome: a healthy or at least an improved or stabilized state of the patient. This *change in paradigm* increases the transparency of processes. The same is valid for a learning process where the outcome of the learner–i.e. the acquisition of knowledge, skills, and competencies–is the starting point for designing the curricula and syllabi, considering the type of learner. Obviously, such processes allow for a substantial quality enhancement system because the outcome is well defined and the means are always measured in terms of effectiveness and efficiency in the light of the desired outcome [13]. They have to be SMART (specific, measurable, achievable, relevant, and timed).

The following examples, case studies, and viewpoints of CEOs are outlined to substantiate this *outcome* approach and to hightlight innovative procedures of business organizations to design supply chains that meet their needs.

Examples of Business Organizations and their CEOs

IBM

IBM is said to have been one of the first to use the term eBusiness in 1997, when it started to rethink its businesses in terms of the potential of the Internet [36] and changed its processes successfully. Operations that needed two hours in 1981 are accomplished today in one second.

Their worldwide complex supply chain structure is managed according to an On-Demand-Strategy. Production starts at their Fulfilment Center after an order has been received. More than 33,000 suppliers operate and distribute on behalf of IBM. This make-to-order system is web-based and integrates all ICT structures. The processes are monitored electronically and are therefore totally transparent, which allows for very effective quality control and early detection of deviations. Human resource and other business functions are completely outsourced; the business organization is fully focused on its core competencies.

IBM is said to save between 5 and 7 billion dollars per year. Their basic idea was not to analyze individual processes but to analyze the *modules of the enterprise* only. A module is made up of processes, employees, and technology (linking primary and support activities). For each module, the internal processes, achievement through cooperation, and outsourcing are defined [37].

From this case, the following key terms should be discussed in the light of the healthcare sector:

– *fulfillment center*
– *module*

Approach by José Ignacio López de Arriortua

López was definitely one of the most controversial managers in the 1990s. He used to be an extremely successful purchasing manager, first for General Motors Corporation (GM) and then for Volkswagen AG. His success at GM triggered Volkswagen to offer him a spectacular contract, which prompted GM to file a lawsuit against Volkswagen. López was said to be the first who selected the suppliers not on the basis of relationship or outsourcing agreements but solely on outcome–the quality and price he had targeted before he negotiated the deals. "He cared not a whit about long-standing relationships with GM suppliers, even when those suppliers were GM subsidiaries. He put those wanting to do business with GM through relentless rounds of bidding, then demanded that the survivors hit even lower marks. When they squawked that they couldn't meet his impossible targets, López sent teams of efficiency experts to their plants to teach them how to save steps in the manufacturing process." ([38], p. 92). This was not all. López went even further and replaced line and staff positions with employees of tier-1 suppliers–that is, he changed supplier relations, supply chain management, and the management of plant operations. The major drawback of this successful cost-cutting effort according to critics was the short-term orientation ([39], p.1). What is left today is the target-pricing approach that has become one element of an outcome orientation.

The following key terms should also be discussed in the light of the healthcare sector:

– *target pricing*
– *supplier relations*

Another example of organizations and their development of new business strategies is the following case, outlined by Marc Helmold in October 2005, Purchasing Manager of the Ford Motor Company / Mazda Motor Corporation in Hiroshima, Japan, at that time.

Ford Motor Company and Mazda Motor Corporation

Fierce competition and increasing globalization have significantly changed the face of the automotive industry. The need to develop more and more customized services and products with shorter lead times have forced enterprises to develop new strategies from the design phase of a vehicle to the point of mass production. Ford Motor Company (Ford), for example, has introduced a new Global Production and Development System

(GPDS) by adapting the system of Mazda (MPDS), which is a partner of the Ford group. This system is a benchmark in terms of speed and efficiency and is characterized by

- lean, standardized manufacturing processes
- highly motivated, multi-skilled employees across functions
- a successful system of recycling parts
- effective knowledge management

GPDS was implemented on all new vehicle programs by September, 2005. Whereas the former system focused only on the vehicle itself, GPDS distinguishes between the lower body and upper body of a vehicle. The diagram in Figure 2-12 outlines the structure and processes of GPDS.[7]

Because GPDS covers areas from the conceptual idea of a vehicle, engine, or transmission (Program Start) to the point of mass production (Job 1), the upstream supply chain management has been highly affected by this new approach. Whereas the Ford Product Development System (FPDS) needs up to 27.5 months, the Mazda system is much faster. The Volvo Production and Development System (VPDS) is also not able to compete with the Mazda Production and Development System (see Table 2-1). The Ford group aims for a lead time of approximately 12 months.

As a consequence of GPDS, suppliers are selected and contracted at an early stage to bring in highly capable and cost-effective, state-of-the art technology and know-how. This involvement covers areas such as development, quality, and the entire supply chain

---

[7] Consult Ford GPDS Guidelines in 2005.

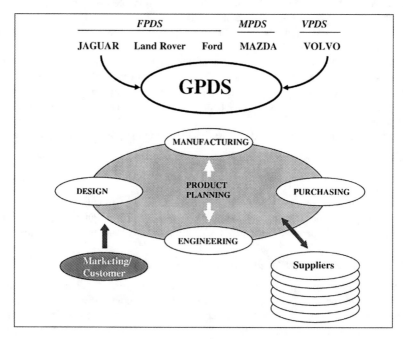

FIGURE 2-12. Global Production and Development System (GPDS).

TABLE 2-1. Lead time of Ford, Volvo and Mazda.

Production and Development System	Lead Time
Ford	25–27.5 Months
Volvo	22–25 Months
Mazda	17–18 Months

management of suppliers. A specific focus is put on success factors such as platform concepts, commonality, corporate part groups, and compatibility across the consumer business groups of Ford, Jaguar, Volvo, Rover, or Mazda. Benefits are seen in:

- the reuse of under-body architecture across programs and brands
- higher quality verification during the prototype phases
- reduced tooling lead times
- fewer engineering changes after concept phase and Job 1
- reduced product and engineering costs, prototypes, and resources.

Based on the fact that more and more value-adding operations in the production cycle of vehicles or power train components–such as engines or transmissions–are outsourced to external suppliers and systems suppliers, GPDS has also severe impacts on the upstream supply chain management and supplier relationships [40]. As the suppliers are now involved at an early stage of product development and expected to support all milestones throughout the supply chain, an effective supply chain synchronization of the material and information flow will become one essential criterion for the successful roll out of GPDS within the Ford Motor group. The process of involving the suppliers now starts at the design concept phase, establishing an early program sourcing strategy. To accomplish this, it will be necessary to create close relationships and strategic alliances with suppliers through the supply chain [41]. If suppliers are considered real partners who actively contribute as a learning organization and strive for innovations and improvements, GPDS will be successful [42].

In addition to the aforementioned issues–the following key terms from this example should be discussed in the light of the healthcare sector:

- *lean, standardized processes*
- *involvement of suppliers / customers*

easyInternetcafé Ltd. (eIc)

easyInternetcafé is an organization under the umbrella of the easyGroup, founded by the Greek entrepreneur Stelios Haji-Ioannou. Other companies in the group are easyJet, easyCar, easyCinema, easy.com, easyMoney, and easyValue. More companies with the *easy* brand are planned. easyInternetcafé was founded in 1999 (in those days called easyEverything) as a chain of cafés taking advantage of the Internet boom in those years. At the beginning, the cafés were established in high-volume street locations in the European Union (in the United Kingdom in particular) and the United States, fully equipped and owned by easyInternetcafé. The decline of the "dot-com boom" affected the development of the organization and caused deep inroads which became obvious when the business was turned into a franchising arrangement. The franchisees had to bear the costs of the property and hardware. This not only cut down the fixed costs, but also allowed the organization to focus on those activities of their supply chain that they could do best: to open about 10 stores per week, smaller in size, which did not have to be staffed, over a period of 2-3 years. easyInternetcafé focused on their core competence and outsourced all the noncore activities. "Their core competence was thought to be the yield management business model applied to the Internet café business and the proprietary hardware and software to implement it[...] elc only needed to research and award franchises and deliver the equipment to the franchisees. All other activities which were earlier undertaken by elc, were now the responsibility of the franchisees." ([43], p. 6). The question that easyInternetcafé is currently pondering is to which extent the purchasing and equipping of the various stores should be outsourced as well.

Further key terms to be added to the discussion in the light of the healthcare sector:

- *core business*
- *core competencies*

SMART and UPS

The example of easyInternetcafé tests the boundaries of outsourcing. The guiding principle for their business appears to be to focus on what they can do best, their core competencies, and try to outsource those activities which may be part of the core business–e.g., equipping the café–but not necessarily their core competence. In the past years, more and more examples can be seen in which organizations use outsourcing as part of their strategy rather than focusing on outsourcing only those activities which are not their core business. Whereas traditional outsourcing can be understood as outsourcing a noncore function to a third party, transformational outsourcing underlines the strategic objectives of the organization. Cutting costs and increasing efficiency by outsourcing is no longer the key driver. Increasing strategic options and being able to implement them appears to be much more at the forefront of thinking today. These options can be cut costs, but can also be much more, "enhancing quality of operational processes" or "differentiating the company from competitors." ([44], p. 1). Transformational outsourcing, it appears, affects the whole organization. It also requires the third party to become much more involved in businesses of the organization, which means that a new problem may evolve: the integration of different company cultures [44].

The production and sale of the "Smart" automobile underlines a transformational model in which the *main* organization adds only a relatively small proportion of the operational value added, in this case about 15% [45].

The author of the case study extended the scope for logistics service providers when describing the logistics of UPS and raised the question of whether or not they move towards *4PL* (i.e., involving a fourth party), in this case a logistics supplier. "The fourth party logistics service provider (4PL) participates in supply chain coordination instead of providing operational logistics and fulfilment services, like a traditional third party logistics provider (3PL) would." ([45], p. 1). This extension has a major effect on the outsourcing organization and its partner, as it means that the service provider (partner) becomes much more integrated into the customer's supply chain and its performance and strategy. Specific benefits can be identified, including "[...] increasing value to customers, strengthening customer relations, and escaping the drive towards commoditization of logistics services." ([45], p. 1). Thus, the logistics service provider becomes more of a coordinator rather than an operator of assets in service to the customer [46]–i.e., "service providers are aiming to evolve from the mass services segment towards the professional services segment." [47]. In summary, this can be demonstrated in the process-oriented supply chain (adapted from [21, 47] in Figures 2-13 and 2-14).

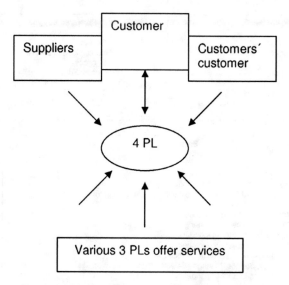

FIGURE 2-13. Development of supply chain scope 4PL I.

In the latter models, the 4 PL coordinates with the manufacturer on the one hand and the logistics operators on the other. The manufacturer itself designs the supply chain strategy and has to coordinate with customers and the 4 PL. Finally, the logistics operators have to coordinate with 4 PL and perform all logistics activities necessary.

Figure 2-14 includes a contract between a manufacturer and the 4 PL. Whereas the manufacturer designs the supply chain strategy and coordinates with customers and 4 PL, the 4 PL additionally has to coordinate with logistics operators that have to perform the logistics activities. According to van Hoek, UPS uses this system with Cisco Systems. "UPS Logistics receives notification when products are ready for shipment from contract

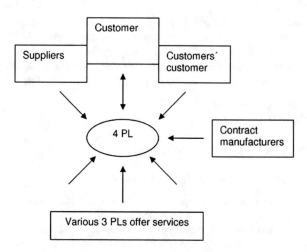

FIGURE 2-14. Development of supply chain scope 4 PL II.

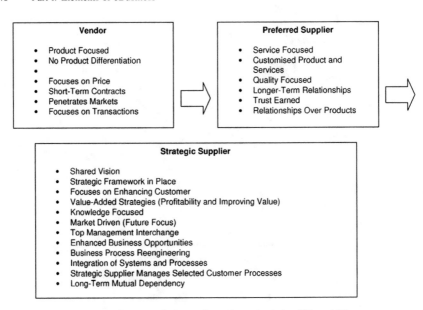

FIGURE 2-15. Strategic supplier alliance evolution ([9], p. 148).

manufacturers to the Cisco plant. These products are then collected within 24 hours from one of more than 20 sites around the world. UPS books aircraft into the continent, and receives product into a dedicated 86,000 square foot European logistics center, owned and operated by UPS." ([47], p. 9). With the support of optimization software, the number of deliveries and congestion at the loading dock can be reduced. The order status is communicated to Cisco directly so that they can inform their customers immediately. All movements are registered in both the UPS and Cisco systems. Similar arrangements could be made with a multinational pharmaceutical company or with a group of smaller pharmaceutical organizations.

The latter two examples, in particular, highlight the change of relationships between parties in a supply chain. Caslione and colleagues [9] characterize the development as a "Strategic Supplier Alliance Evolution," identifying the major concerns of what they call *vendor, preferred supplier, and strategic supplier*" (see Figure 2-15).

Additional key terms to be considered within the healthcare sector:

– *transformational outsourcing*
– *strategic alliances*

Conclusions and Recommendations

Lessons learned for the health care sector

The examples outlined in this chapter have shown a wide scope of opportunities that have one idea in common: meeting the individual needs of the organization. It may therefore be concluded that each party in the supply chain of the health care sector has to identify its specific needs when answering the following key questions ([16], p. 443):

What?

- Doing everything in-house on one extreme, to outsourcing everything at the other extreme?
- Outsourcing only trivial activities on one extreme, to outsourcing even core activities at the other extreme?

Who?

- How many suppliers will be used by the operation?
- How close are the relationships?

As for any other industry, these two dimensions appear to be valid for the health care sector as well, as the following lessons learned from the previous examples seem to indicate. In answering these questions, the scope of the supply chain is understood in a wide sense–i.e., comprising not only the primary but also the support activities as outlined in this chapter.

Lessons Learned from Business Organizations and their CEOs

It should first be determined to what extent the cases and examples outlined earlier in the chapter (examples of business organizations and their CEO: IBM, López, Ford, easy Internet café) could be applied in the healthcare sector as well. The message from SMART and UPS (see example in the text) will be considered separately because of their newness and significance.[8]

A Vision for Health Care: The "On Demand" Strategy   At the very least, the *make-to-order* principle of IBM's supply chain appears to fit the health sector as well. The demand is initiated by the patient with a health-related problem. The fulfillment center could be a hospital, solely as the infrastructure (i.e., building and furniture, medical equipment, IT infrastructure). Practitioners, nurses, and other personnel would be the suppliers that *service* the patient on site. When the patient leaves the hospital, transportation and other patient needs (defined as modules) would be assigned to network partners near the patient's home, depending on the type of illness. Medicine would be distributed directly via third parties, such as pharmacies and other providers of medical supplies, who would also act as partners in the relationship. The medicine would be delivered in the quality and quantity the patient needs. No prefabricated packages would be distributed; the portions would be customized by the third party (e.g., pharmacy). With a virtual hospital proposed some years ago, this is not as new an idea as one might think. The innovative approach has been put in place–in a less rigorous manner, however–in hospitals and in the home care sector.

Scope of Development: Bundling Orders   López' approach could be turned the other way around. The purchasing power of hospitals should be strengthened so that they are in a position to negotiate much more favorable contracts with suppliers (supplier relationships) that are advantageous for both parties (target pricing / target costs). Initiatives to place larger orders through cooperation have been in existence for some time. GPOs in the United States, procurement hubs in the United Kingdom, and purchasing cooperatives in Germany all have one goal in common: to achieve economies of scale by

---

[8] The key terms taken from the various examples are printed in italics.

bundling orders. Competition law, however, has to be respected. Purchasing cartels may be allowed if competition is not distorted and the relevant market is not dominated by one or a few parties. If trade between member states of the European Union is affected, E.U. competition law has to be applied, independent of where the organizations are located [35].

Cutting Lead Times: Standardization and Outsourcing   The lessons learned from Ford and Mazda appear at first to be more difficult to transfer to the health sector. Nevertheless, it may be reasonable to identify lean standardized servicing processes (*clinical pathways*) and cross-functional activities (information technology, materials management, pharmacy). In both areas, it is essential that all partners, suppliers, and customers, get involved to improve efficiency without endangering effectiveness. With the help of ICT, a competent knowledge management is of key importance. This may improve service quality and also decrease time lost for ineffective and inefficient cooperation between the various parties involved in value chain activities.

The approaches of López and Ford have something in common: lean thinking and target pricing / costing. Nigel Edwards, the policy director of the NHS confederation, highlights in a special report of the Financial Times, "Lean's focus on delivering care is a refreshing antidote to benchmarks, targets and the traditional approach to management." ([1], p.1). Robert Bruce, author of the article, underlines the situation by using the example of the pathology department at Bolton hospital in the United Kingdom, which had grown over the years in a very unsystematic way. "It conducted thousands of tests a day but results took longer than they should, patients were unhappy and staff felt under constant pressure." An expert team looked into the matter and found out that the department used a "batch-and-queue system...that meant a 24-hour turnaround was the minimum[...]"([1], p.1). The solution was obvious: redesign of rooms and reallocation of equipment so that "processing times were cut from between 24 and 36 hours to between two and three hours. Fewer staff were required and the space needed could be reduced by 50 percent." ([1], p.1). Bruce concludes that this way of reform, initiated from the inside, works much better than changes imposed from the outside. On this basis, costing as well can be significantly improved.

Strategic Move: Focus on Core Competencies   The concepts outlined in the easyInternetcafé case could be linked to the IBM case to the extent that a company could offer treatment sites on street corners. This concept could also relate to recreation centers and the like. Following this example, however, the core business would need to be defined (the activities oriented towards a business area) but defining the core competencies would be much more important. This is part of a strategy analysis made by an increasing number of hospitals. Johnson and colleagues [14] pinpoint core competencies as those capabilities which enable the organization to outperform competitors on the basis of their ability to best meet the needs of customers (critical success factor). What does this mean in the health care sector? Does it refer to a specific medical knowledge or other non-subject-related competencies? This has to be individually defined by the healthcare providers themselves (see Chapter 11).

Lessons Learned from Transformational Outsourcing

The Move from 3 PL to 4 PL   There is no reason to believe that the 3 PL and 4 PL models could not be applied to the healthcare sector as well. This does not have to be restricted to logistics services, but can basically be organized in terms of any of the chain processes and activities.

In the example illustrated in Figure 2-6, all services are outsourced to a first-tier supplier (e.g., a medical supply center) that offers customized drugs and other medical products together with consultancy service related to the products and their use in patient treatment, food, and maintenance (see Chapter 11). It may, if necessary, require that several second-tier suppliers *purchase* treatment, medical supplies, and other products and services according to the needs of the patient.

The model detailed in Figure 2-13, for example, may consist of a pharmaceutical manufacturer, a wholesaler as its customer, and a hospital. All three parties require logistics support. This can be coordinated by a logistics center acting on behalf of a number of logistics providers. The logistics center may, for example, supply all products to a wholesaler, but at the same time arrange for meeting the needs of all parties of the supply chain in terms of supply quantities and delivery times. This is a further development of the model outlined in Figure 2-4 and will be dealt with in Chapter 11.

The model demonstrated in Figure 2-14 also includes a contract that is agreed upon between the 4 PL and a manufacturer, or several who produce materials for the supplier. It is characterized by a close cooperation between the fourth party and a pharmaceutical enterprise. The pharmaceutical organization designs the supply chain strategy, and has to coordinate with hospitals and wholesale and retail pharmacies that may be either general or specialist businesses. The logistics operators offer their products and services to the 4 PL, who decides on the necessary activities. The 4 PL also has contracts with manufacturers to produce on behalf of the pharmaceutical company.[9]

The 4 PL models, in particular, require a high-level information system. Supply chain management information systems are crucial in achieving the objectives to decrease costs and increase the responsiveness of a supply chain [48]. McLaren and colleagues disclosed that the application of information systems in the management of supply chains can increase operational efficiency and flexibility and improve internal and external planning and analysis [48]. This, however, requires adequate equipment, software, and most importantly the competence of the organization to operate the information system. This entails an interdisciplinary approach to competitive strategy, supply chain management, and interorganizational information systems.

These models stress that the boundaries of value and supply chains have become flexible due to the changing roles of suppliers and customers, supported by the developments of ICT. This is best characterized by *transformation outsourcing* and the formation of *strategic alliances* in an abundant variety of forms.

Supply Chain Management in Healthcare   Generally speaking, it can be said that the principles of a supply chain in the manufacturing industry can be transferred to healthcare. Adaptations, however, have to be considered. Some of them are due to distinct governance frameworks related to the extent to which the healthcare sector is independent. "The governance framework describes whom the organisation is there to serve and how the purposes and priorities of the organisation should be decided." ([14], p. 613). Accordingly, the following ideas might not be able to be applied in a given situation without the existence of an adequate framework. Other differences

---

[9] Although this might not be an issue yet in healthcare, it should be noted that the *4 Parties models* (Figures 2-13 and 2-14) do not just regard the technical side. People of different national and organizational cultures have to be respected as–enhanced by the developments of IT systems–communication takes place worldwide.

remain, however. The manufacturing industry moves *products* to process them, and health management (as a part of the service industry), moves *processes* to a spot to treat a person who needs them (e.g., is bound to a hospital, home, or has had surgery)– moving a product to be processed versus moving processes to a product. The supply chain, to this extent, may be comparable with clinical governance.[10] In such models, all stakeholders are included to identify the quality as the outcome, which the patient interprets as being *healthy* (see section entitled "A New Way of Thinking", and the Stirling Model for Clinical Governance [49]).

Production planning and demand management are different. Both the *product* (treatment and care) and the demand for the product have a much greater variability in healthcare than in other industries. The manufacturing approach, which comes closest to healthcare, is *make-to-demand* and handles a considerable demand variability in a given time period.

Yet another distinction between manufacturing and healthcare is the incomplete control of all factors contributing to good clinical outcomes. While the evolving good can always be seen in a manufacturing product's value chain, with the activities in it or on it always directly proved, this is by no means the case in the healthcare arena. The variance in clinical outcomes depends not only on the input and quality of the service, but on factors inherent to the patient, such as her physical and mental state, individual drug tolerance, and compliance. In primary care, a particular problem arises: the physician sees the patient only at certain points in time, such as when he is in the surgery. After leaving the surgery, the patient (and thus also the outcome) are *out of his control*–that is, the effectiveness of medical care is like a black box. In contrast to the hospital setting, there is obviously a lack of information in the supply chain in primary care due to the restricted control of the patient's behavior.

Electronics may partly change this situation and *open the black box*. In home care, for example, physiological parameters of a patient can be measured and transmitted by telemedicine devices and allow the physician to monitor the patient's physical state. A patient's compliance in following the medical regime can also be made more visible to the physician. An electronic pill-box, for example, informs the doctor to which degree the patient follows the specifications of the treatment [50]. Another tested possibility is that patients are sent an SMS message via mobile phone to remind them to take their medication [50]. In London, a wireless network has been created that links 7,000 users in the eight hospitals of central London. It was established to move to a completely paperless, electronic patient record system. In this way, physicians can get information about a patient wherever they are [51]. With examples like these, it becomes obvious that IT systems will allow the introduction of a seamless information chain comparable to a chain of a manufacturer, to the extent that a complete monitoring of the processes is possible as they become transparent. This does not, however, mean (as it is more likely in a supply and value chain in manufacturing industry) that the outcome will be perfect. There will be the risk that, although the activities have been performed

---

[10] It has to be admitted that talking about human beings in terms of processes and products rather raise objections than support. However, it has to be considered that many activities on a patient are not possible unless the service is moved towards him – wherever he or she is. Whereas an activity in the manufacturing industry is basically made step-by-step, healthcare always has to deal with a person who may not be able to be shifted according to most cost-efficient manufacturing processes but has the "processes" have to be shifted instead where the patient is, independent of any possibility to consider efficiency issues.

faultlessly, the patient may not get better. This is the risk that is much higher in this sector than in other industries where the effect of operations can be anticipated much easier. Overall, the effectiveness of a treatment can be seen much better, and necessary "corrective actions" initiated much earlier. In fact, with the new technology, patients may not have to stay in hospitals because they can be at home and be monitored by the doctors from their surgeries. To this extent, the patient himself is empowered to play a greater role in administering his own medical care [52]. This example very strongly stresses the integration of support and primary activities as discussed before. In fact, the supply chain does not end with the product being delivered to the clinical unit, but extends further into the clinical domain.

The most important difference between manufacturing and healthcare, however, touches the ultimate purpose of healthcare and requires a differentiation between the manufacturer's and the healthcare provider's perspectives. While a supply chain managed by a manufacturer seeks to optimize the added economic value, a supply chain governed by a healthcare provider focuses on the added clinical value. Traditional supply chain approaches, therefore, may remain valid for a manufacturer of medical supplies. Yet, in order to incorporate the healthcare provider's point of view, a new supply chain model specifically geared for the healthcare industry needs to be developed (see Chapter 14).

Other Effects on Healthcare   Other areas of a supply chain in the public sector are also affected. They might as well have an effect on healthcare. This, however, is the subject of a separate investigation and cannot be dealt within the scope of this chapter. Internet-based networks, closed communities centered on a particular global customer or supplier, electronic tendering, and virtual buying partnerships are terms that might crop up in healthcare soon because they have led to significant cost reductions elsewhere. It is assumed that administrative costs alone could be reduced by 25–75%, and the purchasing prices by 10–30% [53]. A global procurement strategy, for example, focuses on global supply chain integration, global eProcurement and global strategic supplier alliances, independent of the type and size of business organizations [9]. "Today, global procurement and its supply chain managers look at the business of the company in the aggregate, and cross-disciplinary decision making is replacing functional silos in all their markets globally." ([9], p. 135) Other issues, however, will then have to be considered even more than they are now: great distances and diverse languages, cultures, currencies, local trade regulations, and so on (global sourcing will be addressed in Chapters 12 and 13 in detail).

Responsibility Division and Tiers – What Triggers the Processes?

The attempt is made to identify some of the potential partners in the supply chain and how they are, or may be, interlinked, taking eBusiness into account. One simple possibility is to start with a final customer. In the first example, the supply chain is triggered by the consumer (i.e., the patient) who arrives at an office of a physician or is admitted to a hospital. It is then launched by a healthcare professional either by ordering a treatment or by prescribing a medicine. Only in the case of over-the-counter (OTC) drugs or non-prescription drugs, or other products patients purchase themselves is the supply chain is initiated by the consumer.

However, practically speaking, only in case of special or customized products does the healthcare professional trigger the chain on behalf of an individual patient. In any

TABLE 2-2. The supply chain interaction matrix in the healthcare sector*.

		Role of the supplier			
		Manufacturer	**First-tier Customer** *Hospital*	**Second-tier Customer** *Pharmacy*	**Third-tier Customer** *Patient*
Role of the Buyer	**Manufacturer**	**B2B** *Relationship* • buying *ebusiness example* • electronic order-to-payment cycle • searching product information on the web	**B2C$_1$** *Relationship* • knowledge transfer *ebusiness example* • electronic clinical trials	**B2C$_2$** *Relationship* • less common	**B2C$_3$** *Relationship* • non existent
	First-tier Customer *Hospital*	**C$_1$2B** *Relationship* • buying *ebusiness examples* • electronic order-to-payment cycle • searching product information on the web	**C$_1$2C$_1$** *Relationship* • sharing a pharmacy or warehouse *ebusiness examples* • electronic order-to-payment cycle • electronic logistics services • searching product information on the web	**C$_1$2C$_2$** *Relationship* • outsourced pharmacy or warehouse *ebusiness examples* • electronic order-to-payment cycle • electronic logistics services • searching product information on the web	**C$_1$2C$_3$** *Relationship* • non existent
	Second-tier Customer *Pharmacy*	**C$_2$2B** *Relationship* • buying *ebusiness examples* • electronic order-to-payment cycle • searching product information on the web	**C$_2$2C$_1$** *Relationship* • less common	**C$_2$2C$_2$** *Relationship* • less common	**C$_2$2C$_3$** *Relationship* • non existent
	Third-tier Customer *Patient*	**C$_3$2B** *Relationship* • information retrieval *ebusiness examples* • web-based patient information system	**C$_3$2C$_1$** *Relationship* • information retrieval *ebusiness examples* • web-based patient information system	**C$_3$2C$_2$** *Relationship* • Buying *ebusiness examples* • Web based ordering (online pharmacy)	**C$_3$2C$_3$** *Relationship* • information exchange *ebusiness examples* • discussion forum and chat

* The 1st, 2nd etc. tier suppliers are not separately listed in this matrix.

other case, it is the healthcare-providing organization that initiates it, estimating the demand from experience or from business analysis.

Many more participants may then get involved once the chain has started to move.

Table 2-2 is an attempt to summarize possible links between the various partners in a supply chain. In contrast to the manufacturing industry, these relationships are rather flat and less hierarchical, which makes a distinction between the various tiers more difficult. To identify types in the healthcare supply chain(s), the criterion applied is whether or not the liaison is with the final link in the supply chain, involving the ultimate consumer, or with one of the prior links in the supply chain, involving two commercial businesses.

Table 2-2 shows the relationship between selected stakeholders within the supply chain that are all customers from the manufacturer's point of view, but which may become suppliers themselves. Figure 2-16 illustrates the interactions between all stake-holders based on their business activities (proposed by Ursula Hübner, see also Chapter 14).

It is obvious that the diagram in Figure 2-16 is nothing but an overview of potential relationships. If one considered the networks involved, the respective supply chains

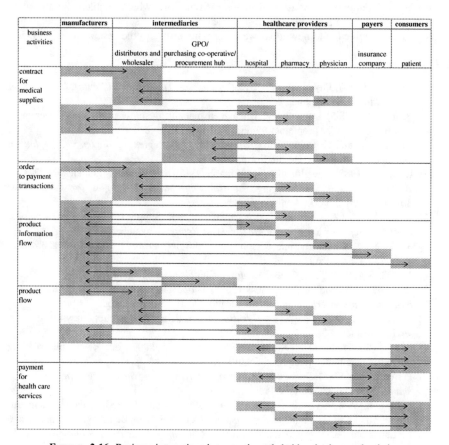

FIGURE 2-16. Business interactions between the stakeholders in the supply chain.

of the partners involved, and all possible supply chains, the links in total cannot be demonstrated in such a table. All connections, however, can be supported by the Web. Further developments will definitely happen, but cannot yet be fully anticipated. What is important is that the changes are not only accepted as a reaction, but that the affected parties try to become part of the mainstream and actively design the relationships in their supply chain–i.e., they manage it. Horst Weber from Deloitte Consulting (operations excellence), who participated in "Virtual roundtable, 2010: What is going to happen in the forthcoming 6 years? (translated from German)," which was organized by the German corporations of Logistics (Deutsche Gesellschaft für Logistik mbH) and Competence Site (NetSkill AG), stipulated the future need of integrating a purely logistical view with the value chain of the whole organization and a stronger link between strategic and operational optimizing tools [54]. The health care industry will not be excluded from these changes. Obviously, some of the issues of this paper will still be topical in the years to come.

Acknowledgement

The author would like to thank Ursula Hübner, the editor of this book, for her understanding and patience demonstrated in long discussions which enabled the author to better understand the particularities in healthcare. Fruitful results emerged, challenging insights were gained, and new ideas were born–hopefully to the benefit of the reader.

References

[1] Bruce, R. (2006) Physician, heal thyself. *Financial Times Special Report, Management Accountancy*, 7 September, 1.

[2] Beattie, A. (2005) Outsourcing, Unchained malady: business is becoming ever more exposed to supplier problems. *Financial Times*, 25 August, 9.

[3] Niehoff, W. and G. Reitz, (2001) *Going Global Strategien, Methoden und Techniken des Auslandsgeschäfts*. Berlin: Springer.

[4] Levitt, T. (1983) The globalisation of markets. *Harvard Business Review*. **61**, 92–102.

[5] Hoecklin, L. (1995) *Managing Cultural Differences, Strategies for Competitive Advantage*. New York: Addison-Wesley.

[6] Mazel, J. L. (2004) New Study Reveals Changes in Supply Chain Management Best Practices. *Supplier Selection & Management Report*. November, 1.

[7] Slack, N., S. Chambers, and R. Johnston, (2001) *Operations Management*. 3rd edn. Harlow: FT Prentice Hall.

[8] Yip, G. S. (2003) *Total Global Strategy II*. Englewood Cliffs: Prentice Hall.

[9] Caslione, J. A. and A. R. Thomas (2001) *Global Manifest Destiny - Growing your business in a borderless economy*. Chicago: Dearborn Publishing.

[10] Wikimedia Foundation (2006) *E-Business*. Available from <http://en.wikipedia.org/wiki/E-Business> [Accessed 25 July 2006].

[11] Bitpipe (2006) *eBusiness*. Needham: TechTarget. Available from: <www.bitpipe.com/tlist/eBusiness.html> [Accessed 25 July 2006].

[12] Porter, M. E. (1985) *Competitive Advantage: Creating and Sustaining Superior Performance*. New York: The Free Press.

[13] Gehmlich, V. (2005) European Credit Transfer System (ECTS), Grundsätze, Instrumente, Risiken und Chancen des Systems. Teil D 3.2. In Benz, W., J. Kohler, and K. Landfried (eds). *Handbuch Qualität in Studium und Lehre, Evaluation nutzen – Akkreditierung sichern – Profil schärfen*. Stuttgart: Dr. Josef Raabe.

[14] Johnson, G., K. Scholes, and R. Wittington. (2005) *Exploring Corporate Strategy.* 7th edn. Englewood Cliffs: Prentice Hall.

[15] Ellram, L. M. and M. C. Cooper, (1993) The Relationship Between Supply Chain Management and Keiretsu. The International Journal of Logistics Management (4) 1–12. Quoted in: Lambert, D. M., S.J. García-Dastuque, and K. L. Croxton. (2005) An evaluation of process-oriented supply chain management frameworks. *Journal of Business Logistics.* **26,** 25–51.

[16] Slack, N., S. Chambers, and R. Johnston, (2004) *Operations Management.* 4th edn. Harlow: FT Prentice Hall.

[17] Simchi-Levi, D., P. Kaminsky, and E. Simchi-Levi. (2000) *Designing and Managing the Supply Chain.* Columbus: McGraw-Hill.

[18] Ayers, J. B. (2001) *Making Supply Chain Management Work: Design, Implementation, Partnerships, Technology and Profits.* Boca Raton: Auerbach Publications.

[19] Monczka, R. M., R. J. Trent, and R. B. Handfield. (1998) *Purchasing and Supply Chain Management.* Mason: South-Western.

[20] Wisner, J.D., G. Keong Leong, and K.-C. Tan. (2005) *Principles of Supply Chain Management: A Balanced Approach.* Mason: South-Western.

[21] Lambert, D. M., S. J. García-Dastuque, and K. L. Croxton. (2005) An evaluation of process-oriented supply chain management frameworks. *Journal of Business Logistics.* **26,** 25–51.

[22] Lambert, D. M., M. C. Cooper, and J. D. Pagh. (1998) Supply Chain Management: Implementation Issues and Research Opportunities. The International Journal of Logistics Management. **9,** 1–19. Quoted in: Lambert, D. M., S. J. García-Dastuque, and K. L. Croxton. (2005) An evaluation of process-oriented supply chain management frameworks. *Journal of Business Logistics.* **26,** 25–51.

[23] Hammer, M. (2001) The Superefficient Company. Harvard Business Review. (79) 82–91. Quoted in: Lambert, D.M., S.J. García-Dastuque, and K. L. Croxton. (2005) An evaluation of process-oriented supply chain management frameworks. *Journal of Business Logistics.* **26,** 25–51.

[24] Quinn, F. J. (2001) A New Agenda for the Decade: An Interview with Michael Hammer. Supply Chain Management Review. **5,** 36–40. Quoted in: Lambert, D.M., S. J. García-Dastuque, and K.L. Croxton. (2005) An evaluation of process-oriented supply chain management frameworks. *Journal of Business Logistics.* **26,** 25–51.

[25] Day, G. S. (1996) Aligning the Organization to the Market. In: Lehmann, D. R. and K. E. Jocz. (1996) Reflections on the Futures of Marketing: Practice and Education. Cambridge: Marketing Science Institute. Quoted in: Lambert, D. M., S. J. García-Dastuque, and K. L. Croxton. (2005) An evaluation of process-oriented supply chain management frameworks. *Journal of Business Logistics.* **26,** 25–51.

[26] Lee, H. L., V. Padmanabhan and S. Whang. (1997) The Bullwhip Effect in Supply Chains. *MIT Sloan Management Review.* **38,** 93–102.

[27] Understanding Shared Services (2006) *Financial Times.* 8 September.

[28] Lester, T. (2006) Sharing services for better results. *Financial Times Understanding Shared Services.* 8 September, 2.

[29] Vernon, M. (2006) Engaging with suppliers and partners for success. *Financial Times Understanding Shared Services.* 8 September, 10.

[30] Thomas, K. (2006) Providing better public services at lower cost. *Financial Times Understanding Shared Services.* 8 September, 6.

[31] Hodgetts, R. M. and F. Luthans, (2000) *International management: culture, strategy and behavior.* 4th edn. Columbus: McGraw-Hill.

[32] About Inc. (2006) *Logistics / Supply Chain*. New York. Available from: <http://logistics.about.com/> [Accessed 14 April 2006].

[33] Johnson, G. and K. Scholes. (2001) *Exploring Corporate Strategy*. 6th edn. Harlow: FT Prentice Hall.

[34] Alexandrou, M. (2006) *IT Project Manager in New York*. West Harrison. Available from: <http://www.mariosalexandrou.com> [Accessed 25 July 2006].

[35] Steiner, J. (1990) *Textbook on EEC Law*. 2nd edn. London: Blackstone Press.

[36] Alexandrou, M. (2006) *eBusiness Definition*. West Harrison. Available from: <http://www.mariosalexandrou.com/definition/ebusiness.asp> [Accessed 25 July 2006].

[37] Kümmerlen, R. (2005) Der sechste Sinn. *Log.Punkt*. (1) 14-18.

[38] Bloodfeud (1997) *Fortune*. **135,** 92.

[39] Moffett, M. H. and W.E. Youngdahl. (1998) *José Ignacio López de Arriortúa*. Glendale: Thunderbird, The American Graduate School of International Management.

[40] Proff, H. and H. Proff. (1998) *Strategien für die Automobilindustrie - Ansatzpunkte im strategischen Management und in der Industriepolitik*. Wiesbaden: Gabler.

[41] Liker, J. and T. Choi. (2005) Fordernde Liebe. *Harvard Business Manager*. **27,** 60–72.

[42] Liker, K. (2004) *The Toyota Way: 14 Management Principles from the World's Greatest Manufacturer*. New York: McGraw-Hill.

[43] Menachof, D. and T. Kedia, (2005). *Logistics and Project Planning at easyInternetcafé Ltd*. London: Case Business School, City University.

[44] Baxter, A. (2005) Outsourcing steps up to a new level. *Financial Times*, 01 June, 1–4.

[45] Van Hoek, R.I. and H. A. M. Weken. (2000) *SMART (car) and smart logistics: A case study in designing and managing an innovative de-integrated supply chain*. Lombard. Available from: Council of Supply Chain Management Professionals. <http://www.cscmp.org/Downloads/CaseStudy/SmartCS.pdf> [Accessed19 April 2006].

[46] Bumstead, J. and K. Cannons, (2002) From 4PL to managed supply-chain operations. *Logistics and transport focus*. **4,** 18–25.

[47] Van Hoek, R. I. (2004) UPS logistics and to move towards 4PL – or not? Lombard. Available from: Council of Supply Chain Management Professionals. <http://www.cscmp.org/Downloads/Education/04LECREMKO.pdf> [Accessed 12 January 2006].

[48] McLaren, T. S., M. M. Head, and Y. Yuan. (2004) Supply chain management information systems capabilities. An exploratory study of electronics manufacturers. *Information Systems and E-Business Management*. **2,** 207–222.

[49] Herbert, D. W. (2000) Clinical Governance. In Scholes, K. and G. Johnson (eds.) *Exploring Public Sector Strategy*. Harlow: FT Prentice Hall, 137

[50] Nairn, G. (2005) Medical information in the digital age. *Financial Times Understanding Medical Innovation*, 24 November, 4.

[51] Stewart, A. (2005) University College London Hospitals. *Financial Times Understanding Medical Innovation*, 24 November, 5.

[52] Colyer E. (2005) Modern healthcare at the touch of a button. *Financial Times Understanding Medical Innovation, 24 November*, 14.

[53] Schinzer, H. (2004) E-Procurement im Public Sector. *Wisu Das Wirtschaftsstudium*. **33,** 1188–1191.

[54] Weber, H. (2004) *E-Interview zum Virtual Roundtable „SCM 2010: Was wird sich in den nächsten 6 Jahren tun? "mit Dr. Horst Weber*. Bremen: Deutsche Gesellschaft für Logistik, Köln: NetSkill. Available from: <http://logistics.de/logistik/scm.nsf/0502D5B00AFACBF8C1256EF3002C3DCF/$File/vr_scm_horst_weber.pdf> [Accessed 31 July 2006].

3
Business Process Analysis

STEFAN JUNGINGER AND EVA KABEL

Executive Summary

Process orientation is a powerful instrument in achieving the goals of eBusiness–i.e., a seamless, efficient flow of information, goods, and money supported by interorganizational information systems. The idea of employing information systems to support business processes is paralleled by the development of workflow management systems (WFMS) that possess knowledge about the business processes and thus are capable of controlling the use of information systems for performing particular tasks within the process. During the management cycle of business process analysis (BPA), *as is* and *to be* processes are designed, modeled, and evaluated according to their intended purpose. Depending on the granularity of the model, this may result in a multitude of interwoven processes. Process landscapes are therefore used to structure different levels of process models in an effort to maintain an overview of the entirety of the processes.

Modeling, analysis, and evaluation are often performed with special database-based modeling tools. In comparison to pure drawing tools, these tools provide sophisticated mechanisms for evaluating and maintaining large quantities of business process models. The tools not only differ in their functionalities, but also in the modeling languages they employ. Although efforts are being made to create a standard modeling language with BPMN or UML, no general standard has been achieved to date.

Several concepts exist with regard to BPA. In this chapter, we will introduce a framework for a generic approach based on the steps of criteria definition, information acquisition, analysis, design, and evaluation. Different techniques can be used to evaluate the modeled processes. Path analysis, volume analysis, and workload analysis, in combination with process simulation, serve to calculate important quantitative parameters such as process time, waiting times, or manpower requirements. A further application area is activity-based costing to determine cost drivers and, among other things, to calculate product and service prices.

In terms of improving process quality, Six Sigma is a clearly defined methodology used in many industries, including healthcare, and often leads to significant results.

Concerning eBusiness applications, a specific approach using so-called *cooperation charts* is presented that aims at the challenge of interorganizational processes. The cooperation chart focuses solely on the communication channels between the organizations involved, leaving out details about their internal processes. If these details are needed, however, workflows may be modeled separately on a more granular level. Supplementing cooperation charts, swim lane diagrams are useful to depict the activities of different partners collaborating in a business process, in particular to highlight the interfaces between these activities. Attention, however, should be paid to the fact that BPA is not feasible on entirely abstract levels and still requires enough details to unfold its power in optimizing processes.

Introduction

Since the beginning of the last decade, process orientation has gradually gained importance [1]. The idea of process orientation focuses on business processes spanning several organizational units, as opposed to focus on the functions and the departments in charge of these functions (see Figure 3-1). Since then, numerous methods for analyzing and improving business processes have been developed. This is reflected in key phrases such as *business process analysis* and *business process re-engineering*. To date, these methods have gained wide acceptance and have become part of the academic education of IT and business management professionals. Fifteen years ago, however, they were only known to a few specialists.

eBusiness is a method that usually involves many participants: the customers, the manufacturers, often also distributors, logistics providers, and providers of electronic

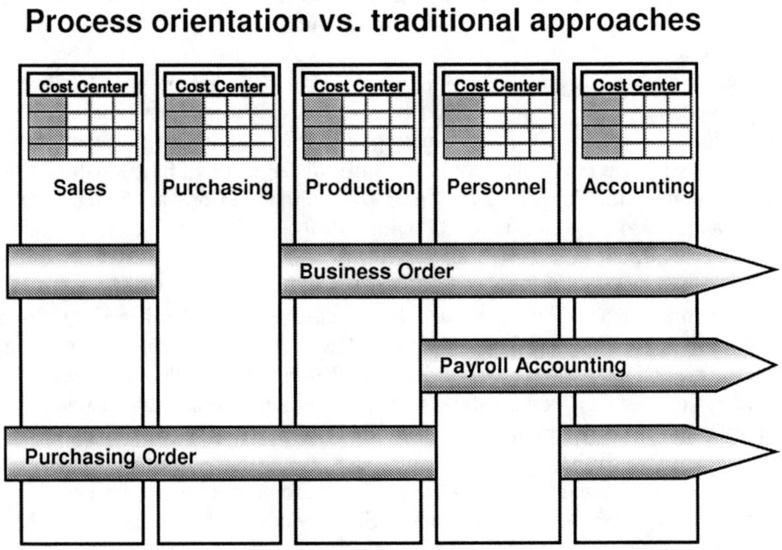

Process orientation vs. traditional approaches

FIGURE 3-1. Process orientation vs. traditional approaches.

market places or online trading exchanges. Because their interaction can become quite complex, the idea of process orientation is a powerful instrument to achieve the goals of eBusiness–i.e., enabling electronic coordination of processes to achieve a better flow of information, goods, and money.

Figure 3-1 shows several business processes crossing different organizational units. For example, the *purchasing order* process is executed by the sales and purchasing departments, by production, and finally by the accounting departments in firms.

Process orientation has also become accepted in the area of information management. The technology primarily responsible for implementing the idea of process orientation is the so-called *workflow management system* (WFMS), joined recently by approaches such as Business Process Execution Language (BPEL). In the healthcare sector, changing to the process paradigm is reflected by the fact that the vendors of healthcare information systems gradually extend their products by workflow components.

The basic concept is that of a system *knowing* the processes and controlling their execution. As shown in Figure 3-2, these systems usually consist of two components. While the processes are defined by experts with the help of the build-time component, and are then translated into an internal representation (e.g., in BPEL), the runtime component controls their execution. This means that the individual participants are given work items by the system that belong to their so-called work lists. These work items contain assignments congruent with the activities of the business process.

Figure 3-3 shows a top-down scheme of BPA integrated into a typical management cycle. Starting from strategic decisions usually made by the top level management, the business processes are (re)designed and documented in a *to be* model. They are then implemented organizationally and/or technically so that they can be subsequently

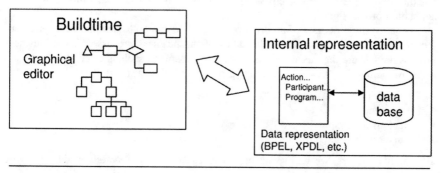

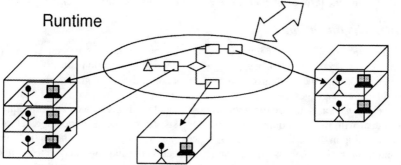

FIGURE 3-2. Process orientation in IT systems.

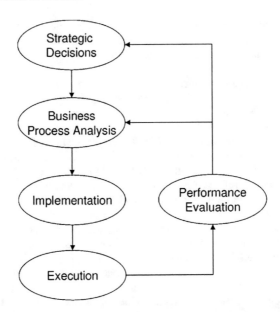

FIGURE 3-3. Classification of business process analysis in a management cycle.

executed. Performance evaluation of newly implemented processes is needed to check whether or not the initial objectives were achieved. It also serves as input for further adaptation or redesign.

To change the processes of an organization, it is common to develop descriptions of the *as is* and especially of the *to be* states of the business processes. These business process models are then used for analysis and assessment, such as calculating time and costs. Modeling thus serves the following purposes in business processes:

- Visualization
- Transparency
- Reduction of complexity
- Simulation

To simplify matters, we will speak of *processes* and *process models* in the following instead of using the term *business processes* and *business process models*.

Chapter Organization

The first section of this chapter introduces the principles of process modeling, starting with the terms *process* and *process model*, describing application areas of process modeling (including the content of process models), and finally giving an overview of the different languages for process modeling. Furthermore, the concept of process landscapes, as well as software tools for process modeling, is presented. The subsequent sections deal with the procedure of process analysis. Based on a generic approach, the role of modeling in the different phases of process analysis is assessed, and an overview of techniques for each phase is given. The fourth section expands on selected techniques for process analysis. Different calculations, simulation, activity-based costing, as well as Six Sigma (a well-known concept for process optimization) are taken into account.

Finally, the application of BPA principles in the eBusiness arena is described, building upon a methodology for implementing eBusiness applications.

Process modeling

Process Modeling Languages, Classification, Examples

Countless definitions for the term *business process* can be found in the literature [2]. In this chapter, and throughout the book, we will use the following definition: "A business process is a set of activities, actors, business objects, resources, and the relationship between them for the production of a product or service." The product created in a process can be destined for external as well as internal customers. Figure 3-4 illustrates the definition by also showing its components and the relationship between them.

A typical example of a process in a hospital is a purchase order (see Figure 3-5). The process usually starts with a requisition note from the requesting department and ends with the execution of the order.

Activities of the process are, for example, *write requisition note*, and *prepare call for tenders*.

Participants in the process are the *requesting department* and *purchasing department*.

Business objects are, for example, *requisition notes* and a *call for tenders*. A *PC client of the materials management system* is an example of a resource used during process execution.

It has to be taken into account that models are meant to serve an intended purpose and this, in fact, applies to any model. The purpose can range from simple visualization to complex simulation, as already mentioned in the Introduction. The language (= display format) of process models is usually graphical, providing symbols for the start and end of a process, for its activities, decisions, resources, and documents. Subprocesses not shown in the model can be referred to by a special symbol and a process may be split

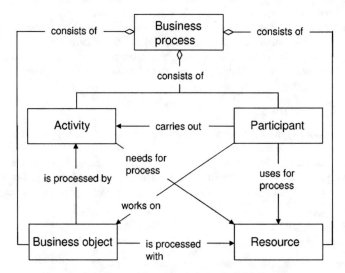

FIGURE 3-4. Composition and relations of a business process.

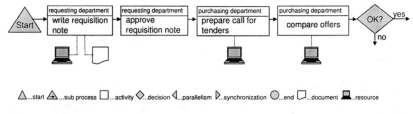

FIGURE 3-5. Extract from the purchase order process (symbols are explained in the legend).

into parallel process tracks and be united again, as depicted by other symbols. The type of symbols used depends on the modeling language. A process model is a directed graph with the individual activities representing nodes of the graph. Further approaches are introduced in the last section.

Process models can be constructed for a variety of application fields. Examples of these are:

– Documentation, e.g., of job and process instructions
– Analysis and reorganization
– Manpower requirements planning, and resource planning
– Monitoring and controlling
– Draft input for *to be* versions
– Specifications for the development and implementation of IT systems

These areas of application determine the content of the process models and the choice of the process modeling language suitable for the particular model and its application. For example, the extract of the *purchase order* process (in Figure 3-5) contains activities and their sequence, their participants, IT resources, and documents.

Unlike data modeling, with entity relationship and class models, no standard of a process modeling language has become commonly accepted until now. The Unified Modeling Language (UML) activity diagrams [3] and Business Process Modeling Language/Business Process Modeling Notation (BPML/BPMN) [4], however, are languages frequently used in process modeling software (see also Chapters 4 and 5). Moreover, common software tools have created quasi-standards through the process modeling languages they offer. Throughout this chapter and the entire book, a simple modeling language, whose symbols are explained below the figures (see for example Figure 3-5), is used.

Process Landscapes

Organizations can typically be described by a multitude of processes. Modeling these processes can lead to a huge number of complex interlinking processes. This is why it has become common to work with so-called *process landscapes* that allow a *bird's-eye view* of the processes of the domain to be modeled. Usually, three types of processes are distinguished (Figure 3-6), thus forming the top level of a process landscape:

– Core processes
– Strategic processes
– Support processes

Core processes describe procedures closely associated with the products and services provided by the organization. In hospitals, the core processes embrace admission, clinical

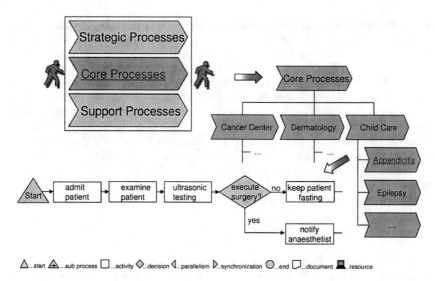

FIGURE 3-6. Process landscape with links to sublevels.

examinations, diagnostics procedures, treatment and nursing care, and discharge or transfer. A sequence of these processes defined for a given disease or diagnosis-related group is called a *clinical pathway* (see also Chapter 9). Strategic processes are the processes that manage and control major changes in the organization, such as controlling the costs and the revenue of clinical cases the hospital has decided to specialize in (see Chapter 10). Support processes manage the resources of the organization, such as supplies that include medical supplies, IT, human resources, or facilities.

Tools for Process Modeling (Functionality, Classification, and Popular Tools)

As already mentioned above, it is common to use specific software tools for process modeling. These tools range from simple drawing tools, such as Visio or MS PowerPoint, to sophisticated, database-based process modeling and simulation tools.

The core functionality of these tools comprises the capability to create a diagram or model of a business process, to change that diagram, and to explore how the process could be improved or redesigned. Diagrams of entire value chains can be generated and then broken down into separate processes and subprocesses to describe a domain comprehensively. This approach is extremely helpful for understanding the mechanisms of how processes and their components are interrelated and work together. Process models consisting primarily of activities are often extended by including resources and participants to show how resources flow into the processes and how the staff and software systems support them. Some process-modeling tools also associate cost data with the activities, thereby give an accounting of the total process costs. Process simulation is another important functionality for exploring the impact of a process on certain target parameters before making actual changes in the organization and its workflow.

The key to discriminating between simple drawing tools and advanced process-modeling tools is whether they store data about the models in a database or a repository. Only advanced modeling tools create data entries in a database. In this way, a box drawn in a process-modeling tool is not simply an image of a box, but becomes an object in a database. Once the box is given a name, the user can begin to record information about the entity the box symbolizes, such as an activity or a resource. With advanced tools, it is also possible to indicate where input comes from and where output goes, and to name the software applications that support an activity. Even more important is the advanced feature that all the data that have been entered once to describe an activity can immediately be imported to a new diagram or a new entity created with the same name. A sophisticated process-modeling tool with this functionality thus serves as an interface for a database that permits organization and storage of information that characterizes the business processes. Well-known tools, such as ADONIS, ARIS, Corporate Modeler, and ProVision all store data about processes and can be used to create and manage a database of information about the organization's processes. Detailed information about these tools can be retrieved from the Internet [5 – 9].

Process of Process Analysis

Modeling processes within a domain requires modeling experience, domain knowledge, and a structured approach to developing the model. Because *process analysis* is a process of its own, it lends itself to description by a process model. Figure 3-7 shows the process analysis value chain and the role of process modeling within process analysis. Usually starting with an *as is* model, process analysis results in one or several *to be* process models.

The framework for a generic approach to BPA includes the following steps of the value chain: criteria definition, information acquisition, analysis, design, and evaluation.

Criteria Definition

In the criteria definition phase, the objectives (including measurable criteria) are defined. Clearly defined criteria are essential for evaluating the *to be* models and choosing the most appropriate one among them that best suits a given purpose. Typical objectives are the reduction of the cycle time or the reduction of costs per process.

Information Acquisition

During this phase, information needed for describing *as is* processes and for designing *to be* processes is collected, usually involving domain experts such as business or healthcare experts. Because the content of the model to be developed depends on

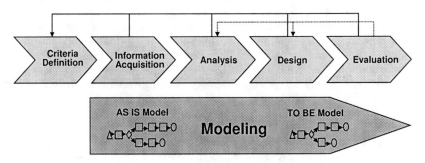

FIGURE 3-7. Overview of the steps of process analysis.

previously defined objectives and the purpose the process model serves, the information to be gathered must be well aligned with the overall objectives. If the people in charge of developing the process model do not have enough domain knowledge, they need to systematically acquire the information. Methods typically employed to capture the information are derived from the empirical methods of the social sciences (see below).

Analysis

Once the information required for modeling has been compiled, it is mapped to an *as is* process model. In a subsequent step, the *as is* processes undergo a thorough validation, consisting of a series of quality assurance measures that check the content of the model, as well as its compliance with the technical modeling guidelines. The major part of the work performed during this phase involves analyzing the model for obvious flaws and weak points, which are then graphically marked in the *as is* model. Media breaks, fractionized activities, and duplication of work are good examples of such weak points that usually result in low process efficiency and efficacy such as long cycle times, high costs, and a high error rate.

Design

Based on the weak points revealed in the analysis phase, solutions for the improvement of the *as is* processes are proposed. Based on this, different alternatives and versions of *to be* processes are developed and depicted in so-called *to be* models. In the eBusiness arena, it is particularly important to determine which parts of the process can be automated and where advanced technology can be used to support communication between the systems, coordination of the tasks, and collaboration between the business partners.

Evaluation

In this phase, the results of the design phase are evaluated in an effort to select the most appropriate model. This implies that the different variations of *to be* models are assessed in terms of their outcomes, which are usually measured by quantitative parameters, including costs and time. The criteria defined in the first phase serve as target values for the outcome parameters and allow the process analyst to choose the model which best fits the criteria.

Which empirical and analytical techniques are used in the individual phases is determined by the targets and the general constraints of the modeling process. Common techniques for the acquisition of information are brainstorming sessions, workshops, interviews, questionnaires, and field observations–all of them involving domain experts.

When designing business processes, it is crucial that the processes meet the predefined objectives. These objectives are deduced from the strategic guidelines and often need to be clarified during the criteria definition phase. In most cases, the emphasis is placed on quantitative attributes such as time, costs, and workload. In the next section, different techniques are presented for analyzing these attributes.

Techniques for the Analysis of Processes

Overview

The analysis of process models can be carried out in different manners–by employing either analytical methods or simulation techniques, among others. Calculations based on analytical methods make use of probability values assigned to process paths, and the frequencies of activities resulting from these probabilities. Furthermore, they include time and cost attributes stored for each activity. A calculation, however, may reach its limits when the process becomes very complex. For example, calculation time can rise exponentially with the number of decisions contained in a process model. A possible solution to this problem is the employment of simulation techniques, where a single process is *executed* very often and the individual execution results are weighted with their respective probability–the higher the number of executed simulation cycles there are, the more accurate the results will be.

When analyzing processes, a multitude of quantitative criteria can be examined. Figure 3-8 gives an overview of the most important ones. Time, costs, and capacity can be further broken down into more specific parameters. Other parameters include the probabilities of given paths and specifications on various calendars holding information about the availability of participants or resources. These criteria should be referred to when defining the objectives–in case costs should be reduced–for example, participant costs, resource costs, and process time could be analyzed together with the overall process costs.

The following sections describe the simulation of processes in greater detail, give an introduction to activity-based costing and present the Six Sigma methodology as a commonly implemented approach to process improvement that utilizes analytical methods, simulation techniques, and activity-based costing methods.

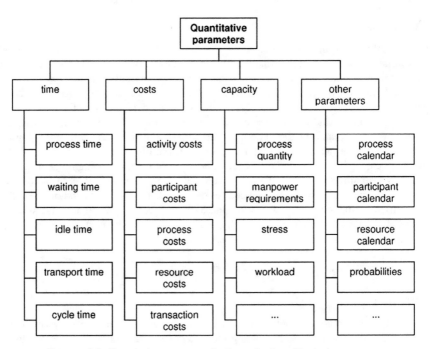

FIGURE 3-8. Quantitative parameters for the evaluation of business processes.

Simulation

Simulation is a term used to denote several techniques that are distinguished by the implemented algorithm. The following sections present these different algorithms.

Path Analysis–Simulation of Processes Without the Organizational Aspect

The simulation-based analysis of processes that disregards a company's organizational structure is called *path analysis*. It requires the process model, including corresponding submodels, the control flow with the respective path probabilities, and time and cost values assigned to the activities, as input. The path analysis may produce several results that answer questions from different perspectives. Technically speaking, its output can be classified in the following three categories:

- Business process results (e.g., the average cycle time or the average execution time of a process)
- Path results (e.g., the average execution time, the average probability of a certain path, or the indication of paths not passed through – *dead* paths)
- Activity results (e.g., the frequency of an activity based on one process cycle)

In Figure 3-9, the frequency of Activity A5 is 0.7. It should be noted that in contrast to probabilities that are connected to decisions and never exceed 100%, the frequency of an activity can be higher than 1.0–for example, when a cut-back loop occurs in the process. This result, being rather obvious, can be recognized immediately in the model. If decisions are nested and the model is large, however, this might be quite different and the option of getting the result automatically may greatly help with analyzing the model.

Figure 3-9 shows an example of a simple process specifying the execution time (in minutes) and the fixed costs (in currency units [CU]) per activity. The model describes two parallel activities (A2 and A3) and a conditional activity (A5) that depends on the result of a decision leading to this activity (A5) in 70% of all cases.

Path analysis for this model is based on two possible paths–one including A5 and the other excluding A5–and calculates the output parameters depending on the path. If the decision falls on the 70% case, the results for this path are:

- Cycle time = 33 minutes (= 5 min + 10 min + 3 min + 15 min)
- Costs = 48.5 currency units (= 10 CU + 15 CU + 10 CU + 10 CU + 0.7 x 5 CU)
- Execution time = 38 minutes (= 5 min + 10 min + 5 min + 3 min + 15 min)

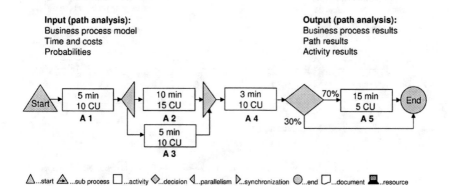

Input (path analysis):
Business process model
Time and costs
Probabilities

Output (path analysis):
Business process results
Path results
Activity results

△...start △...sub process □...activity ◇...decision ◁...parallelism ▷...synchronization ◯...end ▭...document ▪...resource

FIGURE 3-9. Simplified process model used as input for path analysis.

This example illustrates the difference between cycle time and execution time. While cycle time measures the time that is taken from the start to the end of the process, execution time equals the sum of all individual activities' times. Due to the parallel execution of Activities A2 and A3, the cycle time is less than the execution time.

Volume Analysis–Capacity-Oriented Simulation of Processes with the Organizational Aspect

While path analysis focuses only on the process, the capacity-oriented analysis (volume analysis) also builds upon the elements of the organizational structure and upon the quantities of the processes. It also includes the input factors of the path analysis. A specification of the process quantity refers to the number of times a process usually occurs in a given period of time. Among other things, the volume analysis answers the question: "How many participants and how many resources are necessary to execute the described amount of processes?" Given the target volume of process occurrences, typical areas of application embrace manpower requirements planning and the calculation of personnel costs (see Figure 3-10).

In this example, an average wage of 60 CU per hour is assumed for a *clerk* and an average wage of 120 CU per hour for a *supervisor*. This corresponds to 1 CU per minute for the *clerk* and 2 CU for the *supervisor*.

When these basic rates are applied to the process model, a total of 44 CU for staff costs is calculated. Distinguishing between the two different paths is unnecessary as the probabilities are included as weights for calculating the staff costs per activity, when applicable. The following sums of products show the calculation in detail:

$$44 \text{ CU} = 5 \text{ min x } 1 \text{ CU/min} + 10 \text{ min x } 1 \text{ CU/min} + 5 \text{ min x } 1 \text{ CU/min} + 3 \text{ x } 1 \text{ CU/min} + 0.3 \text{ x } 0 \text{ CU/min} + 0.7 \text{ x } 15 \text{ min x } 2 \text{ CU/min}.$$

The staff costs per activity are calculated by multiplying the execution time in minutes with the personnel costs per minute.

Calculating staff costs per process might be quite easily performed in a simplified example such as the previous one; however, it definitely is tedious for large process

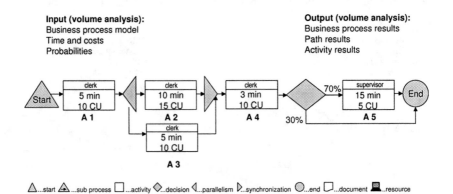

Figure 3-10. Simplified process model including specifications of the staff used as input for the volume analysis.

models such as those usually developed under real conditions. Thus, automatic computation of staff and other costs can be very helpful.

Workload Analysis - Dynamic Simulation of Processes with the Organizational Aspect

In contrast to path and volume analysis, workload analysis takes the time axis into consideration. The relation to time materializes by retrieving time-relevant data from a calendar. In workload analysis, the processes, participants, and resources each have to possess a calendar. A process calendar describes the trigger intervals that start corresponding processes using statistical distributions. A participant calendar contains the period(s) of a participant's daily availability, during which the participant may execute the process activities allocated to him. A resource calendar describes the time during which a resource is available for usage by the participants.

The major task of the workload analysis consists of the determination of waiting times that can arise during the execution of activities if the activities cannot be executed immediately. This means that the delegation of activities to the participants leads to so-called *waiting queues*. The participants (and resources) select the activities to be performed from their waiting queues by defined strategies (e.g., by prioritizing activities). The waiting times of the activities therefore depend on the individual participant's waiting queues and are thus an important simulation result.

The workload analysis primarily answers the following questions:

1) How is the process cycle time changing?
2) Where are the bottlenecks in the execution of processes?

By providing the answers, different scenarios can be gauged by comparing targeted business results with simulation results. In fact, scenario analysis is the chief application of this approach (see Figure 3-11).

The participants described in the organizational model are assigned roles that determine the type of activities each participant is expected to execute. In Figure 3-11,

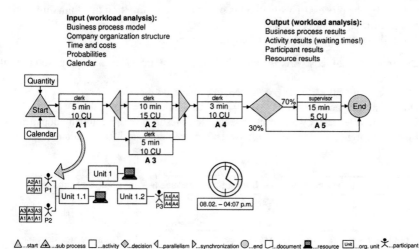

FIGURE 3-11. Schematic example of a process model including information of the organizational structure and calendars used in a workload analysis.

Participants 1 and 2 are assigned the role of *clerk* and therefore receive the tasks assigned to the clerk role. The waiting queue on the left side of the participants symbolizes the activities each particular participant still needs to execute at the observed moment in time (08.02., 04:07 p.m.).

As shown in Figure 3-11, the workload analysis relies heavily on appropriate input data. Due to the effort associated with collecting these data, workload analysis only makes sense for certain well-defined applications where the input data are easily available, such as analyzing the workload in call centers. Through the progressive usage of information technology, however, it is to be expected that we will be able to measure valid input data—such as handling and process times–more easily. This will consequently stimulate the use of workload analysis in other application areas.

Process Costing/Activity-Based Costing

Generalizing the calculation method for staff costs by including other types of costs leads to activity-based costing (ABC). It is based on the assumption that activities consume a variety of resources—not just labor, but also things like materials, equipment, software, or floor space. Costs incurred with all resources required, therefore, would have to be included in a comprehensive calculation. In activity-based costing, the different types of costs have to be first categorized and then allocated to resources and cost centers. After this has been done, cost centers need to be identified to execute each activity or subprocess (see Figure 3-12).

ABC needs frequencies or quantities as input data that can be gained both through simulation or analytical methods. In practice, however, the analytical approach is more common.

As Figure 3-12 shows, costs can be calculated on different aggregation levels. In addition to the direct costs (e.g., material, labor costs), the indirect costs (i.e., the costs of non-value adding processes such as administration or management and other overhead costs) can be allocated to the core processes. One way of achieving this is through splitting the indirect costs proportionally to the direct costs—i.e., the resources consumed by the process. This method is based on the assumption that high direct costs correlate with high indirect costs.

The following are typical areas of application for ABC:

- Determination of cost drivers and their influence on costs and consumption of resources
- Identification of the effects process changes have on the costs
- Documentation and controlling of capacity utilization
- Evaluation of efficiency and costs due to idle times in selected company departments
- Benchmarking (e.g., comparison between cost centers and different branches)

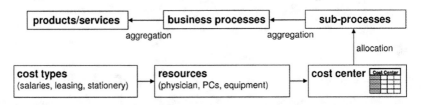

FIGURE 3-12. Allocation of costs and resources to business processes.

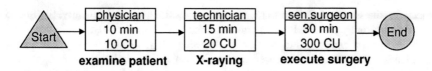

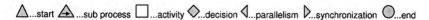

FIGURE 3-13. Simplified example for the calculation of process costs showing the participant, the duration of the activities, and the cost unit rates.

– Calculation of product and service prices
– Appropriate settlement of internal services (internal billing)
– Base for strategic decisions (e.g., *make or buy*, outsourcing)

ABC is often not carried out on the level of detailed process models but rather in a more abstract form using aggregated charts.

Figure 3-13 shows a simplified example of ABC without allocating the costs of non-value adding processes or other overhead costs. The staff costs are calculated by multiplying the wages per minute by the activity duration in minutes (see the example after Figure 3-10). All other direct costs are included in the average rate of, for example, 20 currency units (CU) per x-ray radiograph in the activity *x-raying*. This average value corresponds to the yearly sum of all direct costs (except for staff) divided by the number of x-ray radiographs per year (cost driver). In this example, the yearly non-staff costs originate from the yearly amortization of the *x-ray equipment* resource and further embrace materials costs and operating costs (e.g., service and maintenance contracts). The cost unit rates of the resources used during the activities *examine patient* and *execute surgery* are obtained in the same way as for *x-ray equipment*.

The calculation of the process costs in in Figure 3-13 is based on the following hourly wage rates in currency units (CU):

– Physician: 120 CU (2 CU per minute)
– Technician: 60 CU (1 CU per minute)
– Senior surgeon : 180 CU (3 CU per minute)

Computing the staff costs as described above, and adding the cost unit rate per activity, results in the following equation for the total process costs of 455 CU:

$$455 \text{ CU} = (10 \text{ min} \times 2 \text{ CU/min} + 10 \text{ CU}) + (15 \text{ min} \times 1 \text{ CU/min} + 20 \text{ CU})$$

$$+ (30 \text{ min} \times 3 \text{ CU/min} + 300 \text{ CU})$$

These costs comprise all direct costs–i.e., costs of all resources allocated to the process.

Six Sigma - a Methodology for Process Improvement

Six Sigma is a clearly defined methodology for improving processes that has been yielding significant results in various domains. Originating in the manufacturing arena, it has now spread to other industries, including the healthcare sector [10]. It combines quality management and project management techniques with statistical methods. The idea behind Six Sigma is to achieve business success by quickly reaching predefined objectives–the so-called Critical to Quality objectives (CTQs). Consequently, Six Sigma projects are usually designed for a period of three to six months only.

The term *Six Sigma* refers to the Greek letter *sigma* (σ), which generally symbolizes statistical variation within measurements. It is also the symbol that denotes process variation. Two parameters are used to determine variation in the Six Sigma methodology: Defects per Million Opportunities (DPMO), and its standard deviation σ. To identify the number of defects in a process, a sufficient number of samples is taken and evaluated using statistical methods. The observed number of defects is then projected to an output of one million. The Sigma level indicates the probability of a defect occurring in the process and can be derived from the DPMO by using statistical tables. If only 3.4 defects occur in one million opportunities, the process output has reached the desired quality corresponding to the Six Sigma level.

One of the main concepts of Six Sigma is the modified approach to a defect in a process or product, resulting in a different answer to the question: "What is acceptable quality?" It is not internal specification limits that determine the quality of a product but the customer's demands. A defect is everything that does not meet the customer's demands, such as a time delay or a quality defect in a product. Six Sigma distinguishes between three problem-solving strategies:

– DMAIC (Define Measure Analyse Improve Control) cycle to improve existing processes (and products)
– DMADV (Define Measure Analyze Design Verify) cycle for the complete redesign of existing processes (and products)
– DFSS (Design For Six Sigma) cycle for the design of new processes (and products)

Figure 3-14 shows the different steps of the DMAIC cycle.

Six Sigma can be regarded a *toolbox* that contains the techniques described above and provides a concept for integrating the various methods of business process analysis. In addition, Six Sigma is characterized by its strong focus on the customer's point of

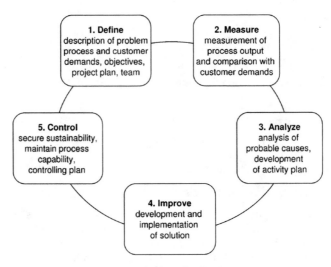

FIGURE 3-14. DMAIC cycle.

view. The DMAIC cycle might therefore be regarded as a special instance of the process model for process analysis as illustrated by Figure 3-7. For further reading, the reader is referred to the literature [11, 12].

BPA in eBusiness

eBusiness, which often spans several departments within an organization and spans at least two separate organizations, pursues the process rather than the functional approach. It comprises both the internal and external business processes that are geared to fulfilling the customers' needs and that are supported by electronic media in achieving their goal (see Chapter 1). In eProcurement and supply chain management, the focus is primarily on interorganizational processes involving participants from various organizations. As has been shown in Chapters 1 and 2, organizations purchasing materials online or managing a supply chain have several options for shaping the relationship with their partners. At the one extreme, the parties involved interact on an ad-hoc basis and on demand, maintaining an arm's length relationship. Other companies may develop tight bonds and appear as a virtual company on the market. The internal coupling between organizational structures also varies, and is strong within profit centers, yet decreases as the structures become larger.

Figure 3-15 shows a continuum ranging from intraorganizational to interorganizational structures with various degrees of cohesion. In terms of process modeling, two important differences between intraorganizational and interorganizational processes need to be considered:

1. Special attention has to be paid to the interfaces between the participants.
2. When designing interorganizational processes, the participants may not want to disclose details of their internal structures.

The process-modeling languages described so far reach their limits when it comes to depicting external eBusiness processes because they do not provide concepts for designing the interfaces between the participants and encapsulating internal parts of the processes that cannot be seen by the outside world. Two more process-modeling approaches, therefore, are presented, namely cooperation charts and swim lane diagrams.

Cooperation charts are designed for describing the interaction between different participants at the top level (see Figure 3-16). The numbered arrows between the participants show the interaction between them and correspond to the activities of the process. For reasons of simplicity, cooperation charts consider only the linear flow of activities, disregarding decisions and parallelisms.

Legally dependent participant			Legally independent participant			
Holding	Group	Profit Center	Virtual Company	Strategic Partnership	Supplier / Producer	Ad hoc interaction

intra-organizational ◄──────────────────► inter-organizational

FIGURE 3-15. Different categories of participants.

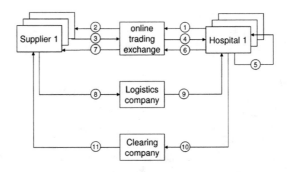

Legend:
1 send order - 2 forward order – 3 send order acknowledgement - 4 forward order acknowledgement –
5 modify order - 6 send modified order - 7 forward modified order – 8 place order with logistics company –
9 send shipment note – 10 authorize payment - 11 forward payment

FIGURE 3-16. Cooperation chart.

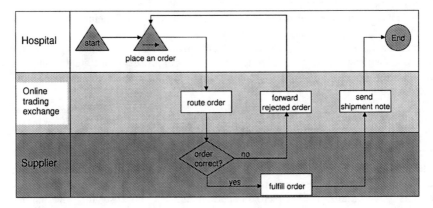

FIGURE 3-17. Process using swim lanes.

Swim lanes are commonly used to illustrate the participants of a process and the interaction between them (see Figure 3-17). In contrast to cooperation charts, decisions and parallelisms can be included in the process. When using swim lane diagrams, however, care should be taken not to design the processes in too complex a manner. Otherwise, the graphical representation may become very difficult to understand and the overview might disappear. Activities should be shown in an aggregated form as subprocesses.

When applying BPA to eBusiness scenarios, all three approaches for process modeling can be combined to the best advantage. Modeling, therefore, should be performed at the following three levels linking the models on each layer (see Figure 3-18):

- Level One: a cooperation chart shows the interaction between the different participants
- Level Two: the process is modeled in more detail using swim lane diagrams to show the participants and their workflow
- Level Three: single subprocesses are modeled in a granular fashion and are analyzed in detail pursuant to the procedures described above

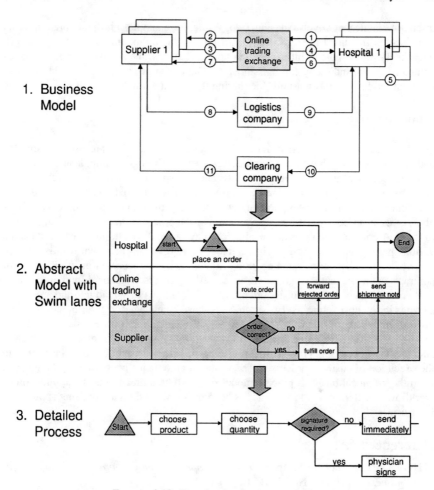

FIGURE 3-18. Three levels of process modelling.

The entire eBusiness process is designed at Levels One and Two by a process analyst who has an overview of all participants, their interactions, and the essentials of the workflow at each participant's site. These models serve as common ground for discussions between the participants when shaping the process. In contrast to the first two models, the detailed process models of Level Three are generated by each individual participant separately. They are not meant to be disclosed to the other partners.

Quality, in regard to the process, can be achieved through service-level agreements (SLAs). A typical example for an SLA in eProcurement is the definition of an *answer time* in which the suppliers have to fulfill the order.

Using the Level Three models, the different participants are able to analyze and optimize their own detailed processes according to their needs. In the logistics sector, for example, mathematical analysis and process simulation are commonly used for planning and optimizing routes, and finding the shortest paths and other applications. While process analysis at Level Three allows for direct changes of the processes, this is often not practical at Levels One and Two. While, for example, a hospital might have an influence on the direct interface between itself and the online trading exchange, it will most likely not be able to influence the interface between the supplier and the logistics company except indirectly through an SLA. The different participants might also use different modeling tools not built for sharing their data and their models.

Conclusion

eBusiness deals with interorganizational business processes that are usually complex and interwoven. Making business processes explicit through the application of BPA helps to obtain a higher degree of clarity and transparency that is so much needed. A first step towards more transparency in processes is achieved when determining the interaction between the different actors and modeling them in cooperation charts. BPA also serves as an instrument for the evaluation of the processes in order to make changes to them. A complete analysis and evaluation may prove difficult, however, because the various participants involved might be reluctant to disclose their own details. On the other hand, it is becoming quite common to include business processes in the annex of contracts to ensure that the partner works according to agreed standards and procedures.

It can be expected that process orientation will continue to spread into the area of IT systems in the near future. BPEL–as an XML-based language for describing a business process in which most of the tasks represent interactions between the process and external Web services [13]–is a move towards a smooth transition from merely modeling and simulating business process to configuring workflow-based IT systems assisting in the execution of business processes. The vision of automatically configuring IT systems from the graphical business process model may still be a dream, but the application of workflow-based information systems has become a reality and is a promising application in eBusiness.

References

[1] Hammer, M. and J. Champy. (1993) *Reengineering the Corporation A Manifesto for Business Revolution*. New York: Harper Collins.

[2] Davenport, T. H. (1993) *Process Innovation: Reengineering Work Through Information Technology*. Boston: Harvard Business Press.

[3] Object Management Group (OMG) (2006) *UML® Resource Page*. Needham. Available from: <http://www.uml.org> [Accessed 01 September 2006].

[4] Object Management Group (OMG) (2006) *Business Management Process Initiative*. Needham. Available from: <http://www.bpmi.org> [Accessed 01 September 2006].

[5] BOC Information Systems (2006) *Adonis*. Wien. Available from: <http://www. boc-eu.com> [Accessed 01 September 2006].

[6] IDS Scheer (2006) *Aris Platform*. Saarbrücken. Available from: <http://www.aris.com> [Accessed 01 September 2006].

[7] Casewise Systems Inc. (2006) *Corporate Modeler*. Mount Laurel. Available from: <http://www.casewise.com/products/corporate-modeler/index.php> [Accessed 01 September 2006].

[8] Proforma Corporation (2006) *ProVision modeling suite*. Southfield. Available from: <http://www.proformacorp.com/Products/process.asp> [Accessed 01 September 2006].

[9] Microsoft Deutschland GmbH (2006) *Visio*. Unterschleißheim. Available from: <http://www.visio.org> (Accessed 01 September 2006].

[10] Wilkerson Porter, A. (2005) *Six Sigma Takes Root at North Carolina Baptist Hospital*. Winston-Salem: Wake Forest University School of Medicine. Available from: <http://www1.wfubmc.edu/articles/Six+Sigma> [Accessed 01 September].

[11] Pyzdek, T. (2003) *The Six Sigma Handbook: a complete guide for green belts, black belts, and managers at all levels*. Columbus: McGraw-Hill.

[12] George, M. L. (2003) *Lean Six Sigma for Service: How to use lean speed and Six Sigma quality to improve services and transactions*. Columbus: McGraw-Hill.

[13] Object Management Group (OMG). (2006) *Business Process Modeling Notation*. Needham. Available from: <http://www.bpmn.org> [Accessed 01 September 2006].

Part II
Technical Background

4
Integrated Information Systems

Martin Staemmler

Executive Summary

When establishing eBusiness based on effective supply chain management (SCM) between organizations, both organizational and technical issues need to be considered so that questions such as the following can be answered:

- Who is going to operate the eBusiness platform?
- Which and how many partners are connected?
- To which degree is each partner's site integrated and what is the level of dependency between the systems?

This chapter begins by presenting the functionality of integrated health information systems in hospitals (HIS$_h$) and materials management (MM) systems. An assessment carried out on the level of integration between HIS$_h$ and MM systems revealed that the current level of integration was quite low. It also showed that there was a strong mutual dependency between the way eBusiness is conducted and the technological approach used to implement the integration. As a result of this observation, the chapter provides some background information on system architecture, recommending loosely coupled information systems based on modular building blocks (components) and web-based services (service-oriented architectures). In addition to these design considerations, integration requires some common language for cooperation between information systems, typically represented by standards for data representation and communication protocols. The chapter, therefore, presents EANCOM, the current and future versions of HL7, and integration services for linking proprietary information systems. Finally, from a systems operation's perspective, tools are presented to support the management and maintenance of the potential complexity of linked information systems, both on the level of business processes and of the technological integration architecture.

Introduction

Integrated information systems are one of the basic prerequisites for managing an enterprise and for enabling eBusiness methods to be applied across organizations. In the first section of this chapter (*Integrated Information Systems in Healthcare*), the current state of development and the functionality of information systems in healthcare are reviewed, and an initial assessment on the level of integration is provided. In practice, integration needs support on two levels:

(i) Technical level–system integration relies heavily on the existence of appropriate standards and system architectures being able to make use of such standards. The second and third sections of this chapter (*Achieving Information System Integration and Messaging Standards in Healthcare*) address system architecture and standards in detail, respectively.

(ii) Organizational level–system integration has to be supported by tools (see the last section, *Tools Used for Supporting Integration*) which analyze and model business processes and allow the management and maintenance of such typically complex integrated system environments.

Integrated Information Systems in Healthcare

Development of Information Systems in the Healthcare Domain

From a business perspective, information systems in healthcare were initially built to be used on a secondary level for administrative and organizational purposes and not to be used on the primary level for supporting patient care. With the advent of 1) computer-based diagnostic and therapeutic systems (e.g., vital-sign monitoring, medical imaging, laboratory automation), 2) the request for documentation and information retrieval (electronic medical records, management of medical knowledge), and 3) a shift from reimbursement schemes to case-based costing, however, both patient care and hospital management have started to use information systems extensively in their daily work. Key issues such as guidelines, clinical pathways, evidence-based medicine, and outcome analysis are fostering the importance of information systems in general, and for medical services in particular. There is also the need to compile information that is kept separately in different information systems. For example, information typically provided by the materials management system (e.g., batch numbers of vaccines and blood products, serial numbers of medical devices and implants) needs to be recorded by the clinical information system and be maintained together with clinical data in the electronic patient record (EPR). The EPR takes over the role of a data repository that allows different applications to access all patient-related information in an integrated manner. Many hospitals are currently working on how to implement an EPR system in their IT environment. The importance of the EPR is underlined by the fact that a growing number of countries are setting up national plans for EPR systems to both aid the flow of information supporting the complete care process within a healthcare organization, and to facilitate shared care across organizational borders.

Chapter 10 in this book pinpoints the demand for integrated data analysis to optimize purchasing and materials management and to support the hospital's overall strategies.

From a technological perspective, the first hospital information systems in the seventies possessed a simple structure based on a monolithic architecture and used mainframes as a hardware platform. Because they were used exclusively for administrative and accounting purposes, there was no need for integration. Following the change from mainframes to midrange computer systems, and as a result of the organizational structure of larger hospitals, information systems were scaled to so-called departmental systems. These systems served the particular needs of a department (e.g., radiology, laboratory, intensive care) and represented more or less stand-alone systems that were not interoperable with or integrated into other departmental information systems. As a result, patients were identified differently in each departmental system, using IDs from separate number ranges with no possibility to collect or combine the information available for one person from all separate departmental systems into one record. To compensate for this drawback, the concept of federated departmental systems was introduced in the early 1990s [1]. Federation, which allows cross-referencing of one patient in several departmental systems, relies on 1) one system acting as a master for assigning patient IDs and 2) a so-called *communication server* supporting interoperability. Typically, the system architecture of larger hospitals shows the communication server in the center managing point-to-point and point-to-multipoint communication between the separate departmental systems. With the increasing number of departmental systems, this approach has proved to be complicated and expensive. This is due to 1) the number of partners involved, 2) the proprietary communication protocols used and 3) in particular, the tight coupling between the different information systems leading to strong dependencies. Even though a large number of hospitals are still using federation, the following two developments can be observed.

Comprehensive Single Vendor Systems

Vendors of HIS_h offer largely integrated systems providing dedicated modules targeted to meet individual departmental needs (e.g., internal medicine, surgery, gynaecology, oncology, and so on). These integrated systems generally use a coherent database model to keep administrative and/or medical data, provide an identical *look and feel* for the graphical user interface of all modules, and support domain-oriented applications. Despite the flaws in the internal architecture, the system appears well integrated and seems to need very few links to the functions of other information systems that are (not yet) available in the integrated system. As expected, this integration and centralization leads to an increase in complexity and is difficult to maintain from a vendor's point of view. From a user's point of view, the individual modules might not be *best of breed*, because there might be other products which better satisfy a particular domain's needs.

Loosely Coupled Multiple Vendor Systems

The requirements of health telematics, extensive cooperation between hospitals in a trust or health maintenance organization (HMO), and the request to reduce complexity have motivated the development of distributed hospital information systems. The *distribution* may separate the administrative functions from the clinical functions, as it is seen in hospitals that use systems from different vendors for each aspect. Extending this line of thought, the use of so-called components (see next section) leads to a much looser coupling for dedicated applications and appears to be the current strategy of most of the HIS_h vendors for their latest and/or future product releases.

The following sections will look at the functional requirements in more detail and consider technological issues for achieving the development mentioned earlier.

Integrated Hospital Information Systems: Functional Requirements

Healthcare information systems in particular those in hospitals (HIS_h) usually cover two application aspects: 1) management issues and 2) clinical issues. The term *clinical* mainly refers to all functions required by medical doctors and caregivers for inpatient and outpatient treatment, and focuses on assisting in the healthcare provision

TABLE 4-1. Overview of HIS$_h$ functions.

	Information Management	Patient Care		Enterprise

Administrative	HIS administration
	- building/rooms structure
	- organizational structure
	- person/role/access rights
	- catalog/classification
	  systems
		Patient management
		- master data/index
		- admission, discharge,
		  transfer
		- coverage
		- medical controlling
			Order
			management
			- order entry
			- scheduling
			- order status
			- service catalog
				Enterprise management
				- accounting
				- finance
				- controlling
				- human resources
				- asset management

Clinical	Interaction/integration
	- laboratory
	- radiology
	- pharmacy, blood bank
	- telemedicine services
	- ... further information
	  systems
		Health
		record/documentation
		- patient history/archive
		- diagnosis/treatment
		  documentation and
		  classification
		- nursing
		  plan/documentation
		- reports (lab, radiology,
		  ...)
			Treatment support
			- treatment plans
			- clinical pathways
			- workflow system
			- decision support
			- knowledge base
			- outcome analysis
				- facility management
				- materials
				  management/supply
				  chain support
				- reporting, statistics
				- enterprise resource
				  planning
				- quality management

process. Management functions mainly relate to administrative tasks like admission, discharge, and transfer (ADT) processes, accounting, purchasing, controlling, materials management, asset management, reports, and statistics. The boundaries between the two types of functions are not always clear and depend on the HIS$_h$ being used. In some organizations, each of these aspects are implemented by an individual information system, and are linked by means of standard protocols (HL7) and/or a dedicated system (EAI system, see next section). Table 4-1 groups the HIS$_h$ functions by their focus and by the usage domains (IT professionals in charge of the information management, clinical staff providing patient care, staff managing the enterprise, and so on).

Integrated Materials Management Systems: Functional Requirements

In the following section, the focus is on the materials management (MM) system as the core component aiding integrated eBusiness. An integrated (MM) system is the backbone for supplying all kind of goods to different organizational units (OUs) in a hospital. It not only deals with the processing of orders and delivery to users, but also supports the logistics, financial, and controlling aspects involved.

In a more detailed definition a MM system may be characterized as an electronic system supporting the internal processes associated with

- Defining and meeting the demand of a material
- Requisitioning, including managing rules and rights for requisitioning
- Sourcing (i.e., selecting a supplier)
- Tendering
- Ordering

- Managing delivery notes
- Managing the inventory/inventories
- Delivering the materials to the requesting units
- Managing returns

In addition, modern MM systems allow information to be exchanged with a supplier while the order is being carried out. This includes receiving order acknowledgments and any information associated with the delivery status, finally leading to the delivery note. It also accepts information sent to the supplier for changing or cancelling an order. Because the MM system provides such services, it constitutes a major component within a supply chain.

MM systems need to be integrated with the financial system and a controlling system in order to manage external invoices and internal cost center-based analyses.

From an end user's point of view, the system is expected to provide a (potentially personalized) catalog of available materials that allows the user to search for and select required materials, order them, and monitor the status of order processing. To make such a scenario possible, the MM system maintains a material master record for each material. This master record describes the material's properties (including images of the product) and is typically based on the vendor's product documentation and specifications. For use in an MM system, a catalog entry also amends the material master record for packaging sizes, order quantities, and rules of approval that take into account the product costs and/or the legal requirements. This holds true, in particular, for pharmaceutical products or medical devices. Usually materials are grouped according to their application domain (e.g., medical surgical supplies materials, medical devices, drugs, office products), and they may be contained in domain specific subcatalogs. Furthermore, the catalog might offer so-called material sets that represent a combination of selected materials serving a dedicated (recurring) task in a care unit. Customizing and updating the catalog(s) is a continuous exercise for the MM system administrators. As will be shown later (Chapter 10), it is recommended to involve the suppliers in updating the catalog and to keep the number of materials and suppliers as low as possible.

During customization of an MM system, the different storage facilities have to be identified and configured, either as central storage, peripheral storage, or in an organizational unit such as a cabinet (for keeping medical products or pharmaceuticals) on a ward. The configuration includes specifying minimal and maximal storage limits and capacities together with rules for refilling automatically or on demand based on given thresholds. In particular, storage management has to cope with the fact that some of the materials in a hospital need specific storage conditions, are subject to expiration dates, or need to have serial numbers and charge identifiers recorded.

From the user's point of view, a selection of materials results in a material requisition that may be related to the organizational unit or to a particular clinical case. Case-related requisitions assign the material to a particular patient for cost-related and/or legal reasons. Anesthetics that are subject to the narcotics act, or drugs for chemotherapy, for example, require approval by authorized persons and a detailed record of each application to a patient. Assigning expensive pharmaceuticals or medical devices to a patient allows treatment-related costs, which are required by health insurance companies in the context of DRG-based remunerations, to be calculated. In contrast to this detailed approach, the cost of materials charged to the organizational unit are distributed more or less evenly to each case based on a given calculation scheme. Chapter 10 expands on the practical issues of applying these methods in a hospital environment.

Due to the different storage facilities, the requisition may be processed locally, centrally, or may result in an external order. To control the individual storage facilities, the MM system has to provide a material requisition card and delivery notes for each requesting organizational unit, as well as for selecting the materials at a storage facility. Furthermore, the MM system also must process ad hoc orders sent directly to the vendor by a clinical unit. These ad hoc orders should typically consist only of dedicated medical consumables, devices needed in emergency cases, or materials needed by only a few organization units.

Assessment of the Level of Integration

As can be seen from the previous sections, there is a great demand for system integration. Integration requires cooperation, which in its turn promotes a win-win situation for the partners involved. It may also lead, however, to a mutual dependency between partners because of the technical and organizational approach used for integration. Figure 4-1 aims to categorize integration and dependency by means of six criteria together with an estimation of the current state of integration in each criterion (see line connecting the axes in the polar graph).

Referring back to the beginning of this section, rating the current state of affairs by using specific criteria shown in Figure 4-1 clearly demonstrates a need to improve the level of integration of HIS_h and MM information systems. This demand is reinforced by the worldwide introduction of diagnosis-related reimbursement schemes (DRG), which require material costs to be assigned to each case and also call for extensive documentation in the patient's records. Together with the need to minimize the length of stay in hospitals, SCM has to ensure that the required material is delivered on time and that no prolonged patient stay occurs due to supply problems.

Modern architectures, like the service-oriented architecture (SOA), will be able to compensate for the observed low level of HIS_h/MM integration. Furthermore, they will provide the means to support the efficiency and flexibility needed to effectively implement a seamless supply chain that includes hospitals and other healthcare providers, suppliers, distributors, online trading exchanges, and group purchasing organizations or purchasing cooperatives.

This development reflects the increasing demand of internal and external integration, starting with coupling different information systems within an organization and extending to integrating the world outside.

Achieving Information System Integration

Introduction

The growing demand for communication across organizations in the context of integrated delivery of care or in the context of eBusiness, not only entails creating standards but also designing information systems for communication. As a result, SOA and component-based software technology are key issues in the discussion about current and future development of enterprise resource planning (ERP) systems and health information systems (HIS). To better understand the benefits obtained from these approaches, one has to take a step back and assess the development from early software architectures up to the concepts currently implemented and those proposed for the future. The development presented in the following paragraphs is closely coupled with both 1) the availability of high performance servers, low-cost PC systems, and high bandwidth

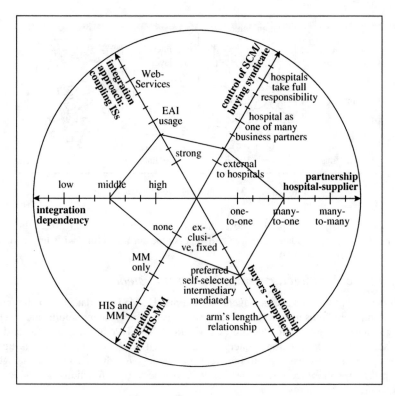

Figure 4-1. SCM – HIS$_h$ – MM technical and organizational integration.

networks, and 2) software development paradigms like object-oriented design (OOD) and distributed computing, together with sophisticated tools to support the software development process.

Monolithic Architecture

Monolithic systems for providing ERP functionality and managing administrative data in healthcare organizations were implemented using mainframe computers from the beginning of the 1960s till the 1980s. Due to the limited (and expensive) hardware resources, these systems were optimized to use memory resources and available data storage capacity more efficiently, which led to squeezed data structures and low-level programming for time-critical functions. The user interface was also purely text oriented and used application/task-dependent screen layouts (masks) with text fields that were placed in fixed positions on the screen for user interaction. From an architectural perspective (see Figure 4-2a), data resided mainly in sequential files that formed a kind of persistence layer. The business logic was reflected by strongly interrelated functions (f1, ..., fn) that were able to access data themselves, process it, and present it to text-oriented terminals.

The major drawback of this architecture is the overall interdependency of data storage, functions, and user interface. The complexity hinders system modification and expansion

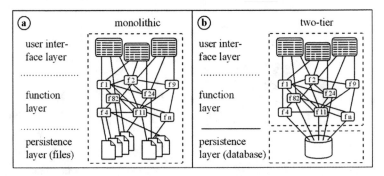

FIGURE 4-2. Monolithic and two-tier architecture.

because it is difficult to predict how changing one function would affect the entire system. As a result, updates are avoided or become an adventure with unpredictable outcomes incurring high costs.

Monolithic Architecture with Database System

With the advent of database management systems (DBMS) and databases using entity relationship paradigms to manage data and relations in tables, the monolithic architecture changed into a two-tier architecture (see Figure 4.2b). Through a quasi-standardized interface (e.g., using structured query language (SQL)), the database layer is tightly coupled with the business logic in functions and the user interface. The disadvantage of having the user interface interwoven with the business logic functions was addressed by three-tier architectures.

Three-Tier Architectures

Motivated by networks with sufficient bandwidth at acceptable costs, and by the widespread use of PCs as intelligent terminals, the user interface became a separate layer, thus establishing a three-tier architecture (see Figure 4-3).

The user interface also started to migrate into a graphical user interface with graphical elements such as buttons, edit and list boxes, scrollbars, and dialog windows. The

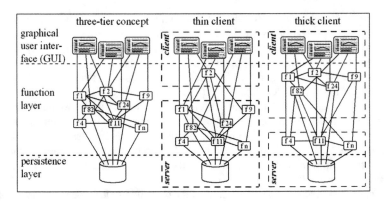

FIGURE 4-3. Three-tier architecture concept implemented as thin or thick client.

business logic layer and its functions remained monolithic. They could be executed either on the database server side or on the PC-based client side. A so-called *thin client* assigned most of the processing to the server. This resulted in small amounts of data passing through the network to the client and reducing the computational requirements of the client to a minimum in an effort to deal primarily with handling the graphical user interface. On the contrary, a *thick client* (sometimes also called a *fat client*) did most of the processing itself. In this way, it reduced the server load to mainly data provided and managed by the database, but also increased the network traffic considerably (e.g., when updating large tables like *article master* or *patients*).

This three-layer architecture is the one mostly used in current ERP and HIS$_h$ systems. While the thick client approach was initially preferred, a transition toward thin clients can be observed today for the following reasons: 1) thin clients require less maintenance at each PC's location, thereby reducing the effort for the IT department, 2) decrease of the cost/performance ratio for server systems, 3) availability of so-called terminal servers (e.g., Microsoft Terminal Server, Citrix Metaframe) allow the computational resources for clients to be centralized to a cluster of central servers with each server handling up to 30 clients, and 4) application service provisioning (ASP). Assessment of the three-layer architecture reveals benefits with regard to the graphical user interface layer and the persistence/database layer and their interfaces, but the business logic still builds a monolithic block. This deficiency might be less dominant when looking at a single information system (e.g., the management information system within a hospital information system or a laboratory system), but becomes more prominent when cooperation and communication for such an information system are required.

Cooperative Information System Architecture

Cooperation between information systems is a major requirement in eBusiness. At least two information systems are typically involved (at the vendor and the buyer site) and are potentially supplemented by the information systems of a purchasing organization or cooperative, a carrier or shipping service, a clearing center, and others. Broadening the view from one information system towards multiple cooperating information systems may be envisaged as a merging of all business logic functions of the individual information systems involved. This could be visualized as implementing all functions again, which of course is impossible. There are several methods to maintaining the architecture of each information system, and they differ in their invasiveness.

- The only intrinsic interface available is the graphical user interface. By wrapping an existing information system and mimicking the user input, and interaction via separate processes, an interface can be provided that allows access to the system's functions. The available functions, however, are limited to those accessible via the graphical user interface.
- Extending the information system by a dedicated interface which supports a single function (e.g., order entry) is a tedious, but alternative option and still provides a proprietary solution.
- Developing an Application Programming Interface (API) is a more generic way of accessing an existing information system. It takes a lot of work, however, and needs to ensure a failsafe access to the internal business logic via the API.
- Even though APIs result in well-defined interfaces, they do not guarantee interoperability between information systems. Data items and their representation, as well

as function calls, might need translation services, which are usually provided by an additional engine in the communication path (a so-called *communication server* or *enterprise integration application (EAI) server*). EAI servers are quite common in health environments to interlink the various systems used.

• Provided that the functionality of an information system allows separation into individual modules, an information system could be split into components, each of which is equipped with well-documented interfaces for both data format and data representation and for the protocol.

Each of the five methods paves the way to a component-based approach with, however, strongly varying granularity of the component: from a complete information system as such, to a single function of the previously monolithic information system. From a technological viewpoint, a variety of methods (see Table 4-2, representatives) exist, typically summarized in the concept of so-called middleware. Asynchronous communication uses the exchange of messages (message-oriented middleware, or MOM). According to Spahni and collaborators [2], three generations of middleware can be identified (Table 4-2) for synchronous communication.

As seen in Table 4-2, middleware acts as a broker, facilitating transactions between information systems and thereby supporting system integration. The evolution of middleware generations shows the development from early proprietary approaches to state-of-the-art techniques, relying on web-based tools and information reference models.

As a recommendation, new developments should use web services that provide maximum flexibility and are able to encapsulate healthcare specific services of the third generation for easy communication, using standard protocols such as Hypertext Transfer Protocol (HTTP) and Hypertext Transfer Protocol Secure (HTTPS).

TABLE 4-2. Middleware generations for information system cooperation.

Generation	Description	Representatives*	Domain
First	Remote functions or methods identified by their name	SUN RPC[1] SUN Java RMI[2]	unspecific
Second	Resource localisation for object-oriented services, usually using a broker or directory	OMG CORBA[3] MS COM/DCOM[4] MS NET Framework W3C WSDL[5], SOAP[6]	unspecific
Third	Applications based on services standardized within a domain-specific reference model	OMG CORBAmed[7] CEN HISA[8] EN 13606[9] HL7 RIM[10]	healthcare domain only

*Legend: [1]SUN Microsystems: Remote Procedure Call (RPC),
[2]SUN Microsystems: Remote Method Invocation (RMI),
[3]Object Management Group (OMG): Common Object Request Broker Architecture (CORBA),
[4]Microsoft Cooperation (MS): (Distributed) Component Object Model (COM), (DCOM),
[5]World Wide Web consortium (W3C): Web Service Definition Language (WSDL),
[6]Simple Object Access Protocol (SOAP),
[7]like OMG CORBA but targeted for the medical domain,
[8]European Committee for Standardisation (CEN): Hospital Information System Architecture (HISA),
[9]European Standard (EN) 13606: "Electronic Healthcare Record Communication",
[10]Health Level Seven (HL7): Reference Information Model (RIM)

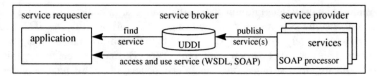

FIGURE 4-4. Use of Web services in a SOA.

Service-Oriented Architecture

Service-oriented architectures (SOA) or enterprise service architectures (ESA) rely on Web services, together with an information representation using XML, and Simple Object Access Protocol (SOAP) to link to service objects, Web Service Description Language (WSDL) to describe the interface of a web service and Universal Description, Discovery, and Integration (UDDI) to locate the web service requested.

Figure 4-4 depicts the interaction required to use a web service. A service requester finds a service published via UDDI–a procedure similar to looking up a phone number in a telephone directory. Obtaining the interface description represented by WSDL from the service provider, the requester may access and use the service via SOAP. By accessing multiple services from more than one service provider, the requester is able to build a dedicated application using components. For communication, an underlying network infrastructure (like Ethernet) is required along with standardized protocols like HTTP or SMTP, which simplify communication across the enterprise borders, and even through firewalls.

SOA leads to a multi-layered architecture with the ability to 1) wrap existing information systems and make their functions available as services and 2) add or combine services to build new applications (Figure 4-5). For example, data mining applications or online analytical processing (OLAP) need to access multiple information systems to perform the required analyses.

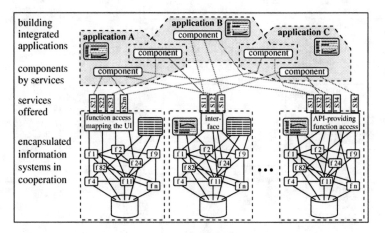

FIGURE 4-5. Building new applications with aggregated services in components.

SOA allows an easy integration with external partners. In contrast to a tight coupling between information systems imposed by using RPC, RMI or APIs, the SOA approach also leads to a loosely coupled system with high flexibility and efficient reuse of components. This may be of particular importance for eBusiness, where the organizations involved tend to avoid strong mutual interdependencies, but still require cooperation and interoperability between their legacy information systems.

Messaging Standards in Healthcare

Introduction

The use of standards significantly simplifies the process of establishing communication between information systems. The most prevailing standards in the medical domain are Health Level Seven (HL7) for message exchange between information systems, and Digital Image Communication in Medicine (DICOM) for medical images. European Article Number Communication (EANCOM), primarily developed outside healthcare, is now also applied to business transactions within the healthcare industry. Figure 4-6 gives an example of how these messaging standards are used within a hospital and for performing eBusiness.

EAN Communication (EANCOM)

Electronic Data Interchange (EDI) has proven its applicability in a variety of markets that require simplified order-entry, processing of orders and delivery and managing of invoices and contracts [3]. Originating from the United Nations, EDI for Administration, Commerce and Transport (EDIFACT) serves as a standard for data exchange but has grown over time and become quite complex due to the large number of messages and domain-specific implementations. EANCOM [4], as a documented subset of EDIFACT,

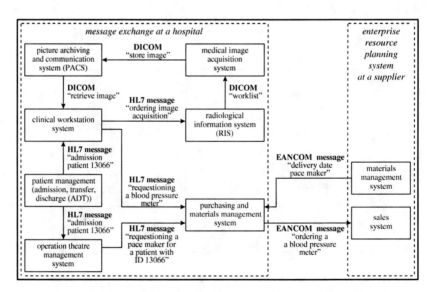

FIGURE 4-6. Example for the application of messaging standards in healthcare.

TABLE 4-3. Comparison of EANCOM and EDI-based HL7 order messages.

EANCOM	Message ORDERS	HL7 event OMN^007	nonstock requisition order msg.
UNA	separators (:+.?')	MSH	separators (|^~\&)/reference
UNB	message header	[{SFT}],[{NTE}]	software, notes and comments
UNH	msg. type/reference	PID,[PD1],[{NTE}]	person ID, add. demographics
BGM	message start	[PV1,[PV2]]	patient visit, add. info
[{DTM}]	order date/delivery	[{IN1,[IN2],{IN3}}]	insurance, add. info
[{NAD}]	order filler/placer	[GT1]	guarantor
[CUX]	currency	[{ALl}]	allergy information
LIN	order item	ORC	common order
[{PIA}]	add. product info	[{[TQ1],[{TQ2}]}]	timing/quantity/order sequence
[IMD]	add. product ID	RQD,[RQ1],[{NTE}]	requisition detail
[{MEA}]	product size / unit	*RQD segment*	requisition line number
QTY	quantity ordered		item codes (internal, external, hospital)
[DTM]	delivery date		requisition quantity, unit of measure
[PRI]	price		dept. cost centre, item natural account code
[CUX]	currency		deliver to ID (delivery location)
UNS	separation		date needed (deadline for delivery)
UNT	message reference	[{OBX,[{NTE}]}]	observation details
UNZ	message end	[BLG]	billing segment

Legend: xxx segment type xxx, [yyy] optional segment yyy, {zzz} repetitive usage allowed for segment zzz

simplifies the implementation by reducing the number of messages by a factor of four. EANCOM relies on messages using segments to group data elements by contents. The segments constituting a valid message depend on the message type. For example, the ORDRS message contains segments for the order placer, the order filler, the date/time, the order number, and the order itself, using an article number (e.g. EAN). An example is given on the left side of Table 4-3. The EAN (see Chapter 6) fulfils a basic requirement by identifying each product by unique sequence of numbers, e.g. a 13-digit number, plus one check digit [5].

Health Level Seven (HL7) – Versions 2.x

HL7 is a comprehensive standard that describes messages to be exchanged between different application systems in a healthcare organization. It comprises a wealth of single messages covering clinical, as well as management, issues and thus is capable of not only integrating clinical systems, but also integrating clinical and management information systems within an organization. Although HL7 is not an eBusiness standard itself, it builds a major element of integrated information systems that constitute the foundation of eBusiness procedures.

HL7 has enjoyed approximately 15 years of development, extensive world-wide use of its 2.x versions (comparable to standards from the American Society for Testing and Materials (ASTM) in the United States), and is looking ahead to a new concept being implemented with version 3.0 [6].

HL7 versions 2.x rely on messages being exchanged between applications. Messages are initiated by so-called trigger events that result in a message consisting of mandatory and optional segments sent from one application (e.g., the patient management system in Figure 4-6) to one or more other applications (e.g., the clinical workstation system and the operation theater management system in Figure 4-6). The type of segments included in a message is determined by the type of trigger event. Table 4-3 gives an example for a general clinical order (on the right). Segments represent a collection of related elements, like patient demographic data or the details of an order. Elements might be mandatory or optional, and repeating items is possible (e.g., for telephone numbers). Coding of a message may use the typical EDI representation or, for the newer 2.x versions, segments and elements using tagging based on XML.

HL7 specifies nearly 150 events and messages that relate to the following activities:

- Admission, discharge and transfer of patients (ADT, 62 events)
- Order entry (13)
- Queries, financial management (9)
- Observation reporting (9)
- Medical records (11)
- Scheduling (11)
- Patient care (9 messages)
- Laboratory automation (13)
- Personal management (9)

It also specifies some messages for communication purposes like *acknowledge* or *not acknowledge*.

As the list reflects, HL7 is intended to transmit both clinical and management information. It thus embraces, for example, data elements for laboratory results, clinical findings, and case reporting, together with data elements for billing and requisitioning.

Table 4-2 shows an example of an HL7 version 2.5 order message (on the right) and, in particular, a non-stock requisition message [7]. Besides providing reference to the patient (PID, PV1, IN1, GT1, ALI), the common order (ORC) segment contains information about the order status, order authorization, order placer, and filler demographics (name, address, contact data), together with date/time of the order/transaction. The requisition segments (RQD, RQ1) are shown in greater detail in the form of a list of items (reference to internal, external and hospital-related catalogs, accounting) that provide detailed order information for each item. Finally, the message is terminated with the billing (BLG) segment. Comparing an HL7 message with an EANCOM order message, as seen in Table 4-3, illustrates the medical domain-specific approach taken by HL7 on the one hand, and the generic similarities for orders like order placer and filler reference, order details, pricing, and billing, on the other hand.

This example demonstrates that HL7 allows a set of information consisting of clinical information and materials-related information to be transmitted, and is thus perfectly suitable for integrating information. It should be mentioned that the delimitating factor is often not HL7, but rather the applications not being able to process all relevant information properly. For example, if the electronic patient record system is not capable of processing materials information, or vice versa, the materials management system will provide no entries for patient and case identifiers. Even the best standard possible would not help to overcome communication problems in such a case.

Health Level Seven (HL7) – Version 3

HL7 V2.x versions show an increasing number of events and messages, thereby following a primarily demand-driven approach, and potentially endangering cohesion and successful integration. Furthermore, the transmission of messages as such does not facilitate a common understanding at the sender's and receiver's site. To provide this so-called semantic interoperability, the message content has to be based on a reference information model being available at the communication partners' sites. To fulfil this

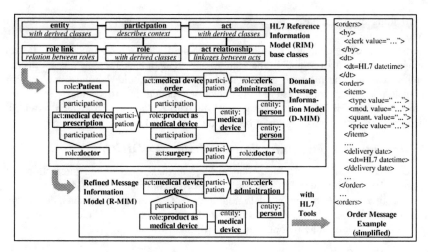

FIGURE 4-7. HL7 V3 methodology using a simplified example.

requirement for future-proof message design, HL7 V3 established a new methodology to specify, develop, and maintain messages (see Figure 4-7).

HL7 V3 relies on a generic, abstract, and object-oriented reference information model (RIM) with six base classes, namely: 1) entity, a physical information object in the healthcare domain; 2) role, the role an entity can take for a specific action; 3) participation, the way of expressing the involvement in an activity; 4) act, the activity performed; 5) role relationship, the representation of an interaction between entities related to their roles; and 6) act relationship, a means to build a sequence of subordinate acts that then form a more complex act (see Figure 4-7, top left).

An example that demonstrates the use of these basic classes is shown in Figure 4-8.

Instead of a demand-driven message design, such as in V2.x's making use of pre-defined messages, HL7 V3 allows messages of any new kind to be built. In a first step, domain-specific information is recorded using approaches like a story board (Figure 4-8), and it is then mapped to the classes of the RIM, resulting in a domain message information model (D-MIM), as shown in the center of Figure 4-7. The D-MIM covers the complete domain and is used later to derive refined message information models (R-MIMs) as subordinate models for specific purposes (e.g., message exchange for the order of a medical device). Each R-MIM defines the structure and contents of a message (sketched as a resulting message on the right in Figure 4-7).

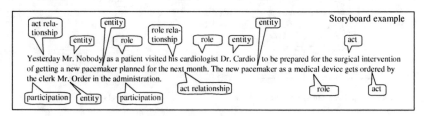

FIGURE 4-8. Storyboard example using the base classes of the RIM.

Providing an XML-based message–as a result of the development steps shown in Figure 4-7–not only facilitates the specification of the message format, but also the interpretation of its contents. Using XML technology allows for a much more flexible exchange of information and is the state-of-the-art approach for machine-to-machine communication. The message generated in the example could therefore be sent from the materials management system to the electronic patient record system.

In conclusion, HL7 V3.0 is an emerging standard replacing V2.x, which provides a vision for integrated information in healthcare within and across organizations.

Digital Image Communication in Medicine (DICOM)

DICOM has become the de facto standard for medical images and interaction with imaging devices. Because DICOM only indirectly contributes to MM aspects (e.g., contrast agents used in computed tomography (CT) or magnetic resonance imaging (MRI) examinations), it is only mentioned in this chapter for the sake of completeness. Detailed information may be obtained from [8] and [9].

Integration Services

Enterprise application integration (EIA) systems, or so-called *communication servers*, are widely used for HIS_h as an exchange platform for data and messages (see Figure 4-9).

Due to the fact that the communication server is located in the center, the number of communication channels varies only linearly (Figure 4-9, right) with the number of information systems (n). If a central integration service is not used, the number of channels equals n^2-n, and thus is significantly larger (Figure 4-9, left).

Initially, the systems were based on proprietary applications being able to 1) to receive data via various hardware interfaces (e.g., serial, file shares, Ethernet, …) and using a variety of protocols, 2) analyze and parse the data according to rules predefined by the user or already provided by the vendor of the system, 3) individually map each data item to an output format, 4) transmit the data to the receiving application through the appropriate interface, and 5) provide control for monitoring transmission failures and errors together with statistical functions for analyzing the traffic. This design had some

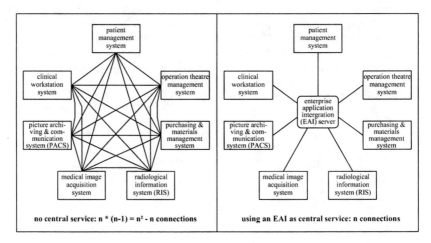

FIGURE 4-9. Comparing system integration without and with a central device.

intrinsic drawbacks. The use of one server limited the availability and scalability, and cooperation between applications only supported point-to-point topologies.

Today, EAI systems/communication servers internally follow the well-known paradigm of publish and subscribe. This means that an incoming message is analyzed and parsed and gets published to interested communication partners subscribing to this type of message, who thereby become receivers of the outgoing message. Each partner receives this message in the required data format and protocol. As an example, one can imagine the message of an admission of a patient being forwarded from the patient master system to the telephone, meals, laboratory, and radiology systems.

To implement the *publish and subscribe* paradigm, input and output queues are used extensively to store data in the event that outgoing connections are temporarily unavailable. To match the requirements of availability and scalability, such an integration service can be distributed on more than one hardware system.

To maintain and manage the complexity of the integrated systems, an EAI usually provides some low-level support based on configurations. To have an overview, however, tools–as presented in the following section–should be used.

Tools that Support Integration

Introduction

Hospital and health information systems today aim for user-specific, integrated access to the modules that assist the users in performing complex administrative, medical, and care giving tasks. This section of the chapter starts with an introduction to the tools used for managing the complexity and continues with a description of key functions provided by HIS_h and MM systems.

Business Process Representation

To represent a functional, procedural view of the specific system, typical approaches such as Scheer's event-driven process chains (EPCs), UML-based sequence or transaction diagrams, or the ADONIS process notation (see Chapter 3) are used. Whereas UML diagrams are more appealing for people trained in computer science, the EPCs and ADONIS® notation are easily understood by people providing care to patients. As was shown in Chapter 3, there is no standard for describing processes, and the decision of which notation to use often depends on the people using the diagrams (see above) and on the information systems themselves. Some providers of information systems prefer certain notations, such as SAP utilizing EPCs to model the processes associated with using SAP's R/3 ERP system. Figure 4-10 compares all three notations.

Very similar to the ADONIS models, an EPC graphically depicts the events that are required to initiate the execution of an activity leading to one or more resulting events, which in turn might serve as a trigger for further activities (see Figure 4-10, left). The process flow, controlled by the states given by the events, allows for branching and merging with typical operations like *and, or, exclusive or*. By using the ARIS toolkit [10] to interactively generate EPCs, this task of business process modeling (BPM) is supported by adding responsibilities for each activity and the required information items, as well as–with an extension of ARIS–a simulation option for *executing* the process chain based on available resources and initiated appropriately. The resulting model is kept in an organization-wide repository, thereby supporting reuse of basic procedures by other departments.

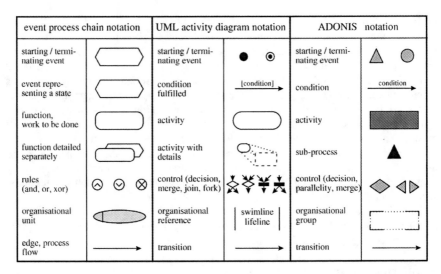

FIGURE 4-10. Basic notations used by EPC and UML, compared with ADONIS notation.

Similarly, UML sequence diagrams represent processes as they are accomplished by instances of classes that reflect entities of the real world, such as persons or systems. They depict the activity of each object and, in particular, the information passed between objects–typically, as messages. Three types of interactions based on messages are supported:

- Simple–transfers the control to a different object
- Asynchronous–without waiting for the execution
- Synchronous–waiting for the execution.

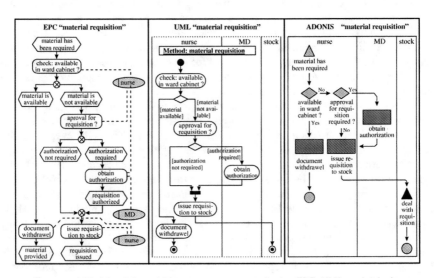

FIGURE 4-11. Material requisition process represented using EPC, UML, and Adonis.

UML uses further diagrams to monitor the state of an application and represent the responsible actions for a task. As a result, it provides a high degree of granularity by allowing for different views, and usually paves the way to implementation by a system developer. Figure 4-11 shows the same scenario (e.g., the *material requisition* process), using an EPC (on the left), a UML activity diagram (in the middle), and an ADONIS model (on the right).

Integration Representation

In addition to the EPC, UML, and ADONIS diagrams focusing on the workflow, there is a need to establish a view on the structure of the information system that supports the workflow and business processes. This perspective allows the chief information officer (CIO) to maintain an overview of the various system components and their interaction.

To assist the CIO's request for up-to-date documentation, Winter has developed the $3LGM^2$ tool [11], which has both an operational and strategic objective. From an operational perspective, the usage of $3LGM^2$ may answer the following questions:

- Which business function is implemented by which information system?
- How is it mapped to the hardware and network resources for seamless operation?

From a strategic point of view, it supports the long-term plans for the information system structure by identifying the weaknesses and the potential of the system to combine and/or optimize the use of the IT resources. The $3LGM^2$ features three layers to model enterprise functions [12, 13], as shown in Figure 4-12.

- Domain layer–models *enterprise functions* and *entity types*. Enterprise functions may use or create information about an entity of a given entity type (e.g., an order).
- Logical tool layer–holds *application components* that represent dedicated *tasks* within an application. Communication is achieved by component-to-component interfaces, or between a component and the user by means of a user interface. As an example, one could consider the ward component sending an order to the pharmacy system.
- Physical tool layer–supports the two upper layers and contains *components* (servers, network) or *people* (e.g., for handling paper-based orders).

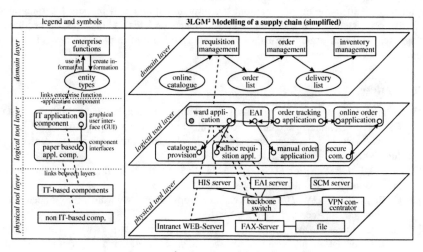

FIGURE 4-12. $3LGM^2$ example of a supply chain (simplified).

- Links between functions of the domain layer, with application components of the logical tool layer, reflect the relations *can support*, *based on*, or *triggered by* (e.g., the order is supported by a generic application component customized for the usage *order*). Similarly, a link from the logical tool layer to a processing component in the physical layer represents the mapping of an application component via a configuration to a processing component. For example, the configuration specifies the hardware that should be used for execution of the application component.

Due to the links provided between layers, questions such as the initial one can be answered using the provided 3LGM^2 tool. Its query function allows both a graphical and a list-oriented presentation of dependencies between the layers, which proves to be of particular use when crossing institutional boundaries (e.g., for material management and telemedicine).

Conclusion

Integration as a prerequisite for enabling successful supply chain management and eBusiness cooperation has to be achieved in a multilevel approach. On the *system level*, integration should be based on system architectures supporting loose coupling of the information systems involved. On the *application level*, modular or component-based software designs will facilitate state-of-the-art web-based services. Both levels need to rely on standardized protocols and information representation, as available (e.g., HL7, ASTM, DICOM, and EANCOM). Besides these standards guaranteeing technical and, to a certain extent, semantic interoperability, integration also has to be fostered on an *organizational level*. From experience, the most effort may have to be invested in solving the organizational issues. Identification and documentation of key processes using typical practices (e.g., event process chains by ARIS, UML activity diagrams, and ADONIS process mapping) will, on the one hand, allow bridging of the different heritages of the people and organizations involved. On the other hand, they will pave the way for integration based on appropriate decisions made concerning technical issues. Finally, by keeping the process documentation up-to-date and using tools (e.g., 3LGM^2) to record and to maintain information, the implementation will prepare the integrated information systems for updates and changes. These updates and changes are needed to adopt technical and organisational changes and pursue and implement new eBusiness opportunities.

References

[1] Grimson, W., D. Berry, J. Grimson, G. Stephens, E. Felton, P. Given, and R. O'Moore. Federated Healthcare Record Server-the Synapses paradigm. Available from: <https://www.cs.tcd.ie/synapses/public/html/technicaldescription.html> [Accessed 16 June 2006]
[2] Spahni, J., J. R. Scherrer, D. Sauquet, and P.A. Sottile. (1998) Middleware for healthcare information systems. *Medinfo* 1998; 9 Pt 1: 212–216.
[3] UNECE (2006) *UN/EDIFACT*. Available from: <http://www.unece.org/trade/untdid/welcome.htm> [Accessed 3 November 2006]
[4] GS1 Germany (2006) *EANCOM*. Available from: <http://www.gs1-germany.de/internet/content/produkte/ean/ecommerce_edi/eancom_2002/index_ger.html> [Accessed 3 November 2006]

[5] GS1 Germany (2006) Available from: <http://www.gs1-germany.de/internet/content/ index_ger.html> [Accessed 18 April 2006]

[6] Health Level 7 (2006). Available from: <www.hl7.org> [Accessed 5 March 2006]

[7] Health Level 7 (2003) *HL7 Standard, version 2.5, Chapter 4* (July 2003) Available from: <www.hl7.org> [Accessed 5 March 2006]

[8] Digital Imaging and Communication in Medicine (2006) Available from: <http://medical.nema.org/> [Accessed 2 May 2006]

[9] HIMSS (2006) *Integrating the Healthcare Enterprise.* Available from: <www.himss. org/ASP/topics_IHE.asp> and <www.ihe-europe.org/> [Accessed 5 March 2006]

[10] IDS Scheer (2006) *ARIS Platform.* Available from: <www.ids-scheer.com> [Accessed 21 April 2006]

[11] Universität Leipzig (2006) *Three-layer graph-based meta model to describe, evaluate and plan health information systems.* Available from: <http://www.3lgm.de/en/> [Accessed 21 April 2006]

[12] Wendt, T., B. Brigl, and A. Winter. (2003) Modeling Hospital Information Systems (Part 1): The Revised Three-layer Graph-based Meta Model 3LGM². *Methods of Information in Medicine.* **42**(5), 544–51.

[13] Wendt, T., A. Häber, B. Brigl, and A. Winter. (2004) Modeling Hospital Information Systems (Part2): Using the 3LGM² Tool for Modeling the Patient Record Management. *Methods of Information in Medicine.* **43**(3), 256–67.

5
Achieving Interorganizational Connectivity

Ursula Hübner

Executive Summary

Electronic business between enterprises requires interorganizational connectivity–either between humans and machines, or between machines and machines. Whereas human-machine communication in eBusiness reflects the B2C scenario, where the customer orders products via a web browser, machine-machine interactions are common in B2B scenarios, where two machines exchange business messages. Due to asymmetries in size and levels of technical sophistication among the business partners, however, B2C-like scenarios are also found in B2B. In healthcare, such scenarios are quite common, particularly with small hospitals that have business relations with large manufacturers, and vice versa. Methods aiming to establish electronic business communication for a critical number of enterprises therefore need to cover all levels of connectivity, from simple Internet access to the interoperability between ERP and HIS_h systems.

Before deciding on the technical method that is most appropriate for their case, business partners have to be clear about whether they wish to establish end-to-end communication, or just want to utilize a central hub, such as an Internet trading exchange. This question is closely related to the question of where the catalog, the main component of any electronic business interaction, should reside. Due to the disadvantages of end-to-end communication, hub-based approaches are the method of choice in healthcare today. The hub manages a central multivendor catalog, which is fed by the suppliers regularly and thus kept up-to-date. The hub also manages connectors between various systems and permits Web-based or fax-based access to its system. Internet trading exchanges in healthcare enable business partners to carry out each step of the order-to-payment process, supported by electronic means. They do not, however, provide mechanisms for negotiations and other activities in the early phases of business transactions.

When aiming at the interoperability of information systems–either in an end-to-end mode or involving the information system of the hub–using standards is the most appropriate way to cope with the heterogeneous system environments of the business partners. eBusiness is traditionally rooted in EDI, a family of standards providing a plethora of business messages including messages for purchase orders, advance shipping notifications, and invoices. EDI messages can be written as XML documents today, but there are also new, purely XML-based standards supporting business transactions such as UBL (xCBL) and cXML. In contrast to these transaction-oriented standards, business process standards such as RosettaNet and ebXML pursue a more comprehensive approach. They make use of the messaging concept, but include information about the business processes underlying the messages and about the business partners' profiles.

Modern architectures of ERP systems place much focus on integration methodology and business processes orchestrating applications internally (A2A) and across enterprises (B2B). Integration is thereby understood as the result of loosely coupling different systems, and is guided by the principles of the service-oriented architecture (SOA) and the use of open standards. Examples (such as SAP's exchange infrastructure, and Oracle's fusion architecture) are given to illustrate these approaches.

With ERP providers abandoning proprietary strategies, with open standards being supported by the systems, and with low-level methods being available to reach different types and sizes of business partners, interorganizational connectivity is also becoming achievable on a large scale. Healthcare-specific online trading exchanges will continue to play a major role in this process and will evolve as the essential component within an infrastructure that constitutes the basis of all business transactions.

Introduction

The idea of interorganizational information systems (IOS) has long been seen as a conceptual framework for systems supporting business cooperation between enterprises, in particular for aiding B2B transactions and supply chain management. Furthermore, an IOS need not be a self-contained system. It can be an extension of an existing corporate information system permitting connectivity. Practical realizations of the IOS concept [1] reflect the full range of business scenarios and different types of technical implementations possible. Chatterjee and Ravichandran [1] hence argue that interorganizational systems are diverse and multidimensional in nature, and propose the dimensions of *relational support*, *control over IOS*, *integration with internal systems*, and *technology specificity* to classify IOS:

- Relational support–from arm's length type of relationships to selected/strategic partnerships
- Control over IOS—From no financial control and no decision making on the side of the users to complete user ownership
- Integration with internal systems–from no to full integration with internal information systems
- Technology specificity–from a widely accepted common solution to a proprietary system that is specific for a single organization

Extending this line of thought, there is no single technical systems architecture that enables enterprises to cooperate, but there are a variety of options to pursue depending on the purpose. In this chapter, we will use the IOS concept as a main idea that covers all cross-enterprise technical realizations.

Irrespective of their particular nature, the need for accessing shared information resources is common to all interorganizational information systems. Therefore, system architects have to tackle the issue of system integration, which is particularly challenging in a heterogeneous landscape of systems. Coping with heterogeneity within an organization is already a demanding task; however, connecting applications across enterprises requires even greater effort as different technologies are often involved.

Employing standards is the most effective way of achieving integration between heterogeneous platforms. With this background, eBusiness has stimulated the development of a variety of standards with industry consortia and official standardization bodies. These developments have resulted in a series of standards that are used in certain (technical) environments, are (partly) overlapping, and compete with each other. Thus, the harmonization of existing standards–achieved by whatever means–still remains an issue.

Often the impact of standards is judged by the size of their current user base. However, as eBusiness technology is evolving rapidly, standards have to keep pace with or get ahead of new developments–leading to new concepts and paralleling new technical developments. In fact, these new standards have had less chance to pervade the market in terms of the number of users than the old ones. Yet another challenge originates from the use of legacy systems that either do not support standards or only support older types of standards.

Despite these problems, standards are the most powerful means of achieving connectivity, and this chapter will expand on existing standards and will give an outlook for advanced standards.

eBusiness–as a phenomenon–is largely defined by the number of business partners and thus exploits its potential only with a critical number of participants. Although the adoption of Internet technology has reached a significant level and has thereby paved the way towards a greater use of eBusiness methods, not all business partners possess the highly sophisticated IT solutions that facilitate electronic business transactions. Therefore, eBusiness solutions must not preclude these partners by requiring a high level of technical sophistication. On the contrary, system suppliers must come up with pragmatic and inexpensive concepts for connecting the majority of users. This is a particular challenge in the healthcare industry, where there are many small enterprises operating alongside the large players. This holds true for both the healthcare providers and the suppliers, but particularly for the providers.

Finally, it should be kept in mind that eBusiness technology serves the purpose of supporting partners in healthcare in the process of conducting routine business and to make new, economically (and clinically) useful approaches for business collaboration possible. It should therefore be as unobtrusive for the end user as possible, and must not itself become a barrier to adopting eBusiness. In this chapter, we will briefly touch on the B2C type of business interaction before focussing on the B2B type.

B2C

B2C business transactions have pervaded daily life in many countries of the world, and companies such as Amazon.com are widely known. Technically speaking, these applications are realized by so called online shops that are either proprietary solutions made possible by an ERP system, or built and managed via an application server. B2C solutions are characterized by a web-based front end that allows the customer to browse through a catalog, select items, move them into an electronic cart, and process the

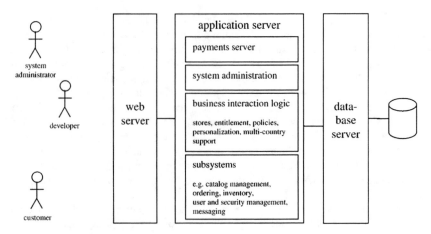

FIGURE 5-1. Application server environment – example (based on [2]).

payment. Information to the customer (i.e., the current status of the order) is sent via email. Typically, there is no integration with any client software or back-office software on the customer's side. B2C solutions can also be adopted for B2B scenarios if no deep integration is required or possible.

A common way of developing, deploying and executing online shops is making use of application server (AS) software available on the market (e.g., WebSphere by IBM, AS 10g by Oracle, WebLogic by BEA), or with an open source product (e.g., JBOSS). Application server products come with a development environment and a run-time environment; some of them are already prebuilt for eCommerce solutions. In general, application servers are a means to separate the presentation, the business logic, and the data management layer, thus making scalable solutions possible. Many of them are based on Java to Enterprise Edition (J2EE), now Java Platform Enterprise Edition (Java EE)–a specification for a software architecture supporting Java-written, transaction-based, Web applications. Figure 5-1 shows an application server-based B2C environment.

System administrators and developers access the system via dedicated tools, and the customers simply use a Web browser to run the application. Application servers may be integrated with legacy systems at the supplier's end.

B2B

EDI – The Roots of eBusiness

Long before the Internet and, in particular, the Web became common media for conducting business electronically, eBusiness partners used EDI as a technological platform. EDI is still used by big firms for example in the automotive industry. In this context, EDI typically refers to two features that are often used in combination: a messaging standard, and a network for transporting the messages. EDI messages (the first feature of the EDI definition) can be either written as ANSI ASC-X12 messages [3], which is widely used in the United States, or as UN/EDIFACT (ISO 9735) messages [4], which is predominantly used outside the United States (e.g., Europe). Both EDI message families comprise a plethora of message types covering many industries–i.e., more than 315 in the case of X12 and more than 200 in the case of EDIFACT. To reduce the complexity of the EDIFACT messages, subsets for different industries were developed from the pool of EDIFACT messages, such as EANCOM for consumer goods, EDIFICE for the electronics industry, and ODETTE for the automotive industry. EANCOM (see Chapter 4) is the subset of choice used in healthcare. In other words, EDI is not a single messaging standard, but rather a concept with several realizations.

The second feature of the EDI definition refers to the network. It is actually totally detached from the EDI messaging standard. In the old days of electronic business, so-called value-added networks (VANs) were exclusively utilized for transmitting the messages. Today, VANs still exist and are used for this purpose, but there are other networks, particularly the Internet, that have become a viable alternative. VAN providers charged their customers a fee depending on the number of transactions, which led (and still leads) to statements about the high costs of EDI. In summary, the term *EDI* does not have one single meaning, and one needs to clearly scrutinize what it actually means in a specific context.

This ambiguity has caused several misunderstandings. One of them refers to the alleged antagonism of EDI and XML. In fact, EDI semantics can be phrased either by pursuing the ISO 9735 convention [5], or can be formulated as XML schemas. This notation difference does not affect the contents of the message, but rather the automated interpretation of its contents (i.e., the interpretation of the data elements). Whereas the classic notation requires the software to *know* the meaning of a data element, the XML notation provides the structure together with the message.

Another misunderstanding concerns the connection between EDI, the Internet, and the Web. EDI messages–using whatever notation, being stored in a file or sent in a synchronous manner–can be transmitted across any network (a VAN, the Internet (TCP/IP), or any other network). Results from a European survey show that nearly equal numbers of companies use classic EDI, Internet EDI, or both [6].

WebEDI is yet another term that has caused some confusion. Today, WebEDI is generally accepted to denote a solution for manually capturing EDI data via a Web browser [7, 8].

Irrespective of its many meanings and different implementations, EDI constitutes a family of standards. It is recognized as the common denominator of eBusiness applications, particularly holding true for the past, but also still for today's applications in some industries.

eBusiness Standards

Over the years–as technology has evolved and Web applications and services have become available–many more standards have evolved that are relevant to eBusiness. In general, it may be said that eBusiness is a test case for demonstrating the use of standards. Unlike enterprise information systems, which can be based on a single technical architecture, eBusiness automatically brings together heterogeneous partners with different technological backgrounds for conducting business–regionally and globally. Technological solutions thus have to make sure that 1) relevant information is exchanged on time, securely, and without failure across organizational borders; 2) the data are readable, non-ambiguous, accurate, and meaningful; and 3) the information sent between the partners supports the business processes on both ends. A set of standards – not a single standard – is typically utilized for safeguarding these individual requirements. To understand the contribution of each individual standard for achieving electronic business interactions, it is helpful to distinguish between different types of standards (i.e., technical versus business standards), and among these standards to classify them according to their major focus. In the following, we concentrate on business standards and adopt the five categories suggested by Quantz and Wichmann [9]. These categories are *standards for identification, classification, catalogs, transactions*, and *processes* (see Figure 5-2).

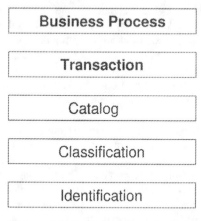

FIGURE 5-2. Stack of eBusiness standards.

TABLE 5-1. Standards overview.

Transaction Standards	Process Standards
EDIFACT Standards including subsets such as EANCOM (http://www.gs1.org/productssolutions/ecom/eancom/) EDIFACT: United Nations (UN) standard/International Organisation for Standardization (ISO) standard	ebXML (http://www.ebxml.org) standard developed by joint efforts of OASIS (Organization for the Advancement of Structured Information Standards) and UN/CEFACT (United Nations/Centre for Trade Facilitation and Electronic Business)
ANSI ASC-X12 (www.x12.org) American National Standards Institute (ANSI) standard	RosettaNet (http://portal.rosettanet.org/cms/sites/RosettaNet/index.html) industry standard (targeting the High-Tech industry)
xCBL – XML Common Business Library (www.xcbl.org) industry standard	
UBL – Universal Business Language (http://www.oasis-open.org/committees/tc_home.php?wg_abbrev=ubl)	
OASIS (Organization for the Advancement of Structured Information Standards) industry standard	
cXML – commerce XML (www.cxml.org) industry standard (Ariba)	

This chapter focuses on transaction and process standards, while Chapter 6 presents and discusses identification, classification, and catalog standards. Table 5-1 gives an overview of transaction and process standards.

EDIFACT and X12 are standards originating from the EDI family, but also include an XML version. All other standards are purely XML-based. Table 5-1 focuses only on the most common standards, but illustrates the multitude of existing standards.

Due to the historical developments of eBusiness, some standards are more common than others. Consequently, after about two decades of development, EDIFACT and X12 standards naturally still have a larger user base than the younger XML-based standards. This, however, might change in the years to come [6]. In addition, eBusiness standards are far from being finalized and it is expected that further developments will take place–not necessarily resulting in totally new standards, but rather in a consolidation of existing standards. UBL, for example, is an advancement of xCBL. Furthermore, not all existing standards are listed in Table 5-1. Besides those contained in Table 5-1, various other activities take place in different countries that need to be watched in terms of acceptance and adoption by the industry.

X12 and EANCOM are standards both discussed and used in healthcare. For example, most of the electronic transaction standards mandated or proposed under the Health Insurance Portability and Accountability Act (HIPAA), including those related to healthcare insurance, are X12 messages [10]. EANCOM messages (such as the ORDERS message–see Table 4-3) are promoted by GS1–Healthcare User Group (HUG) as supply chain messages. Although the ORDERS message is the most widely known, EANCOM comprises many more messages including [11]:

- Master Data Messages (party and product information)
- Business Transactions Messages (quotation, purchase order, transportation and logistics, invoice and remittance advice)
- Report and Planning Messages
- Syntax and Service Report Messages
- Security Messages (secure authentication and acknowledgment message, security key, and certificate management message)
- General Messages

In contrast to transaction standards that describe more or less isolated messages, business process standards address an entire environment in which supply chain partners cooperate. In other words, while transaction standards focus on the definition of the syntax and the semantics of messages, process-oriented standards aim at including the technical and business constraints that define the environment for exchanging the messages. They are therefore sometimes also called frameworks. Among the most widely known frameworks for business processes are RosettaNet and ebXML (Table 5-1).

RosettaNet is an industry standards organization that develops specifications for business processes and technical elements for interoperability and communication between the different IT systems of the business partners. The standards embrace

- Multiple Messaging Services, building upon existing XML-based messaging systems
- Partner Interface Processes (PIPs)
- A directory for the retrieval of information related to the PIPs
- Dictionaries containing PIP properties
- The RosettaNet Implementation Framework, describing the technical handling of PIP messages (packaging, routing, transporting)
- Trading Partner Implementation Requirements

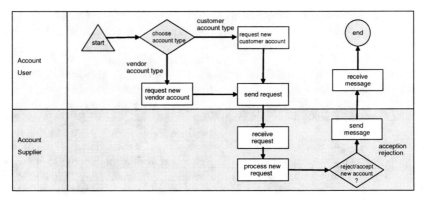

FIGURE 5-3. RosettaNet Partner Interface account setup process (based on [12]).

Figure 5-3 shows an example of a PIP–in this case, the process of setting up an account between a supplier and a customer. The accounts contain relevant business information (location and contacts) that is made available electronically once a partnership agreement is in place.

Developed by companies from the high-tech industry, RosettaNet is a standard (still) less used in healthcare today. It is, however, applicable to healthcare in principle and it demonstrates the characteristics of process standards very well. For this reason, it was included in this description.

Another process-oriented standard is ebXML. Developed by OASIS and UN/CEFACT, ebXML is a high-level process standard for binary or multiparty collaboration within a business community. ebXML is described in more detail in the "Outlook" section of this chapter.

End-to-End Connections versus a Central Hub

Advantages of a Central Hub

Classic EDI-based eBusiness assumed a business interaction between a limited number of partners only, primarily between two partners exchanging messages (order, advance shipping notification, invoice). As SCM concepts concern not only logistics, but pervade the entire order fulfilment process and beyond (see Chapters 2 and 14), business transactions are no longer regarded as a dyadic (binary) activity, but encompass the interaction of a whole variety of partners along the supply chain. Business process standards such as RosettaNet and ebXML clearly reflect this trend and stay abreast of these changes. Aligned with SCM is the concept of business collaboration or cCommerce (see Chapters 1 and 14), which extends the set of classic dyadic transactions by multiparty activities.

Besides this new approach in eBusiness, which requires new technical solutions for its implementation, there is a technical problem associated with traditional enterprise-to-enterprise communication because simple end-to-end connections soon reach their limits. If a business partner wants to trade with hundreds of other partners electronically, he would have to establish and maintain interfaces between all those partners, which is a costly and technically difficult endeavor. This problem is solved by installing a central hub to which all partners are connected and which serves as a digital turntable for receiving and forwarding messages. An electronic hub is an example of a self-contained interorganizational information system. The concept of a central hub was already extensively discussed in Chapter 4, in the context of enabling communication between heterogeneous systems within a hospital. It is generally applicable, however, to any kind of communication or EAI problem, and may also be exploited for B2B purposes.

eBusiness is familiar with two kinds of these hubs, in fact–electronic market places and technically oriented exchanges. While electronic marketplaces allow the entire business cycle, including negotiations, to be automated, technically oriented exchanges (such as the ones most common in healthcare) focus on supporting the later phases. They provide the technical interfaces, perform data clearance, manage the catalogs, and handle inbound and outbound messages, but do not support any negotiations. Among the Internet-based trading exchanges in healthcare, the Global Healthcare Exchange (GHX, *www.ghx.com*) is the largest and operates worldwide in the United States, in Canada, and in Europe (mainland Europe and the United Kingdom). Chapter 7 details other Internet-based trading exchanges. Electronic marketplaces are uncommon for procuring medical supplies. If utilized at all in healthcare, they play a role in procuring supplies other than medical (e.g., office supplies).

Figure 5-4 gives an overview of technical B2B enablers in healthcare. Because Internet-based trading exchanges play a major role in connecting suppliers and providers, the term is printed in bold.

Collaborative procurement hubs (CPHs) are an emerging type of intermediary that manages interorganizational information systems in the healthcare industry in the United Kingdom. Arranging for electronic auctions and aggregating purchasing volume, they definitely support the early phases and resemble classical electronic marketplaces.

A portal is a Web-based platform owned by one of the business partners or by a third party that allows business processes to be supported and integrated–often in a personalized way. The term is neutral with regard to the business logic it supports, and could fulfil the function of either an electronic marketplace or a technically oriented exchange.

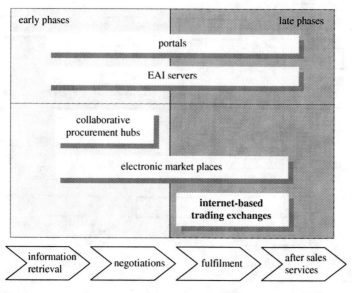

FIGURE 5-4. Technical B2B enablers in healthcare and their contribution to the business processes.

Typically located within an organization to make the integration of different applications possible, EAI servers do not exactly stand between the business partners like a portal managed by a third party. They may also permit one partner, however, to connect to several outside partners by providing converters and connectors to common ERP systems or to marketplaces and exchanges [7]. EAI servers, like portals, may support any type of business interaction depending on the information systems and the applications to which the EAI server connects (Figure 5-3).

Location of the Catalog

The location of the catalog is one of the most critical issues of B2B and is tightly coupled with the question of how connectivity is achieved. Not only is the catalog the guarantor for added value because it enables data to be error free, but catalog management also requires significant resources (staff, time, equipment). Furthermore, it serves as the semantic link between the business partners. In other words, the catalog is the key for steering eBusiness activities. Bearing this in mind, a distinction is made between sell-side approaches, buy-side approaches, and the hub-based solution (Figure 5-5). We speak of sell-side approaches if the supplier provides and manages his catalog, and of buy-side approaches if the customer (healthcare provider) imports the catalogs from his suppliers and merges them into one multisupplier catalog from which he makes his orders. In the case of a hub, the catalogs are managed by the hub that imports the catalog data provided and updated by the suppliers. To be able to import catalogs from different

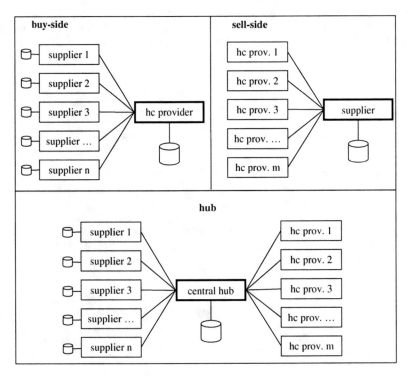

FIGURE 5-5. Buy-side vs. sell-side vs. hub – catalogs depicted as tons.

sources, a mandatory common data structure must be agreed on by all suppliers who feed the catalog.

When ordering via an electronic catalog, the catalog can either stay with the site or can be duplicated and sent to the customer prior to ordering. The latter solution is the method of choice with low-band networks. If customers browse online in the remote catalog, they can do so via a server-based application designed to display the catalog (and handle the cart) or via their local procurement solution, which is made possible by a mechanism called PunchOut or RoundTrip (see Chapter 6).

Levels of Integration

B2B Scenarios

Technical B2B solutions have to accommodate for different eBusiness scenarios. These scenarios often reflect different sizes of enterprises and thus different electronic capabilities. They also depend on business decisions, such as whether certain functions are outsourced to a third party (see Chapters 2 and 11). In principle, there are two categories of users: 1) those that operate a complete HIS_h or ERP system with materials management and/or sales functions incorporated, and 2) those that do not have such a system or run only a rudimentary information system with no materials management/sales function or whose information system does not allow any proper integration. The latter category of users has often outsourced purchasing and materials management to a third party and just wishes to place orders. Both types of users exist on the hospitals' side, as well as on the suppliers' side, and solutions must consider any of these scenarios. This can result in quite technically simple approaches, as well as highly sophisticated solutions. Table 5-2 depicts the four relevant scenarios. Except for Scenario D, which requires a hub, all other scenarios can be technically implemented either in an end-to-end way or by utilizing a hub.

In **Scenario A,** the healthcare provider has no means of sending and receiving electronic messages with the help of an information system due to any of the reasons mentioned above. In contrast, the supplier or the exchange to which the provider is connected possesses full electronic capabilities. In this sense, Scenario A is similar to an online shop solution or a portal typically found in B2C scenarios. The healthcare provider thus needs to become equipped with a device that permits the connection to the supplier's site or the hub (see Figure 5-6).

The simplest approach for such a device is a Web browser, through which the user invokes a server-based application in the information system of the supplier or the hub. The application may either start an electronic form, into which the order data are typed manually (called WebEDI, if data are structured via an EDI convention), or may display the user interface of an ordering application which accesses a catalog and handles the

TABLE 5-2. B2B scenarios – technical perspective.

		Supplier	
		Rudimentary electronic capacities	Integrated information system
Healthcare Provider	Rudimentary electronic capacities	Scenario D	Scenario A
	Integrated information system	Scenario B	Scenario C

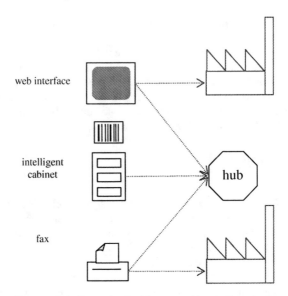

FIGURE 5-6. Connecting healthcare providers in Scenario A.

electronic cart. No additional software is installed on the client's side and thus there is no software requiring any maintenance by the healthcare provider. Another device that allows requisitioning or ordering by the healthcare provider is a cabinet (see Chapter 9), in combination with a barcode reader for capturing the information (type and quantity) about the items needed and a software system that stores and transmits the information to the supplier's (or the exchange's) system. The electronic orders may be transferred via synchronous or asynchronous methods. In both cases, the browser and the cabinet solution, the supported transactions are requisitioning and ordering. In the case of the browser-based solution, it also includes receiving information about the order status, line-item status, and line exceptions (for visual inspection by the user). Periodical reports on all transactions made can also often be retrieved from a website.

Yet another, even simpler, approach is a fax order. Here the device is a fax machine on the client's side and a fax server on the supplier's side. The fax server manages the inbound faxes and stores them for further analysis. For information on electronic fax orders to be treated as structured data (e.g., an EDI message), the fax documents need to be translated by character recognition software.

In **Scenario B,** the supplier can be reached electronically (via the Web), but has no ERP system in place and the healthcare provider wishes to communicate electronically. In this case, the purchasing or materials managing system produces an electronic order that is converted into a text document to be faxed or emailed to the supplier. In return, the supplier may email business documents back to the healthcare provider. Alternatively, suppliers may connect to a central application hosted by a hub via a Web browser. This allows them to access purchase orders placed electronically and to respond electronically (e.g., order acknowledgment, advance shipping notification, invoices).

Scenario C is the most sophisticated and technically challenging approach. Integration may be achieved by asynchronous procedures, in particular by exchanging file-based messages or by synchronous solutions (e.g., remote procedure calls). Chapter 4 describes the full range of approaches for integrating systems by implementing cooperative information system architectures and service-oriented architectures. In this chapter, we will present and discuss common methods employed in healthcare eBusiness (see "Integration of Local Information System with Hub" and "Integration of Information Systems" in this chapter).

Only this scenario allows for a true bidirectional communication between two systems exchanging structured business information electronically, such as purchase orders, order acknowledgements, order status, advance shipping notifications, delivery notes, delivery acknowledgements, and invoices. It is the basis for completely automating the order-to-payment cycle, and it is the method of choice for a seamless integration of the data accompanying B2B processes into one's own information system for business analysis.

Scenario D is a combination of the first two scenarios, where both partners possess only rudimentary electronic capacities (i.e., Internet access). Nevertheless, this scenario may be supported electronically via an electronic hub (marketplace or exchange). Although none of the parties processes the data electronically in a back-office system, there is added value for both parties. That is to say that this method ensures the generation of clean order data because the healthcare provider may access up-to-date catalog data residing on the site of the hub.

These four scenarios reflect different levels of integration with the fax and Web interface ranging at the lowest level, and synchronous communication between two information systems at the highest level.

Integration of Local Information Systems with Electronic Hub

Hub systems can be built with various tools by either using dedicated development and run-time systems for electronic marketplaces, using AS technology or using an EAI server as the kernel. In all cases, the marketplace system must provide means for connecting to heterogeneous buyers' and sellers' information systems. In contrast to integrating two or more information systems (ERP and HIS_h), the challenge here is establishing and maintaining connectivity with a large number of systems and providing robust and secure mechanisms for handling a high throughput. Typically, this is achieved by a connectivity platform as part of the hub system that communicates with connectors implemented at the external sites (see Figure 5-7). Inbound messages are transformed in the external connector, such as from a proprietary format to a standard XML format, before they are sent to the hub. This relieves the hub system from transforming the large bulk of inbound messages itself and thus reduces the system's workload.

Messages are then validated against the hub's catalog, which serves as the reference. Fields to be checked in a purchase order typically include the product number, the unit of measure, and the supplier's division. In case this review results in discrepancies, pre-established rules or other resources are invoked for correcting the data. Only clean messages (e.g., purchase orders) are forwarded to the supplier. The sending party is notified about the corrections made so that relevant changes can be made to the local item master. This process is sometimes referred to as *cleansing*. In advanced scenarios, a mechanism triggers the updating of the local masters once the central catalog has been changed. Purchase orders can also be validated against customized catalogs containing only contracted items. This requires the system to be able to access contract data. Systems incorporating contract management also allow for price validation, which is particularly relevant, so that correct invoices can be generated.

healthcare provider   hub   supplier

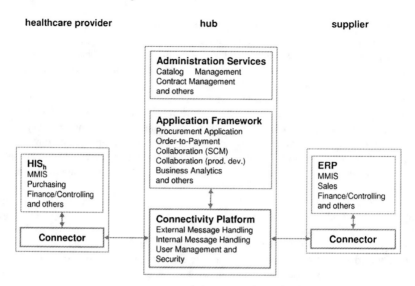

FIGURE 5-7. Hub structure.

The GHX, for example, manages a multivendor catalog with normalized data–the AllSource Catalog–which contains up-to-date entries and thus makes sure that incorrect orders due to outdated product information are avoided. GHX also provides contract management via its Contract Center.

A message bus, which is part of the connectivity platform, handles the routing of the messages internally (to and from the applications) and externally to the message recipient.

Depending on their business orientation, hubs offer various applications such as supporting the complete order-to-payment cycle (including status monitoring), which is the most common application, but also permit electronic collaboration, bidding, auctions (not for medical supplies), and other advanced solutions. Integration between a local information system and a hub typically involves efforts on both sides. The following list illustrates the practical steps made for integrating an online trading exchange (in this case GHX) and is an extract from a report on the seven steps made at Leeds Teaching Hospitals [13].

3. GHX Setup and Configuration Completed
    Project Planned, staffed and kicked-off
    Client Registration (IDs/Cross Reference Tables/Routing Tables) at GHX and existing Member's systems
    Configuration of GHX servers for new customer completed by GHX
    Special development-related setup and configuration
4. Customer Setup and Configuration Completed
    Connectivity Solution Operational & Tested - communication server installed and tested through firewalls (for communication between the hospital and GHX)

Application Solutions Operational – ERP[1] application upgraded and configured with GHX functionality

Testing Readiness Checklist Complete / 'Integration' Readiness Assessment Complete

Testing of Overall Solution Complete (unit testing and end-to-end)

5. Master File Reconciliation Completed

Hospital provides catalogue extract to GHX, GHX matches items against GHX AllSource catalogue, Supplier identifies wrong and obsolete item numbers and provides correct item information

Hospital updates ERP Item Master with correct item numbers, unit of measures, quantity of each and descriptions

Supplier adds missing items to GHX AllSource catalogue

6. Go Live

Configuration of GHX Production environment

Go Live Readiness Checklist Complete

Configuration/cut-over to new customer Production environment

Successful Production Order

Roll-out schedule agreed

The previous example demonstrates that integration is not just a question of connecting two technical systems, but revolves to a large degree around data synchronization.

Integration of Information Systems

While Chapter 4 gives an overview of general methods for achieving integration, this chapter illustrates some of the common methods for allowing two ERP systems to communicate with each other in a B2B scenario. We will present the approaches taken by SAP and by Oracle as examples to demonstrate integration strategies of two world-leading ERP providers with a significant user base in the healthcare industry.

With the evolvement of SAP's software products from a client server-based ERP system to a family of products based on the principles of service-oriented architectures, *integration* has become a topic that is addressed by an integration framework (see exchange infrastructure in next section) rather than by single techniques.

In many B2B installations involving SAP R/3, however, external applications (SAP and nonSAP solutions) are connected via the following direct methods:

- Business Application Programming Interfaces (BAPIs)
- Remote Function Calls (RFCs)
- Intermediate Documents (IDOCs)

Originating in object-oriented programming methods, BAPIs are the methods within SAP Business Objects Types (BO). BOs are assigned to Business Components, for example the BO *employee* is assigned to the Business Component *Human Resources* (HR). BAPIs, which permit the access and manipulation of Business Objects, thus represent interfaces at the business level of communication. Technically speaking, BAPIs make use of Internet services, CORBA, and DCOM environments (see also Chapter 4). In the case of Internet-based communication, they are used to implement cross-enterprise communication via the SAP Business Connector (BC) or Internet Application Components [14].

---

[1] ERP refers to the management functionality within the HIS_h.

The remote function call (RFC) concept allows the programmer to call functions located in a remote system. RFCs are implemented in ABAP, the SAP programming language. In fact, BAPIs are technically based on RFCs. Both BAPIs and RFCs belong to the category of synchronous communication methods.

IDOCs are SAP's approach to implementing EDI-type messages. They strongly resemble EDIFACT messages; however, they need to be converted to become fully EDIFACT compliant. Similar to EDIFACT, there are the INVOICE IDOC for invoices and the ORDERS IDOC for purchase orders, just to name a few examples. IDOCs, like other messages, are typical implementations of asynchronous communication. In addition, IDOCs serve as the asynchronous interface of BAPIs, which can generate IDOCs for this purpose. To use IDOCs in a Web environment, the SAP Business Connector converts IDOCs into XML documents, and vice versa. It is also responsible for receiving and sending the documents. In the case of an IDOC-to-XML conversion, the new XML file (e.g., in xCBL format) is transported–via HTTP, HTTPS, file transfer protocol (FTP) or the small mail transfer protocol (SMTP) used in emailing–to its destination. In the other case (XML-to-IDOC), the IDOCs are either transferred to the SAP system using transactional RFCs, or written into a directory from where they could be read by an application [15]. Generally speaking, the Business Connector cannot only be employed to convert IDOCs into XML documents, but must also be able to convert into any other format and vice versa once configured for that task.

All three integration methods (i.e., BAPIs, RFCs and IDOCs) used in an isolated manner lack the flexibility required in changing B2B environments, which typically make extensive use of the Internet.

With the announcement of ESA in 2003–now called Enterprise SOA–SAP has committed itself to moving its products towards full support of SOA fundamentals with the expectation of gaining the flexibility which characterizes modern component-based software architectures and allows business partnerships to be changed. Serving as a technical platform, SAP NetWeaver includes the Exchange Infrastructure (SAP XI)–an environment for connecting enterprise internal systems (application-to-application or A2A) and cross-enterprise systems (B2B). It supports several B2B standards, such as RosettaNet (see earlier). The Integration Server (see Figure 5-8) is an XI run-time component that illustrates the connectivity capabilities of XI using industry standards (industry protocol adapter).

Besides RosettaNet, SAP also supports standards common in healthcare. Data conversion for EDI, HL7, and HIPAA-compliant messages is made possible by using an adapter module of the Adapter Engine.

Figure 5-8 shows that integration is not simply a methodology of handling and converting messages, but that it also exploits additional information provided by the Integration Repository and Integration Directory. This includes information about the business scenarios and the business processes, in conjunction with information about the profiles of the business partners and about the specific type of collaboration they have agreed upon.

Oracle, originally a pioneer for relational database management systems, has become a major player in the ERP market. It maintains several ERP product lines–its own ERP product, Oracle E-Business Suite, and PeopleSoft's products, including the JD Edwards product line (since acquiring PeopleSoft Corporation). Oracle's strategy to provide mechanisms for business integration of various types is expressed in the Fusion Architecture and Fusion Applications [17]. The Fusion Architecture–featuring the use of Web services to loosely couple different applications–consists of an Enterprise Service

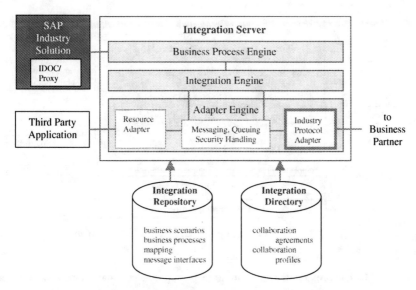

FIGURE 5-8. SAP XI Integration Server (based on [16]).

Bus, a Service Registry, the BPEL (Business Process Execution Language) Process Manager and Workflow, Business Rules, the Web Service Manager, and a tool for business activity monitoring. Central to making integration possible, the Enterprise Service Bus allows messages to be passed in both synchronous and an asynchronous manners. Messages are transformed, routed, and delivered following either a point-to-point or a publish-and-subscribe pattern. The Service Registry is devised as an online directory and a service broker for Web services, interfaces, and so-called integration points for applications. It thus also functions as a catalog for B2B protocols.

Technically, the Fusion Architecture (as a concept) is realized by the Oracle Fusion Middleware–a portfolio of products including tools for integration and process management [18], as well as for B2B collaboration. Figure 5-9 shows the major components of Oracle Fusion Middleware, with those modules highlighted that relate to integration and business processes.

It allows the business partners to define, configure, manage, and monitor the electronic exchange of information. Major industry standards, such as RosettaNet, ebXML, and EDI (X12 and EDIFACT) are supported by providing adapters. For healthcare-specific applications, there are converters for HL7 and for U.S.-specific standards and regulatory requirements such as HIPAA (X12) and the National Council for Prescription Drug Programs (NCPDP) format.

Both SAP and Oracle show that integration concepts have become central in their system architecture. Integration is understood in a wide sense, embracing application-to-application (A2A) integration, as well as cross-enterprise B2B integration. This perspective of integration is technically supported by the commitment of both companies to open standards–in particular, the SOA, which is not restricted to a special integration scenario, but applicable to integration tasks in general. The concept of business processes steering integration has influenced both approaches.

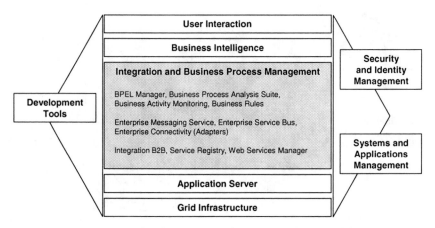

FIGURE 5-9. Oracle Fusion Middleware – excerpt (based on [18]).

SAP and Oracle provide dedicated solutions to supply chain management within their ERP systems that make use of the B2B integration concepts.

The outlook provided in the next paragraph returns to the standards issue and adopts a general perspective on the future of B2B and a generic support of the underlying business processes.

Outlook

ebXML was mentioned briefly earlier in this chapter as an advanced and generic process standard. In this section, we will expand on it and give evidence of where ebXML is used in healthcare. ebXML is a set of loosely coupled specifications that aim at making business collaboration possible. By collaboration, ebXML means a set of transactions between the business partners. Transactions are defined as business document flows between business partners. A sequence of transactions (order and transition) is called a Business Process Choreography in ebXML language [19]. Central to ebXML is the registry concept that allows for a centralized, as well as *federated* approach for organizing a registry. A registry is a physical information system which stores XML and non-XML documents and their metadata (see also [20]). It is to be distinguished from a repository where the registered objects are actually kept. When used for enabling business collaboration to take place, the registry holds the business scenarios and the partner profiles (i.e., the partner's ebXML capacities and constraints). Registered business partners can be *discovered* by their business scenarios. In the subsequent steps, business arrangements are to be agreed upon before transactions may begin [21, 22]. Figure 5-10 shows a simplified ebXML interaction scenario.

In ebXML, business processes are generally described by the Business Process Specification Schema (BPSS), which serve as a bridge between process modeling and software specifications (see Chapter 3[2]). BPSS instances point to the definition of business documents (e.g., a purchase order document) that are generated from the so-called

---

[2] BPSS like BPEL, mentioned in Chapter 3, are also referred to as choreography languages. They are based on XML, thus they can be processed by a business partner's software application [23].

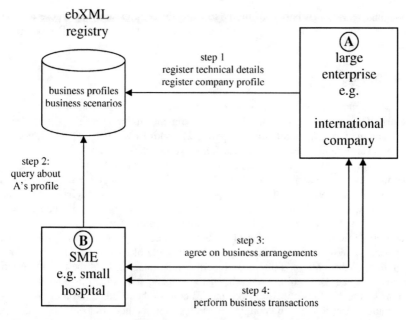

FIGURE 5-10. The ebXML interaction scenario – simplified [based on [21]].

core components (CC) or from other specifications. The BPSS is incorporated with, or referenced by, the Collaboration Protocol Profile (CPP) and the collaborative partner agreement (CPA) of the trading partners involved. Instances of the profile and processes (i.e., those profiles and processes that apply to a specific business partner) are stored in the registry and are thus searchable for other partners.

Once partners *have found* each other and agree on specific transactions, they reference the BPSS instance in the CPA. The registry and its services are specified in the registry information model (ebRIM) and the registry services specification (ebRS). Other ebXML specifications are the ebXML requirements (ebREQ), the technical architecture (ebTA), and the messaging service (ebMSG).

Due to ebXML's generic nature, its use is not confined to classic B2B collaboration scenarios, but is also applicable outside the business domain. For example, ebXML has been tested by incorporating patient care-related HL7 messages (see Chapter 4) as a payload [24]. The ebXML registry concept has also been exploited by "Integrating the Healthcare Enterprise" (IHE)[3] in its specification for storing cross-enterprise healthcare documents (electronic health records) and enabling documents to be shared [25]. This approach has been extended by utilizing BPSS from the suite of ebXML specifications for describing healthcare workflows [26]. In the United Kingdom, ebMSG–the messaging service of ebXML–is a key component of the Transaction and

---

[3] IHE is an initiative of the American College of Cardiology, the Healthcare Information and Management Systems Society (HIMSS), and the Radiological Society of North America (*www.ihe.net*).

Messaging Service that is part of the NHS Care Record Service [27]. These and other examples demonstrate the recognition of ebXML, or parts of the specification suite, in healthcare [28].

Conclusion

In this chapter, different technical realizations of interorganizational information systems (IOS) were presented. Following the dimensions proposed by Chatterjee and Ravichandran [1]–i.e., 1) relational support, 2) control over IOS, 3) integration with internal systems, and 4) technology specificity–we saw that B2C approaches adopted for B2B transactions allow quite a low level of integration with internal systems, and thus make the customer rather independent of the supplier. This characterizes arm's length relationships, or a low level of relational support. In return, customers have little control over the IOS. From the customer's point of view, the technology is not specific because it is based on Web technology. From a supplier's point of view, the technology can be quite specific depending on the IT system selected. B2B cooperation, pursuing the end-to-end pattern of connectivity, is often an example of a case with a high degree of integration, as this pattern is often combined with an integration of the two information systems involved. Depending on the intensity of using standards, this approach can be more or less technology specific. Both parties control their end of the IOS and need to make mutual decisions when changing the integration method. Indeed, due to the great effort involved for setting up and maintaining the interconnectivity, this approach only makes sense in selected cases to support strategic partnerships. B2B scenarios making use of a hub try to avoid these deficiencies. Common exchanges in healthcare, such as GHX, provide mechanisms for both a low and a high level of technical integration, thus being flexible in terms of the specific needs of the organization. They also support various models of relational support, including a rather loose business interaction (e.g., placing an order) and a rather close business relationship (e.g., managing a consignment warehouse). Equity members of the GHX (both suppliers and healthcare providers) can exert control over the system. Thus, GHX is unspecific and neutral with regard to this dimension. Other exchanges, such as GSG (Gesellschaft für Standardprozesse im Gesundheitswesen) in Germany, are governed by the healthcare providers who have control over the system in terms of the decisions made and with regard to the finances. Whether or not the technology used by the exchanges is specific greatly depends on the perspective. All hospitals connected to GSG utilize SAP R/3 solutions within their HIS_h, thus GSG makes use of a widely implemented technology in German hospitals. In contrast, GHX needs to serve a heterogeneous system's landscape. Like in the case of GSG, GHX technology is specific. It constitutes a de facto standard, however, due to the large customer base of GHX in the United States.

In fact, many approaches made in the healthcare arena converge towards the exchange model, because it is the only one that is expected to generate the critical number of users needed to be successful.

Although exchanges are a classic type of IOS, it can be argued that they actually serve as an IOS infrastructure. Borman [29] argues that the nature of an IOS is that of an infrastructure, as opposed to a system. An infrastructure, he says, is characterized by the features 1) providing support to activities –not providing applications; 2) being flexible and adaptive; 3) having a limited scope–not serving all purposes, and 4) providing an advantage. Bearing in mind what has been stipulated in the introduction–i.e., that eBusiness technology in healthcare must work in an unobtrusive manner–exchanges will evolve from a system to an infrastructure. With hospital/health information systems and ERP systems becoming more and more pervasive in the healthcare industry, exchanges will not need to provide applications because they will then come with the information system. Thus, their scope will narrow down to supporting business processes, handling the messages, managing the catalog(s) and clearing the data. Connecting to a huge diversity of heterogeneous systems, exchanges in healthcare have proven already to be flexible and adaptive. With the increasing adoption of eBusiness standards, exchanges will have to provide and maintain less diverse methods for connecting the users. Their particular advantage in healthcare is subject to a series of investigations, also described in Chapters 7, 12 and 13 of this book. Thinking of exchanges as technical infrastructure paves the way to understanding them as commonplace, routine means for conducting business.

References

[1] Chatterjee, D. and T. Ravichandran. (2004) Beyond the Exchange Models: Understanding the Structure of B2B Information Systems. *Information Systems and e-Business Management.* **2,** 169-186.

[2] Ganci, J. (2003) WebSphere Commerce V5.5 Architecture. IBM Redbooks Paper. Available from: <http://www.redbooks.ibm.com/redpapers/pdfs/redp3730.pdf> [Accessed 20 November 2006].

[3] The Accredited Standards Committee (ASC) X12 (2006). *X12.* Available from: < http://www.x12.org/> [Accessed 11 November 2006].

[4] United Nations Economic Commission for Europe (2006). *UN/EDIFACT.* Available from: <http://www.unece.org/trade/untdid/welcome.htm> [Accessed 11 November 2006].

[5] United Nations Economic Commission for Europe. *CHAPTER 2.2 - Electronic data interchange for administration, commerce and transport (EDIFACT) - Application level syntax rules.* Available from: <http://www.unece.org/trade/untdid/texts/d422_d.htm#p1> [Accessed 15 November 2006].

[6] European Commission, Directorate General for Enterprise and Industry (2005) *Special Report e-business Interoperability and Standards: A Cross-Sector Perspective and Outlook.* Bonn: empirica. Available from: <http://www.ebusiness-watch.org/resources/documents/TR03_Interoperability_2005_web.pdf> [Accessed 01 September 2006].

[7] Seeburger Business Integration (2006). Available from: <http://www.seeburger.de/> [Accessed 11 November 2006].

[8] GS1 Germany (2005) WebEDI. Available from: <http://www.gs1-germany.de/Internet/content/produkte/ean/ecommerce_edi/webedi/index_ger.html> [Accessed 12 November 2006].

[9] Quantz, J. and T. Wichmann. (2003) *e-Business-Standards in Germany: Assessment, Problems, Prospects.* Berlin: Berlecon Research. Available from: <http://www.berlecon.de/research/reports.php?we_objectID=125> [Accessed 01 September 2006].

[10] U.S. Department of Health and Human Services. *Centers for Medicare and Medicaid Services – Glossary.* Available from: <http://www.cms.hhs.gov/apps/glossary/default.asp?Letter=X&Language=English> [Accessed 10 November 2006].

[11] GS1. *GS1 EANCOM Technical.* Available from: <http://www.gs1.org/productssolutions/ecom/eancom/technical/> [Accessed 19 November 2006].

[12] RosettaNet. *PIP 1A1: Request Account Set Up*. Available from: <http://portal.rosettanet. org/cms/sites/RosettaNet/Standards/RStandards/pip/c11/seg1a/index.html> [Accessed 20 November 2006].

[13] NHS - The Leeds Teaching Hospitals. *e-Commerce at Leeds*. <http://www.leedsteac hinghospitals.com/sites/supplies/sevensteps.php> [Accessed 19 November 2006].

[14] SAP. *General Introduction to BAPIs (CA-BFA)*. Available from: <http://help.sap.com/ saphelp_46c/helpdata/en/61/f3f0371bc15d73e10000009b38f8cf/frameset.htm> [Accessed 12 November 2006].

[15] SAP. *Communication Using Industry Standards*. Available from: <http://help.sap.com/ saphelp_nw04/helpdata/en/9b/5d989b236e4a4e8067446b103b05fa/content.htm> [Accessed 12 November 2006].

[16] Buxmann, P., W. König, M. Fricke, F. Hollich, L. Martin Diaz, and S. Weber. (2004) *Inter-organizational Cooperation with SAP Solutions*. Berlin: Springer.

[17] Oracle (2006) *Oracle Fusion Architecture and Oracle Fusion Applications – An Oracle Technical White Paper*. Available from: <http://www.oracle.com/ applica- tions/fusion.html> [Accessed 10 November 2006].

[18] Oracle. *Oracle Fusion Middleware*. Available from: <http://www.oracle.com/ technology/products/middleware/index.html> [Accessed 12 November 2006].

[19] UN/CEFACT (2003) *ebXML Business Process Specification Schema V1.10 2003*. Available from: <http://www.untmg.org/dmdocuments/BPSS_v110_2003_10_18.pdf > [Accessed 19 November 2006].

[20] Breininger, K. *ebXML registry*. OASIS ebXL Registry TC. Available from: <http://xml.coverpages.org/EbizXMLRegistry200310.pdf> [Accessed 10 November 2006].

[21] Hofreiter, B., C. Huemer, and J. H. Kim (2006) Choreography of ebXML business collaboration. *Information Systems and e-Business Management*. **4**, 221-243.

[22] Webber, D. (2004) *The Benefits of ebXML for e-Business*. IDEAlliance XML 2004 Conference and Exposition, Washington, DC. Available from: <http://www.idealliance.org/proceedings/xml04/papers/44/webber.html> [Accessed 10 November 2006].

[23] Hofreiter, B. and C. Huemer (2006) From a UMM Process Model to a Business Environment Specific ebXML Process. *Journal of Electronic Commerce Research*. **7**(3), 138-153.

[24] UN/CEFACT and OASIS (xx). *ebXML in healthcare*. Available from: <http://www.ebxml.org/news/pr_20010509.htm> [Accessed 20 November 2006].

[25] Dogac, A., G. B. Laleci, Y. Kabak, S. Unal, S. Heard, S. Beale, P. L. Elkin, F. Najmi, C. Mattocks, D. Webber and M. Kernberg. (2005) Exploiting ebXML registry semantic constructs for handling archetype metadata in healthcare informatics. *International Journal of Metadata, Semantics and Ontologies*. 1(1), 21-36.

[26] Dogac, A., V. Bicer, and A. Okcan (2006) *Collaborative Business Process Support in IHE XDS through ebXML Business Processes*. The 22nd Inter- national Conference on Data Engineering, Atlanta, GA. Available from: <http://xml.coverpages.org/ebXML.html> [Accessed 10 November 2006].

[27] OASIS, BT (2004) Case Study: UK National Health Service NPfIT uses ebXML Messaging. Available from: <http://www.ebxml.org/case_studies/NHS- ebMSG-casestudy-041206.pdf> [Accessed 21 November 2006].

[28] Cover Pages (2006) Technical Report – XML in Clinical Research and Healthcare Industry. Available from: <http://www.kor.dk/borge/inflate.php?url=

http%3A%2F%2Fxml.coverpages.org%2Fhealthcare.html&style=top> [Accessed 19 November 2006].

[29] Borman, M. (2006) Developing, and Testing, a Theoretical Framework for Interorganizational Systems (IOS) as Infrastructure to Aid Future IOS design. *Information Systems and e-Business Management.* **4**, 343-360.

6
From Product Identification to Catalog Standards

Frank Brüggemann and Ursula Hübner

Executive Summary

The purpose of standards is to meet one of the greatest challenges in eBusiness–
the diversity among the technical systems in use, the processes executed by the
various partners, and the structure and meaning of the information exchanged. This
chapter focuses on standards that help in understanding the meaning of a message.
This implies that the items included in the message are uniquely identified, named
properly, classified correctly, and used in the appropriate context. Interpreting
messages correctly is the most essential prerequisite for sustainable process
automation in eBusiness. Standardized information has an impact on all electronically supported business processes, not just those that are entirely automated–with
electronic product catalogs constituting their core element. The latter ensure
that product information can be easily updated and distributed on a large scale.
With standardized, updated information becoming regularly available, all supply
chain partners–manufacturers, distributors, wholesalers, resellers, and health care
providers–are in a position to optimize their processes, building on accurate and
structured data to be transmitted along the supply chain and be further analyzed
for business and patient-care purposes.

Covering the lower layers of the stack of eBusiness standards, this chapter
expands on identification standards, classification systems, nomenclatures, and
catalog standards. The following major examples in each category,

- EAN·UCC and HIBCC for identification standards
- UNSPSC, NHS-eClass, eCl@ss, ATC/DDD,GPI, EGAR for classification systems
- UMDNS and GMDN for nomenclatures
- PRICAT/PRODAT (EANCOM), xCBL, cXML, and BMEcat (only shortly) for catalog standards

are described in terms of their scope, structure, and the organization in charge
of the standard. Not surprisingly, there are several standards in each category,
making it difficult for the user to decide which one to choose.

No attempt is undertaken to evaluate the standards, however the authors try to give a pragmatic answer to the question of what a good standard is, concluding that a bad standard is a standard not used. Phrased in a positive way, this means that the usage, and the reason why a standard is or should be used, forms the criteria for deciding which standard is more appropriate than the other. It is clear that analyzing the requirements derived from its practical application is therefore mandatory before coming to any conclusion. Further issues to be considered are whether the standard is specific to healthcare or not ,and what type of organization(s) stand(s) behind the standard. It is concluded that independent of whether the standard is healthcare-specific or not, it is the expertise of the organization in healthcare that finally counts.

The question is raised as to whether a global registration authority in charge of all supply chain standards in healthcare is needed to overcome current deficiencies in the standards area, and to assist in speeding up the adoption of eBusiness and supply chain methods in healthcare.

Introduction

One of the greatest challenges in eBusiness is the diversity among the technical systems in use, the processes executed by the various partners, and the structure and meaning of the information exchanged. The only way of achieving the necessary degree of harmonization at the various levels is by reaching consensus among the parties and utilizing standards. While the previous chapters focused on technical standards for message exchange (e.g., SOAP), on business standards for transactions in healthcare (e.g. EANCOM, HL7), on workflow management (BPEL in Chapter 3), and on process management (RosettaNet, ebXML), it is the aim of this chapter to describe and discuss existing approaches to standardize the semantics of exchanged messages. Understanding the meaning of a message implies that the items included in the message are identified uniquely, named properly, classified correctly, and used in the appropriate context. Interpreting messages correctly is the most essential prerequisite for sustainable process automation in eBusiness.

Standardized information, however, has a bearing not only on technical matters but also on nearly every business process. With structured and standardized information establishing the foundation of electronic catalogs, product information can easily be updated and distributed on a large scale. Suppliers may use electronic catalogs for optimizing their marketing, sales, logistics processes, and after-sales services, while healthcare providers may use them for sourcing, requisitioning, ordering, and providing detailed information to the end users–in particular, the clinicians.

A variety of modern electronic media such as the Web or optical media are useful vehicles for distributing product information along the supply chain from the manufacturers to the end customers.

As a result, effort associated with developing and enforcing such standards is less of an academic exercise but clearly has an impact on the practical way of conducting business by exploiting the power of the standards for creating electronic catalogs.

Benefits of the Electronic Catalog

With eCatalogs replacing the printed editions, a significantly greater number of potential buyers can be reached at a fraction of the cost incurred for the paper version. Providing comprehensive product information to customers constitutes the basis for the electronically supported procedures in marketing, including customer relationship management–activities that are becoming common business practice. These are, in fact, the greatest benefit from the manufacturers' point of view. Not only are the manufacturers themselves affected. In comparison to paper-based catalogs, electronically readable information ensures greater accuracy and productivity in communications among all supply-chain partners. To date, channel partners like distributors, resellers, and others who provide pre-sales and post-sales support on uncountable stock keeping units (SKUs) have to identify and process product information with no common structure and contents collected from hundreds of suppliers. This effort, duplicated by each distributor in the channel, makes the aggregation and dissemination of product information an expensive and inefficient proposition. The lack of standards required for creating eCatalogs, including standardized machine-readable product descriptors, leads to inefficiency and higher product prices.

With standardized, updated information becoming regularly available, all channel partners are, in principle, in a position to optimize their distribution processes. This will permit better inventory management and forecasting, and, in combination with eBusiness platforms, utilization of data for market analysis and standardized market share information on a broad basis.

The healthcare providers can also make use of standardized information retrieved from eCatalogs in multiple areas: at the operational level in requisitioning, purchasing and regular reporting, but also at the strategic level in analyzing aggregated data for the purpose of medical and corporate planning and controlling. In fact, most healthcare providers today do not know the exact spending volume of the supplies used in defined patient-care processes, and are therefore not capable of identifying candidates for strategic suppliers and strategic products. Structured information on classified products that are uniquely identified and well described forms the ideal basis of the master items database that enables healthcare providers to distribute and analyze their data according to their needs in a flexible manner. Providing access to the master items database from a series of IT-supported applications, such as requisitioning systems and electronic patient record systems, in a customized and controllable manner allows Central Purchasing to delegate a highly automated order process to the staff on the ward. They simply need to identify the product and to trigger the internal requisition or the external order. Having detailed product information at their fingertips helps clinicians get answers to clinical questions and choose the right product.

What applies to single healthcare providers also holds true for purchasing cooperatives and any kind of group purchasing organization. As demonstrated above, the free availability of standardized machine-readable information through electronic catalogs and directories connected to search engines and enterprise applications leads to tangible benefits for all players in a supply chain.

eCatalogs, however, do not come entirely free of charge. They require structured planning and investments to be made in terms of the resources necessary for inserting, deleting, and updating data. There are various options regarding who should be responsible for such kinds of data maintenance activities. Some claim the healthcare providers should not give away the responsibility for the data they depend on, but others state that the best solution is capturing all data at their source–this would make it the manufacturers' duty to take care of the electronic catalog.

What Are Standards?

Overview of Standards

According to CEN and ISO/IEC [1], a standard is a "document, established by consensus and approved by a recognized body that provides, for common and repeated use, rules, guidelines or characteristics for activities or their results, aimed at the achievement of the optimum degree of order in a given context." In the context of information systems and information management, the *degree of order* mentioned in the above definition is equivalent to *the degree of interoperability* between the systems involved. Because interoperability is multidimensional in nature, connecting systems to actually share data, information, and knowledge requires not only one single standard but builds upon multiple standards often arranged as a stack–thus demonstrating an increase in complexity and scope. As shown in Chapter 5, the stack of business-related standards is comprised of identification standards at the bottom, followed by classification systems, standards for electronic catalogs, transaction standards, and finally process standards at the top of the stack.

Covering the lower layers, namely identification standards, classification systems, and standards for catalog exchange, this chapter will begin by providing some definitions for each category and will then continue by describing the most important examples of standards in each category. It is worth keeping in mind that, in some areas, multiple standards aimed at identical, or nearly identical, topics exist and thus compete with each other. It is not the goal of this chapter, however, to resolve this issue by evaluating the various standards. Figure 6-1 gives an overview of the standards to be presented in this chapter.

Name of standards	Identification	Classification	Nomenclature	Catalog	Transaction
EAN_UCC	▓				
HIBC	▓				
UNSPSC		▓			
NHS-eClass		▓			
eCl@ss		▓			
ATC/DDD		▓			
GPI		▓			
EGAR		▓			
GMDN			▓		
UMDNS			▓		
BMEcat				▓	
EANCOM				▓	░
xCBL				▓	░
cXML				▓	░

FIGURE 6-1. Standards (features marked in light grey are NOT described further in this chapter).

Some Definitions

Identification Systems

Identification systems provide a scheme for assigning unique numbers to an entity such as a product, a container, a supplier, and a location. A set of widely accepted standardized rules for generating the numbers is the key to ensuring the uniqueness and consistency of the numbers required for unambiguous identification. The more widespread the products are, the more global the approval of the numbering standard must be. In a global world of trade, only one numbering scheme agreed upon worldwide and used for a variety of products is desirable. In such a case, a network of national agencies has to be established for delivering the numbers or sets of numbers.

Classification Systems

Classification systems are a collection of controlled terms organized in a hierarchical structure. Each term in a classification system is in one or more parent-child relationships to other terms in the system. Good practice limits all parent-child relationships to a single parent, whereby some classification systems allow for a poly-hierarchy, which means that a term can have multiple parents [2].

Classification systems may also be differentiated by the use of attributes associated with each node in the hierarchy. While some classification systems provide such attributes together with possible attribute values, others not only give the name of the node but sometimes couple it with a definition. In the event that nodes are described by a set of attributes with corresponding values, these features are inherited by all nodes at lower levels within this branch of the hierarchy. Typically, the node name is associated with a unique code identifying the node. Most code systems reflect the hierarchical structure with nodes at lower levels in the tree structure consisting of longer codes than those at the upper levels.

In healthcare, a variety of classification systems is widely in use, primarily for coding diseases–notably the International Classification of Diseases (ICD), 10th revision, and therapeutic or diagnostic procedures. Over the last decade(s), patient classification systems such as various diagnosis-related group (DRG) systems have become a common tool in healthcare economics in many countries. They are to be distinguished from classification systems describing a domain of knowledge (e.g., diseases) because they seek to break down patients into cost-homogeneous groups according to their diagnoses and procedures.

Developed for statistical analysis at that time, classification systems gained momentum with the wide adoption of information systems and now serve a variety of purposes, including decision-making support, reporting, controlling, budgeting, and remuneration.

Nomenclatures

Nomenclatures aim at describing a particular discipline or a body of knowledge in as comprehensive a manner as possible. They therefore consist of enumerated objects that are given standardized names and definitions. Ideally, the list of names is controlled by, and available from, a controlled vocabulary registration authority. All terms in a controlled nomenclature should have an unambiguous, nonredundant definition.

In contrast to classification systems, no systematic relationship among the objects is assumed and therefore the names are not arranged according to any particular structure (e.g., a tree structure or hierarchy).

As the boundaries of the term *nomenclature* are becoming blurred, some systems called *nomenclatures* would not match the above definition. While some nomenclatures are structured hierarchically, others have incorporated a logic-based approach that would make them resemble ontologies rather than nomenclatures.

Catalogs

By catalogs, we mean a complete and systematic compilation of information on items arranged as a list or a display in printed or electronic format. Usually the arrangement follows a systematic structure. Information on items contained in the catalog may consist of any type of multimedia data, including text, graphics, images, URL's (links to websites), audio and video files, and applications allowing for simulation and animation. Catalogs may make use of classification and identification systems by assigning a unique identifier, plus a code and a name derived from one or several classification system(s), to each item.

Often catalogs provide an intrinsic view of a domain defined by the organization that publishes the catalog, such as the product catalog of a supplier or the catalog of medical procedures offered by a hospital. Product catalogs may be subdivided into single and multiple-supplier catalogs according to the number of suppliers contributing to the catalog.

Identification Systems

EAN·UCC

Launched in 2005, GS1 is a globally operating not-for-profit organization that develops and promotes, among other things, EAN.UCC standards that combine European, Japanese, and North American tracks of development for identification systems dating back to the seventies.

GS1 came into existence after the U.S. American Uniform Code Council (UCC) and the Electronic Commerce Council of Canada (ECCC) joined EAN International as member organizations and EAN International decided to change its name to GS1– reflecting the global reach of the organization.[1]

The EAN·UCC identification keys embrace the following items:

- GTIN– Global Trade Item Number
- GLN– Global Location Number
- SSCC– Serial Shipping Container Code
- GRAI– Global Returnable Asset Identifier
- GIAI– Global Individual Asset Identifier
- GSRN–Global Service Relation Number
- GDTI– Global Document Type Identifier

Among these identification keys, the Global Trade Item Number (GTIN) is the most well known. It is a non-overlapping identifier for products and services that is unique throughout the world and is designed as a nonsignificant number, meaning that its code does not contain any significant information about the product itself and its features.

In fact, GTIN is not a single structure but rather describes a family of EAN·UCC global data structures that employ 14 digits and can be encoded into various types of

---

[1] For more information, visit www.gs1.org.

TABLE 6-1. GTIN family (source: www.gtin.info).

GTIN Data Structure		Legacy Terminology
GTIN-12	UPC, UCC-12	
GTIN-13	EAN, JAN, EAN-13	
GTIN-8	EAN-8	
GTIN-14	EAN/UCC-14	
GTIN-14	ITF Symbol, SCC-14, DUN-14, UPC Case Code, UPC Shipping Container Code, UCC Code 128, EAN Code 128	

data carriers. Table 6-1 shows the GTIN data structures and the corresponding legacy terminology developed by UCC, EAN International, and the Japanese organization responsible for the Japanese Article Number (JAN).

Numbers behind the acronym GTIN denote the number of digits actually used. In accordance with the 14-digit notation, the leading digits are padded with zeros in case of GTIN-12, GTIN-13 and GTIN-8. GTIN-13 or EAN-13 (old terminology), for example, is composed of a basic number–an article number generated by the supplier and a check digit (see Figure 6-2). GTIN-13 integrates a country and company prefix (basic number) derived from the Global Location Number (GLN)–an identifier for manufacturers and service providers (see upcoming paragraph). The numbers in the individual area (proprietary article numbers) enable the suppliers to code up to 100,000 different products and services. It therefore allows the supplier to distinguish between similar products of various sizes, colors, and other features.

The principles of GTIN are very similar to those of the international standard book number (ISBN) used for identifying books, and there are efforts to match the two approaches for identifying articles. A GTIN-13 code for books, for example, can be compiled from the ISBN-10 code by padding the first three digits with a fixed string and using the last digit as a check sum calculated via GTIN-13. ISBN-10 has been further developed to ISBN-13, making it compatible with GTIN-13.

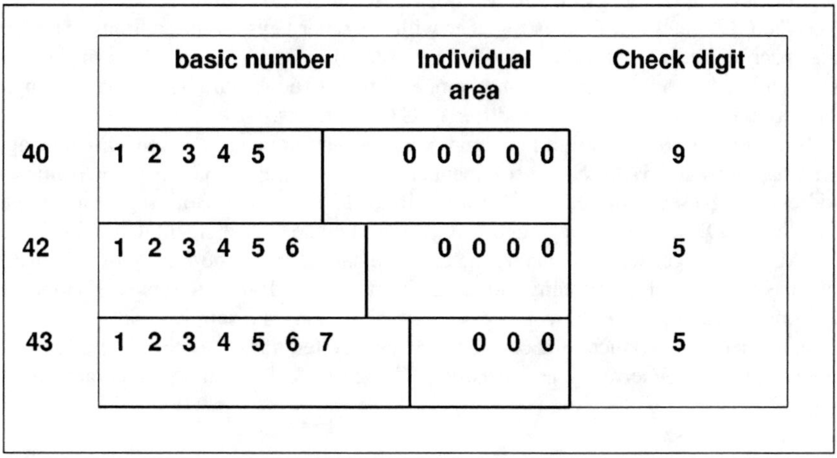

	basic number	Individual area	Check digit
40	1 2 3 4 5	0 0 0 0 0	9
42	1 2 3 4 5 6	0 0 0 0	5
43	1 2 3 4 5 6 7	0 0 0	5

FIGURE 6-2. Global Trade Item Number (GTIN) (www.gs1.com).

res. number	basic number from GLN 2		Individual area	Check digit
3	40	1 2 3 4 5	1 2 3 4 5 6 7 8 9	5
3	42	1 2 3 4 5 6	1 2 3 4 5 6 7 8	0
3	43	1 2 3 4 5 6 7	1 2 3 4 5 6 7	6

FIGURE 6-3. Serial Shipping Container Code (SSCC) (www.gs1.org).

The Global Location Number (GLN) is an identification key used to automatically process the address information of senders and recipients. GLN comes in two versions, with GLN 1 representing a fixed postal address consisting of 13 digits. For example, the following sequence of digits, 4399901883253, identifies the company GSG mbH in Hannover, Germany. In contrast to GLN 1, GLN 2 is more flexible and open in terms of appending additional information. The individual area allows the users to generate identifiers of their own, denoting specific locations or serving other individual demands. The basic number is the same as the one in GTIN.

The Serial Shipping Container Code (SSCC)[2] is another identification key among the EAN·UCC family of keys that identifies items of any package type for transport and/or storage that need to be managed through the supply chain. It is utilized for tracking such items such as packages or containers along the logistics chain. The use of this key in electronic messages (e.g., EANCOM DESADV = Despatch advice or International advance ship notice) enables further automation as the SSCC guarantees worldwide uniqueness in communication. Depending on the length of the company prefix, it is possible to add seven to nine more digits. Figure 6-3 shows the SSCC structure comprising an extension digit, with the basic number derived from GLN 2, the individual area, and the check digit. In contrast to GTIN and GLN, SSCC is 18 digits long and allows for more items to be coded in the individual area.[3]

GTIN, GLN, and SSCC keys together with the other keys are not automatically tied to a specific medium, and thus may be represented in various ways. One of the most common is a barcode attached to the item. Figure 6-4 shows various barcode examples illustrating the use of barcodes in different GTIN formats.

Moreover, the identification keys may very well be utilized in EANCOM messages (see Chapters 4 and 5). GLN is recommended for identifying the parties in the Name and Address (NAD) segment, and GTIN for use in the LIN segment. Both segments are part of the EANCOM ORDERS message. SSCC is used in the GIN segment in the EANCOM DESADV message, which contains the advance ship notice. The family of EAN·UCC keys has been adopted by many industries in more than 100 countries worldwide and has contributed significantly to process automation along the supply chain.

Pharmaceutical products are coded by special systems such as the *Pharmazentral-nummer* (PZN) in Germany and Austria–a 7-digit code that can be integrated into a

---

[2] In Germany, SSCC is more commonly known as NVE (Nummer der Versandeinheit).

[3] For further information on the other identification keys, refer to the GS 1 homepage (*www.gs1.org*).

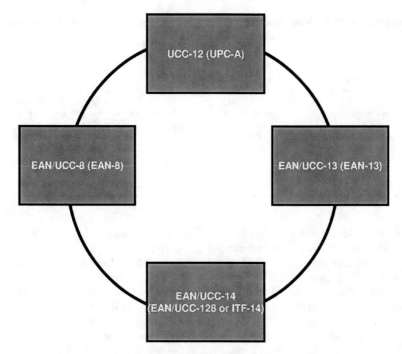

FIGURE 6-4. Barcodes (www.gtin.info).

GTIN or coupled with a GTIN. In the United States, the FDA's National Drug Code (NDC) for pharmaceutical products and the National Health Related Item Code (NHRIC) for medical/surgical devices are directly incorporated into GTIN.

HIBC Standards

Besides the EAN.UCC family of standards provided by GS 1, there is another system for identification keys that is used predominantly in the United States and geared especially to the healthcare industry. Founded in 1983 by major U.S. healthcare associations, the Health Industry Business Communications Council (HIBCC) is an industry-sponsored organization for the development and maintenance of healthcare-specific standards.[4] HIBCC is accredited by the American National Standards Institute (ANSI) and by the European Committee for Standardisation (CEN).

The Health Industry Bar Code (HIBC) Standards consist of two parts:

- Supplier Labeling Standard
- Provider Applications Standard.

The Supplier Labeling Standard [3] aims at providing a code that identifies the labeler, the product code, the unit of measurement embraced in the primary data structure, and additional information inserted at the discretion of the labeler, called *secondary data structure*. The labeler identification is a data element that is controlled by either the

---

[4] For more information on HIBCC, refer to their website at *www.hibcc.org*.

HIBCC or by GS 1 (showing interoperability at this level). The HIBCC version defines the primary data structure as shown in Table 6-2.

TABLE 6-2. HIBC Supplier Labelling Code – primary data structure.

+		HIBC Supplier Labelling Flag Character
4 alphanumeric characters	LIC	labeller identification code
1-13 alphanumeric characters	PCN	labeller product or catalogue code
1 numeric character	unit of measurement	0 = unit-of-use items
		1 – 8 = packing levels above unit-of-use
		9 = variable quantity containers
1 character	link character	calculated from the above characters

The optional secondary data set is used to encode the quantity and/or the expiration date and/or the lot, batch, or serial number of a product.

The Provider Applications Standard [4] defines standard data structures to be used either as a single data structure (see Table 6-3) split, or concatenated–building upon a single data structure (which is not further explained in this chapter). The single data structure, in fact, describes the *where* and the *what* (see Table 6-3).

Table 6-3 shows the broad variety of pieces of information that can be coded by the Provider Applications Standard, ranging from business and product information to patient and clinical information. It does not define the structure, nor does it propose a

TABLE 6-3. HIBC Provider Applications Standard - single data structure.

1 or 3 character(s)	"where"	flag(s) indicating where the data structure is located, for example
		A = device affixed to a patient
		B = patient care record
		C = specimen container
		D = direct patient image item
		E = business record
		and others
1 or 3 character(s)	"what"	A = Labeller Identification Code (LIC)
		B = service identification such as nursing unit, operation room, patient room
		C = patient identification
		D = specimen identification
		E = personnel identification
		F = administrable product identification such as ID's for drugs, blood components and IV fluids
		G = implantable product identification such as ID for pacemakers, artificial organs, prosthetic devices
		...
		I = medical procedure identification
		...
		O = purchase order number
		and others
Variable length	contents	data defined by the application
1 character	check character	modulus 43 check character

coding scheme of the data used in the application. Leaving them untouched, the standard just wraps the application data.

Expressions based on the Provider Applications Standard data structures are utilized to form more complex expressions, such as a purchase order consisting of the LIC of the ordering hospital, the purchase order number, or the purchase order data and the time.

In the United States and in other countries, HIBCC and GS 1 standards are in direct competition with each other. The Association of the Medical Technology Industry in Europe (www.eucomed.be) endorses both standards for bar coding, emphasizing generally that the use of identification standards is the essential prerequisite for both ensuring patient safety and enabling process automation in the supply chain [5]. Indeed, both standards coexist in hospitals worldwide, and are supported by various barcode readers and software systems [6].

Not only can products be better identified, which reduces the error rate, but packages can also be tracked and traced along their path from the supplier to the end customer, as has been demonstrated convincingly by other industries–in particular, for consumer goods.

Classification Systems

Introduction

When it comes to aggregating product data into meaningful groups, identification systems are of little value because the generated codes do not reveal any information about the product and its features. In such a case, products need to be classified utilizing a standard classification system. In the following, classification systems discussed in the eBusiness context are presented, some of them covering the healthcare industry specifically while others are more generic in nature. Some of them have been established for some time, whereas others are still emerging.

Multi-sector Classification Systems

UNSPSC

The United Nations Standard Products and Services Code (UNSPSC) was the first global initiative for a multisector classification system jointly developed by the United Nations Development Programme (UNDP) and Dun & Bradstreet Corporation (D & B) in 1998. It is owned by UNDP and further developed, maintained, and promoted by the UNSPSC organization that offers membership to individuals or organizations and is funded through the membership fee. UNSPSC is managed by GS 1 US (formerly UCC). The most recent version of UNSPSC is available in English. Translations into other languages–namely German, Dutch, French, Spanish, Japanese, Korean, Chinese, Danish, and Norwegian–exist and are available for different lower UNSPSC versions. Since version 6.0315, the Electronic Commerce Code Management Association (ECCMA) and the UNDP versions of the classification have been harmonized and integrated into one single system. Change requests, edits, deletions, and movements of segments can be posted by any individual or organization to technical advisors of these segments after becoming a member of UNSPSC. UNSPSC encourages members to translate the recent version, or comment on both the breadth and depth of the nodes in the hierarchy.

The hierarchy of the UNSPSC system consists of five levels: segment, family, class, commodity, and business function (see Table 6-4). The UNSPSC structure follows an

TABLE 6-4. The Structure of UNSPSC.

Segment
The logical aggregation of families for analytical purposes
   Family
   A commonly recognized group of inter-related commodity categories
      Class
      A group of commodities sharing common characteristics
         Commodity
         A group of substitutable products or services
            Business Function
            The function performed by an organization in support of the commodity

TABLE 6-5. UNSPSC example.

Hierarchy	Category Number	Title
Segment	42000000	Medical Equipment and Accessories and Supplies
Family	42240000	Orthopaedic and prosthetic and sports medicine products
Class	42241500	Casting and splinting supplies
Commodity	42241505	Orthopaedic casting rolls or tapes
Business Function	12	Manufacturer

increasing granularity in the description of product features (i.e., characteristics intrinsic to the product, irrespective of how the product is used).

All UNSPSC entities are identified by a unique 8-digit numeric code and a 2-digit suffix that indicates the business function. The code reflects both the hierarchical level (segment, family, class, and commodity) and the membership in a given category, as shown in Table 6-5.

The UNSPSC Business Function (BF), encoded by a 2-digit number–the Business Function Identifier (BFI) –reflects the kind of relationship between the company and the product category, as shown in Table 6-6. UNSPSC thus permits the conveyance not only of product intrinsic information but also–to a limited extent–of information about the current business context of the product.

As a result of its goal to cover a very wide area of application domains, segments addressed by UNSPSC range from live plant and animal material to

TABLE 6-6. UNSPSC Business Function Identifier.

BFI value	Business Function
10	Rental or Lease
11	Maintenance or Repair
12	Manufacturer
13	Wholesale
14	Retail
15	Recycle
16	Installation
17	Engineered
18	Outsource

furniture and furnishings. In healthcare, UNSPSCP may be utilized for healthcare-specific items, in particular, for medical supplies as well as for nonhealthcare-specific products such as food and beverages, cleaning equipment and supplies, office equipment, sports and recreational equipment, information technology, and electrical equipment.

Table 6-7 shows the list of healthcare-specific segments in UNSPSC.

TABLE 6-7. UNSPSC segments specific to healthcare.

code	segment title
1200000000	Chemicals including bio-chemicals and gas materials
4100000000	Laboratory and Measuring and Observing and Testing Equipment
4200000000	Medical Equipment and Accessories and Suppliers
5100000000	Drugs and Pharmaceutical Products

The UNSPSC organization seeks to foster the adoption of its code for use in healthcare by Group Purchasing Organizations (GPOs), manufacturers, distributors, and health care providers. To this end, it is cooperating in the United States with the Coalition for Healthcare eStandards (CHeS), an organization that promotes the use of open data exchange standards in the healthcare industry.

NHS-eClass

Within the English National Health Service (NHS), a multiproduct-type classification system called the NHS-eClass System is recommended particularly for use in eProcurement scenarios. It consists of a three-level hierarchy and systematically covers all product types typically purchased by healthcare providers, including healthcare-specific (see Table 6-8) and non-specific items. It has been mapped to the UNSPSC system and is freely available from the NHS Purchasing and Supply Agency website.[5]

TABLE 6-8. NHS-eClass example.

E	Dressings
...	...
EI	Adhesive Wound Dressings
EIA	Plasters washproof
EIB	Plasters washproof blue
EIH	Plaster elastic fabric
EIJ	Non woven fabric backed
EIK	Non woven fabric backed intravenous
EIR	Wound closure strip

---

[5] For more information on the NHS Purchasing and Supply Agency, refer to their website at *www.pasa.nhs.uk.*

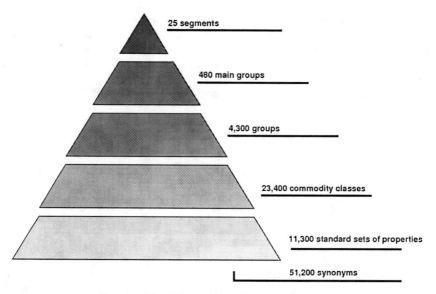

FIGURE 6-5. eCl@ss structure (from www.eclass.de).

eCl@ss

eCl@ss, distinct from NHS-eClass, is a multiindustry product classification system developed in the wake of eBusiness. Starting as a primarily German classification for supporting eBusiness activities of small and medium-sized enterprises (SMEs), the new business model of the eCl@ss association, eCl@ss e.V, reflects the move towards a global and open approach to accommodating international offices and offering membership to individuals and organizations. The organization is financed by the membership fees.

The current version of eCl@ss has been translated into several languages and is available in German, English, Italian, French, Spanish and Chinese. Mappings to other classification systems–to UNSPSC, among others–have been announced. A services and products ontology based on eCl@ss has been published recently [7].

eCl@ss is characterized by a four-level hierarchical classification system with a key-word register of 75,000 terms in 25 segments (see Figure 6-5). In contrast to other classifications, eCl@ss allows for the specification of product properties.

The segments cover different industries, such as automotive technology, electrical engineering, information technology, the chemical industry, and laboratory technology.

In healthcare, eCl@ss is primarily used for nonhealthcare-specific products, such as office supplies, and has been implemented in major German Internet-based trading exchanges in healthcare.

Pharmaceutical Classification Systems

Anatomical Therapeutic Chemical Classification System

The Anatomical Therapeutic Chemical Classification System (AT, or ATC and ATC/DDD) is one of the established classification systems in healthcare and is used for the classification of drugs. It is managed by the World Health Organization (WHO)

Collaborating Centre for Drug Statistics Methodology at the Norwegian Institute of Public Health,[6] which is directly linked into the WHO headquarters in Geneva. The ATC code was first published in 1976, with its infancy dating back to the late 1960s when Norwegian researchers–the Drug Utilization Research Group (DURG)–identified the need for an international classification system for pharmaceutical products at a symposium in Oslo. The ATC/DDD system is designed as a tool for presenting drug utilization statistics for various purposes such as

- Improving drug use
- Drug safety assessment
- Drug costs, pricing, and reimbursement
- Marketing

Practically speaking, this implies analyzing sales data of wholesalers, the number and type of drugs dispensed at pharmacies, drugs prescribed by office-based physicians in combination with other patient data, drug consumption by patients, or drug consumption per DRG in a hospital.

Drugs coded in ATC are divided into different groups according to the organ or the functional system they act upon, and/or their therapeutic and chemical characteristics. The ATC classification system classifies drugs into groups at five different levels of granularity and uses–if possible–names from the list of International Non-proprietary Names (INN) for biological, pharmaceutical, and similar products administered by the WHO. A non-proprietary name is also known as a *generic* name. The first level of the code is based on a letter for the anatomical group, and consists of one letter. There are 14 main groups that can be found in Table 6-9.

The second level describes the pharmacological/therapeutic subgroup encoded by two digits (see Table 6-10). The third and the fourth levels refer to the chemical/pharmacological/therapeutic sub-group, each adding one letter to the full code. Finally, the fifth level denotes the chemical substance with its code consisting of two more digits (see Table 6-11).

---

[6] For more information about the Collaborating Centre for Drug Statistics Methodology at the Norwegian Institute of Public Health, please refer to their website at *www.whocc.no/atcddd/*.

TABLE 6-9. ATC codes for level one.

A	Alimentary tract and metabolism
B	Blood and blood forming organs
C	Cardiovascular system
D	Dermatologicals
G	Genito-urinary system and sex hormones
H	Systemic hormonal preparations, excluding sex hormones and insulins
J	Anti-infectives for systemic use
L	Antineoplastic and immunomodulating agents
M	Musculoskeletal system
N	Nervous system
P	Antiparasitic products, insecticides and repellents
Q	Veterinary drugs
R	Respiratory system
S	Sensory organs
V	Various

TABLE 6-10. ATC details of segment "A" – second level (complete list).

A	Alimentary tract and metabolism
A01	Stomatological preparations
A02	Drugs for acid related disorders
A03	Drugs for functional gastrointestinal disorders
A04	Antiemetics and antinauseants
A05	Bile and liver therapy
A06	Laxatives
A07	Anti-diarrhoeal, intestinal, anti-inflammatory / anti-infective agents
A08	Anti-obesity preparations, excl. diet products
A09	Digestives, incl. enzymes
A10	Drugs used in diabetes
A11	Vitamins
A12	Mineral supplements
A13	Tonics
A14	Anabolic agents for systemic use
A15	Appetite stimulants
A16	Other alimentary tract and metabolism products

TABLE 6-11. ATC details of segment "A" – all five levels (examples).

A	Alimentary tract and metabolism			
A01	Stomatological preparations			
	A01A	Stomatological preparations		
		A01AC	Corticosteroids for local oral treatment	
			A01AC01	Triamcinolone
			A01AC02	Dexamethasone
			A01AC03	Hydrocortisone
			A01AC54	Prednisolone, combinations

TABLE 6-12. ATC example for metformin.

A	Alimentary tract and metabolism (1st level, anatomical main group)
A10	Drugs used in diabetes (2nd level, therapeutic subgroup)
A10B	Oral blood glucose lowering drugs (3rd level, pharmacological subgroup)
A10BA	Biguanides (4th level, chemical subgroup)
A10BA02	Metformin (5th level, chemical substance)

Table 6-12 shows the hierarchy of antidiabetic drugs containing the chemical agent *metformin* (plain metformin preparations).

By means of supplementary information about the defined daily doses (DDD), the ATC system is extended to the ATC/DDD system. DDD is defined by the WHO as the assumed average maintenance dose per day for a drug used for its main indication in adults. The purpose of this system is to serve as a tool for drug utilization research in the effort to improve the quality of drug use.

Other ATC classifications are ATCvet for veterinary medicinal products, and ATC herbal for herbal remedies.

Specific Classification Systems for Medical-Surgical Products and Medical Devices

Introduction

The following two classification systems specifically cover the area of medical-surgical products and medical devices.

GPI

The GPI classification system is a German proprietary standard for medical-surgical supplies and medical technical devices. It has been developed by IMS Health, its present owners, and has been adopted by major Internet-based trading exchanges in healthcare. This system is used by German healthcare providers and purchasing cooperatives in their effort to analyze the purchasing volume. It consists of 13 major groups broken down into seven levels. Currently, there is no translation into other languages, nor is it mapped to other classification systems.

EGAR

The aim of the European Generic Article Register (EGAR) project, started by the European Committee for Standardisation (CEN) in 2002, was to establish a standardized classification system for medical supplies supporting the tendering process—in particular, in the public area [8, 9]. Often, tendering suffers from a lack of common understanding among the suppliers and the customers about the items included in the tender. The aim is to achieve this understanding by a brand-neutral generic product description embedded in a hierarchical structure.

The basic methodology of CEN was to involve both suppliers and healthcare providers in the building up and maintenance processes of the register in an effort to find a practical European solution for the growing electronic market in healthcare.

EGAR is hierarchically structured, consisting of three data elements at the lowest level: the Generic Article Number, the Generic Article Description, and the Price Unit.

The Generic Article Number contains a four-step hierarchy. The highest level is the main group, followed by the intermediate group, the product group, and finally the Generic Article. As in every classification, a Generic Article exists only once in EGAR. The EGAR Generic Article Number is an 11-digit code with the first two digits representing the main group, the second two representing the intermediate product group, the next three digits representing the product group, and the last four digits representing the Generic Article Level.

The following example illustrates the EGAR structure:

1. **Main Group:** Medical Disposals 65
2. **Intermediate Product Group:** Syringes and needles 65 69
3. **Product Group:** Needles, epidural 65 69 230
4. **Generic Article Level:**

Generic Article No.	Generic Article Description	Price Unit
65 69 230 0010	Needles, epidural, 16 G	PCE
65 69 230 0015	Needles, epidural, 17 G	PCE
65 69 230 0020	Needles, epidural, 18 G	PCE

The Article Description is a 70-character field containing the following sequence of data elements:

- Neutral description of the article derived from the Product Group
- Material
- Type
- Format, size, length, etc.

During the EGAR pilot, 7,000 codes and designations for articles in the medical sector were developed. In accordance with the EGAR concept, the goal for the EGAR data structure was to supplement the Global Medical Device Nomenclature (GMDN), described in the next section, for use in tendering [8, 9]. It remains to be seen how the results of the EGAR pilot will be exploited in the future.

Nomenclatures

Universal Medical Device Nomenclature System (UMDNS)

UMDNS is an international nomenclature for medical devices used for many purposes, including eBusiness applications–in particular, electronic procurement and electronic commerce, as well as hospital inventory and work-order controls, national agency medical device regulatory systems, and medical device databases. It is owned and managed by ECRI, a collaborating center of the WHO, for–among other things–the development and maintenance of "a Universal Medical Device Nomenclature System (UMDNS) and, in the context of global harmonization efforts" for the "work on its compatibility with other medical device nomenclatures, particularly the Global Medical Device Nomenclature (GMDN)."[7] ECRI cooperates regarding the UMDNS terminology, with various U.S. institutions such as the National Library of Medicine, the Healthcare Information and Management Systems Society (HIMSS) and the Committee on Data Standards for Patient Safety of the Institute of Medicine (IOM).

Global Medical Device Nomenclature (GMDN)

The Global Medical Device Nomenclature (GMDN) is a collection of terms used to describe and catalog medical devices. The terms compiled in the GMDN are derived from various international sources, most notably the Universal Medical Device Nomenclature System (UMDNS). GMDN was developed in an EU-funded research project, under the auspices of CEN, and in cooperation with the International Organization for Standardization (ISO). This standard, which is recognized by CEN/ISO, is managed by the GMDN Agency–a not-for-profit organization functioning as a hub for the maintenance and running of the nomenclature. Most industrialized countries have committed themselves through legislation or participation in the development process to using GMDN as the preferred national nomenclature for medical devices. In the United States, the FDA is currently working towards a possible adoption of GMDN [10].

In contrast to multilevel hierarchical classification systems aiming at the statistical analysis of aggregated data, the GMDN mainly serves legal purposes in those European countries requiring manufacturers to classify their products using the GMDN.

The GMDN, therefore, consists only of two levels: the Device Categories, the major group level, and the Generic Device Groups–the actual nomenclature level at which

---

[7] The ECRI was formally known as the Emergency Care Research Institute. For more information about this center, consult their website at *www.ecri.org*.

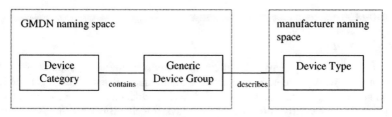

FIGURE 6-6. GMDN – simplified data model.

TABLE 6-13. GMDN – Device Categories.

Code	Term
01	Active implantable devices
02	Anaesthetic and respiratory devices
03	Dental devices
04	Electro mechanical medical devices
05	Hospital hardware
06	In vitro diagnostic devices (IVD)
07	Non-active implantable devices
08	Ophthalmic and optical devices
09	Reusable instruments
10	Single use devices
11	Technical aids for disabled persons
12	Diagnostic and therapeutic radiation devices
13	Obsolete terms

the generic device names are listed. Products to be classified are given a name from the Generic Device Groups. In addition, however, there is a Device Type containing manufacturer-specific information about the make and type of a product outside the GMDN naming space. It can be included as mandatory information required by a product register. Figure 6-7 shows the data model underlying the GMDN [11].

Of the 20 possible device categories, 13 are currently used and are shown in Table 6-13.

The Generic Device Groups consist of three types of terms:

- The preferred term supplied with a definition
- The template terms that collectively groups all preferred terms that have an identical character string up to a certain character position, as denoted by the symbol
- The synonym terms

Fluidized bed, for example, is a synonym for the preferred term *bed, air fluidized*, and *heartstarter* is a synonym for the template term *defibrillator, <specify>*. The template term *centrifuge, <specify>*, for example, groups the preferred terms *centrifuge, blood bank, centrifuge, cell washing, centrifuge, cytology, centrifuge, general-purpose laboratory*, and others [11].

The terms in the Generic Device Groups coded by five digits consist of sequential cardinal numbers that do not carry any significant information about the classified object and therefore merely serve as a unique identifier.

As suggested by EGAR, GMDN terms are supplemented by the EGAR data structure to be used in generic electronic tendering [8, 9].

Catalogs

Introduction

While identification systems, classification systems, and nomenclatures provide a semantic framework for representing product and product-related data at a generic level, they do not manage actual manufacturers' data. These data are kept in catalogs, usually along with the codes derived from the generic systems. In eBusiness, any type of transaction between suppliers and customers relies on mutually interpretable product data that are typically kept in electronic catalogs. Once generated at the supplier's site, they are communicated to the customer in a fashion that depends upon where the catalog data should reside. They can either stay with the supplier who makes them available to the customer during run time (see "PunchOut" concept), or they can be physically distributed to the customers directly or through any eBusiness hub (Internet-based trading exchange, electronic marketplace) for further electronic processing. In integrated eBusiness solutions (see Chapter 5), the communication of catalog data is a typical machine-to-machine exercise, and therefore requires standardized data to be understood at both ends. Most solutions for catalog data exchange either have a simple structure based on text elements delimited by typical separators (e.g., tab stops, colons, and commas), or are part of transaction standards. Among the less-advanced solutions, the comma separated values (CSV) format or word processing and spreadsheet application formats are very common and still outnumber more sophisticated approaches [12].

EDI-based Standards

Besides the transaction-oriented messages EANCOM primarily provides, such as the purchase order message ORDERS, it also defines messages for exchanging catalog data. The messages used for this purpose are the Price/Sales Catalog (PRICAT) message, and the Product Data (PRODAT) message.

The PRICAT message may be used in different scenarios relating to handling catalog data. Irrespective of the scenarios, it generally conveys descriptive, logistic, and pricing information about a product. The message might be designed to indicate general information valid for all customers (i.e., the standard catalog), or to indicate information specific to one customer only (i.e., the customized catalog). A PRICAT message can also be compiled to contain information about all products a supplier offers (i.e., distribution of a catalog), or to hold information about a single product or a limited number of products (i.e., catalog updates). The message may feed a central database (the electronic catalog, or may be used for one particular instance of a business transaction only. The following example, extracted from a more comprehensive example,[8] provides some insight into the construction of a PRICAT message, using the typical sequence of segments for structuring self-contained information blocks. Table 6-14 describes the contents of the message in more detail. As can be seen, the EAN.UCC identification keys, the GLN, and the GTIN are incorporated in this message.

The supplier sending the message is identified by GLN 4012345500004. The recipient of this message is identified by GLN 5412345000020.

The message sent on the first of January 2002 has been given the reference number PC12123 [...]. The price list currency is specified as euros.

---

[8] See *www.ean.se*.

TABLE 6-14. PRICAT message – excerpt from example (http://www.ean.se).

UNH+ME000055+PRICAT:D:01B:UN:EAN008'	Message header
BGM+9+PC12123+9'	Price/sales catalogue number PC12123
DTM+137:20020101:102'	Message date 1st January 2002
NAD+BY+5412345500020::9'	Buyer is identified by GLN 5412345500020
NAD+SU+4012345500004::9'	Supplier is identified by GLN 4012345500004
CUX+2:EUR:8'	Price list currency is euros
PGI+2'	Product group containing no price group
LIN+1+1+8711113000000:SRV'	Line 1 is an addition of the product identified by GTIN 8711113000000
IMD+C++CU::9'	The product is a consumer unit
IMD+F++:::SCALPEL TYPE AX157'	Product description
MEA+PD+AAA+GRM:98'	Weight of the product is 98 grams
MEA+PD+LN+MMT:170'	Length of the product is 170 mm
TAX+7+VAT+++:::21+S'	Product is subject to VAT at the standard rate of 21%
PRI+AAE:400:CA:SRP'	The suggested retail information price, excluding allowances /charges and taxes, is 400
PAC+++BX'	Product is packaged in a box
...	...

The first occurrence of the LIN segment is used to describe one [...] product, the scalpel type AX157, that is new to [...] the recipient of the message. This article is identified by GTIN 8711113000000. The article is a consumer unit packed in a box. The suggested retail price of the product is 400 EUR and VAT is charged at 21 per cent. [...].

Whereas PRICAT explicitly contains information on terms and conditions, such as prices, PRODAT is used to transmit the detailed technical and functional data of a product by just referring to other lists or messages for price information.[9]

XML-based Standards

EDI-based and XML-based messages need not be contradictory because, in principle, any EDI message can transformed into an XML message. By XML-based standards, we mean standards specifically designed for implementation in Internet-based eBusiness applications that support XML (see also Chapter 5).

XML-based catalog standards are typically included in families of eBusiness standards such as xCBL and cXML–two recognized transaction standards that are also supported by major Internet-based trading exchanges in healthcare.

Initially developed by Veo Systems, and further refined by Commerce One, Inc. at that time, XML Common Business Language (xCBL) was designed to model the information requirements for eBusiness transactions (B2B) by building on existing EDI standards. Among other things, the standard includes documents related to the product catalog. The aim of the following short section is to give a very brief overview of an xCBL Product Catalog document, which consists of:

- CatalogHeader–providing administrative information about the catalog, such as provider, expiry data, version, default currency, information whether single supplier or multisupplier catalog, and others
- CatalogSchema–containing optional creator-configured information on the structure of the products, which is a typical XML feature

---

[9] See PRODAT examples at *www.ean.se*.

- CatalogData–serving as a container for a data set related to an actual product. This data set embraces information about various product IDs, the unit of measurement, the manufacturer, product details, product price, reference to a contract, etc.[10]

Commercial XML (cXML), an eBusiness standard developed by Ariba, Inc., is a document exchange protocol for electronic business transactions between buying organizations, suppliers, intermediaries, and service providers *(www.cxml.org)*. Transactions as defined by cXML consist of documents comprising and embracing typical business information such as an order or a catalog. cXML is designed for a concept called *PunchOut*, which describes an eProcurement scenario where the catalog data remain at the supplier's site, and in which a buyer accesses the supplier's catalog through his own procurement software, selects items while the procurement software maintains a connection to the supplier's website, and collects pertinent data for submitting the order. xCBL and other standards support similar concepts. Among them, Open Catalog Interface (OCI), which is a standard developed by SAP, integrates external catalogs into R/3 supplier-relationship management (SRM) applications.

Finally, BMEcat should be mentioned as a catalog standard for exchanging data. Initially developed in Germany by the Federal Association for Materials Management, Purchasing and Logistics (BME), it now receives attention outside Germany also, including in the United States. BMEcat 2005 features comprise.

- Support of external catalogs (i.e., OCI, PunchOut, RoundTrip)
- Enhanced product model for complex, configurable products
- Enhanced price model (i.e., dynamic pricing)
- Enhanced product description for logistics purposes
- Multilingualism
- Multisupplier catalogs
- Compatibility with lower versions

The following example illustrates some of these features. Written in XML, it is quite easily readable by human users.

```
<CP><?xml version="1.0" encoding="ISO-8859-1"?>
<!DOCTYPE BMECAT SYSTEM "bmecat_new_catalog_1_2.dtd">
<BMECAT version="1.2"
xmlns="http://www.bmecat.org/bmecat/1.2/bmecat_ new_catalog" >
  <HEADER>
  <CATALOG>
  <LANGUAGE>English</LANGUAGE>
  <CATALOG_ID>QA_CAT_002</CATALOG_ID>
```
          ...various pieces of information about catalog version, name, creation date, time,
currency
```
  </CATALOG>
  <BUYER>
```
          ...buyer information
```
  </BUYER>
  <SUPPLIER>
```
          ...supplier's information

---

[10] Readers interested in further details are referred to the xCBL homepage for the complete information structure and examples (*www.xcbl.org*).

```
</SUPPLIER>
</HEADER>
<T_NEW_CATALOG>
<ARTICLE mode="new">
<SUPPLIER_AID>Q20-P09</SUPPLIER_AID>
<ARTICLE_DETAILS>
          ...various article descriptions
<MANUFACTURER_NAME>Concurrent Limited</MANUFACTURER_NAME>
</ARTICLE_DETAILS>
<ARTICLE_FEATURES>
<REFERENCE_FEATURE_SYSTEM_NAME>UNSPSC5.02</REFERENCE_FEATURE
_SYSTEM_NAME>
<REFERENCE_FEATURE_GROUP_ID>44121505</REFERENCE _FEATURE_GROUP_ID>
</ARTICLE_FEATURES>
<ARTICLE_ORDER_DETAILS>
<ORDER_UNIT>1</ORDER_UNIT>
</ARTICLE_ORDER_DETAILS>
<ARTICLE_PRICE_DETAILS>
          ...information about price, currency, etc.
</ARTICLE_PRICE_DETAILS>
<MIME_INFO>
<MIME>
          ...multimedia information, i.e. images
</MIME>
</MIME_INFO>
</ARTICLE>
</T_NEW_CATALOG>
</BMECAT>
```

All XML-based standards, regardless of their origin and focus, share the advantage of being self-explanatory and supporting multimedia data [13].

Outlook

Products developed, tested, purchased, and used in patient care always appear in a specific context that is not reflected by identification systems, classification systems, nomenclatures, and catalogs. To analyze all factors influencing a product-related action, however, such as the use of a certain drug or device in curing a disease, the context must become visible. Models aiming to represent a comprehensive view of healthcare-related actions, persons, items, and other entities are gaining importance with the demand for integrated healthcare information systems.

The Systematized Nomenclature of Medicine (SNOMED) is the most well-known approach to providing a consistent medical terminology, and is based on the work of the College of American Pathologists (CAP). First published in 1975 as a nomenclature, it has adopted a more logic-based structure (called SNOMED Reference Terminology) and has been merged with the NHS Clinical Terms (the Read Codes) to form SNOMED CT. SNOMED CT consists of 11 concepts representing the various aspects of medicine, including drugs and devices (see Table 6-15).

TABLE 6-15. SNOMED concepts.

T	Topography	Anatomic terms
M	Morphology	Changes found in cells, tissues and organs
L	Living organisms	Bacteria and viruses
C	Chemical	Drugs
F	Function	Signs and symptoms
J	Occupation	Terms that describe the occupation
D	Diagnosis	Diagnostic terms
P	Procedure	Administrative, diagnostic and therapeutic procedures
A	Physical agents, forces, activities	Devices and activities associated with the disease
S	Social context	Social conditions and important relationships in medicine
G	General	Syntactic linkages and qualifiers

Every concept is interrelated with other concepts. These interrelationships include hierarchical relationships (such as a *kidney disease* IS_A *disorder of the urinary system*) and also permit multihierarchies and attributes (such as an *appendicitis* HAS FINDING SITE, namely *appendix structure*).

SNOMED codes are incorporated into the data records of the dm+d database–the NHS dictionary of medicines and devices. In the United States, the FDA decided to include SNOMED codes (of the Problem List Subset within SNOMED) for use in product labeling. These efforts were undertaken to support the implementation of a national e-Health record of all American citizens in the next decade.

Although it is not being developed as a terminology standard, but rather for supporting the HL7 data exchange standard V3.0, the RIM included in HL7 V3.0 (see Chapter 4) is a formal approach of interest in this context as it describes entities of the medical world and their interrelationships. With a growing demand for integrated information throughout a healthcare enterprise, the RIM may also serve as a common data model referred to by different healthcare information systems. Ongoing work explores the possibilities of using SNOMED CT within HL7.

Conclusions

Overview

Motivation of Standards Revisited

Identifying, naming, and classifying products in a standard manner are not academic exercises but a business necessity in eBusiness, as Aberdeen Research and the Gartner Group make clear. Aberdeen [14] stated at the end of 2004 that "Data visibility is the major challenge for the majority of programs despite the significant progress of e-sourcing and e-procurement." And Gartner [15] predicted that "By 2013, standardized ways of describing products will prevent errors and help manufacturers, distributors and retailers cut costs. Implementation will not be cheap, but the payoffs will be too big to ignore."

In other words, *standardization and the strengths of all participants in the supply chain combined to achieve this goal will ensure the success of eBusiness in health care as well.* It also makes clear that standardization requires concerted efforts and resources in order to make the benefits happen.

Combined Efforts

As has been shown above, there are standards in each of the categories used by the healthcare industry. Some of them are more common and others less common, and often depend on the country in which they are being used. The major question of standardization is, in fact, not whether there are standards but how to achieve globally recognized and used standards.

There are examples of combined efforts to bring together already existing standards such as the EAN·UCC family of standards in the area of product identification, to strive for a global nomenclature of medical devices in the area of classifications and nomenclatures (UMDNS and GMDN), and the combination of terms originating from SNOMED and from the NHS Clinical Terms to form SNOMED CT. These activities reflect the understanding that not one single standard will eventually prevail, but that existing standards should somehow be merged or made interoperable (e.g., by mapping the standards), or should be dealt with by the same organization so that a new standard derived from existing standards can evolve more easily.

What is a Good Standard?

A Pragmatic Answer

The next question of standardization is whether there are good and bad standards, and whether there are general criteria to distinguish the good from the bad. There are formalisms describing the desiderata of standards [16], against which existing standards can be measured.

A rather simplistic, but in the end pragmatic, answer to this question is

A bad standard is a standard that is not used.

This statement leads us to the question of why a standard is employed.

Purpose of Use

In fact, the main question to be resolved from a practical point of view is whether the standard fits the purpose for which it is intended. For example, a classification with a steep hierarchy might be generally desirable. This degree of detail, however, might not be necessary for business analysis requiring only a few levels of abstraction–it might, however, be so for scientific analysis. Another issue is representation. If a nomenclature does not represent the complete domain, manufacturers (for example) who are not able to find the appropriate terms for their products would find the entire system inappropriate for the purpose of giving generic names to products. In all these cases, the main application and the purpose of the standard must determine which one to choose. Another issue would be flexibility of use. Generally a desirable feature for a standard, it does not prove useful if the application does not require flexibility. For eBusiness in healthcare, one has to bear in mind that standards must often serve a two-fold purpose–supporting the supply chain and business analysis, and supporting patient care–which admittedly does not make the decision easy.

In any case, before making a decision about a standard, the applications of the standard, including specific requirements, have to be stated clearly.

Healthcare Specific vs. Unspecific Standards

Considering the use of standards raises the question about how specific a standard should be. As shown previously, there are multiple-industry standards and standards specific to healthcare. To make a general assumption that healthcare-specific standards fit healthcare applications best would be too simple an approach. For example, if the purchase volume of medical products is compared with the volume of various other types of nonmedical products also purchased by a healthcare provider, a cross-industry classification would seem more suitable than a healthcare-specific classification. If indepth information about medical entities, such as a drug or a device, has to be named and coded, healthcare-specific standards are more likely to contain relevant terms and codes. Sometimes, a look behind the scenes of the organization that develops the standards reveals helpful information.

Standards Organization

There are all sorts of schemes on how to classify standards by the organizations that develop them, such as

- De facto standards vs. de jure standards, meaning standards that evolved (e.g., TCP/IP) vs. standards that have been approved by an officially recognized standardization body (e.g. ANSI, CEN, ISO)
- Standards developed mainly by the industry vs. standards developed by a consortium consisting of various stakeholders
- Standards approved by consensus vs. standards that are primarily developed by one organization and then adopted by others
- Free available standards (open standards) vs. standards requiring licence fees

These four schemes are overlapping and nonexclusive, and do not fundamentally reveal anything about the quality of the standard.

By involving partners with different backgrounds and perspectives, supply chain applications tend to require standards approved by consensus among a variety of stakeholders to take different views into account. Furthermore, organizations developing and maintaining standards to be used in healthcare must incorporate a team of experts from the healthcare industry, or must ally with organizations that provide such teams.

So the question actually is, "Has the standard been developed with enough expertise from the healthcare industry?" rather than "Is it a healthcare-specific standard?"

Need for a Global Registration Authority?

It has been argued that the rather slow speed in adopting eBusiness and supply chain methods in healthcare was caused by deficiencies in the standards area. Deficiencies can be anything ranging from a lack of standards to a jungle of existing standards, and from unawareness of standards availability to noncompliance with existing standards.

These deficiencies could be overcome by concentrating all efforts on standardizing the electronic supply chain in one single global authority that would raise the awareness of the need for standards as well as develop, maintain, and promote them. Such an authority would not only be responsible for one type of standard but for all types of standards necessary for streamlining the entire supply chain to meet business and patient-care requirements. Best practice from successfully established systems in other sectors indicates one common denominator–namely the willingness and the combined strengths of all relevant participants, plus a global registration authority. These facts speak in favor of a similar authority in the healthcare industry.

The main issue today, therefore, is who the perfect driver for healthcare supply chain standards might be. To ensure the broadest possible support and success for such a global registration authority, all stakeholders must be involved (i.e., health care providers, suppliers, distributors, online trading exchanges, and other intermediaries as well as scientific organizations). Experts from these different types of organizations must cover issues of information technology and management, logistics, and patient care to embrace all relevant aspects.

The main hindrances preventing companies from supporting standards must be identified and eliminated. Among well-known factors hampering standards are costs, little compatibility with other standards, no multiple-language support, and fixation on one technology. Thus, the standards provided by such an authority would have to overcome these barriers. In detail, this means that if one assumes that costs are a main source for impeding the use of standards, the global registration authority should promote open, freely available standards. This means that the standards would reside in the public domain and the code set could be used without any licensing fees.

Cross-mapping to other standards should also exist. With the key factors for global acceptance being multiple-language support, the terms provided must be available in English, French, Spanish, Italian, German, Japanese, and preferably also Russian and Chinese. These terms have to be updated on a regular basis. In addition to conventional bar coding methods, new technologies such as Radio Frequency Identification (RFID) tags must be supported by the standards.

There is a growing demand for global transparency within the supply chain. More and more companies such as manufacturers, distributors, and the healthcare providers explicitly express their urgent requirements for standards to identify, name, and classify products. To achieve such goals, the different needs and perspectives of the various stakeholders must be bundled–including those of the healthcare providers. Only by reaching a consensus between the different parties will these standards be accepted. In fact, acceptance building is the main challenge for an authority aiming at standardizing the supply chain. One of the most recent approaches in this area has been made by the Healthcare User Group (GS1 HUG), which integrates the different stakeholders on an international basis by trying to lead the healthcare industry towards the utilization and further development of standards. In 2007, GS1 HUG and HL7 joined forces to synchronize their developments with the ultimate goal of reducing medical errors and of increasing the effectiveness of the healthcare supply chain by using standards.

Considering the current situation, it seems there is little to lose and much to gain from standardizing the supply chain in healthcare.

References

[1] European Commission, Directorate General for Enterprise and Industry (2005) *Special report e-business interoperability and standards: A Cross-sector Perspective and Outlook*. Bonn: empirica. Available from: <http://www.ebusiness-watch.org/resources/documents/TR03_Interoperability_2005_web.pdf> [Accessed 01 September 2006].

[2] Berglund, D. J., Hirs, W., L'Hours, A. and Sykes, C. (2002) *The Who Family Of International Classifications And Its Relationship To Clinical Vocabularies*. Geneva: World Health Organization. Available from: Australian Institute for Health and Welfare <http://www.aihw.gov.au/international/who_hoc/hoc_02_papers/brisbane83.pdf> [Accessed 06 October 2006].

[3] American National Standard Institute (1997) *The health industry bar code (HIBC) supplier labeling standard*. Phoenix: Health Industry Business Communications Council. Available from: <http://www.hibcc.org/AUTOIDUPN/docs/ Supplier Standard.pdf> [Accessed 01 September 2006].

[4] American National Standards Institute (1996) *The health industry bar code (HIBC) provider applications standard.* Phoenix: Health Industry Business Communications Council. Available from: <http://www.hibcc.org/AUTOIDUPN/docs/ ProviderStandard.pdf> [Accessed 01 September 2006].

[5] Eucomed (2004) *Eucomed Position Paper on Bar Coding for Medical Devices.* Available from: <www.hibcc.org/PUBS/Position%20Papers/Eucomed%20Bar%20 Code%20Position%20Paper_04.pdf > [Accessed 22 November 2006].

[6] Geisendorf, N. (2006) Identifikationstechnik – Zwischen den Welten. *Klinik Management Aktuell.* (12) 42. Available from: <www.kma-online.de> [Accessed 01 September 2006].

[7] Hepp, M. (2006) Products and Services Ontologies: A Methodology for Deriving OWL Ontologies from Industrial Categorization Standards. *International Journal on Semantic Web and Information Systems.* **2**, 72-99.

[8] European Committee for Standardization (2002) *Workshop Agreement CWA 14446: European Generic Article Register - Conceptual description of EGAR, working Methodology and relation to the tendering and procurement process in the healthcare sector.* Brussels. Available from: <ftp://cenftp1.cenorm.be/PUBLIC/CWAs/eEurope/ECHOP/cwa14446-00-2002-Mar.pdf> [Accessed 01 September 2006].

[9] European Committee for Standardization (2002) *Workshop Agreement CWA 14445: European Generic Article Register - Conceptual description of EGAR, working Methodology and relation to the tendering and procurement process in the healthcare sector.* Brussels. Available from: <ftp://cenftp1.cenorm.be/PUBLIC/CWAs/eEurope/ECHOP/cwa14445-00-2002-Mar.pdf> [Accessed 01 September 06].

[10] Emergency Care Research Institute (2005) *Automatic Identification of Medical Devices.* Plymouth Meeting. Available from: United States Food and Drug Administration <http://www.fda.gov/cdrh/ocd/ecritask4.pdf> [Accessed 01 September 2006].

[11] Global Medical Device Nomenclature (2003) *A Technical Introductory/User Guide for the GMDN Version 2003.1.* Oxford. Available from: <http://www.gmdn.org/GMDN_Technical_2003v2.pdf> [Accessed 01 September 2006].

[12] Quantz, J. and T. Wichmann (2003) *e-Business-Standards in Germany: Assessment, Problems, Prospects.* Berlin: Berlecon Research. Available from: <http:// www.berlecon.de/research/reports.php?we_objectID=125> [Accessed 01 September 2006].

[13] Bundesministerium für Wirtschaft und Arbeit (2003) E-Standards. *e-f@cts - Informationen zum E-Business.* (15) 1-8. Available from: Webweiser für Entscheider <http://www2.webweiser.net/wps/ecm/dl/down/open/ecm/ef3c15a679e128114740c58b 915b0e8bcb731a016ffbd67f7bab94623a8876a9f4e21b631607579c06361780d05f42bd/ efacts_15 _nov03.pdf> [Accessed 17 October 2006].

[14] Aberdeen Group (2004) *Addressing Costs Beyond Price – The MRO Category Spend Benchmark Report.* Boston. Available from: <http://www.aberdeen.com /summary/report/benchmark/CSMMRO_JP.asp> [Accessed 06 October 2006].

[15] Hope-Ross, D. and A. White. (2003) Product Content and Data Management Promises Savings. *Achieving Supply Chain Exchange through Technology.* (5) San Francisco: Montgomery Research. Available from: <http://www.ascet.com/ documents.asp?d_ID=2003> [Accessed 01 September 2006].

[16] Cimino J. J. (1998) Desiderata for controlled medical vocabularies in the twenty-first century. *Methods of Information in Medicine.* **37**, 394-403.

Part III
Applications and Experiences

7
The Evolution of eBusiness in Healthcare

KAREN M. CONWAY AND RICHARD PERRIN

Executive Summary

The inefficiencies in the healthcare supply chain are well documented, with a 2001 study stating that lack of data synchronization and visibility in purchasing data results in considerable errors and rework. A 1996 report also identified billions of dollars in potential savings through process improvements.

As early as the mid-1980s, healthcare suppliers and providers in the United States attempted to utilize technology to streamline the purchasing process, but the lack of an open architecture and limited transaction capabilities prevented those efforts from delivering the anticipated value. The advent of the Internet resolved many of the technological challenges, but overzealous marketers promoted unrealistic expectations, creating another round of disillusionment.

There were some healthcare providers and suppliers who recognized that by working together, often through trial and error, they could build the technology and change business processes to benefit all involved in the supply chain. At the turn of the century, numerous companies offered Internet-based trading exchanges to electronically connect hospitals and suppliers and enable them to conduct business with one another electronically and more efficiently. With market consolidation, one such trading exchange eventually garnered the trust and involvement of enough trading partners to begin delivering value.

As in other industries, hospitals and suppliers utilizing eBusiness to streamline the supply chain have experienced value in areas such as:

- Faster order processing times
- Lower order processing costs
- Fewer invoice exceptions
- Reduced off-contract or maverick spending
- Increased staff productivity

Achieving value from eBusiness requires hospitals to maximize the percentage of ordering done electronically, and to automate as much of the purchasing process–from requisition to payment–as possible. Perhaps most importantly, hospitals and suppliers need to synchronize their product data to reduce errors that can delay product shipments and result in costly and time-consuming invoice exceptions.

Focus on the supply chain as an opportunity for cost savings is expected to increase, as supply costs continue to rise, in part due to greater usage of high-priced medical devices in treating an aging population. Because the selection of these devices is most often left to the physician, there is a need for greater collaboration between clinical and materials departments to identify the best products for patient care at the best price.

Access to more comprehensive and accurate purchasing data, made possible through eBusiness, can assist in this process. With a more comprehensive understanding of their overall purchasing, healthcare providers can better determine actual procedure costs, analyze patterns of use, and make future product choices that support both clinical and fiscal objectives.

The limitations of some materials management systems has hampered greater use of eBusiness in the healthcare supply chain, as well as the ability to access the kind of data needed for more strategic supply chain activities. Some healthcare systems are addressing this problem by converting to new, multimillion dollar ERP systems, while others are utilizing Web-based applications to extend the functionality of their existing systems.

Lack of industry standards, such as universal product numbers, and the inability of materials systems to fully utilize such standards, has also limited automation of the supply chain. Industry observers say, however, that with a critical mass of trading partners now conducting business with one another electronically, and many across the same technology platform, there is an opportunity to increase industry adoption of standards.

Once the technology is in place to conduct eBusiness, the successful use of such systems depends to a large extent on how well those involved in supply chain activities are willing and able to change business processes accordingly. With the supply chain the second highest expense for most hospitals, the potential exists for eBusiness to make a significant difference in rising healthcare costs. Enabling eBusiness between trading partners is only the beginning, but it lays the foundation for greater collaboration, increased efficiencies, and cost savings for all involved.

Introduction

The inefficiencies in the healthcare supply chain have been well documented. According to the 2001 Anderson study, "The Value of eCommerce in the Healthcare Supply Chain," the lack of data synchronization and visibility in purchasing data results in 40% of a hospital buyer's time and 68% of an accounts payable worker's time spent on manual processing and rework. That same study says 52% of all re-work could be eliminated through eCommerce [1].

Using technology to automate procurement practices and improve operational efficiencies is not a new concept in healthcare, despite the fact that it has only recently become relatively more common. Today, the majority of hospitals in the United States and other countries (most notably Germany, the United Kingdom, and Canada) are purchasing at least a portion of their supplies electronically through one or more of the following methods: vendor websites, direct EDI connections with individual suppliers, and/or an Internet-based trading exchange. Despite consistently strong growth in the percentage of purchasing handled electronically, there is a considerable variance among hospitals in terms of the benefits they are achieving through their eProcurement initiatives. Two key variables appear to be:

- the degree to which hospitals have redesigned business processes to maximize the value of technology implementations
- whether they have provided adequate and ongoing training for users

Healthcare providers that have successfully changed how work is done to make electronic ordering the preferred purchasing methodology are discovering that the value extends beyond the benefits of process automation. A better and more comprehensive understanding of total purchasing has enabled some hospitals to document quantifiable savings by reducing maverick or off-contract purchases, identifying new contracting opportunities, standardizing products, and ensuring that facilities are paying the correct and best price for the products purchased.

This chapter describes the evolution of eBusiness in healthcare and the current challenges and opportunities. To this end, interviews were conducted with supply chain and materials managers of U.S. hospitals and healthcare systems. The results of those interviews are presented below, highlighting the achievements made and the problems encountered. Mainly focusing on the experience in the United States, this chapter also aims at providing a broader perspective by outlining the general constraints of eBusiness in healthcare and referring to countries outside the United States.

A Short History of eBusiness in Healthcare

The Early Days

The first attempt to automate the healthcare supply chain in the United States dates back to the early 1960s, when American Hospital Supply Company (AHSC) first provided hospital customers with IBM data phones to transmit orders via phone lines using pre-punched cards–one for each item purchased from AHSC. Over the next twenty-five years, AHSC (which later became Baxter Healthcare Corporation) continued to enhance its electronic ordering capabilities. In 1987, the company introduced ASAP Express, which enabled hospital purchasing departments and multiple vendors to send and receive purchase orders (POs) and purchase order acknowledgements (POAs) using a single computer-based system. At the time, then Baxter Senior Vice President Richard Egan predicted that the ASAP Express system would result in "Total automation of hospital logistics, virtually eliminating the clerical aspects of purchasing." Baxter also anticipated significant changes for suppliers. Michael Hudson, president of Baxter's Hospital Systems division, predicted that ASAP Express would "level (the) playing field," giving "no advantage to any one vendor." Hudson added that "suppliers must compete in other areas such as product line breadth, distribution capabilities, and value-added services." [2].

The market shared Baxter's high expectations. By 1994, more than 2,300 hospitals and 1,500 suppliers were reportedly using ASAP Express, while similar systems launched by Baxter's competitors–such as Abbott Laboratories' Quik Link–had also entered the scene [3]. Despite strong adoption of those early systems, healthcare purchasing remained a highly manual business process. At that stage in the evolution of eBusiness in healthcare, the problem was not the concept, but the technology. The costs for vendors to maintain the systems were high, and hospitals were increasingly dissatisfied with closed systems that required proprietary formats, and offered only two basic electronic transaction sets: POs and POAs.

The First Wave of Adoption: Enter the Internet

By the late 1990s, the Internet, with its scalable, open architecture, was considered the solution. Bolstered by the 1996 Efficient Consumer Healthcare Response (ECHR) study–that predicted billions of dollars in savings from improvements in healthcare supply chain efficiency in the United States alone–and dot.com euphoria in the financial markets, literally dozens of companies were formed, each touting their ability to help hospitals dramatically reduce supply chain costs at the speed of the Internet. Some of these companies offered very specific services, such as online auctions for used capital equipment, while others were created to provide online trading exchanges, similar in concept to the earlier offerings from Baxter and Abbott where multiple buyers and sellers could conduct business with one another. A number of these early Internet-based companies were capitalized by public stock offerings and fell victim to the dot.com bust, while others were sabotaged by their own marketing campaigns.

Many of the earliest eBusiness adopters in healthcare and other industries based their decisions "less on well-honed business cases and more on a frenetic and irrational desire to be viewed as 'e' savvy and, in some cases, to cash in on the outrageous market valuations of pioneering eProcurement vendors." [4] Vendors fueled this irrationality with aggressive marketing messages that far outpaced the functionality of their solutions. When their over-inflated promises of near immediate savings failed to materialize, the market began to doubt that eProcurement was worth making the financial investment or changing well-established business practices.

There were a handful of visionaries within healthcare who approached the decision more thoughtfully. They understood that implementing eBusiness practices in the supply chain would necessitate closer working relationships with their trading partners to identify, often through trial and error, what steps needed to be taken to realize process efficiencies and, more importantly, to increase visibility and collaboration across the entire supply chain. These organizations recognized that supply chain optimization using eBusiness would be more of an evolution than a revolution, and would require certain progressive steps to be taken along the way.

Market consolidation among companies offering Internet-based trading exchanges came quickly in the United States. By 2001, only five exchanges existed in healthcare. Three of the four survivors were closely aligned with group purchasing organizations (GPOs): Neoforma (Novation), Medibuy (Premier), and Broadlink (Broadlane). The fourth, HealthNexis, was owned by major healthcare distributors, and the fifth, Global Healthcare Exchange (GHX), was founded by major healthcare manufacturers. Over the next two years, GHX merged with both HealthNexis and Medibuy, bringing distributors, hospitals, and GPOs into its ownership mix. In 2006, GHX also acquired Neoforma, converting the sole publicly held exchange into a privately held company, and increasing the percentage of hospital ownership in GHX. GHX and Broadlink, meanwhile, continued a strategic alliance that had been formed in 2002 to allow hospitals connected to Broadlink and suppliers connected to GHX to conduct business with one another electronically without having to connect to more than one exchange. The resulting exchange was not what most people envisioned when they think of an electronic marketplace. In other words, it was not a place where buyers can shop and compare products and prices. Instead, it was primarily a platform for connecting trading partners, with additional services to reduce errors and automate business processes.

Market consolidation among electronic trading exchanges in healthcare has also occurred globally. In Germany, for example, after years of severe competition for both healthcare provider and supplier customers, only a handful of large Internet-based trading exchanges survived (GHX and Medical Columbus, and pharmaMall for pharmaceutical products). With purchasing cooperatives gaining momentum in Germany, it remains to be seen how the online trading exchange market will evolve in the near future (see also "Group Purchasing Organizations" in this chapter).

As the market consolidated, Gartner Vice President Michael Davis said that allowing more trading partners to participate in a single supply chain solution would generate greater efficiencies: "Through the elimination of redundant investments, improved integration, and synchronization of data, healthcare organizations should be able to better manage their supply chain processes and begin to recognize cost efficiencies." [5] Although Davis was speaking about the U.S. market only, many observers now wonder if further consolidation on a global level might result in a single exchange for all of healthcare worldwide. With many suppliers already operating globally, this level of guaranteed interoperability might make sense, but such an exchange would need to accommodate the diversity among healthcare systems and market regulations that can vary not only by country but also jurisdiction.

The Second Wave of Adoption: Building Trust and Critical Mass

Market consolidation alone was not enough to drive market adoption. Because of the differences in ownership among the initial exchanges, many players in the market were concerned that they were either too *supplier* or too *GPO-focused*. Some of those fears were alleviated as GHX expanded its ownership base to include representatives from across the entire supply chain. Still, skeptics waited to see if the consolidated exchange would adhere to its commitment to treat all members with neutrality and "to reduce supply chain costs and to improve efficiencies for all."

Demonstrating value required a critical mass of participants to begin transacting business with one another. As expected, the supplier-founded exchange initially attracted more suppliers, while those exchanges started by GPOs were able to attract more providers at first, drawing upon GPO membership. With market consolidation, however, the number of trading partners using a single exchange increased, as did the percentage of purchasing flowing through an exchange as opposed to the other eBusiness methodologies, primarily direct EDI connections and proprietary supplier websites (see Chapter 5 for more information on these methodologies). Baxter Healthcare Corporation reported that orders received via an exchange increased five-fold in just two years. Johnson & Johnson Healthcare Corporation increased the number of purchase orders it received via an exchange by 90% in 2005, while Boston Scientific Corporation realized 70% growth during that same time period.

Many manufacturers are encouraging their customers to consider eBusiness as more than just a means to place orders. Tools that provide real-time, online order status and shipment tracking, electronic invoices, and data synchronization to ensure pricing and data accuracy deliver additional value in areas such as increased productivity and error reduction. One manufacturer's eCommerce Director explained, "We're trying to use the technology to provide even more efficiency and service to customers. Our goal is to streamline the supply chain and realize a shared commitment to reduce healthcare costs for the ultimate benefit of patients. By helping caregivers manage their transactions in a more efficient and effective way, eCommerce enables them to spend more time on what they do best, with is caring for patients." [6]

More healthcare systems are also encouraging their suppliers to join them in doing eBusiness via an exchange. In fact, several large integrated delivery networks (IDNs) in the United States require suppliers to be able to receive orders via an exchange as a condition of doing business with them.

In 2002, Gartner Research accurately depicted in the chart in Figure 7-1 that true eBusiness would eventually rise from the disillusionment caused by the dot-com shakeout, and organizations effectively incorporating eProcurement as part of their business processes would begin to learn how to optimize the supply chain.

Aberdeen Research confirmed that prediction in 2004, stating that "Once viewed as the poster child for the dot-com bust, Internet-based procurement automation (eProcurement) had been quietly delivering measurable value to enterprises in the form of reduced material and operating costs, improved compliance, and increased total spend under management."

Although the Aberdeen report, "E-procurement Benchmark Report: Less Hype, More Results," did not specifically address healthcare organizations, hospital purchasing departments that have embraced eProcurement are experiencing many of the same value points as their supply chain counterparts in other industries, including:

- Faster order processing times
- Lower order processing costs
- Fewer invoice exceptions
- Reduced off-contract or maverick spending
- Increased staff productivity

Many healthcare organizations, especially large systems with multiple facilities, anticipate even greater value from more comprehensive and accurate purchasing data. With this data, they can, among other things, anticipate demand and budget supply costs

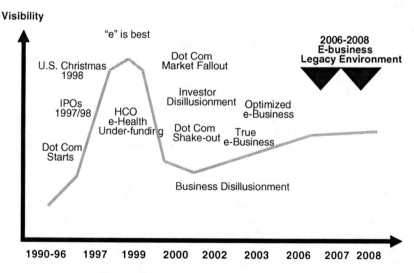

FIGURE 7-1. The Internet: from hype to value.

accordingly, identify product lines that qualify for new contracts or better-tier pricing, and even analyze product utilization by facility, by department, and by procedure (see also Chapter 10).

eBusiness Essentials: The Building Blocks to Achieving Value

Although there is growing awareness of the value of eProcurement for healthcare, the process required to fully realize the benefits is not as well understood. The following are the steps that hospitals in the United States have taken to increase operational efficiencies and reduce supply chain costs through use of an Internet-based trading exchange.

Essential #1: High Percentage of Electronic Transactions

An Internet-based trading exchange enables both hospitals and their vendors to establish one connection through which they can reach multiple trading partners.

Without an exchange, hospitals and suppliers interested in conducting business electronically have to establish and maintain separate EDI connections with each of their trading partners, and in some cases incur additional costs to utilize a VAN for communication services. American suppliers and hospitals estimated that they could avoid $5,000 to $15,000 USD for each trading partner reached through an exchange as opposed to a direct EDI connection.

Utilizing an exchange places less burden on hospital IT staff to establish and maintain trading partner connectivity. The disbursement manager for a four-hospital, regional health system in the eastern United States says it used to take hospital personnel several weeks to establish EDI connectivity with a single vendor, compared to an hour or less of staff time when connecting to a new supplier through an exchange. Given the time and financial resources required to establish direct connections, most hospital and health systems not using an exchange only maintain connectivity with a few, primary vendors.

Most hospitals in the United States and many other countries work with thousands of vendors, although only a small percentage of those suppliers account for the majority of their purchasing. For example, a 12-hospital system in Colorado purchases products from more than 2,000 suppliers but conducts most of its business with only 200 vendors. The majority of those top 200 vendors have the technological capabilities to integrate their order management systems with an exchange. Smaller, niche suppliers without an EDI infrastructure can participate by using web browser-based tools to send and receive POs, POAs, and electronic invoices. The vice president of sales for a small water and air filtration supplier said having "electronic invoicing capability makes it easier for smaller suppliers to compete with more technologically sophisticated companies." Hospitals that seek to maximize the percentage of orders processed electronically can also utilize tools that convert their EDI orders sent through an exchange to orders that are received via fax by suppliers not participating in the exchange. Then, when the supplier returns an acknowledgement via fax, it can be converted back to an EDI transaction after passing through the exchange. Similar tools are available for suppliers working with customers only capable of sending and receiving fax orders. By sending more of their orders through an exchange, hospitals and suppliers can not only standardize ordering procedures but can also capture data on more of their total purchasing, which in turn can be used for better contract negotiation, demand planning, and budgeting.

Essential #2: Data Accuracy

Simply establishing connectivity does not guarantee improved efficiencies in the healthcare supply chain. Lack of data synchronization between the myriad buyers and sellers and other supply chain business partners, such as group purchasing organizations, is a fundamental source of inefficiency in the healthcare supply chain. Without addressing this problem, electronic commerce can actually exacerbate inefficiencies by passing inaccurate data faster and increasing the number of mistakes that must be corrected manually after the fact. Scott Tiazkun, an analyst with the market research firm IDC wrote, "With all these players, there's a great potential for poisoned data. If you don't have the basics down, all this infrastructure is for naught." [7]. The following statistics illustrate the magnitude of the problem and its associated costs for hospitals and suppliers:

- 70 to 80% of all product transaction errors are directly related to inaccurate product information [8].
- Typically, 20-40% of invoices have discrepancies and as much as 40% of an accounts payable clerk's time is spent reconciling invoices (based on studies conducted by Global Healthcare Exchange at more than 160 hospitals).
- Average cost (shared by hospitals/suppliers) to research and correct a single order reconciliation exception ranges from $15 to $50 [9].
- A study of 1,200 companies found that, on average, a manually processed order was nearly seven times more expensive to process than an electronically synchronized order [9].

To avoid these problems, hospitals and healthcare systems are advised to cleanse their item masters (the internal databases of the products they purchase most frequently) before ordering products electronically. Cleansing involves matching their data to product information held by manufacturers and deleting duplicate entries and obsolete items.

True data synchronization requires access to a reliable source of *truth* for accurate product data, which ultimately comes from the manufacturers. Efforts are underway to establish a central repository of supplier-verified product data to synchronize information across the supply chain. Use of such a repository in the retail industry has reduced purchase order error rates from 11% to less than 2%, according to the Healthcare eBusiness Collaborative.

An Internet exchange addresses the need for data accuracy by conducting an *eCommerce readiness* process with all healthcare providers before they go live on the exchange. This entails comparing the information contained in a hospital's item master with data maintained and verified by suppliers in the exchange's product content repository. Providers are then notified about corrections that need to be made to their product data. During this process, an average 35% rate of inconsistency has been found between hospital and manufacturer data.

Once an item master is cleansed, healthcare organizations need to put policies and procedures in place to maintain data accuracy. Manufacturers continually introduce new products to the market while removing others, and mergers and acquisitions among suppliers result in changes in both product and vendor data. Too often, hospitals have spent considerable sums of money, often in the hundreds of thousands of dollars in the United States, to have their item masters cleansed only to discover that their data was once again inaccurate soon after the cleansing process had been completed. A purchasing agent at a small hospital in northeastern New York State described this phenomenon quite simply: "It's like cleaning your house. If you only do it once, it will just get dirty again." The hospital conducts quarterly scrubbings of any new data added to its item master and runs periodic reports to make sure buyers are adding items in a standardized manner. Buyers are instructed to always list the noun describing the product first, followed by other attributes such as size or color. That way, if a buyer is looking for a pen, he or she can search on the word *pen* to find a list of applicable items. If the item were listed instead as a *blue pen*, a similar search would not find the item. The key is building quality into the process from the start, rather than trying to fix problems after the fact.

Without standardized product descriptions as often the case with medical supplies–the lack of unstructured and unclassified data can become a severe barrier for searching items and for computing statistics (see Chapter 6).

An added benefit of data cleansing and synchronization is a more manageable item master. By eliminating obsolete and duplicate items, one IDN reported reducing the size of its database from 75,000 to 45,000 items, while virtually eliminating errors in purchase orders sent through the exchange.

Essential #3: Process Automation

Fully automating the procurement process requires more than just the ability to send and receive POs and POAs. Maximum efficiency is achieved when eBusiness tools can be used from the point a product is requisitioned through to when the invoice is processed for payment. This requires healthcare providers to view the supply chain as an enterprise-wide operation, involving clinical, purchasing, and accounts payable departments.

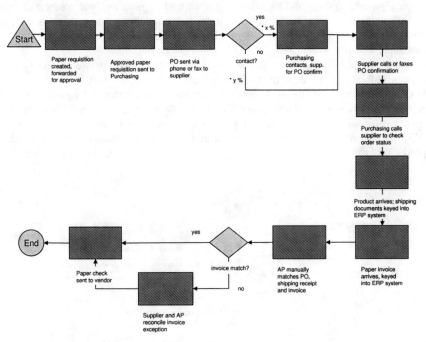

Legend: * in x% of the cases a contact is necessary, in y% of the cases no contact necessary

FIGURE 7-2. Manual purchasing process.

In a manual environment, considerable time is spent on materials management-related functions both before and after orders are actually sent to suppliers. Each step in the process increases the time and cost to process an order, as well as the potential for errors. For example, clinical staff must find the right product, prepare the paper requisition, seek necessary approvals, and follow-up on order status. Purchasing staff, in turn, must convert the paper requisition into a PO to be sent to vendors, while accounts payable clerks must re-key paper invoices into their financial systems. Contracting staff, meanwhile, have the challenge of keeping the latest contract information in their systems to ensure they are paying the correct price. Figure 7-2 depicts a simplified example of a manual order process.

All of these steps contribute to data entry errors. When information on POs and invoices does not match, purchasing and accounts payable staff–along with their counterparts at vendor organizations–are tasked with determining the cause of the discrepancies. In a fully integrated eCommerce solution, many of the above steps can be eliminated, as illustrated in Figure 7-3.

Simplifying the ordering process and reducing errors helped one Chicago-based IDN reduce its transactional costs from $75 USD to approximately $10 - $30 USD per PO.

Online Requisitioning

With an online requisitioning system, clinicians can send requisitions to the purchasing department electronically, and, with customized workflows, requisitions that meet pre-established approvals can be converted into purchase orders without any manual intervention. Clinicians can then monitor the status of orders from their desktops to determine when a product is expected to arrive or be notified if there are backorders and other arrangements need to be made. This facilitates the scheduling of procedures, and eliminates the need to call buyers to determine if a product has been ordered successfully and when it will arrive.

Some requisitioning systems enable clinicians to more easily source products using customized catalogs by department. This not only saves clinicians time, but also helps hospitals maximize the amount of products purchased on contract and therefore at lower prices. Often, when clinicians cannot find the product they are looking for in the item master, they will place a special order for a noncontracted product at a higher price. When there are no internal policies regarding item master changes, they will add a product to the database, negatively impacting the accuracy of the data. Before one

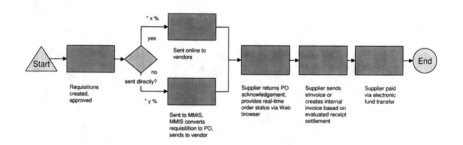

Legend: * in x% of the cases order is sent directly, in y% of the cases via MMIS

FIGURE 7-3. Electronic purchasing process.

St. Louis-based healthcare system had implemented an online requisitioning system, more than 50% of the system's orders were for so-called specialty items or products ordered without a standard item number. This meant the healthcare system was likely to pay higher prices for products and unable to capture important purchasing history data. By improving sourcing and increasing contract compliance, the healthcare system realized more than $1 million in incremental annual savings.

Order Processing

Electronic ordering saves buyers considerable time by enabling them to manage by exception. With direct EDI connections, hospitals can send POs electronically, but staff must review printed order confirmations sent by suppliers line-by-line to identify any problems. With an electronic order management system, they can receive real-time notifications when there is a problem that must be addressed, such as a backordered item, or an item number or price discrepancy, while allowing error-free orders to proceed in an automated and touchless fashion. By proactively addressing problems, buyers can avoid costly invoice exceptions and the need for time-consuming reconciliations. Utilizing an exception-based order management system has reduced the amount of time buyers at a 225-bed hospital in Baton Rouge, Louisiana spend verifying PO exceptions from 10 hours to 45 minutes per day.

Many hospitals reported utilizing this *free time* to redirect staff activities to more value-added work, such as identifying new contracting opportunities, reviewing inventory par levels, and analyzing product utilization. The director of Purchasing and Supply Chain Systems at a Chicago children's hospital reorganized his staff to enable purchasing agents to spend more time understanding how to better serve clinical departments. He reduced the number of agents from seven to four and promoted two of the seven to purchasing managers, which has enabled him to spend less time on day-to-day ordering and more time on managing the department. He also moved several employees into the operating room (OR) to work as inventory supply technicians. According to the director, "If a supply is needed during a procedure, the technician can get it, rather than a clinician having to leave the OR. That way, clinicians can spend more time on what they do best, patient care."

Further efficiencies can be achieved through linkages between internal point-of-care dispensing systems, materials management systems, and vendors. At a three-hospital system in Chicago, when a nurse takes a product from one of their automated supply cabinets, the inventory is automatically decremented, creating a requisition in the materials management information system (MMIS), which generates a PO to replace that product and sends it through the exchange to the system's primary distributor. Once the order is filled, the product is delivered to the receiving dock and taken directly to the supply cabinet. Meanwhile, the IDN and its distributor can capture data to facilitate better demand management.

Accounts Payable

Improved data accuracy and electronic invoicing also saves considerable time for accounts payable staff. On average, hospitals can reduce the amount of time spent manually entering paper invoices by 25% and researching invoice discrepancies by 75%. Fewer invoice problems also enable hospitals to pay suppliers faster and qualify for early pay discounts. One IDN realized a 1% early pay discount on $16 million US spent annually with its primary distributor, while another says it pays vendors utilizing an exchange nearly twice as fast as those that it conducts business with manually. That can result in significant savings for suppliers, as well. A supplier with a turnover of $750 million that successfully decreases its Days Sales Outstanding (DSO) by one day would yield a return of $185,000 on an annualized basis, assuming a 9% cost of debt.

Challenges and Opportunities in the eBusiness Environment

Economic Issues

Material Costs Matter

Hospital expenditures account for one third of total U.S. spending on healthcare, which is approaching 17% of the gross domestic product, and that percentage will likely continue to rise as the population ages. With average supply costs representing approximately one third of a hospital's total operating budget (31% in the United States and 33% in Germany), improving supply chain efficiencies can have a dramatic impact on controlling rising healthcare costs, not only in the United States but in other countries as well. Figure 7-4 depicts the breakdown in operating expenses for a typical hospital in the United States.

According to the American Hospital Association, one third of U.S. hospitals are operating in the red, and total hospital operating margins have fallen 34% since 1997. Schneller, Smeltzer, and Burns point out that, as a hospital's second largest expense, supply chain management is increasingly recognized as a key opportunity for organizational improvement [10]. Holmes and Miller further contend that "the application of eCommerce to the healthcare arena is one solution to educating, informing, and more efficiently utilizing scarce resources to sustain the health of a nation," which in turn can have a "direct impact on economic growth and political stability." [11].

IT Spending in Hospitals and Healthcare Systems

Despite this compelling case for change in how hospitals purchase products, "supply systems at many (U.S.) healthcare providers get short shrift because of tight budgets

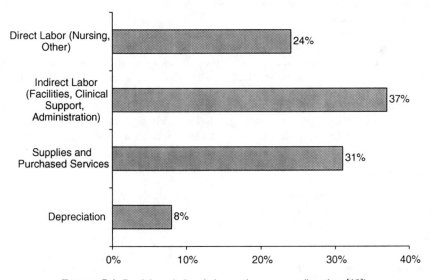

FIGURE 7-4. Breakdown in hospital operating expenses (based on [10]).

and a management bias in favor of clinical or patient systems." [7]. In the United States, hospital information technology (IT) departments are faced with competing priorities, often driven by government mandates, and few have the resources to devote to supply chain improvements. Until recently, U.S. healthcare institutions have invested less in IT than other industries. Healthcare's average expenditure of just 2% of revenues is less than half of that spent by the financial industry [12]. German hospitals, meanwhile, spend approximately 2.7% of their yearly revenue on healthcare information systems, which include both management and clinical applications [13].

There are signs that this is beginning to change, as healthcare IT and business executives begin to forge closer working relationships than their counterparts outside healthcare. According to a recent Forrester Research study, hospital IT budgets were expected to grow by 4.8% in 2006, compared to just 4% in other enterprises [14]. Nearly three quarters of German hospitals anticipate that percentage to grow in the coming year [13].

Much of the growth in the United States is being driven by clinical informatics, as opposed to supply chain initiatives, but that too could change as the relationship between the supply chain and the quality of patient care, as well as the bottom line, is more fully recognized. For example, "when supplies are not available or are unacceptable, the (healthcare) organization faces increased risk that it cannot perform a function or that a function will be performed improperly," while "for many procedures, good materials contribute to great (patient) outcomes." ([10], p. 6) The relationship between clinical and supply chain functions is discussed further in Chapter 9.

Variation in Patient Needs and Lack of Standardization Limit Cost Control Initiatives

The role of clinicians in selecting what products to buy and the variation in patient needs uniquely impact a healthcare supply manager's ability to implement cost-control strategies. Schneller and Smeltzer [10] pointed out that in most industries, once product decisions were made, standardization prevailed, and the supply chain was managed by sourcing professionals. In healthcare, two patients with the exact same malady may have very different, or changing, needs, forcing hospitals to stock many different kinds of basic products such as sutures.

Figure 7-5 shows the rising costs (since 2002) for implantable devices for one IDN in the United States.

Lack of standardization increases in the arena of high-cost, specialty medical devices such as orthopedic implants and cardiac stents. As medical technology evolves, new, higher-priced, higher-tech items are continually being introduced to replace older technology. For example, patients with irregular heart rhythms used to be treated by having a pacemaker implanted. Today, an increasing number of patients are receiving implantable cardiac defibrillators, which are approximately four times more expensive than pacemakers. Specialty medical devices now comprise approximately 40% of an average hospital's total supply costs, and that percentage is expected to grow to 60% as an aging population undergoes more procedures utilizing these devices.

Many hospitals try to control costs by negotiating lower contracted prices for these devices with specific suppliers, but the final decision on which device to use is usually made by the attending physician. Supply chain executives at some hospitals are making an effort to work more closely with physicians to mutually identify clinically acceptable products that can be placed on contract. Others have adopted the (at times controversial) and legally sensitive practice known as *gain sharing*, in which doctors are rewarded

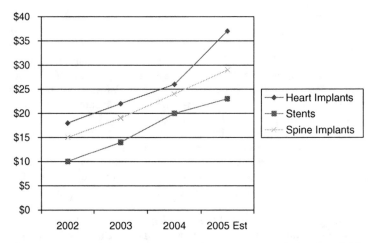

FIGURE 7-5. Costs of implantable devices (data source: one U.S. American IDN).

for achieving verifiable cost savings. eProcurement tools can assist with these efforts by making it easier for clinicians to identify the products that are on contract and for materials managers to validate that they are being charged the correct contract price during the transactional process. These tools, combined with better data on clinical outcomes by product, can facilitate decision-making to choose the best product at the best price (see also Chapter 10).

Technical Issues

The limitations of some MMISs to accommodate eBusiness functions within the complex healthcare environment further hamper supply chain improvement programs. The director of materials systems for one of Chicago's largest healthcare systems, who was interviewed for the study, said, "Some materials systems in use today are based on old manufacturing models. They are adequate for simple procurement functions, such as reordering and inventory, but they do not provide easy access to the kind of data needed for more strategic supply chain activities."

For this reason, some healthcare organizations have chosen to convert to state-of-the-art ERP systems, but the process can be extremely expensive and requires a significant investment of time. A large Catholic healthcare system in the western United States spent $120 million on a failed attempt to standardize to a single ERP application across its 40 hospitals and medical centers. The system then spent an additional $54 million to implement another vendor's system. The second attempt was a success, with the healthcare system projecting a 144% return on investment in eight years [15].

Other healthcare systems have chosen instead to employ Web-based applications that expand the functionality of their existing mainframe legacy systems. These systems operate on the application service providers' (ASP) server, which places less burden on hospital IT staff. The ASP is responsible for installing any upgrades, and hospitals can take advantage of new functionality with little effort beyond training staff on how to utilize the new features.

A lack of industry standards, such as universal product numbers (UPNs), as well as the inability of some materials systems to fully utilize such standards, has also hampered efforts to automate the purchasing process. Healthcare in the United States is still very fragmented, with more than 5,500 hospitals each transacting business with thousands of suppliers. There is no predominant organization in healthcare analogous to the role that a large retailer such as Wal-Mart plays in the retail sector to drive adoption and usage of industry standards. After nearly two decades of talking about the need for industry standards with little progress, the vice president for standardization and contract administration for a large for-profit healthcare system and its GPO reported, "With a critical number of hospitals and suppliers transacting business over a single electronic trading exchange, we are finally in a position to drive widespread adoption of standards. Working together as an industry, we have the potential to standardize how we identify products and trading partners in the transactions we send through the exchange." Greater adoption first requires more manufacturers to assign UPNs to their products, and the vice president says hospitals need to demonstrate their commitment to utilizing the standard by ensuring their materials management systems can store them.

People Issues

Lack of adequate training, coupled with a failure to change business processes, contributes to the greater than 70 % failure rate for IT implementations in healthcare. The corporate director of materials management for a 3-hospital IDN in Chicago said hospitals "try to force feed old business practices on top of new technology, rather than redesigning how work is done to optimize what the new tools have to offer." That is much harder to do, the director said because it involves changing how employees perform their jobs in an environment where "personnel are often reluctant to leave old work flow processes and switch onto a new system." The director added, "It requires a commitment to training, especially for employees who have been doing their work *the old way* for many years." [16].

A St. Louis-based IDN has tried to make it more convenient for employees to change behaviors to comply with new contracting policies. "We want to make it so easy to do the right thing that buyers don't want to order off contract," explained the IDN's vice president of supply chain operations. The 13-hospital IDN now utilizes an online requisitioning system with a front end that the vice president said "looks a lot like Amazon.com" and was much easier for clinicians to use than the *green screen* view afforded by its legacy system. With the new system, preparing a requisition now takes 5 minutes instead of 15, while improving sourcing and resulting in fewer off-contract purchases.

Changing business processes and assuming new responsibilities can be daunting for some personnel, but more satisfying for others. When one buyer, a study participant, joined a North Carolina IDN ten years ago, she said she bought whatever the clinicians wanted, with little attention paid to the price. Now, with less clerical workload, she could spend more time working with clinicians to find the best product for patient care at the best price. "When you know what you are buying and why, you can do your job better and with more satisfaction," said another buyer at the same healthcare system who also participated in the study.

The Role of eBusiness in Procurement Strategy

eBusiness and Sound Purchasing Strategies

Utilizing a single ordering platform, such as a trading exchange, enables hospitals to standardize business practices and aggregate purchasing information on a greater percentage of their purchasing, even across organizations with disparate technology.

Hospitals cannot control supply costs until they know what they are spending, on what, and with whom. Understanding what products were purchased and received, for how much, and how they were used, provides information essential to determining actual procedure costs, analyzing patterns of use, and making future product choices that support both clinical and fiscal objectives. One healthcare supply chain expert clarified it this way in the interview, "If the gauze pads that cost $6 provide no better outcomes than those that cost $3, why buy them?" This again underscores the need for accurate data on both purchasing and clinical outcomes, and greater collaboration between clinical and materials functions within healthcare organizations.

Auto ID and Capture Technologies Increase Collaboration and Visibility

The use of new technologies to increase accuracy and data synchronization across the supply chain is "not only changing the way companies operate internally, but is also altering the relationship between…suppliers, customers and other business partners." [12] If the experience of other industries is any indication, this may yield the greatest savings for both hospitals and their suppliers. For example, when the grocery industry began using automated check-out stands to scan universal product codes, the estimated net benefits (after implementation costs) were said to equal nearly 3% of sales. Using standardized codes to uniquely identify products provided trading partners with increased visibility across the entire supply chain and yielded nearly twice the savings as a result of better inventory control and demand management [17].

Expanded use of auto identification and data capture (AIDC) technologies in healthcare, such as barcode scanning and radio frequency identification (RFID), can provide benefits analogous to those experienced by the grocery industry. Many hospitals and suppliers are already using barcode technology for specific applications, such as tracking product usage and ensuring that patients receive the proper medication. The value of RFID, according to one of the purchasing and supply chain systems directors in the study, will not be fully realized until the software is capable of more completely manipulating the data and more products are identified with UPNs. He explained in the interview: "When we are all using the same identifiers, we can track products from the acquisition of raw materials for manufacturing through to the point when they are used in patient care. With full visibility, we can anticipate product shortages because we will know in advance when there is a lack of necessary raw materials. Without that kind of visibility, we don't know there is a problem until a supplier sends a backorder notice."

The Role of Group Purchasing Organizations (GPOs)

United States

Collaboration in the healthcare supply chain involves more than just buyers and sellers of products. The majority of U.S. hospitals utilize the services of a GPO, not only to negotiate better contract pricing by leveraging the purchasing volume of the GPO's combined provider membership, but also to assist with issues that impact purchasing decisions and supply chain costs, such as measuring clinical outcomes, developing spend metrics, and managing Diagnosis Related Groups (DRGs) for reimbursement.

During the early days of the dot-com boom, many GPOs in the United States took a proactive role in creating eCommerce exchanges for their individual hospital members, hoping to garner critical purchasing data to track contract compliance (among other things) from transactions conducted over an exchange. What they failed to realize was 1) that many hospital members were reluctant to share such data and 2) that funneling all of their purchasing through a single exchange would not be practical for hospitals anytime in the foreseeable future. Some order types, such as consignments that require additional patient and product information, are difficult to automate. Also for many hospitals, pharmacy and blood products are still ordered through channels separate from materials management.

As the exchange market consolidated, many of the GPOs traded ownership in their own exchanges for shared ownership with other GPOs, hospitals, and vendors in a single exchange. By reducing the number of exchanges and broadening the ownership base in the remaining exchange, they were able to reduce the total cost of ownership for all involved.

Today, most of the major GPOs in the United States are working to create a consolidated contract management tool for their provider members. By providing hospital-specific contract data to the exchange, their member hospitals can validate, during the transactional process, that the prices used in purchase orders and purchase order acknowledgements match their latest contract price on file. With real time notification, hospitals can address the discrepancies before they become costly invoice exceptions. Aggregated purchasing history reports made available through exchanges also enable hospitals to identify when their purchasing volume affords new contracting opportunities, and to ensure price parity across multiple facilities.

Having a single industry tool for contract price validation is particularly useful to hospitals that utilize more than one GPO and/or negotiate some contracts directly with manufacturers, because they can use a single tool to store and manage all of their contracts. The Anderson study found that being able to validate contract pricing early in the process could enable hospitals to avoid overpaying suppliers by 2 to 7% for the products they purchase [1].

Most GPOs and manufacturers also support the development of a single industry platform for reaching agreement on hospital or system-specific tier pricing commitments. Ensuring that all impacted parties (hospitals, manufacturers, distributors, and GPOs) have access to the same data improves collaboration and minimizes rework.

While GPOs in the United States are collaborating more in areas related to contract commitment and price validation, they continue to differentiate themselves through their expertise and offerings in other areas, such as providing the necessary clinical knowledge to help hospitals choose the best products for both patient care and the bottom line. Some other commonly offered services include:

- **Benchmarking**–members can utilize a central database to compare their performance with comparable institutions that represent best practices related to clinical, administrative, and financial operations, as well as patient outcomes
- **Consulting Services**–members receive support in areas ranging from specialized clinical services to reengineering selected business processes and contracting for financial auditing services
- **Biomedical Equipment Maintenance**–group purchasing contracts are offered for biomedical repair and maintenance services, including regulatory compliance and safety testing and inspection
- **Clinical Education Programs**–these programs include providing clinical pharmacists to assist with the development of cost-reduction strategies and standardization of hospital formularies, as well as research to help evaluate the effectiveness of therapeutic equivalencies

- **Information Systems**–several GPOs provide their members with favorable contracts for the acquisition of systems for materials management and other hospital functions
- **Insurance and Risk Management Programs**–these programs help member hospitals manage insurance expenses through the provision of cost-effective coverage designed to meet individual needs

Germany

In Germany, strong cost pressures exerted by the DRG-based financing of hospitals made bundling the purchasing power of an otherwise fragmented medical supplies market an attractive means to reduce materials costs. Today, large healthcare systems, for-profit hospital chains, and an increasing number of hospital purchasing cooperatives are taking advantage of aggregating the demand side and pursuing a much more professional approach to procurement.

There are different types of purchasing cooperatives in Germany: binding and non-binding; those that specialize in particular items; and those that support the full range of products. Although about 70 purchasing cooperatives currently exist, roughly half of supplier sales are influenced by just 20 purchasing consortia [18]. The smaller the degree of product differentiation, the higher the volume of products purchased under these group purchasing conditions will be.

The purchasing consortia differ from GPOs in the United States in terms of both their organization and financing schemes, as they are typically smaller and more strongly controlled by the hospitals. They face similar problems, however–most notably in areas such as monitoring contract compliance, standardizing products, and needing structured data to analyze buying patterns.

How much group purchasing in Germany is associated with eBusiness remains a moot point. Whereas Kruetten and colleagues [18] deny any linkage, the purchasing consortium COMPARATIO, consisting of major North German university hospitals, has established its own Internet trading exchange, called GSG.

United Kingdom

In the United Kingdom, the National Health Trust (NHS) previously regarded group purchasing as a national, as opposed to local, activity. The Purchasing and Supply Agency (PASA) of the NHS sought to negotiate contracts for all hospital trusts, assuming it could achieve better agreements as a result of greater demand pooling. The difficulty for PASA was that the contracts were negotiated at a distance from the trusts. Without their involvement, the trusts were less committed to work with the PASA-negotiated contracts. Instead, the trusts negotiated individual contracts with suppliers, and rather than creating a single, common market, the PASA approach resulted in more fragmentation within healthcare.

With ongoing restructuring of the NHS, responsibilities have shifted to the regional level, and collaborative procurement hubs (CPH) have been established to counteract these deficiencies. The mission of the CPHs is to enforce the use of group contracts by 1) controlling and directing purchasing from a strategic point of view, 2) engaging the trusts in ongoing discussions and 3) remaining involved in day-to-day transactional activities.

The hub model is more effective than the prior PASA approach because there is not only a smaller geographical distance between the trusts and the purchasing organization but also because clinical advisors work more closely with the clinical end users than they do with the procurement managers. The goal is to more closely align stakeholders with the contracts by getting them involved at the beginning and arriving at contracts that are shaped by the users.

Because CPHs have only been recently implemented in the English NHS, work is still underway to establish a link to electronic business transactions. The first success in the electronic domain, however, has been documented. The CPH in Greater Manchester Area is conducting electronic auctions for computers and other equipment. It remains to be seen whether there will also be auctions for medical supplies in the near future.

In all three countries, there are ongoing activities in the group purchasing field. Due to the divergent backgrounds and histories, however, the group purchasing activities vary to a great extent. While GPOs in the United States are trying to differentiate themselves through the types of services offered, German purchasing cooperatives are struggling to increase their influence in the market. In the United Kingdom, the centralistic approach proved to be ineffective, with regional contracts now considered the best way to achieve user satisfaction and contract compliance. Although both regional in nature, the German and English approaches are different, with the English focusing on the clinical user and the Germans more on the professional purchasing manager.

Conclusion

The healthcare supply chain serves a critical role in ensuring the quality of patient care, as well as the financial health of a nation as a whole. Improving operational efficiencies and controlling rising healthcare costs requires system integration and standardized purchasing processes across the myriad organizations that make up the supply chain, including suppliers, group purchasing organizations, hospitals, and other healthcare providers. Historically, the supply chain has been highly fragmented, with little coordination among the various players, or between the purchasing-related functions within individual organizations. In the wake of declining margins, hospitals are taking a more holistic approach to the supply chain to improve efficiencies and foster greater cooperation, information sharing, and process integration among clinical, purchasing, and financial operations. At the same time, technology is being implemented to improve how hospitals work with their vendors and group purchasing organizations.

Technology, however, is only a means to achieve supply chain objectives. Greater trust among stakeholders is fundamental to organizations being able to utilize new technology to its greatest potential. Enabling eProcurement between trading partners is only the beginning, but it lays the foundation for greater collaboration, and with only about 30% of healthcare purchasing currently handled electronically, the potential for continued improvement is considerable.

Acknowledgment

The information provided in this chapter was based on the experiences of studies conducted with more than 200 hospitals transacting business electronically with suppliers. We would like to thank these organizations for providing specific examples of what they have learned in the process in terms of how to utilize eProcurement to its full potential: BJC HealthCare, Cape Fear Valley Health System, Centura Health, Children's Memorial Hospital, HCA, Resurrection HealthCare, Terrebonne General Medical Center, and Woman's Hospital of Baton Rouge.

References

[1] Lacy, R. G., K. J. Connor, P. F. Carane, A. R. Gonce, K. A. Reid, and J. R. Harter. (2001) *The Value of eCommerce in the Healthcare Supply Chain.* Chicago: Arthur Andersen.

[2] Konsynski, B. and M. Vitale. (1991) *Baxter Healthcare Corporation: ASAP Express.* Boston: Harvard Business School.

[3] Marshall, C. L. and J. J. Sviokla. (1996) *Baxter International: OnCall as Soon as Possible?* Boston: Harvard Business School.

[4] Minahan, T. A. (2004) *The E-procurement Benchmark Report: Less Hype, More Results.* Boston: AberdeenGroup

[5] Global Healthcare Exchange (2002) *Global Healthcare Exchange and Medibuy Sign Definitive Merger Agreement.* Westminster. Available from: <http://home.ghx.com/NewsPressReleasesDetail.asp?info_id=403> [Accessed 17 October 2006].

[6] Baxter International Inc. (2005) *Baxter Again Named Supplier of Year by Global Healthcare Exchange.* Deerfield. Available from: <http://www.baxter.com/about_baxter/sustainability/sust_stories/stakeholder/stk_ghx_supplier_award.html> (Accessed 17 October 2006].

[7] Anthes, G. (2005) *On the Mend.* Framingham: Computerworld. Available from: <http://www.computerworld.com/action/article.do?command=viewArticleBasic&articleId=99058> [Accessed 17 October 2006].

[8] Healthcare EBusiness Collaborative (2002) *Healthcare Product Data Synchronization Business Case.* Available from: <http://www.hcec.org/index.php?query=43> [Accessed 17 October 2006].

[9] Hagemeier, G. (2004) The cost of bad healthcare supply data. HCEC Bulletin – Health Care eBusiness Collaborative 9/13/2004.

[10] Schneller, E. S. and L. R. Smeltzer. (2006) *Strategic Management of the Health Care Supply Chain.* San Francisco: Jossey-Bass.

[11] Holmes, S. C. and R. H. Miller. (2003) The strategic role of e-commerce in the supply chain of the healthcare industry. *International Journal of Services Technology and Management.* **4**, 507-517.

[12] Chen, J. C. H., M. Dolan, and B. Lin. (2004) Improve processes on healthcare: current issues and future trends. *International Journal of Electronic Healthcare.* **1**, 149-164.

[13] Hübner, U., B. Sellemann and A. Frey (2006) *IT-Report Gesundheitswesen - Teil A: Befragung der Krankenhäuser.* Osnabrück: University of Applied Sciences Osnabrück.

[14] Brown, E. G. and W. McEnroe, (2006) *Hospital IT And Business Execs Share Technology Buying Decisions.* Cambridge: Forrester Research. Available from: <http://www.forrester.com/Research/Document/Excerpt/0,7211,37999,00.html> [Accessed 17 October 2006].

[15] Havenstein, H. (2005) Health Care Provider Nears End of 10-Year ERP Journey. Framingham: Computerworld. Available from: <http://www.computerworld.com/softwaretopics/erp/story/0,10801,107180,00.html> [Accessed 17 October 2006].

[16] Mieczkowska, S., M. Hinton and D. Barnes, (2004) Barriers to e-health business processes. *International Journal of Electronic Healthcare.* **1**, 47-59.

[17] KPMG Consulting (2000) *Industry Standard Numbering Systems in the Globalization of Supply Chains and Markets.* New York: KPMG Consulting.

[18] Kruetten, J.M., F. Rautenberg and M. Liefner, (2005) *Future Relevance and Consequences of Hospital Purchasing Cooperatives for Medical Technology Suppliers in Germany.* Bonn: Simon-Kucher und Partners. Available from: Bundesverband Medizintechnologie <http://www.bvmed.de/stepone/data/downloads/55/a5/00/study_purchasing.pdf> [Accessed 17 October 2006].

8
An Integrated Strategy for eProcurement: The Case for Leeds Teaching Hospitals

Keith E. Lilley

Executive Summary

The study of eProcurement at the Leeds Teaching Hospitals is not a review of technology—a misconception that many readers could reasonably make. The success at Leeds is a business process reengineering project that has used technology at the heart of the process to make the business work.

The primary challenge for the Hospital Trust was to manage the value of its procurement activity and not simply the cost. The environment within which procurement operated was closely allied to the pressures that the whole of the National Health Service (NHS) was experiencing—increasing demands from a host of customers, including but not exclusively patients, where resources are finite. Overlaying this environment was a range of additional pressures, including the vast numbers of experts of whom many are international leaders within their field.

Leeds, like many other NHS and commercial organizations, had many other challenges to address. The information systems within the organization were mixed in terms of quality and their application. Systems were not always joined up, but had been directed to address particular business problems within a narrow area of the organization.

The challenge for the procurement service was to improve procurement outcomes where these pressures applied. A range of procurement contracts existed, with many of the markets mature, and prices when benchmarked were good. Like all procurement operations, there is always room for improvement, but incremental changes in such an environment are more difficult to realize.

Added to this was the need to take cost out of the procurement administration and engage the internal purchasing customer. Without customer buy-in, purchasing outside the organization lacks commitment. Mixed messages for supply organizations allow greater opportunities for prices to increase. In addition, the cost base of purchasing concentrated on costs and not added value.

177

The factors described above will be recognizable to many organizations. Identifying the challenges for the Trust was only the first stage of the process. Suppliers for the Trust wanted greater certainty and the value that comes from such certainty. The process of procurement from order to payment can be lengthy. Governments have recognized this by publishing purchase-to-pay standards for larger organizations dealing with SMEs. By reducing the cost base of the Trust, there was an opportunity to improve the suppliers' cost base at the same time. These mutual benefits of improved transaction processing were a primary motivation in the eCommerce project. Through careful negotiation, Leeds had the opportunity to secure these process improvements, and realize some of these benefits to be shared by the supplier in the form of reduced prices and supply chain improvements.

This study examines the business process improvements that created a virtuous circle at Leeds for its procurement service. The methodology employed to engage internal customers in simple, effective and intuitive purchasing systems that supported their business gave confidence to the customer. Managing the supply chain effectively allowed the Trust's procurement team to collaborate more closely with expert customers, having gained their trust through massive process improvements. The corollary to this was to move the purchasing agenda upstream from process, and to concentrate on value-added activities such as contracting.

The improvements for Leeds were facilitated by understanding that technology was vital to the success of the business. Conversely, the technology was not the business driver, unlike many businesses that adopt eCommerce. Leeds made significant distinctions in examining the differences between the electronic marketplace, B2B solutions, and the applicability of the deeply integrated business process adopted here. Often this analysis is ignored or given insufficient critique. The consequence is usually a less favourable outcome. This is not the case at Leeds.

Introduction: Why eProcurement Means Transforming the Transactional Nature of Procurement

Within the vast majority of NHS procurement services, the placing of orders is labor intensive and is very much the driver for the operation. In a number of organizations, there has been some automation, including a limited number of remote requisitioning processes, utilizing data input on PC desktops or handheld PCs.

Most of the NHS has experienced relatively low levels of investment in IT to support the financial functions, which includes procurement. IT investment has largely been directed toward patient care, again with a few notable exceptions.

As a consequence of this and many other factors, the ability for organizations to trade electronically is mixed. The drive for eProcurement at Leeds Teaching Hospitals came about not as a solution to deliver all the perceived benefits of good procurement practice, but as a logical step of the development of good procurement practice.

eProcurement can not be divorced from the mainstream of procurement processes but is complimentary to it. For the Leeds Teaching Hospitals, NHS Trust, and other organizations to adopt operations that are effective and efficient, the process must deliver the service design that is required. This is supported by operations management researchers, who state *"many services involve the customer in being part of the transformation process."* ([1], p. 123).

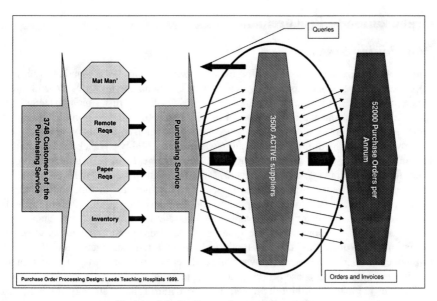

FIGURE 8-1. Purchase order processing design.

This is certainly the case within the healthcare setting, where the requisitioner is based within many and varied departments spread throughout the organization. Figure 8-1 demonstrates the process of service that existed within the organization. Many NHS organizations are significantly less mature, and whose provisioning systems are quite basic. It also identifies the target area for administration savings within the *ellipse*. To understand what processes are effective, an analysis was necessary.

Process commences with the identification of demand from the customer. In Leeds, there are nearly 4,000 customers using the service from a staffing compliment of 16,000. Figure 8-1 illustrates that there are four main provisioning methodologies:

- Materials management—products are managed by a dedicated team of purchasing staff who replenish stock to predetermined levels, utilizing hand-held computer technology (bar codes) to capture demand.
- Remote requisitioning—takes place using a PC desktop interface that provides electronic data input to the organization's Oracle ERP system.
- Paper requisitioning—planned to be phased out.
- Computerised inventory systems—write directly to the ERP system.

The purchasing service utilizes 3,500 active suppliers, and places some 52,000 purchase orders per annum.

An analysis was undertaken to evaluate the administrative costs of this service, including creditor payment costs. When compared with other NHS organizations, Leeds was seen to be performing well, with a 52% (PASA data analysis) first match invoice rate (the invoice and purchase order were found to match at the first attempt). Within United Kingdom industry, this also represents good comparative performance. This data also clearly showed that a further 48% of expenditures needed to be addressed to reduce costs and improve service.

Organization of Procurement

Provisioning Systems

With such a large and diverse workforce and *primitive* means of transacting processes (paper requisitions), concerns were evident in terms of managing maverick expenditures. This activity was not restricted to purchasing outside of the Trust's main systems, but occurred as a consequence of human error and human nature. In addition, the historical nature of the procurement process remained largely unchanged for many years.

Conversely, two methods of provisioning were already highly advanced. These can be seen in Figure 8-2, which shows that inventory management was fully computerized at Leeds together with materials management. Materials management is a process whereby Procurement staff requisition products on behalf of the internal customer, utilizing bar code technology and hand-held computers. The supplier(s) of goods via this methodology were originally restricted to two prime wholesalers (this subsequently changed to include all contracted suppliers). The range of goods were predetermined, as were the maximum stock quantities. Both of these systems required cataloged items that were maintained regularly. This situation was quite different from the majority of procurement activity that entailed purchase ordering direct from suppliers.

Chandler [2] identified the relationship that "structure follows strategy" as long ago as 1962. The strategy within the Trust needed to be to facilitate the automation of procurement and significantly increase compliance with expenditure limits with new and existing contracts. Delivering change presents a range of implications that can work against the required goal. Woodward's 1965 study [3] found that technology and structure were closely related, and the work within Leeds represents this theory in practice. With the introduction of computerized requisitioning systems, the ability of the organization to change its procurement process was possible.

While no formal analysis has been undertaken regarding the ease that internal customers (requisitioners) found with these new systems, it was clear in staff interviews that the new systems were quickly adopted. This may be explained by additional studies that followed Woodward's work, such as that of Charles Perrow [4]. Perrow argued that technology could be analyzed as to the extent to which the technology was predictable, and not the extent to which the technology was complex. Within the Leeds experience, the technology was much easier to navigate than the inevitable bureaucracy that accompanies the traditional procurement process. As a consequence, rapid implementation has been experienced as the process is perceived as simple and intuitive.

When considering its structure, Leeds can be described as vertically and horizontally differentiated, as shown in Figure 8-3.

Figure 8-3 develops the notion of layers of management within such a large and complex organization. Computerized requisitioning systems brought order as they presented the user with a fast and friendly user interface. The requisitioner logs on to their PC, and can then requisition from a custom catalog that is tailored to their agreed-upon requirements. This can eliminate the human error often seen by procurement as *maverick* buying. It does not, however, thwart staff that are determined to go around established systems.

In the example of Wilson and Rosenfeld's organization [5] with high vertical differentiation, delivering a custom catalog to the customer exerts managerial control because the customer can only buy what they see. Simultaneously, the service provided by this system is faster, easier, and communicates progress at all stages. Experience has shown with this solution that change was easy to sell based on process improvement

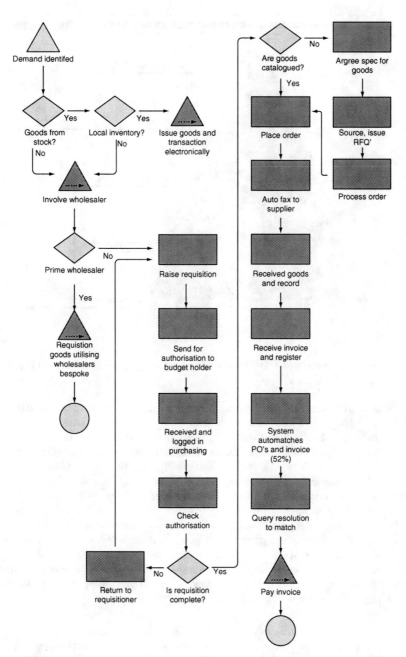

FIGURE 8-2. Simplified administration/requisition process flow for Leeds Teaching Hospitals.

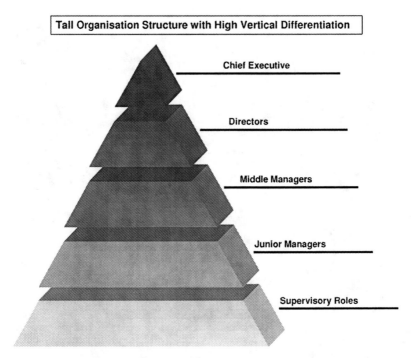

Tall Organisation Structure with High Vertical Differentiation

Chief Executive

Directors

Middle Managers

Junior Managers

Supervisory Roles

FIGURE 8-3. Organizational differentiation at Leeds Teaching Hospitals (based on [5]).

for the customer, while delivering managerial control. The *nondecisions*, as described by Bachrach and Baratz [6], are at work here.

Each individual brings with them their own self interest set to the organization, and this is particularly the case within Leeds, with over 600 consultant medical staff, all experts in their own field. The change delivered by this first step within the internal process of procurement was deceptive, because it provided processes that delivered a greater degree of control for the individual customer while simultaneously delivering control for the organization.

The introduction of this technology and its rapid adoption as seen within Leeds has changed the nature of the procurement power within the organization. Two power relationships now exist (see Table 8-1). The introduction of this system occurred organically with adoption driven by user acceptance and marketing by customers converted to the system. The power relationships were key to eProcurement supporting the standardization of process to allow automation to take place.

TABLE 8-1. The power relationship within the procurement process for transactions.

Central Control	Customer Control
The items available for the customer to requisition	*Timing of requirements*
The supplier to be used	*The quantity to be requisitioned*
The price and contract arrangement in place	

While these system changes have delivered progress in process change, the internal challenge of procurement remains to ensure that the organization buys the right items. The challenges of catalog management, standardization, and variety reduction remain firmly on the agenda.

This change was one of the important building blocks for successful eProcurement, because the development of a clean catalog was essential for the requisitioning *front end* of the procurement process. Power has definitely changed, although the shift could not be described as total, nor should this be the aim, because the development of a catalog range genuinely occurs best with the involvement of the expert client. Commodity products that do not require such expert user input, however, are no longer a procurement challenge when managed through this system.

Administration: The First Benefit Horizon

The NHS Purchasing and Supply Agency identified a range of benefits that they believe will accrue following the deployment of eCommerce (PASA eCommerce strategy/eProcurement [7]). The headlines are similar to those that are researched here, but no estimate of cost reduction and savings was made. Toy [8] described the problems that are associated with return-on-investment (ROI) analysis, stating that most eCommerce projects over promise and under deliver. Toy recommends that organizations put monitoring systems in place to analyze ROI and the progress that has been made from Day One.

Verespej [9] cites savings within the telecommunications sector as between 15% and 40% saved on MRO (Maintenance, Repair and Operations) items. Within Leeds, it is too early to release cash benefits within the Purchasing Department. The supplies strategy document also clarifies that when resources are released they will be redirected to information management, which is what has happened to date. This process is intended to promote the development of the virtuous circle, to provide more cataloged items that take less time to order and thus free up more staffing resources.

Systems Strategy to Deliver Administration Benefits

Introduction

Figure 8-2 illustrates the process flow of information. Like most organizations, Ward and Griffiths describe information management as, "a 'legacy' resulting from a less than strategic approach to information systems/information technology in the past." ([10], p. 1).

Leeds was no different from many organizations in this respect, and the need to integrate much of the process flow was essential to delivering the levels of improvement required. Scrapping the organization's existing systems was not an option based on cost alone. Although many of the systems worked well, they simply did not have the level of integration required for the organization. This was a key driver in streamlining process improvement.

GAP Analysis

A GAP analysis is illustrated in Table 8-2. This was a very useful tool for examining the strategy for systems. After analyzing the organizations' Business Plans for 1999–2000 and 2000–2001, the Trust was seen as diverse and required a greater focus on corporate

TABLE 8-2. GAP analysis for Leads Teaching Hospital, NHS Trust.

CHARACTERISTIC	DETAIL	CURRENT POSITION	DESIRED POSITION
Size	• Largest Trust in the UK • Represents approx. 1% of whole of the NHS • National specialities and Regional specialities • Historic financial difficulties with overspending the norm	• 15000 staff and annual turnover of around £600 million per annum • Expenditure approx. £150million non pay p.a. • Leader in the provision of certain services within the NHS and lead center for Teaching and Research • Anticipated overspend each year of £10 to £15 millions	• Bring the organization into financial balance • Continue to develop and deliver services of the highest quality • To utilize all resources to the best advantage and reduce waste which can be directed toward direct patient care • Reduce expenditure on bought in goods and services by a minimum of 3% per annum
Structure	• Many tiers within the organization: vertically differentiated • Large organization with many Clinical Directorates (34) plus administration support • Nearly 400 staff utilizing the purchasing service via a number of routes	• Organized to deliver effective patient focused services • Bureaucratic necessitated to support public accountability: but could be streamlined • Based on 8 sites with 6 main hospitals • Modern in healthcare terms, traditional in business terms	• Improve business processes • Reflect modern practices within the business environment • Deliver efficiency in organization and healthcare structure
Style	• Sharing of access to support services such as Human Resources Finance and Procurement	• Federation of clinical departments working and 'trading' together • Support systems which are designed and delivered to support the main aim of excellence in healthcare, but delivered seamlessly and which support these aims within the existing resources	• Integrated organization whose determinant is excellence in healthcare

(Continued)

TABLE 8-2. *(Continued)*

CHARACTERISTIC	DETAIL	CURRENT POSITION	DESIRED POSITION
Skills	• Highly complex organisation with expertise at all levels • Leading practitioners in management and healthcare delivery • Leading practitioners within teaching and research	• Professional knowledge • Political awareness within a highly politicised environment • Within procurement high number of professional qualified staff and IT expertise	• Integrate the expertise that exists within clinical and business arenas • Clearly defined and easy navigable processes which allow skilled staff to undertake their core role Automate processes where possible to reduced costs and deliver predictable results
Staff		• Executive Directors with national profile • Clinical experts • Business specialists • Nursing staff (6000) • Support staff both admin' and facilities	• Truly integrated management team • Business process becomes to norm to support healthcare agenda: clinical experts to support this • Clinical excellence becomes to norm, managerial staff to support this • Customer service to the fore
Systems	• Purchasing (Oracle 10.7) • Payment and Accounting (Oracle 10.7) • Hand held computing/ data capture: bar code technology • data analysis	• Good systems including latest generation ERP system Oracle 10.7 • Procurement information systems working well, but integration at reporting (post event) in the main • Developing data reporting tool SPAMMIS (Supplies Purchasing and Materials Management Information System) • Highly developed intranet and network with over 5000 connections	• Integrated reporting and data analysis • Systems that support easy and effective management of large amounts of data • Less manual intervention • Easy to use and effective • Strategic data to move the procurement agenda forward • Seamless data integration
Shared Goals		• Business strategy and clinical strategy do not converge • Have sufficient funds to deliver healthcare needs for our patients • Eliminate waste and concentrate on the organisations core agenda	• Integrated business and healthcare strategy • Engage staff effectively within both areas of the organizations agendas • Service and quality focus • Reduce our cost base to remain effective

goals. The Supplies Strategy (2000–2001) identified the specific issues of information management for procurement that are also considered in the GAP analysis.

Some of the specific issues for procurement to consider are the following:

- Size—the largest U.K. healthcare provider, the Trust has great resource opportunities but huge challenges in terms of financial position. A recurring problem with overspending provides great focus for the procurement discipline within the organization as a whole. During difficult financial times, procurement finds many new friends, which is a similar theme across the NHS
- Structure—Size and complexity are the main obstacles to business integration for the Trust. As assessed earlier the organization was both vertically and horizontally differentiated
- Style—seen as a federation of clinical services operating separately, support functions were seen as ancillary to the process of healthcare delivery rather than a facilitator of them. The goals described by the business planning process required a seamless and integrated approach to the organization's primary goal
- Skills—with vast skills resources, the plans identified the need to harness this expertise in automated and facilitated environments. This contrasted with the existing bureaucracy
- Staff—seen as the organization's strength, a truly integrated management approach was necessary to deliver the required outcomes. This was not the original position, with independent working seen as the norm
- Systems—good systems foundations existed, but little was found in terms of an integrated approach for financial functions. Success delivered elsewhere within the Trust with information systems for direct management of healthcare had been achieved. The infrastructure of the organization's communications and Intranet were seen as a major plus
- Shared Goals—goals were mainly focused on functional areas, and not corporate/organizational aims. The Trust wished to engender greater cross-functional working and delivery of an integrated approach

The GAP analysis was useful in understanding some of the challenges facing the Trust, and the procurement function in particular. This contextualization also helps with the analysis of what needed to happen for the organization within its wider business goals.

SWOT Analysis

To further analyze the environmental factors, a SWOT analysis was undertaken.

SWOT Analysis

Strengths

Forward-thinking culture
Track record of procurement success: consistent delivery against national targets
IT skills available
High-level commitment to procurement function

Weaknesses

Mature marketplace for many procured items meant continuous cost reduction was difficult
Excellent working relationships with suppliers, but changing systems is difficult without supplier support

Poor integration of information

Huge amounts of data to manage if success is to be achieved

Little capital investment available

Opportunities

Suppliers may be as interested in the administrative cost reductions as Leeds: some had indicated empathy in discussion with the Trust

Current technology was now more able to deliver integration than at any time

Business model could demonstrate that lower administrative costs for the Trust would generate competitive advantage when selecting suppliers

Threats

Pressure to keep the service running at a time when investment is required to modify the process

Required capital investment unknown: could the project be too expensive to deliver meaningful results?

Suppliers may not be ready, or may be unwilling to change

From the SWOT analysis, many organizational goals can be seen as target areas. The weaknesses are actually drivers for the organization to deliver more effective procurement, with the challenge being the delivery of this goal.

The lack of integrated systems and data management was a real issue for the organization during 2000–2001. Of particular concern was the relationship management with suppliers of the Trust, because the project could only have limited success if the other party would not work with the organization to deliver these goals.

A major plus, however, was that the analysis of the internal administrative costs were such that similar percentage returns might be possible for suppliers. If so, the case for change would be easier to navigate with these external organizations.

These two analysis tools have demonstrated that the goal of reduced administration costs is achievable. Indeed, the culture of the organization points towards these goals being supported at a macro level. Within such a diverse organization, the task for procurement was to devise a strategy for information management. With effective management of the organization's data, the practical steps for eProcurement would be overcome.

Clean Catalog

Drivers for Data Management

Figure 8-2 maps the administration process for procurement. Within the process, there is a concentration on the administration of procurement and not the value-added elements for the organization. Porter's value chain [11] is a useful model in assessing the drive for a clean catalog (see Figure 8-4). In Chapter 2, the value chain concept was presented as an overarching model for describing all processes in a hospital with the clinical processes as primary activities. Value chain-based analysis can be performed on all levels of an organization. Figure 8-4 shows the purchasing department's specific value chain, which focuses on purchasing activities as primary activities.

Particularly for purchasing, there is an emphasis on the effective processing of procurement demands quickly, which is necessitated by the need to ensure that the

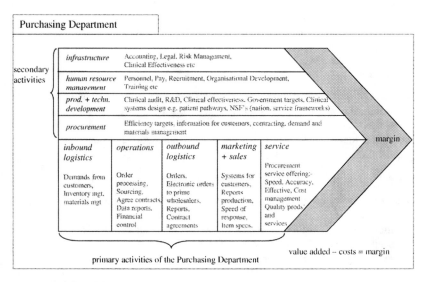

FIGURE 8-4. Value chain to analzse the procurement process within Leeds.

hospitals continue to function. Materials requirement planning is difficult, because patients can not be planned in the same way as typical production. Over time, however, reliable supply provisioning can respond to these demands with appropriate inventory and demand management systems. This can be seen in the Materials Management service provided within the Trust, where inventory is reduced by up to 80% (Leeds Teaching Hospitals Supplies Strategy, 2000–2001).

Activities concentrate less on the value-added areas and more on the process controls. This is evidenced by the manpower employed in each area, with approximately 69% of office-based staff undertaking these roles compared to those negotiating contracts.

The strategy clearly identified the need for the service to release personnel from these administrative activities and redirect resources to the value-added processes. Accompanying this drive for change, the procurement function adopted a comprehensive training initiative. This included sponsoring staff to undertake the Chartered Institute of Purchasing and Supply qualifications, and resulted in their achieving the Investor in People award in the spring of 2002.

The value chain was extremely useful in highlighting the drivers for change, particularly when considering the investment for IT. It could not be considered alone, as there are many value chains within the organization, particularly with the horizontal differentiation as represented by the clinical directorates. One of the most significant elements of this tool was the identification of the importance of data to the organization. Ward and Griffiths commented that, "to maximise performance a business needs to match demand and supply precisely. This explains why firms have been pushing IS/IT tentacles outwards to capture this information earlier and more accurately." ([10], p. 221).

The first building block for eCommerce within Leeds was the development of a clean catalog. This sounds much easier than reality would testify. If the eCommerce project was to be a success, it needed to concentrate on an area that was both high profile and high value to gain high-level commitment. The danger with such a strategy was that failure would also present high-risk issues.

The area chosen for the project was the cardiac catheter laboratories at Leeds General Infirmary. This is Europe's largest suite of cardiac labs, with five operating theater rooms. The service delivers interventional cardiac procedures, including angioplasty, stenting, ablation, and implantation of pacemakers and implantable cardiac defibrillators. The labs spend around £30,000 per day, ostensively on consumable items, and a further £20,000 per day on implantable products.

The inventory was fast moving, and recorded by the purchasing department's computerized inventory management system. The positive element in choosing this area was that the products were well managed internally with a good catalog.

The Catalog

A computerized inventory was a good starting point for implementation. The catalog worked well, but was not truly clean. The catalog range was fixed in accordance with the contracting cycle. For the purposes of eCommerce, the catalog had to contain the attributes described in Table 8-3.

Developing this level of information was not easy within the existing ERP system, so the decision was made to develop a cleaning area for the catalog prior to loading this within the Trust's ERP system (Oracle 10.7). This decision proved critical in the success of delivering change. While it was first thought, naively, that the Trust would present the majority of problems in delivering a clean catalog, suppliers also presented a number of challenges to the Trust. Effectively, they needed to re-engineer their processes to ensure that they presented clean information each time they transacted with the Trust. This administration was the basic process in any procurement relationship, but one that equally challenged the suppliers. The net effect of two bad databases is a high-cost administrative process, particularly as each transaction would need to be resolved before any invoices could be paid. Commenting in Hospital Materials Management, GHX Vice President of Marketing Bruce Johnson stated that, "hospitals aren't the only the only ones with inefficiencies within their supply chain." [12].

SPAMMIS (a SQL server-based database) was developed as a consequence by the Trust, to manage the necessary clean data. Extensive discussions took place with suppliers to ensure that the data maintained by both parties was correct. This meant changing relationships with suppliers to include customer services staff in addition to the sales and marketing staff. Relationship management was an unexpected challenge in delivering eCommerce, but one that played a major role.

Ward and Griffiths [10] commented that effective information management presents many problems, including data that resides on multiple databases, proprietary databases, and data that is of poor quality, resulting in a legacy of many years of uncoordinated

TABLE 8-3. The Clean Catalog.

Number	Attribute for Clean Catalog
1	Description matching suppliers
2	Orderable part number matching suppliers
3	Searchable part number match suppliers
4	Price match
5	Unit of purchase match
6	Bar code match
7	Leeds stock code

development. The Leeds experience closely supports this view and the need for change was recognized by those suppliers who were approached initially.

Once the two organization's data sets were validated against one another, maintaining the information was relatively easy. Applying simple disciplines that the data remained current for agreed periods of time meant that a structured review of the data set was possible. The key difference in practice was that this was undertaken together.

Many examples of the market relationship exist. The boom of the 1990's that saw the explosion of electronic trading, was largely led by the myriad of new dot-com ventures, such as Amazon.com. These trading relationships brought cataloged items and browsing to the client as an essential element of the offer. EDI, because of its costs, was restricted to B2B relationships and was only of value where volume could justify an ROI. These models, however, are at both ends of the continuum, and the emergence of deeply integrated web portals, such as GHX, provide another perspective for procurement.

Both hierarchical and electronic marketplaces have their place, and usually within the same organization. The differentiation between the utilization of these service provisions is the application for which they are used. The hybrid model for healthcare allows maximum competition while similarly providing compliance and integration.

Market Segmentation

Leeds is a horizontally and vertically differentiated organization. It includes multiple sites and is vast in healthcare terms—some £100million or more larger in turnover than the next largest NHS Trust. It serves a range of recognized healthcare needs, as well as specialist areas. The organization is already segmented by the very nature of what it does. Doyle argues that, "Segmentation increases profit opportunities because different groups of customers attract different values to the solutions offered." [13].

Purchasing must also respond to this, and can use this technique to identify where real value can be added and, of equal importance, where costs can be avoided.

So why segment procurement? The rationale for this approach is demonstrated by Figure 8-5, which shows the relationship between procurement and the numbers of suppliers that are used. As can be seen, there is the recognizable Pareto effect. This broadly accords with an anticipated 80/20 spilt. More interesting is the figure at 70% that shows a distinct element to the supplier base and the concentration of purchasing with the top 106 suppliers. It is on this basis, and at this level, that the route to market has been segmented.

Similar to marketing strategy, these two elements of the supplier base have been identified as having special characteristics, which are significant to the operations strategy for the procurement process. The first 106 suppliers have been targeted by Leeds as the area for deeply integrated eCommerce, but the balance of the suppliers necessitates a different approach.

By combining these elements, the organization is able to determine the eCommerce approach that best suits the associated expenditure. This is not atypical of many organizations, but is particularly pronounced within Leeds as a consequence of the large supplier base.

By referring back to the value chain, the segmentation of operations is applicable to the primary activities identified by procurement. The costs of what Malone and co-authors [14] describe as coordination costs, are the essential area of differentiation. The Trust has decided to differentiate based on the cost benefit of the process.

For Leeds, the models of transaction process are not mutually exclusive but complimentary. By adopting such an approach, strategic sourcing can be maintained while

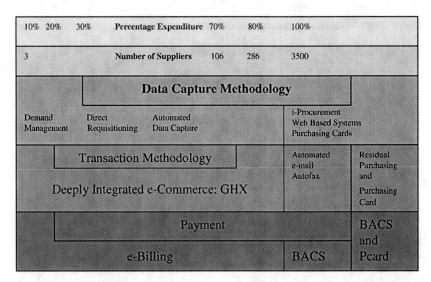

| 10% 20% | 30% | Percentage Expenditure 70% | 80% | 100% |
| 3 | | Number of Suppliers 106 | 286 | 3500 |

FIGURE 8-5. Leeds Teaching Hospital's route to market (based on [17]): selection of eCommerce strategy[1].

the organization automates the lower-value, higher-cost procurement at the tail of the Pareto curve.

So what are the essential differences between the two approaches? EDI was the first electronic trading process to require the means of supporting detailed catalog management by both buyer and seller. If either partner neglected this activity, the process would either fail by drowning in queries, or one of the parties would find themselves trading on terms that they had not agreed to—essentially costing them money.

Electronic markets, such as the U.K.-based UKProcure, operate systems that allow the buyer to access a range of suppliers, and sourcing becomes relatively easy. Price, however, becomes secondary, even if only marginally so, as does cost, because these Web-based systems provide a vendor-managed catalog service only.

The experience at Citius is somewhat different. This Belgium company pioneered the management of catalogs specific to the client, while hosting an eCommerce process that could link many buyers and suppliers together. Citius started trading with a range of office products including consumables, furniture, and equipment. Catalogs were stored on a series of servers on which buyers could have specific data stored, including authorization limits and pricing. Technology was completely hosted by the eCommerce provider. Studies of Citius identified that this methodology delivered a cost savings of 20–45%. The Citius experience broadly accords with the GHX model, with some notable exceptions.

The requirement for the purchaser to maintain a catalog of their required products is a cornerstone of good procurement practice. While Citius provided this service for the buyer, there is always the need to validate the information. Without such validation,

---

[1] BACS: Bank Automated Credit Systems used for money transfer between banking organisations as a means of electronic payment. Purchasing Card: Corporate Credit card using merchant catagories for low cost purchasing spend with some restricted purchasing control.

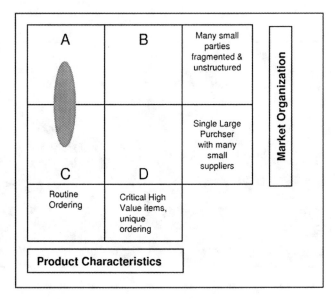

FIGURE 8-6. Purchasing market segmentation (based on [15]).

the purchaser does not always know if they are buying the right item from the right supplier at the right price. The segmentation of the product mix for procurement—a key component of Leeds' eCommerce launch strategy—is described in the next section.

Figure 8-6 shows four market sectors and differentiation to which the various eProcurement offerings can cater. Sector A is often represented by concentrated businesses such as monopolistic or oligopolistic industries. Sector B represents sectors such as construction with high-value and one-off purchases that are relatively unstructured. Sector C represents an area where routine ordering exists and products change very little. Sector D tends to represent one-off purchasing project areas such as large construction projects and event organizations.

The Leeds experience is represented by the grey ellipse. The NHS exists in all of these sectors, but the areas to address for eProcurement appear in Sectors A and B, and this has been the strategic response of electronic marketplace suppliers.

Administration Summary

"By removing the administrative burden of order placing and providing improved management information, e-procurement provides a powerful platform from which to exploit the organizations strategic leverage and undertake major total supply chain cost improvements." ([16], p. 35)

Croom is referring to the experience of BT within the United Kingdom. The initial assessments of eCommerce have more generally hyped the message of savings and improved performance, and early claims have largely exceeded the achieved results. Nevertheless, the eCommerce agenda has delivered some notable beneficiaries and their experience is useful in helping to understand where Leeds can improve, and where it has already delivered optimized benefits.

Few studies have identified the benefits separately by analyzing the various components of eCommerce. The majority of studies have looked at the totality of the implementation. The difference with Leeds is that the benefit process has been incremental. This very much reflects the emergent strategy that Leeds has developed in relation to the project. Johnson and Scholes' emergent strategy model in Figure 8-7 describes the Leeds experience particularly well [17].

The original goal was to reduce administrative costs. New horizons have subsequently emerged, including the facilitation of competitive advantage and supply chain rationalization, which are discussed later.

The model adopted by Leeds recognizes the need for both the hosting of catalog information by the eCommerce supplier, the ultimate vendor, and the buyer. Without these three key components, the management of procurement compliance (i.e., buying contracted goods that are fit for purpose and value for money) is very difficult. With the discipline of all three parties validating copies of the data, trading is an easy process. The Leeds experience has shown that for the organizations connected to the GHX exchange, there have been zero errors since the first transaction on February 4, 2002.

Administrative benefits are significant when viewed on a cost per transaction basis. A key element, however, is achieving critical mass to deliver these benefits through volume to the organization. In this respect, the Leeds experience has shown that preparation is everything, and that growing the database of traded items takes time and effort. Once completed, maintenance is relatively easy with a good working relationship with the vendor.

Eakin [18] cites that benefits from eProcurement are beyond dispute. He further states in a review of overall eProcurement benefits that potential savings are quite different from realized savings. The benefits found within Leeds included

- The cost of raising the purchase order
- Sourcing
- Error rate reduced to zero on all expenditures through the deeply integrated GHX route
- Invoice queries reduced to zero
- Delivery errors reduced to zero—no returns administration required

Toy analyzes the benefits of eProcurement and the return on investment. Interestingly, one important element is the process of catalog management, and he states that "Virtually

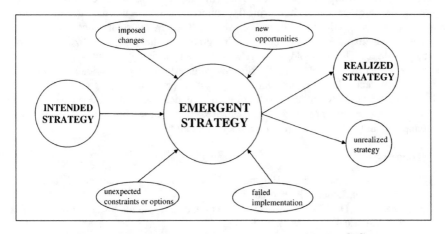

FIGURE 8-7. Development of the emergent strategy (based on [17]).

every company experiences one or more of the following issues…catalogue management has proven to be more difficult and costly than expected." ([8], p. 46)

This view is underscored by Moore [19], who cites research into the U.S. experience of MRO within the chemical engineering industry. Of particular note are his comments regarding the maintenance of the catalog environment, which he sees as the contributory factor for many organizations abandoning the eMRO marketplace. It is not surprising, then, that many buy-side organizations have struggled with the catalog maintenance issue. If the eProcurement provider finds this a major challenge, then matching this data in three places multiplies the problems many times. Fast, accurate, and flexible data management must be a key factor.

This has been achieved at Leeds, and represents one of the critical success factors—the development of the SQL server-based database, SPAMMIS. The SPAMMIS system was a key driver in automating the management of contracted items and as a means of ensuring that data uploaded to the organization's ERP system was always clean. This process was a core requirement of the procurement process—goods and services must match what the vendor believes they are supplying.

The Leeds experience developed a deeply integrated eCommerce solution. This integration was the first of its kind in healthcare, and a leading example of integration across many industry sectors. The key drivers for change were the milestones identified by the failures in previous systems. These included the performance of first-time, purchase-to-pay invoice matching, the high cost of purchasing administration, and the need to improve customer engagement. Relationship management with suppliers played a key part in developing the solutions that were found. The need for suppliers to reduce their own costs, and the recognition that their own processes could be better delivered, provided a real driver for them. Harmonizing these goals and harnessing them to the drive for profits from suppliers gave an additional impetus for change.

The example at Leeds was a genuine virtuous circle, but like all business process, it was not perfect. Progress was dependent upon relationship management and the technology had to work—it did. Selecting the right business process for the right business objective was key to ensuring that the strategy delivered added value.

Customers, suppliers, and technology providers, including internal technology development, all played a significant role in making change occur. The system and process remain live however, and will require regular maintenance. With so many organizational interfaces, relationship management will need to maintained while the technology is being proven. Staff turnover within these critical supplier organizations will need to be monitored, and the relationships that have been established will require constant maintenance.

The Leeds experience was built on integration technologies, utilizing primarily legacy systems. The technology effort was focused on deploying links between these systems to realize benefits. This is perhaps where the real success can be measured in terms of technology. Utilizing existing systems and harnessing their value with the use of SPAMMIS and the GHX solution provided the best platform on which to build. Re-engineering provided Leeds with real and measurable benefits from which purchasing, and the Trust overall, continues to benefit.

References

[1] Slack, N., S. Chambers, C. Harland, A. Harrison and R. Johnston. (1995) *Operations Management.* London, Pitman Publishing.

[2] Chandler, A. D. (1962) Strategy and structure: chapters in the history of the industrial enterprise. Cambridge (MA): MIT Press.

[3] Woodward, J. (1965) *Industrial Organisation: Theory and Practice.* London: Oxford University Press.

[4] Perrow, C. (1967) A Framework for the Comparative Analysis of Organizations. *American Sociological Review.* **32**, 194–208.

[5] Wilson, D.C. and R. H. Rosenfeld. (1990) *Managing Organisations.* London: McGraw-Hill International.

[6] Bachrach, P. and M. S Baratz. (1970) Power and Poverty. New York: Oxford University Press.

[7] NHS Purchasing and Supply Agency (2003). *E-commerce Policy.* Available from: <www.pasa.doh.gov.uk/purchasing/policies/polecomweb.doc> and *eProcurment.* Available from: <http://www.pasa.nhs.uk/eprocurement/> [Accessed 18 November 2006]

[8] Toy, P. W. (2001) The Saving Grace: getting the ROI out of E (Electronic Procurement). Purchasing B2B, Toronto, Jul-Aug. 46.

[9] Verespej. M.A. (2002) E-Procurement Explosion. *Industry Week.* **251**(2), 24.

[10] Ward, J. and P. Griffiths. (1996) *Strategic Planning for Information Systems.* Chichester: Wiley and Sons.

[11] Porter, M. E. (1984) *Competitive Advantage.* New York: Free Press.

[12] DeJohn, P. (2001) Slow and steady wins race to e-success, GHX verifies. *Hospital Materials Management.* **26** (11), 1, 9–11.

[13] Doyle, P. (1994) *Marketing Management and Strategy.* Oxford: Prentice Hall.

[14] Malone, T.W., J. Yates, and R. I. Benjamin. (1989) The Logic of Electronic Market. *Harvard Business Review.* **67**(3), 166–8, 170, 172.

[15] Timmers, P. (2000) Electronic Commerce: Strategies and Models for Business-to-Business Trading. Chichester: John Wiley & Sons.

[16] Croom, S. (2001) *Supply Chain Management in the E-Business Era: an investigation into Supply Chain Strategies, Practices and Progress in E-Business Adoption.* Coventry: S.C Associates.

[17] Johnson, G. and K. Scholes. (1993) *Exploring Corporate Strategy.* Englewood Cliffs (NJ): Prentice Hall.

[18] Eakin, D. (2002) Measuring e-Procurement benefits. *Government procurement.* **10**, 6–12.

[19] Moore, J. (2003) Manufacturers struggle with e-procurement but still see gains. Chemical Engineering Progress. **99**(9), 23.

9
Supply Chain Management on Clinical Units

BARBARA L. VAN DE CASTLE AND GINA SZYMANSKI

Executive Summary

This chapter provides the reader with a discussion of how healthcare supplies can be efficiently managed in a hospital clinical unit. Effective unit supply management involves understanding patient profiles, defining recurrent nursing and multidisciplinary standards of care, facilitating ongoing collaboration between the supply chain stakeholders, and investing in automated supply systems. Partnerships between nurse managers, clinical staff, and materials management staff is critical to the overall success of unit-based supply management and disbursement.

A unique example of supply chain planning and forecasting centered on patient profiles and nursing standards is the expansion of a patient service based on demand and evolving technologies. Peripherally inserted central line catheters (PICCs) are used to provide venous access for many types of patients. In our large, comprehensive cancer center, these catheters are integral to providing long-term therapies to patients while minimizing other peripheral and central catheter-related complications, patient discomfort, and cost. The evolution of PICC catheter technology has been dramatic and, coupled with bedside ultrasound technology, has increased the PICC insertion success rate for trained nurses at the bedside. Our nursing-led PICC team developed an inclusive strategy for improving access to the latest PICC technology for all patients. They redefined the PICC placement standard of care and worked with the supply chain stakeholders, both internal and external, to organize a pilot study. This included purchasing and stocking upgraded PICC catheters and exploring the latest ultrasound technologies. In the short term, it was projected that the upgraded catheter selection and associated placement supplies, and the service expansion by the PICC team, would promote patient and staff satisfaction, decrease central line catheter placement costs and associated complications, and improve patient safety. The accomplishments achieved by the collaboration between materials management, the Clinical Value Analysis Committee, and the clinical nursing staff were immediately measurable. The number of requests for the new PICC doubled, new oncology patient populations were added to the eligibility list, the wait time for PICC placement went from an average of 48–72 hours to 24 hours, nurse satisfaction reports regarding ease of placement and success rate soared, and anecdotal reports from patients related to discomfort and wait time were very favorable. In addition, this inclusive group was able to make their mark in the organization by tackling more difficult outcomes, such as the impact of the supply changes and practice on length of stay and blood stream infection rates, both of which affect the hospitals financial bottom line. This is one of many performance successes our hospital's clinical staff has been able to achieve through an available and engaged supply chain.

Unit profiling of patient demographics and reasons for patient admissions allows materials management to assist the healthcare team in developing a supply inventory that meets patient needs and ensures safe, quality patient care. Communication between unit-based healthcare team members regarding new patient care practices is essential and, together with recurring standards of care, will facilitate supply forecasting and fiscal supply planning. The use of automated inventory management that provides consistent supply availability with minimal shelf inventory and patient specific real time charge capture is a 21st century technology investment that must be considered in future healthcare environments. This chapter provides examples of this technology and encourages the reader to explore options with nursing and materials management in an effort to link standards of care with supplies.

Introduction

An automated system of supply management is the trend in today's hospitals in the United States [1]. Revenue capture in hospitals using automated patient-charge systems or supply-scan systems have risen as much as 95% compared to 70% with manual patient charge systems [2]. Because a primary goal for materials management staff is adding value while reducing costs, it is logical to consider using an automated supply system. Achieving this goal depends on the collaboration and a commitment to more vertical integration of supply chain customers. The disconnect between end users, hospital staff, and the supply procurement process results in product design flaws, a lack of standardization, and supply inventory and delivery cycles that promote hoarding and *shelved* purchase dollars. The disengaged supply chain ultimately affects the care of the patient—the supply consumer.

Supply management on clinical units centers on the needs of the patient. The nurse/unit manager is ultimately responsible for overseeing patient care and ensuring that the multidisciplinary providers have the supplies they need to care for the patient. The organization of nursing care and other disciplines is built around standards of care that define what the patient can expect from the healthcare team in terms of physical care, communication, decision-making and outcomes. Standards of care help drive supply inventory, as does unit-specific patient demographics and reasons for admission. Regardless of the systems for supply inventory, disbursement, and dispensing, supply needs are a collaborative effort between unit staff and the materials management department. It is here that an exclusive electronic focus on information exchange begins to loose value. Instead, a multidisciplinary clinical value analysis team bridges the gap between people and the relationship-distancing technology. Representative multidisciplinary staff executes the dialog necessary to standardize inventory, bring in new value-added products at a cost savings, and create product substitution catalogs that do not interrupt the delivery of safe patient care.

Automated supply stations support the patient care mission of timely and safe quality patient care. These systems ensure supply standardization, supply availability, and fiscal accountability for purchased dollars spent on the supply inventory. Performance reports are useful in understanding overall supply performance and trends by user, and in evaluating cost and revenue targets.

The business of supply management in busy hospital units is complicated at best. Reasonableness, affordability, and value must be central to all supply procurement processes. As healthcare providers, we must embrace our ongoing commitment to the best value at a reduced cost and continue to advance IT applications in the delivery of patient care.

The Difficulty in Achieving the Highest Value at the Lowest Cost

The supply chain is part of a larger healthcare value chain that serves to more vertically integrate producers, purchasers, providers of healthcare, financial intermediaries, and payers in an attempt to simultaneously add value and reduce costs [3]. Healthcare has met with mixed results in trying to achieve the *value at the lowest cost* goal as compared to other industries. This is mainly due to the role of the *end user* in supply procurement, the *not-for-profit* status of the majority of the providers in the healthcare industry, the lack of provider leadership in industry standardization, decentralization of decision-making to the front line, the goal of providers to make technical investments in patient care as opposed to infrastructure, and information system investments [3]. The doctor, the nurse, and the pharmacist drive the ordering of the products—these are the end users that seem to be at the root of the problem in trying to attain the highest value at the lowest cost [3].

The end user has no core competencies in purchasing, contract negotiation, or distribution, nor do they actually pay for the product. The hospital administration, however, has sanctioned decision-making for supply management to this front line where clinical outcomes rest with those who deliver the care. The end user orders products in a way that ensures availability at the cost of *holding or shelving* inventory. This philosophy promotes overstocking, which is tied to a cost. These *dormant* purchase dollars are dollars that can be used towards other expenses. Product selection by this group is based on preference rather than a cost-benefit analysis and what the healthcare provider (the hospital) can afford. End-user autonomy and the public's goals of access and quality have derailed the provider's *best business practice* philosophy for supply procurement [3].

Customers and Consumers in the Supply Chain

To understand the process of supply procurement in hospitals, and specifically on inpatient units, one must first ask the questions, "Who is the customer?" and "What systems are available to support their supply needs?" On an inpatient unit, the patient mix dictates what supplies will be used, in what quantity, and under what conditions. The patient receives, and ultimately pays, for the supplies, Therefore, the patient is the *consumer*. The multidisciplinary healthcare team—predominately the physician, nurse and pharmacist—will advocate for the type and quality of inventory, the amount or volume needed on hand, and how the supplies will be used to deliver care to the patient. This team defines and executes the standards of care, specific for each patient population, and can be considered the *customer* in supply procurement on the inpatient unit. Finance and administrative staff will evaluate expense and revenue reports as well as performance reports generated by automated supply systems. They are also customers in supply procurement.

The inpatient unit manager, ideally an administratively trained nurse, is ultimately responsible and accountable for representing the needs of the unit—a unit is comprised of the patient and the multidisciplinary team. The manager is a supply procurement customer and has a vested interest in the financial impact on the hospital of unit supply costs and revenue. The nurse/unit manager is responsible for knowing and understanding the patient demographics, including the reason for admission as well as the key procedures and standards of care (SOC) that are part of care delivery. The nurse manager must also have working knowledge of the supply budget process. The manager

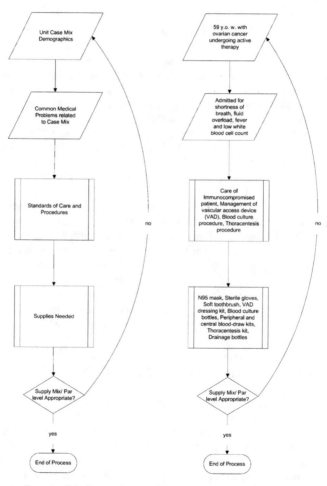

FIGURE 9-1. Forecasting supply usage with clinical information.

needs to contribute to the analysis of supply usage, as well as plan and forecast supply needs as budgets are prepared. The analysis process can be greatly enhanced by having an automated supply system that generates user, usage, and compliance reports for the manager.

Patient demographics, including age, sex, cultural diversity, socioeconomic status, and geographic draw, all contribute to understanding the potential supply needs of patients on an inpatient unit. Admission kits fully stocked with toiletries may be essential in inner-city hospitals with a high incidence of indigent care and socioeconomically disadvantaged clientele. In addition, if the average age of patients admitted to the unit is 45 years of age, the amount and types of incontinence products may be very different than for a predominately geriatric population.

A comprehensive rank-order list of *reason for admission* diagnoses is critical to understanding the supply needs of the patients on the unit. An analysis of the reason for admission diagnoses that represent 70–80% of the admissions will define the common standards of care being provided as well as the supplies that must be made available to the multidisciplinary team. Of note, the reason for admission is different than the patient's overarching healthcare diagnosis. Figure 9-1 shows the process that a nurse/unit manager would utilize to examine the admissions to the unit and common patient problems. The manager must consider the following question, "What are the standards of care that would provide the structure to care delivery and do they dictate the supplies needed for a given problem?" For example, a patient with an overarching healthcare diagnosis of ovarian cancer may have shortness of breath and fluid overload as her *reason for admission* diagnosis. Her reason for admission would predominately drive supply usage during her inpatient stay.

How Standards of Care Facilitate the Planning of Unit Supplies

Quality of care can be achieved through written standards. The organization of care on nursing units, in the hospital, and within the health system is built around standards of care. A *standard of care* defines what the patient can expect from the care delivered by one or more members of the healthcare team. Standards should establish minimum levels of performance with consistent uniformity across individuals and an organization. This uniformity can set expectations for staff, the patient, and third party purchasers of healthcare. Standards should also ensure patient safety [4]. Expectations about performance apply to healthcare organizations and the healthcare professionals in the organization, as well as the drugs and devices the organization uses to deliver care. Expectations for professional performance, and ultimately the performance of the organization, are shaped by professional groups such as the American Nursing Association and the Oncology Nursing Society, as well as purchasers of healthcare, consumers of healthcare, and society [4].

An inpatient unit that admits adult oncology patients with solid tumors for chemotherapy and symptom management issues has a discrete set of SOC and procedures that are provided to patients during their admission. If comprehensive in their development, SOCs will often include procedures and a list of supplies (implicit or explicit) needed to optimize the delivery of care to the patient.

Each discipline—the nurse, the physician, the social worker—can write their own discipline-specific standards of care that relate to the care they provide to the patient. The care processes may be in response to a discipline-specific diagnosis, health problem, or patient care need, or it may relate to a particular point on the continuum of care or a stage of development [5]. Management of patients with a patient-controlled analgesia pump or care of the patient with an immune deficiency are examples of nursing SOCs that delineate nursing actions and standardize supplies. Nursing procedures, such as urinary catheter placement, blood cultures, and vascular access device (VAD) dressing changes, are standardized procedures with predictable supply usage. Discipline-specific procedure books and hospital-specific procedure manuals are also available to guide the nurse or physician in completing a task and using supplies in the step-by-step instructions.

Multidisciplinary team members can also unite and write interdisciplinary SOCs for those care processes for which more than one discipline contributes and for which active interdisciplinary collaboration is central to quality heathcare and positive patient outcomes. Chemotherapy administration is an example of an interdisciplinary clinical SOC, that outlines the roles and responsibilities of different multidisciplinary providers. Each discipline determines part of the provider actions and needed supplies.

Relationships among the Materials Management and the Customer

There is research that supports the belief that environment affects well-being. A book called Relationship-Based Care: A Model for transforming practice [6] discusses organizational management, and work redesign with a patient outcomes orientation. The process of establishing relationships in hospital culture, specifically between the healthcare team and the materials management department, is worth exploring as e-procurement communication opportunities flourish.

Central to caring and healing cultures are relationships; relationships between the members of the healthcare team and their internal (other hospital personnel) and external (the patient and their family) customers [6]. Understanding the interdependencies between both of these relationships and their effects on the patient are essential to understanding how support services, like materials management, support the healing relationship between the patient and the primary health providers. Point-of-care materials distribution allows the nurse to spend more time applying interventions to the patient and less time looking for and retrieving supplies needed to begin the interaction. The possible hazards of electronic communication as the primary interactive tool between hospital materials management departments and the bedside providers should be carefully considered. Verbal and face-to-face communication can help when differences of understanding occur with supply items.

Customers and Production

The role of the nurse/unit manager and the multidisciplinary team in product development and production varies, from no role at all to a significant contribution depending on the relationship between the manager or hospital and the manufacturer. Participating in this phase of the supply chain requires hands-on experience with the product in question. Those healthcare providers who act as independent consultants outside of their role as a hospital or health system employee establish their own contractual relationship with the manufacturer. This relationship may start as a result of the manufacturer meeting a provider who uses their product and is interested in working together on future product development outside of the hospital structure. Involvement of legal staff is important when dealing with manufacturers in this scenario.

Manufacturers are eager to learn from the clinicians who use their product. Some relationships are informal and involve consultative sessions between the manufacturer's key research and development team members and invited hospital end users. Others involve a more formalized relationship where the outcome for both the manufacturer and the hospital are more clearly defined up front, before the relationship begins. Hospitals, as well as their employees, may establish a contractual relationship with a manufacturer that often includes the opportunity to assist in the design features, in addition to serving as a beta test site for the product prototype. Frequently, manufacturer and hospital relationships start because of a customer request for a custom product, or a desire on the part of either party to change or upgrade a current product or build a related product. The manufacturer often seeks information about how the product is currently used. They want to know what is working well and what is problematic related to product use, what the clinicians would change about the current product, and what their *wish list* would be if they could completely redesign the product for the future. They may also want to understand the providers' experience with their competition and what they like most and least about their competition's products. Safety needles and other safety technologies employed to make the needle safe for the healthcare worker to use, is an example of how provider input and experience can drive product development and usage. The evolution of the safety needle from an *active* user-initiated safety mechanism to the availability of *passive* device-initiated safety mechanism came from experiential use with these products.

Research and design engineers generally lack the hands-on functionality experience with medical products in the field. They know what they designed and what the intended use was, but the actual experience by the end user is key to understanding the products' ultimate success and longevity in the market. This type of *grass roots* consultative advice is invaluable to design engineers and the marketing team as they develop and sell their products.

Customers and Purchasing

Vendor contracts and membership in buying groups can be a sensitive and complex business process. For example, the type of non-latex, non-sterile gloves chosen by a hospital may be driven by a contractual relationship, cost, or vendor ability to meet volume demands, rather than provider preference. Participating in this phase of the supply procurement process takes specialized skill and knowledge. The unit/nursing management and the multidisciplinary team should limit their interactions with the vendors to marketing and educational decisions, rather than negotiations to obtain products and determine product costs. These types of discussions should be executed by hospital purchasing agents in advance of a product being brought into the hospital for presentation, testing, and ultimate use. This ensures compliance with existing contractual agreements and ensures the person with the skill and knowledge to negotiate the best price leads the *cost* discussions. What are most effective, and very much a key point, is that a strong, ongoing working relationship exists between the hospital purchasing department and representative multidisciplinary providers. A hospital or health system supply value analysis committee is a credible forum to meet such a challenge.

Distribution of Supplies

The role of the materials management team in the supply distribution cycle includes the movement of supplies from the manufacturer to the hospital or health system materials distribution center (MDC), from the MDC to the central supply department (CSD) in the hospital and from the CSD to the nursing unit supply room. What is important for unit management is the process flow and associated time frames created for the supply distribution cycle.

Corporate distributors may be employed to store bulk volumes of supplies, manage supply inventory, and move products from the distributor's distribution center to the MDC. The assumption, on the part of unit management, is that all supplies needed on the unit are available and ready to be distributed from the MDC. The corporate distributor ensures supply products are available in the agreed-upon quantity, quality, packaging, and time frames to facilitate the hospital's supply distribution cycle. At this distribution level, the nurse/unit manager needs to understand the management of *temporarily out of stock* items, substitution products, and discontinued items. Corporate distributors are effective if substitutions due to temporarily out of stock items are kept at a minimum, and if communication about such events is proactive enough to allow end users to anticipate the change in product. Electronic communication via email or website postings is an effective means for keeping the end user informed of changes, and to survey users about reasonable substitution products if a back-up product has not yet been identified. A hospital-specific distributor Web page that outlines services to the hospital or health system, as well as a full product inventory, would be an important resource for the unit/nurse manager.

The nurse/unit manager is most concerned with the distribution of supplies from the health system's distribution center to the unit. At this level, the nurse/unit manager needs to understand the ordering and replenishment cycle and associated time frames. The assumption is that the nurse/unit manager has identified the unique supply inventory for the specific unit, and that these supplies are available in the MDC to be systematically delivered to the unit. Appropriate and timely distribution of supplies at the unit level occurs when the nurse/unit manager has created a replenishment profile for each item, ensures the order is placed at the appropriate interval, and anticipates and supports delivery and restocking of the supply bins for the unit staff.

Case Study

Historical Progression of Supplies on a Clinical Unit

The technology associated with supply management on inpatient clinical units has evolved over time. In our large (1,000 bed) teaching hospital, supply management has seen many changes. This facility's management structure is decentralized, thus making it more difficult to standardize across the hospital. It does, however, allow for tailoring to individual units and patient populations. System processes have progressed from an open exchange cart with manual patient charging to open and closed automated systems with sophisticated inventory management, patient charging, and reporting capabilities. The progression in our institution began with open exchange carts containing supplies tagged with pink paper tickets. As items were removed from the cart, the nurse placed the pink tickets in patient-specific envelopes. These envelopes were batched and hand-delivered to the finance office for processing when the patient was discharged. This process was nursing-resource intensive and created a backlog of information to be processed by the finance staff.

Supply replenishment advanced to hand-held electronic devices, and was our institution's first introduction to supply replenishment technology. Materials management staff, using handheld devices, went on rounds and reordered stock at a set time during the day. The nurse charged their patients for supplies using a patient-specific supply charge sheet clipped to the end of the patient's bed. The nurse would indicate on the preprinted sheet when a supply item was used. These sheets were batched daily and hand-delivered to the finance office for processing. Daily collection was an improvement over batching supply sheets for an entire admission, but there was still a backlog of information to be processed by the finance office. This replenishment system was also personnel intensive and created inefficiencies in the flow of information.

Our introduction to automation came with the PAR Excellence technology (see Figure 9-2a). A control wand was used to *touch* buttons associated with each supply item taken. The *touch* served two purposes, inventory management and patient charging. This automated system was less personnel-resource intensive, but the nurse was required to actively engage the system by touching the item button. Without a physical barrier, items could be removed without touching the button creating inaccuracies in inventory and patient charging. Figure 9-2b shows a nurse dispensing a supply item using a Touch Probe.

Our current supply-dispensing cabinet is a closed automated system that still requires the nurse to actively engage the system to take supplies. This system, however, eliminates

FIGURE   9-2A. PAR Excellence display for capturing transactions at the point-of-use (with kind permission of PAR Excellence Systems, Inc.).

FIGURE 9-2B. Nurse removing a supply item from an open system (Image Courtesy of PAR Excellence Systems, Inc.).

the problem of not acknowledging an item is being taken. The system requires the staff to identify themselves as a user, identify a patient for which they are removing supplies, and press the *take* button to complete the transaction. If the take button is not touched by the staff, the machine will prompt the staff to do so. Each touch is linked to a specific staff member, encouraging the staff to have a vested interest in touching the items taken. This transaction, when done correctly, results in replenishment of the item and patient billing.

There are two types of material management systems, open systems or closed *barrier* systems. An open system will have unobstructed shelving where supplies are stocked in a container or in drawers, and supplies are freely accessible to anyone who enters the supply area. The staff member is usually required to document the use of an item on the patient's chart. This system is fraught with problems related to waste, unavailable supplies, and lost revenue from staff noncompliance with patient charging. Advantages of an open system are ease of use for a healthcare worker, and ease of replenishment for the supply clerk. If you are using rolling carts, then it is easy to replace one empty cart with a full cart daily.

The barrier, or closed system is a set of drawers or cabinets that are locked, usually with a glass door so that supplies are visible and can be easily located (see Figure 9-3 and Figure 9-4). These systems require the user, as well as the patient, to be identified prior to taking an item. A password or a scanned badge or biometrics such as a fingerprint can be used as identifiers. Supplies are not out in the open and readily accessible. The process of removing supplies can take a few moments longer, but the learning curve with use of the system is short. The ability to charge for items as part of the removal process makes up for the additional time.

FIGURE 9-3. Cabinet system Pyxis cabinet – copyright ©2004 Cardinal Health, Inc. All rights reserved. With kind permission of Cardinal Health, Inc.

These systems have a built-in emergency release so that when patients' acuity changes rapidly, all cabinets can be unlocked for quick access to all areas of supplies. Common manufacturers of these open and closed systems are Omnicell, PAR Excellence, and Cardinal Health Pyxis Products (see Table 9-1 for Web addresses for these companies).

Unit-based supplies stocked by the central supply service need a *replenishment profile* to ensure product availability. Whether an open or a closed system is used, and whether the type of inventory management and patient charging system is automated or manual, each supply item needs a replenishment profile. The profile includes a description of the item and the associated item hospital identification number, and the par level (or the *fully-stocked* amount) to be made available on the unit. In more sophisticated automated systems, the profile can further be defined to include the *re-issue level*, or the point at which the item is reordered to bring the total number of the items back up to par level, and an *urgent restocking level,* or the point at which the item must be made available

TABLE 9-1. Suppliers of cabinet systems – examples.

Company	Website
Cardinal Health Pyxis Products	http://www.cardinal.com/pyxis
Omnicell	http://www.omnicell.com/
PAR Excellence	http://www.parexcellencesystems.com/main.asp

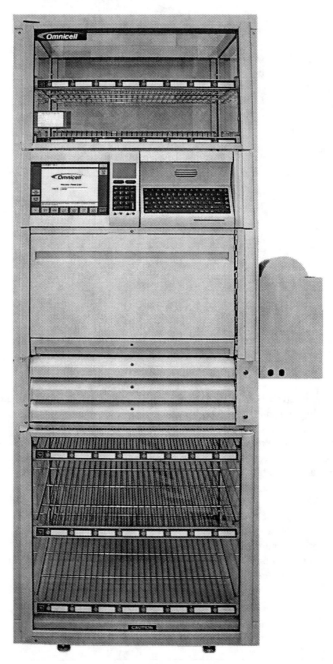

FIGURE 9-4. Omni Rx One-Cell medication dispensing cabinet with Omni Dispenser Module (with kind permission of Omnicell, Inc.).

to the unit immediately rather than waiting for the item to be replenished through the usual mechanism.

Supply levels are primarily determined by the size of the unit supply room. The room size drives the amount of inventory that can be stored at any given time. Par levels are established based on the shelf life, or the length of time (on average) that an established inventory should last. Units with limited space and small supply rooms, or hospitals with a philosophy to keep minimum inventory or *dollars* on the shelves, would be likely to consider a 24-hour replenishment par level. This would require that supplies be inventoried and many supplies reordered every 24 hours, based on the reissue level. A 48-hour par level means there should be enough of each item on hand for a 48-hour period. Supply inventory may occur daily, but replenishment will occur for most supplies every other day. Busy units with high turnover and limited supply storage may need their supply rooms inventoried and replenished more than once a day. Automated systems and finely tuned par and reissue levels facilitate this type of replenishment.

It is the responsibility of the nurse/unit manager to set up supply rooms, including the order and arrangement of related items, to support the end user. Consideration must also, however, be given to the material management staff that replenishes the items. Standardization of supply rooms across the hospital, a department or, at minimum, similar units, facilitates efficiency and accuracy in the replenishment process. Hospital safety literature also speaks to the importance of standardization of supply items, supply room locations on units, and the arrangement of supplies in a supply room across a hospital or health system. Standardization breeds safety in terms of timeliness in locating supplies and in choosing the appropriate supplies for the patient. Each unit should have identical locations for standard equipment so that staff who need to work in different units will be able to find supplies quickly [7].

The nurse/unit manager must work closely with the MDC and the CSD to understand the timing of the inventory and how it relates to supply replenishment on the unit. If par interval periods and reissue levels are set appropriately (24 hour par, 48 hour par, etc.) the time it takes for inventory and replenishment will not matter in terms of supply availability, as long as it happens at the same time every day. Replenishment should occur at a time that is not disruptive to other unit operations. It is key to minimize the gap between the time of inventory and when the supplies are delivered to the unit and restocked. The larger that time gap becomes, the more supplies are being used and the less likely it is that supplies will remain above the reissue level and not reach the urgent restocking level, which creates a flurry of additional manual labor activity.

General maintenance and functionality of a supply room is a collaborative effort between unit staff and the hospital materials management staff. Unit staff should expect supply rooms to be stocked and maintained free of supply overflow, clutter, and trash. Items should be stocked in their appropriate locations. Materials management staff should expect unit staff to utilize the supply management systems appropriately to ensure accurate inventory counts and reload items correctly to prevent inventory errors. The nurse/unit manager should lead the collaborative effort and facilitate an efficient *win-win* process for all staff involved.

Systems to Support the Customer

Value Analysis Group

Medical supply costs represent a significant portion of overall hospital costs. Purchasing the wrong supply products because of inattention to inventory management or value analysis is estimated to cost hospitals upwards of a million dollars annually [8]. Taking the time to analyze cost and quality and ensure the maximum value of purchasing dollars is a process that is overwhelming and requires the efforts of end users as well as a variety of supply administrators.

This university-based teaching hospital created a Clinical Product Value Analysis Committee (CVAC) to meet the challenge of *value* spending in medical supplies across our health system. The committee, lead by a health system clinical products specialist (CPS), united end users from a variety of disciplines and departments, including those from corporate purchasing and the medical distribution center. In addition to designing a process for materials and evaluating all new product requests, the committee led the daunting task of methodically working through the current inventory to look for cost-saving opportunities. A number of the tactical strategies employed in this process were

- Securitizing new product requests
- Standardization – to minimize product duplication
- Written protocols – to ensure the proper use of specific products
- Substitution products – obtained through competitive bidding

The creation of CVAC has reduced the amount of *reckless outside supply orders* initiated at the request of individuals and covered as a departmental expense. In addition to the changes that needed to be made in the supply acquisition process, the cultural change regarding supply resource utilization could not be underestimated.

Standardization with the CVAC

Standardization of medical supply products, and requiring all supplies be obtained through a health system purchasing process, are effective strategies to reduce hospital medical supply costs and ensure quality and safety for the patients and the staff who are using the products. Prior to the CVAC committee, and the development of a new/replacement products requisition process, it was not uncommon for new/replacement products to appear on nursing units without prior staff knowledge or education, leaving them unprepared to manage and use the new product safely. This created staff stress and confusion and often resulted in unfavorable exchanges between the primary user of the product (e.g., the physician) and the nursing staff. Patients' education about the product was delayed and their questions went unanswered. Safe patient care was ultimately compromised as missing information created gaps in nursing performance.

The requirement that education for the nursing staff and other unit healthcare providers be planned and implemented prior to the arrival of a new product, has reduced erroneous supply products showing up on nursing units *unannounced*. In addition, this practice has improved the safe infusion of new supply products into the healthcare system, ensuring training and education of the nursing staff and the appropriate patient education.

The Chemotherapy Gown Story

Through the methodical review of medical supplies currently in our inventory, and with the implementation of a house-wide multidisciplinary chemotherapy administration protocol, it became apparent to the CPS that there were multiple different chemotherapy gowns being issued to nursing staff to administer chemotherapy. The quality and characteristics of an appropriate protective garment are clearly documented in the literature [9, 10]. Some of the gowns that were stocked in our hospitals exceeded the minimum standards for a chemotherapy gown and were more than twice as expensive as what was required. Other gowns were inadequate and did not meet minimum safety requirements for gown characteristics. With input and translation of the available federal and national guidelines by the oncology experts, one gown was selected for chemotherapy administration within our health system.

New / Replacement Product Requisition Process

When a new or replacement product need is identified, a process is set in motion through the completion of a Health System New/ Replacement Product request form. Each product must have a clinical contact person who will serve as the *Shepherd* for moving the product through the process. The form is available online and asks for the following information:

- Contact information
- Product descriptors
- Information to confirm the product is a medical supply (e.g., dressing, syringe) and not classified as something else like a durable medical supply (commode chair, personal assistive devices)
- Usage information

  - anticipated volume
  - use by other departments
  - products that will be eliminated as a result of the new product
  - staff education requirements
  - FDA status

This formalized new/replacement medical supply requisition process that includes documentation requirements is an effective strategy in controlling inventory and due diligence in managing supply dollars (see Figure 9-5).

The form is completed and submitted to the CPS. The specialist reviews the form for content validity, clarifies information with the requestor, and then schedules the requestor to present their product to the CVAC committee, which meets monthly. The presentation is meant to be a brief and organized description of the new or replacement product, the key staff in the use of the product, and the reason for the request. If applicable, a pilot for the new product is planned. New products are piloted by stakeholders from multiple departments. Pilot results are formally evaluated and statistically analyzed. Replacement products can be substituted with a majority vote of the committee, if the product is budget-neutral or a cost savings and there is no requirement for additional staff education or training.

The product request form is simultaneously sent to corporate purchasing to determine the financial impact of the addition or change and to ascertain any contractual conflicts that may exist as a result of bringing in the new or replacement product. If corporate purchasing concedes that there are financial risks or contract conflicts, the CPS may delay the presentation in order to preview the request with the committee and determine its ultimate viability.

If the product request advances, the presentation is made and the plan for implementation of a pilot and roll-out, or an immediate roll-out, is discussed. In almost all cases, existing product must be used up before the new or replacement product is available. The status of all new or replacement product requests are reviewed at each monthly meeting.

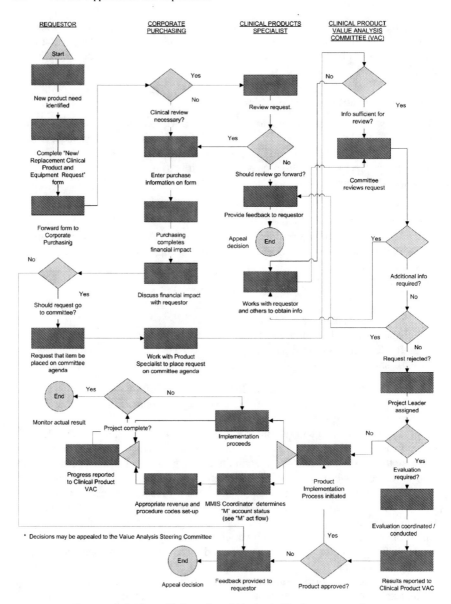

FIGURE 9-5. Flow of information within the facility for a new product.

The Chemotherapy New Product Story

Over the past few years, pharmacy safety literature has described the concept of a closed system for use in mixing, dispensing, and administering chemotherapy. The product was a closed preparation system that minimized exposure of toxic chemotherapy drugs to the pharmacy staff who mixed and dispensed chemotherapeutic agents, as well as nursing staff who administered them. There were several components to the system that were added and changed as the chemotherapy agent progressed from the pharmacy to the nursing unit. At the time, it was the only product of its kind on the market. It had been developed overseas but then piloted, approved by the FDA, and used in the United States for a couple of years. The cost of the multipiece product seemed to be a limiting factor. It was expensive, about $10.00-$20.00 per patient per IV dose of chemotherapy—clearly an additional cost to the chemotherapy procedure. The chemotherapy exposure studies that supported this device, however, were compelling, and the costs of not using the product were very evident. It was these evidence-based findings that were used to persuade pharmacy and nursing leadership to proceed with the purchase.

In the final analysis, it was not the CVAC committee that made the decision to use the product and accept the additional costs that would be incurred by the institution. The committee was the launch pad that prepared the necessary documentation for the next level of review. The product and the implications of its use were reviewed by hospital risk management and pharmacy directors. They would have to assume the additional costs in their supply budgets in spite of no incremental revenue to pay for the device. In the end, it was decided to pilot the product with the intent to use it if the pilot outcomes and evaluation were favorable.

Substituting Products with the CVAC

Cost-effective supply management is the goal of all members in our supply chain team. An end user does not always initiate the substitution of medical supply products. The relationship that our health system has with medical supply vendors and distributors is collaborative and invites dialog regarding new and significantly cheaper replacement products for those already in use. This cost-saving strategy has proven very effective in reducing hospital medical supply costs.

A regular agenda item at our CVAC meeting includes recommendations from our represented distributor regarding product substitution. The recommendation comes with pricing information, health system cost savings based on current usage, and a hands-on *show and touch* that allows committee members who are medical supply users to handle the product and make their own judgments about transferability. Most products are brought in and piloted on a few high volume user units to determine product viability. With a successful product evaluation, the product is quickly moved across the house after the current stock has been completely used up. The only exceptions to using up a product before the new product is available is a) if the hospital is able to get credit for returned stock or b) if there is a safety risk to the patient or provider by delaying the use of the new product.

The survival of a healthcare system depends on cost, quality, and value existing in a balanced equation. Balancing the equation calls for an organization to embrace change, ensuring market strength and position. To be competitive, new forms of technology must be embraced—to be effective and profitable, new structures and processes must be considered [11]. Clinical product value analysis committees yield a structured process to ensure the maximum value is obtained from every purchasing dollar spent on medical supplies.

Supplies and Budget Process for a Clinical Unit

The supply budget process is usually a fiscal year event. Expense budgets going forward are based on inflation and the previous fiscal years' budget. A prescribed performance target is dictated by hospital management. Previously added, but unbudgeted, items are incorporated, as well as items that have been forecasted to be part of the supply landscape within the coming fiscal year. The nurse manager must understand patient volumes and patient days, as well as anticipated growth in volume, as it relates to new programs. Many automated supply stations allow for both inventory management and charging patients for supplies used. The charging component is often unseen to the staff, as it is built into the programming on the back-end without the healthcare provider's knowledge of what is billable and what is not. There is good news and bad news to this back-end approach. It can be argued that supply station users who are not aware of the individual cost of each supply item, especially the expensive ones, may be less vigilant about ensuring they have appropriately recorded the use of the item for a specific patient. The good news is that staff does not need to worry about the ever-changing cost details. Their only focus is to record the taking of an item to ensure it is replenished for the next time. The nurse manager need only focus on, and audit, the proper use of the system by all users so that the system can perform at its peak, ensuring timely inventory replenishment and appropriate patient charging.

Hospital Financial Reports

Hospital financial reports and automated system reports are important supportive documents for the nurse/unit manager with supply management responsibilities.

Many hospital financial reports leave a *gross dollar* paper trail that speaks to the cost and revenue associated with supply distribution and consumption. For these reports to be of any use to the nurse/unit manager, they must reflect supply activity for that manager's unit or cost center, as well as similar units/cost centers for benchmarking and comparison. Financial reports are often produced in layers, each giving more specific details about cost, quantity, and revenue generated. Financial statements that report current monthly, year-to-date, budget-to-actual dollars, along with the previous year's numbers, allow the nurse/unit manager to observe trends and correlate unit volume activities and practice changes with the supply financial picture. The more detailed reports allow the nurse/unit manager to audit and validate the actual supplies used, which are not revealed in broader account reports. Monthly detail reports also allow the nurse/unit manager to observe quantity used for the more expensive or procedure specific supply item. If a chest tube placement procedure happens on an average of two times per month, the nurse/unit manager can observe the unique supplies associated with the procedure and validate quantities used. It is also the supplies that *do not belong* and cannot be tied to the practice on the unit that become the focus of the more detailed reports. Figure 9-6 shows the value of utilizing detailed direct income and expense reports with an example of the total budgeted costs for intravenous tubing and the associated totals.

Automated Systems Report

Automated supply station reports are helpful in demonstrating user trends, replenishment patterns, user compliance, and lost-charge capture opportunities. These systems allow for real-time adjustments to par levels and make it easy to add or delete items from the system. Automated systems can also provide information by a given user, and produce user and group performance trends. This type of reporting lends itself to maximizing cost-effective supply management. Many of these systems have reporting capabilities that can be overwhelming to the end user. The challenge is to find a pre-existing form that functions well in the setting or to design institution-specific reports that are credible and provide decision support for the nurse/unit manger.

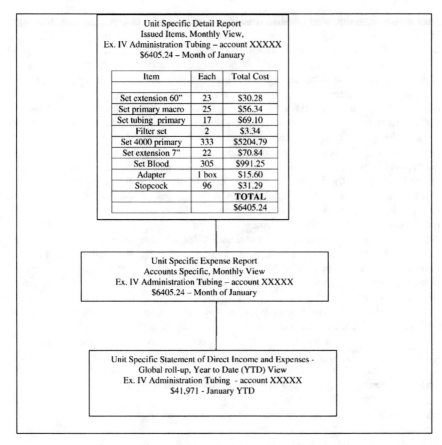

Item	Each	Total Cost
Set extension 60"	23	$30.28
Set primary macro	25	$56.34
Set tubing primary	17	$69.10
Filter set	2	$3.34
Set 4000 primary	333	$5204.79
Set extension 7"	22	$70.84
Set Blood	305	$991.25
Adapter	1 box	$15.60
Stopcock	96	$31.29
		TOTAL
		$6405.24

FIGURE 9-6. Income and expense reports.

Usage reports are often written in terms of par level activity. They can be run for a specified period of time to reflect unit utilization of supplies. These reports are most useful when they are run over a 90 to 120-day period to adjust for spikes in usage related to complex or unique patients and seasonality. Items in these reports can often be sorted by most utilized and least utilized to assist with utilization forecasts, space allocation (especially in limited space supply rooms), and elimination of obsolete items. The materials management department's investment in usage reports allows them to effectively manage the top 20 and bottom 20 supply performers, with little or no effort on the part of staff. Benefits resulting from better management are increased staff satisfaction related to supply availability, increased patient satisfaction related to minimal procedure delays, decreased inventory carrying costs, and maximum revenue generation. The materials management department's investment in usage reports affords efficiencies in the process with minimal additional manual intervention.

Compliance reports are helpful in understanding the units' overall compliance with using the system. Amanda Llewellyn, our Assistant Director of Materials Management at Johns Hopkins Hospital, says that typically, a compliance rate of 90% to 95% is necessary to ensure adequate charge capture and inventory management. Compliance rates below 80% diminish the efficiencies of the system, which necessitates increased manual intervention, limits the accuracy of system-generated reports, and threatens the hospital or health system's ROI. Reports that look at specific user activity patterns yield valuable information about system compliance. User access that frequently does not result in a matching transaction suggests a user compliance issue. This type of user issue is a threat to the integrity of the automated system. Reports can be generated to look at materials management staff compliance with the replenishment process. The lack of regular inventory reconciliation and appropriate inventory adjustments with restocking are also threats to the performance of the automated system.

Finally, lost charges are missed revenue opportunities. Lost charges result from discrepancies in the count of a chargeable item—perhaps the system expects you find ten and there are only five in the cabinet. Lost charges can also be a result of removing stock at the expense of the unit rather than at the expense of the patient using the item or removing an item under *floor stock* rather than under a patient's name. Discrepancy reports can be printed daily and further delineated by user, shift, or patient to maximize the opportunity of correcting the lost charge. Maximizing revenue is an important outcome of the purchase of any automated system. Reports that facilitate a change in unit culture and user behavior, as it relates to supply usage, are critical to the overall performance of the supply procurement and replenishment process and the automated dispensing system.

The success of the information technology investment can be measured by the achievement of projected financial targets, as well as automated system usage and user reports. Ongoing evaluation of performance reports is the responsibility of the materials management staff, the nurse/unit manager, and the finance department. This shared responsibility should be performed both independently and as a group to ensure success with the automated point-of-use inventory management system.

Conclusion

Advances in materials management technology clearly benefit budgets, managers, third-party payers, and administrators. There are benefits for the primary care nurse, but they are less tangible. The ultimate goal is to always have an item at hand when needed. This is a goal that can be accomplished for the bedside nurse through technology.

What computers do best is analyze data, look for trends, and follow rules that can be built based on these trends. An automated system should ideally track the supplies used on a given patient, then link those supplies to the reason for admission. This monitoring would result in having the appropriate supplies automatically delivered to specific units as needed. This approach is very similar to the development of the specific procedure equipment pick-lists and supply carts that are provided for operating room cases. Data mining on the type and quantity of supplies used should generate data for analysis and enable real-time adjustments when admissions of that type come into the hospital. This type of supply forecasting to support inventory and replenishment is currently utilized in less than 25% of hospitals [12].

Another area where information can be effective is timely analysis of charges per unit. Nurse managers deal with *lost charges* on a daily basis due to the difficulty in linking the item used to the patient. If daily charge reports were provided for the manager to verify usage (before the patients and staff have forgotten what supplies were used), there would be tighter control of charging supplies, a tighter control on inventory, and increased revenue for the nursing unit. Anticipatory supply of materials must become a part of our clinical information system(s). This can be accomplished by linking the provider order entry to established steps in patient care standards.

We have discussed census and patient mix on the units in this chapter, but the next step is for decision support systems to be automatically aware of the admission changes and adjust the inventory based on previous needs. An increased incidence of pneumonia patients would mean an increase in the number of suction catheters to the nursing unit. This chapter has shown the reader ways to create inventory that support SOCs. Vendors of material management systems must collaborate with vendors of clinical information systems and nursing to develop tighter control of supplies using an analysis of supplies used.

Acknowledgments

The authors would like to acknowledge the help and guidance of William Kennett, Colleen Cusick, Amanda Llewellyn, Peggy Neidlinger, and Nancy Miner for their support on this chapter.

References

[1] Neef, D. (2001) *e-Procurement : from strategy to implementation.* Upper Saddle River, NJ: Financial Times/Prentice Hall.

[2] Carpenter, D. (2005) A touch of technology begets big savings. *Materials management in health care.* **14**(10), 36–8.

[3] Burns, L. R. and Wharton School Colleagues (2002) *The Health Care Value Chain: Producers, Purchasers, and Providers.* San Francisco: Jossey-Bass.

[4] Kohn, L.T., J. Corrigan, and M. S. Donaldson, (2000) *To err is human :building a safer health system.* Washington, DC: National Academy Press.

[5] Mason, E. J. (1994) *How to write meaningful standards of care.* Saratoga Springs, NY: Delmar Publishers.

[6] Koloroutis, M. (Ed). (2004) *Relationship-Based Care: A Model for Transforming Practice.* Minneapolis: Creative Health Care Management Publishers.

[7] Larson, L. (2003) Putting patient safety in the blueprint. *Hospitals & health networks.* **77**(2), 46, 50, 52–3, 2.

[8] Health Care Cost Reengineering Report. (1998) February **3**(2), 23–5.

[9] Polovich, M. (2004) Safe handling of hazardous drugs. *Online Journal of Issues in Nursing.* **9**(3), 6. Available at: http://www.nursingworld.org/ojin/ [Accessed on 14 April 2007]

[10] Ritchie, M.A., C. McAdams, and N. Fritz, (2000) Exposure Risk in the Handling and Administration of Chemotherapy Agents: A Review and Synthesis of the Literature. *The Online Journal of Knowledge Synthesis for Nursing.* **7**, 4.

[11] Bridges, W. (1991) *Managing transitions: making the most of change.* Reading, Mass.: Perseus Books.

[12] Langabeer, J. (2005) The evolving role of supply chain management technology in healthcare. *Journal of Healthcare Information Management.* **19**(2), 27–33.

10
Business Analysis

MARC A. ELMHORST

Executive Summary

In this chapter, we take a closer look at how to monitor and control the usage and costs of medical supplies in hospitals. By materials management, we mean all materials-related processes comprising procurement (including purchasing and invoice management), materials planning, logistics, and inventory management. In this chapter, however, we mainly focus on procurement issues within materials management. We distinguish between methods at the operational and strategic level of materials management. Whereas operationally oriented methods aim at optimizing these processes, strategic methods seek to put an overall strategic plan into practice that focuses on those issues of materials management that support the overall plan. The description of both types of methods is based on the experience gained at five German university hospitals, and on the current discussions taking place at these hospitals in the procurement area—particularly in consolidating their eBusiness procedures and purchasing activities. The case study at the end of the chapter illustrates the achievements possible and the problems encountered when establishing a data warehouse in one of the university hospitals to improve its business analysis capabilities.

Analyzing the usage and costs of medical supplies always needs to refer to patient care, which constitutes the core processes in a hospital. These are the processes where the medical supplies are used. Although this is widely known and accepted, accessing integrated clinical data linked to materials data still is a big challenge. There are various reasons for this problem. Integrated data need an integrated information management system and a way of thinking that is patient-centered as opposed to department-centered. Only patient-centric organizations can achieve the necessary volume of integrated data for business analysis. In addition, the contribution of materials management in supporting clinical processes, and the fact that medical supplies may exert an important impact on clinical outcomes, must be clearly recognized. This leads to necessary management attention to materials issues, their relation to clinical processes, and to the IT support necessary to analyze relevant information.

Despite these challenges, experience has proven that there is a series of methods providing good measures for optimizing purchasing, managing suppliers and materials, and standardizing the use of materials. At the operational level, the methods presented and discussed embrace

- Methods for optimizing the procurement process
  - o Automating the internal eBusiness transactions, mainly the requisitioning process
  - o Employing an electronic catalog
  - o Automating the external eBusiness transactions
  - o Prioritizing suppliers/concentrating business efforts on the important suppliers
- Methods for product standardization
  - o Reducing the number of suppliers
  - o Concentrating the purchasing values on a few suppliers
  - o Reducing the number of materials
  - o Concentrating the purchasing value on a few products
- Methods for standardizing product use
  - o Using the same materials in several clinical processes
  - o Reducing the number of materials within the same clinical processes
  - o Optimizing the materials costs per clinical case or patient
- Methods for optimizing the results of negotiating with suppliers
  - o Optimizing the purchase price by general volume bundling
  - o Optimizing the purchasing price by volume bundling within ad hoc purchasing group
  - o Optimizing negotiation skills by providing detailed information
- New procurement methods
  - o Using evidence-based purchasing methods

Most of the methods described directly relate to eBusiness applications in a narrow sense or are supported by the data that are enabled by eBusiness methods in a wider sense.

eBusiness, therefore, is not only attractive because of its potential to automate tasks within the procurement process, but also because eBusiness applications have an indirect impact on the analysis methods in terms of increasing the availability of information and decreasing the effort required to generate such information. Electronic product catalogs are a good example of this. At the strategic level, methods to increase the revenue and the quality, and methods for shifting risks and responsibilities to suppliers, are presented. These strategic methods (with the exception of outsourcing warehouse management) relate not only to materials management but, in fact, to the entire hospital. As will be seen in this chapter, both areas contribute to the success of the strategic approach. The methods discussed in detail are:

- Methods for increasing the revenue
  - o Become center of excellence for particular medical treatments
- Methods for increasing the clinical quality
  - o Standardize clinical processes
  - o Reduce complication rates
- Methods for shifting risks and responsibilities to suppliers
  - o Share the risks with suppliers (capitation contracts)
  - o Outsource warehouse management (consignment stores and vendor-managed inventories)

The COINS case study highlights the strategic approach of transforming a hospital into a patient-centered organization pursued by the Medizinische Hochschule Hannover. It illustrates the procedures and techniques implemented to build a controlling information system based on a data warehouse that will assist in monitoring the progress made in transforming the organization. It demonstrates how data from different systems are extracted, how data inconsistencies are dealt with, and gives examples of management reports enabled by the system—in particular, DRG-based reports. It can be concluded that business analysis, including information derived from the core processes of a hospital, is possible and provides management information upon which decisions can be based.

Introduction

In the manufacturing industry, the entire organization, including its IT infrastructure and information management, focuses on the product and the production process—its primary process. Secondary processes supporting the primary process, such as procurement, logistics, and supply chain management are regarded as important components of an entirety contributing to the manufacturing of the product. Consequently, materials are recognized as an integral part of the product or of the process eventually leading to the product. Product categorizations typically used in the manufacturing industry reflect this point of view. Materials add value to the end product, and therefore possess a defined value themselves. This way of thinking is well illustrated by an approach manufacturers employ for setting price limits for a given material. The value a certain type of material (e.g., the headlights of a car) adds to the end product (the car), defines the target price the manufacturer is willing to pay for that material. If the value generated by the headlights is high, the manufacturer would accept a higher price than if the value was less.

Hospitals neither belong to the manufacturing industry nor are patients products. Looking across the boundaries of the healthcare industry, however, might help to understand certain limitations that still exist today and might contribute to overcoming these limitations. More and more hospitals are moving towards a patient-centric organization, focusing on clinical outcomes. Factors strongly impacting an outcome are of high value to the organization. Such factors could range from the skills of a clinical expert or of a team of experts, to a drug or a medical device. Thus, the value of medical supplies should therefore be judged by the degree they contribute to the outcome or to the process leading to the outcome. Patients are not products. Outcomes, however, are products comparable to any other product in the manufacturing industry. Purchasing processes, materials management, and supply chain management also play as important a role in healthcare as they do in other industries—most notably in the manufacturing industry. This awareness is growing among healthcare executives and will finally result in an understanding that all issues of materials management, including procurement, strongly support the medical processes and their applications. The organizational structure and the IT infrastructure within healthcare organizations will have to follow this new awareness. To date, the old gap between clinical and so-called administrative solutions still hinders a seamless flow of consistent information between the IT systems involved. Business analysis aiming at an integrated view is still challenged by a lack of information covering business as well as medical issues.

This chapter, therefore, focuses not only on how to analyze relevant parameters for controlling medical supplies, but also looks at the data sources.

The experience and conclusions presented in this chapter are derived from the results and the achievements of five German university hospitals (Hannover, Göttingen, Magdeburg, Schleswig-Holstein, and Greifswald) in the area of procurement, but particularly in employing electronic methods for purchasing and controlling all processes within materials management. These five teaching hospitals set up a purchasing cooperative (COMPA-RATIO) and an electronic infrastructure to support its activities that consists of a central group purchasing information system (GROPIS) and an online trading exchange operated by the GSG (Gesellschaft für Standardprozesse im Gesundheitswesen).

The case study at the end of the chapter focuses on the controlling information system (COINS) implemented in one of the five hospitals, and summarizes possible achievements and problems encountered.

Controlling Medical Supplies in Hospitals

IT Infrastructure

Typically, the IT infrastructure of hospitals contains horizontal systems for the management of resources such as finances, human resources, facilities, assets, and materials. Horizontal systems are also employed for patient management, such as admission, discharge, and transfer (ADT). The clinical processes are driven by several vertically structured clinical systems specializing in supporting the various medical departments (see also Chapter 4). Modern hospital information systems (HIS_h) seek to support medical processes, thus allowing a coherent look at all clinical data that patients produce during their stay or encounter or over the time of their disease. Electronic patient record (EPR) systems or electronic health record (EHR) systems, which are currently being implemented in a growing number of hospitals, are the core element of a modern HIS_h and the basic prerequisite for such a coherent look. Other processes such as quality assurance, medical controlling, and DRG-based billing strongly benefit from data provided by EPRs or EHRs as they heavily rely on integrated data and IT support. As was shown in Chapter 4, achieving integration within heterogeneous IT systems in hospitals requires system architectures suitable for integration, protocols enabling syntactic and semantic integration, and methods (EAI and communication servers) for actually putting the systems together. The most effective way for compiling data for management purposes is through data warehouse technology because it allows the building of a logical and consistent pool of information composed of data from various sources (see Figure 10-1). This will be further illustrated in the COINS case study at the end of the chapter.

The availability of information (or the lack thereof) affects the ability to control medical supplies within hospitals. In particular, data on costs charged to the patient must be available in order to measure the economic effect caused by this patient or this disease. This also includes information on materials costs assigned to a patient.

For any quality-oriented view, the medical process also needs to be integrated. Improving the availability of information is complex and requires, in most situations, organizational and technological changes. In the long term, materials management needs to have an influence on the continuous development of a hospital's IT infrastructure. Such influences should ensure that

- All material purchased is purchased through a materials management system,
- Information about the usage of all purchased materials is captured and stored
- Medical supplies data can be linked with clinical outcomes and economic results

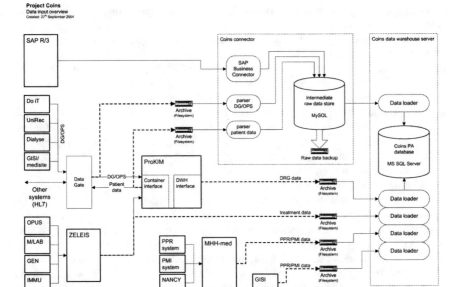

FIGURE 10-1. Systems integration in a heterogeneous environment (example – Medizinische Hochschule Hannover, Germany).

Organizational Matters and Priorities

There are various options for organizing materials management. An organizational structure allowing materials management to support and influence medical processes, increasing the value both can add to the medical process. There are several ways of establishing the best materials management scenario for a given hospital. The most appropriate way of selecting the right method is by allowing materials management to follow the overall strategy of the hospital (see COINS case study), and by deriving an appropriate organizational structure from the strategic plan.

One option is to organize materials management in a central department serving the entire organization. Such a department requires a certain purchasing volume and value to justify the overhead costs associated with such an organization. In addition, this department must be endowed with the necessary skills and power to pursue a centralistic approach for standardizing medical supplies and enforcing ordering discipline. Another option is to join a purchasing cooperative or group purchasing organization. Again, there are various scenarios. Either the cooperative or organization can be responsible for the selection of suppliers, or it can only be permitted to negotiate prices for given products. A third option is to outsource procurement and/or inventory management to a third party.

Besides IT infrastructure and the organizational framework, the purchasing volume, the personal skills of the staff, and the size of the team are determining factors for setting priorities in procurement. The effort required to implement and execute the approach must therefore be considered in conjunction with the expected impact of each procurement scheme. Both purchasing volume and the number of staff are linked to a third variable, which is the size of the healthcare organization. In any case, the procurement method chosen must fit the size of the entire organization.

Smaller hospitals typically have no purchasing value, which justifies the overhead of a materials management department. The diversity of the medical processes they perform is limited compared to those performed in a large or metropolitan hospital, thus the diversity of supplies is limited. One option for such hospitals is to pass over the responsibility of certain purchasing processes to a purchasing cooperative, a group purchasing organization, or a third party organization. This requires a clear organizational definition as to what degree this organization is responsible for the purchasing process and for setting standards for materials and suppliers. Hospitals that are not able or willing to give up product responsibility might decide to occasionally team up with other hospitals to purchase a selected set of products.

Based upon their situation and the purchasing volume, larger hospitals or healthcare systems with a central materials management department have the choice of implementing a mix of methods for purchasing materials. First, supplies used for their most important medical processes should be managed with a high priority. Second, the influence a material has on the medical process and its outcome should be measured, including complication rates, and should influence the decision-making about a product. Third, the effort spent on purchasing materials with small or no impact at all on the medical process should be balanced with any potential savings. Fourth, if a large hospital or healthcare system decides to join a purchasing cooperative, it must be able to enforce procurement guidelines and ensure contract compliance, which is particularly challenging in large healthcare organizations. The reduction of suppliers and the reduction of the number of materials are the key factors in a purchasing cooperative's ability to reduce costs. Fifth, the execution of a hospital's purchasing strategy requires close interaction between clinical staff, materials management staff, and general administration. Thus, a complete understanding of this strategy is needed across all levels. If this strategy is focusing on the impact of a given product on clinical outcomes and process efficiency, it is recommended that feedback loops be implemented after regular evaluations to draw conclusions about whether the expected effects have actually materialized (see also Chapter 9).

Operational Procurement

Measuring the Purchasing Performance and Optimizing the Purchasing Process

Before measuring and optimizing the purchasing process, it is necessary to take a closer look at the steps required for purchasing any material within a hospital. The German Scientific Association for Technology in Hospitals (WGKT) defined a reference model consisting of 11 such steps (see Figure 10-2) for the entire procurement process [1].

Because the procurement process involves different organizations, and the time and effort required for each step within this process is not captured automatically in IT systems, the measurements necessary for optimizing the entire process thus cannot be performed on a day-to-day basis. Questionnaires and/or time measurements are typically employed for collecting the relevant data.

Some indicators can be collected from already available data, such as the number of automated processes vs. not automated processes used in the purchasing process. To measure this, the number of transactions performed with an automated procurement

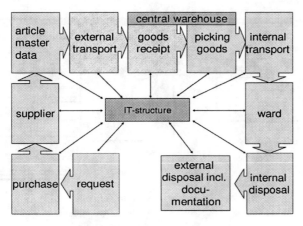

FIGURE 10-2. Eleven steps of procuring.

system is compared to the number of transactions made outside the electronic system. Effort needed to operate the procurement system should also be included in this analysis.

A good example is the requisitioning process. Most hospitals either use an electronic shop solution for browsing the electronic catalog and entering the requisition via keyboard, or a barcode reader-based solution for automatically capturing all relevant data, primarily product type and quantity. Either option is typically part of an individual procurement system or part of a procurement module integrated into an HIS_h. In the electronic shop version, the user selects an item from the products in the catalog. Because such a catalog requires regular maintenance, often only data for supplies that are frequently requisitioned are listed there. Also, an electronic shop might not prove useful for certain materials, such as complex chemicals. The difference between electronically vs. not electronically requisitioned products is measured by comparing the number of lines of all relevant invoices in the financial system with the number of lines in the requisitioning system.

As mentioned above, a large part of the effort of operating a procurement system consists of updating or deleting old catalog entries or inserting new ones within the system itself. This effort can be reduced by involving the suppliers and making them responsible for maintaining the data within a hospital's central materials management systems. Some online trading exchanges provide this functionality as a service that comprises combining and maintaining catalogs from different suppliers. As a result, each individual hospital does not need to contact each individual supplier, which reduces the effort for both sides. This service may include mechanisms for a hospital to maintain complete control of their data.

Using a method such as this helps to reduce breakdowns in communication between the hospital and the supplier, because it ensures that the supplier and the hospital are both using the same identification method and descriptors for any given material.

The following example shows how important it is to harmonize catalog entries. Hospitals and suppliers look at material data in different ways. A supplier's material description focuses, for example, on packages to sell, but a hospital focuses on quantities of use. If the catalog is not harmonized, either party might interpret the quantity differently, which would automatically lead to order errors. Because this method requires close interaction between the supplier and the hospital, it is recommended that hospitals focus

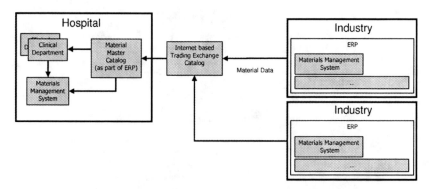

FIGURE 10-3. Unique source of materials data.

on suppliers providing many products that are purchased frequently. The success of this method is measured based on data from the materials management system by counting the number of products bought from suppliers who are responsible for maintaining their own material data within the hospital's procurement systems.

Automating the business processes between the hospital and the supplier is yet another measure in optimizing the procurement process and the information exchange associated with each single step along the way. This embraces the order, the order acknowledgment, the advanced shipment notice, the delivery notice, and the invoice, all of which need to be sent electronically using standard protocols such as EANCOM. To measure this effect, the number of automated transactions per type of transaction (e.g., order and invoice) must be compared to the number of unautomated transactions performed within the same timeframe. This information can be further broken down by counting the lines per transaction for transaction type.

Procurement starts with requisitioning, therefore automating the procurement process must also begin with the implementation of the electronic requisition. There is an urgent need for integrating clinical subsystems and materials management to electronically requisition from the clinical units and match materials and patient data for patient charging. First, electronic catalogs usually stored in a central database of the materials management system must be made available in the clinical units (see Figure 10-3). The most challenging version is to allow requisitioning directly through the electronic patient record system. In particular, if patient data and materials data are to be linked, patient lists and product catalogs must be accessible from a single front-end system. To ensure consistent data, materials and patients must be identified by unique codes in all systems involved.

Categorizing Suppliers

The effort required to conduct business with a supplier varies widely depending upon the materials used within a hospital. In terms of controlling operational procurement, it is sufficient to focus on those suppliers where purchasing efforts (time and resources) promise to produce the highest impact on cost and revenue. Most hospitals, therefore, pursue a strategy that focuses their efforts on a handful of alpha suppliers. Consequently, the hospital must find out which suppliers are good candidates for alpha suppliers. This strategy requires the categorization of suppliers and the definition of different approaches on how to deal with the suppliers in each category. A typical approach for categorizing suppliers is to categorize their products. There are many ways of achieving this—categories could be formed according to purchasing frequency, volume, purchase value, type of product (commodity vs. specialized product), and others. One of the most widely used methods in the manufacturing industry is to categorize suppliers by the importance of the material supplied. A very pragmatic approach is based on three categories:

A material = material is part of the product
B material = material is used in production and influences the product
C material = material has no influence on the product

These categories reflect a typical product-centric perspective. Hospitals moving to a patient-centric organization might easily adopt this approach for their own defining purposes:

A material = material that stays with the patient (implants) or has a proven influence on the outcome
B material = material that influences the patient care process
C material = material that has no influence on patient care

Hospitals typically use a mix of different parameters to categorize their suppliers—very often including total purchase value. In some cases, strategies for selected medical processes may define the importance of a product and its supplier. For example, this might be the case for implanting hearing devices, a specialized medical process in which the hospital wants to acquire a reputation for excellence and allies with the supplier of hearing devices to support them in their effort to reach the goal. Such a supplier could also be defined as a high-priority supplier regardless of the purchasing volume.

There are suppliers with a high purchasing volume who do not become an alpha vendor despite that high volume (e.g., a utility provider for water and energy), because their contribution to patient care is that of a background supplier rather than that of a supplier whose product directly influences clinical outcomes. This example documents the mix of parameters needed for categorizing suppliers correctly.

Once suppliers are prioritized, this information needs to be stored in the materials management system for later analysis. It is useful to keep additional information about the supplier in the database that supplements the category information, such as whether the hospital entertains a research and development partnership with the supplier or whether the supplier is important because his product is used in clinical cases in which the hospital has specialized.

The major consequence of categorizing, and hereby prioritizing, suppliers is a change in the effort invested by the hospital in managing this supplier in terms of time and human resources. Only alpha suppliers receive the greatest amount of attention, and controlling methods must make sure that the effort is proportional to the category.

This implies that the effort per supplier is measured. If such data are available, a simple table summarizing the effort spent in each category gives an excellent indication to which degree the strategy of categorizing and prioritizing the suppliers is executed. If such data are not available, measurable indicators are the number of purchasing transactions compared to the number of meetings with the suppliers in each category. The number of purchasing transactions is ideally further broken down into automated transactions and transactions requiring resources of the materials management department.

Number of Suppliers

Each supplier creates a certain amount of administrative effort in terms of time and human and machine resources. This being the case, a reduction of the number of suppliers correspondingly reduces the overall effort spent during the purchasing process. The effect of this approach is measured by counting the number of suppliers within the materials management system before and after the method has been implemented.

Besides reducing the administrative effort of managing a supplier, there is another impact of this measure. A higher concentration of the purchasing value on a few suppliers is, from the supplier's point of view, an increase in the revenue. This is a good argument for hospitals to be used in price negotiations (see next section).

One could argue, however, that not all suppliers are equal and therefore a given supplier cannot be easily replaced by another supplier. A wide range of suppliers have unique products protected by patents, or sell products that are required for given medical processes, that other suppliers may not provide. Therefore, purchasing managers need to focus on those suppliers who offer products that can be substituted by alternative products offered by other major suppliers of the hospital. These are typically commodity products.

Reducing the number of suppliers should eventually lead to a concentration of a few suppliers for a higher percentage of the purchasing volume. To measure the degree of concentration achieved, the percentages of suppliers providing a given amount of purchasing values are calculated. This relation should increase with time. If data are available, a comparison with other hospitals gives a good indication of the status quo.

An example of a typical relation of suppliers and the value of goods purchased from them is shown in Table 10-1. The fractions indicate an improvement compared to the past, but there is still room for optimization as the benchmarks with the other hospitals show. There is a caveat for comparing data from different hospitals, however, because the degree of concentration of suppliers on purchasing value is strongly influenced by the type of medical services provided. Specialized hospitals may therefore achieve higher rates of concentration than general hospitals. It must be ensured that the hospital being compared is similarly structured in terms of size, case mix, and diversity of medical services provided. In addition, it must be ensured that the definition of a supply is the same in both hospitals [2].

The concentration measures can be refined by selectively looking at groups of suppliers—in particular, the A-material suppliers, or those whose products may influence the clinical outcome. The data required for analyzing the concentration of suppliers are directly derived from the purchasing and materials management system.

Variations of Material

Each material creates a certain administrative effort, therefore a reduction of the number of materials should, in turn, reduce the effort spent during the purchasing process. A

TABLE 10-1. Suppliers in relation to purchasing value.

Fraction of supplier	Fraction of value	Fraction of value in the past	Other hospital
1%	40%	38%	43%
2%	50%	45%	54%
5%	70%	62%	77%
10%	85%	78%	87%

simple approach for measuring the effect is to count the number of materials within the materials management system. As the number of suppliers and the number of materials are correlated, reducing the number of suppliers already has an effect on the number of supplies used, and there may still be variation within the products provided by a given single supplier that needs to be reduced.

Because the materials used in clinical processes largely depend on the type of treatment or care given, the involvement of clinicians is essential for achieving success. A good balance between clinically necessary variation and a concentration on certain products should be aimed for and can only be monitored through close interaction between clinicians and purchasing staff.

A report showing the change in concentration of the purchasing value to a few products over time will give an indication of the degree of success achieved by this method. Because this report only requires information from the materials management system, it should be easily compiled.

An example of a typical relation of products used and the fraction of the total purchasing value is shown in Table 10-2. The data in the table documents an improvement over time and indicates a level of concentration higher than that of the hospital with which the comparison is made. There are limitations to this concentration process, however. Not all products can be used across several clinical processes and it might prove useful to test new products in the market.

In principle, a decision on whether a product is suitable for use in different processes can only be made on the basis of independent clinical requirements for those products. These requirements have to be matched with the features describing products available on the market. These types of analyses are made possible by comprehensive nomenclature and classification systems (see Chapter 6) as they provide standardized group and item descriptors. Comparability between the requirements and the features of a product is ensured if the features defining a product class are detailed enough to describe products properly, yet are generic enough to allow more than one product per group.

Product decisions should be based on the information provided by a materials-oriented report that lists all products by class, and should provide additional information on the number of items used within a given period of time (see Table 10-3).

If the decision was based on the frequency of use, only products A and B would be considered for further analysis. Reports of this kind require a classification system to be implemented within the materials management system and require product catalogs to contain a class code per product. Ideally, manufacturers classify their products as they have the deepest product knowledge.

If the method is employed within a purchasing cooperative, either all member hospitals must refer to the same classification system or at least must agree on a mechanism for

TABLE 10-2. Products used in relation to purchasing value.

Fraction of products	Fraction of value	Fraction of value in the past	Other hospital
0.1%	12%	10%	11%
1%	32%	28%	30.5%
5%	60.5%	51.5%	54%
20%	85%	78.5%	82.5%

TABLE 10-3. Products used in a given class of material.

Supplier	Brand Name	Product Class	Code
		Cardiovascular catheterization kits	42221513
AAA	A	548	
BBB	B	123	
CCC	C	4	
DDD	D	2	

mapping between the different classification systems that are used. In the case of the five university hospitals, the decision was made to use a German classification system provided by several online trading exchanges (the GPI system).

After deciding whether a product may be used across several different processes, the next question is whether several different products should be used within a single process. In general, the success of harmonizing the supplies within a process can be evaluated by the results of a report showing the medical treatment process and the corresponding supplies used within this process. There should be as little product variation as can be clinically justified within identical clinical processes in a hospital. Such harmonization not only affects the reduction of the effort and the costs associated with supplies (economic parameters), but also has a positive impact on patient care (quality parameters), such as less time spent on training clinical staff on different products and a higher level of skills and more experience to be acquired with a well-circumscribed number of products. It needs to be monitored, however, if the decreased variability of supplies used in a given clinical process actually results in a decreased variability of the clinical outcomes and fewer complications. Due to the effort necessary to gauge these effects, this method is employed only in very few areas (see also "DRG-Related Analyses" in this chapter).

The method of reducing the number of supplies is, however, limited by the inherent variation within a single medical process due to the differences among patients.

A combined analysis of the products' use in clinical processes requires information from several clinical IT systems, together with information from materials management and a structured way of linking those pieces of information (see COINS case study in this chapter).

There is yet another aspect of harmonizing product use and reducing the variety of products. A reduction in the number of different materials ordered also creates savings on the supplier's side, therefore suppliers might have an interest in helping hospitals achieve a concentration of the products used.

Optimizing the Purchase Price

Reducing the number of suppliers and the number of products used results in a concentration of products and an aggregation of the purchasing volume, as shown in the preceding sections. Significant volumes lead to more favorable conditions because suppliers are willing to grant better conditions—in particular, lower prices. Only an extremely large reduction of variations in products used allows the hospitals to buy large enough quantities of materials to convince suppliers to give a price discount. Often these quantities cannot be achieved by a single hospital and therefore definitely require a purchasing cooperative to aggregate the purchasing volume.

Besides volume bundling, the negotiation skills of the purchasing manager strongly influence the price to be paid. The key to successful negotiations is information based on a comparison of prices negotiated in other hospitals. This price comparison can relate to the same products of the same suppliers, or it can relate to a group of products consisting of different products from various vendors.

Based on a single product, a comparison of prices achieved by several hospitals for the same product over the same period of time gives a good indication of the improvements. To perform price comparisons between different products in a product group, an attempt must be made to make products comparable. This is achieved by classifying products in groups following the scheme of one of the classification systems. The analysis of products within a class definitely requires a database containing all data from all hospitals involved, such as the GROPIS system implemented in the five university hospitals. Figure 10-4 shows the potential savings for three of the five university hospitals. Depending on the type of medical supply, there were huge differences in the prices paid by the individual hospitals.

Analyzing the price differences can be performed by the cooperating hospitals themselves or by service providers, typically a consulting company. Some online trading exchanges and purchasing cooperatives also offer such services. Data included in these analyses are the average and lowest prices for a single product or product group.

As these data are cumbersome to collect and process, especially if many products are gauged and if product groups are targeted, some hospitals or purchasing cooperatives are focusing on a few products only. Hospitals, realizing that they do not have the purchasing power to influence the price, may team up with one another and form an ad hoc purchasing cooperative to purchase only a few or limited set of products. This method works best with products that are easy to compare. By focusing on products with a high value, this method can create large savings in a relatively short period of time. When the range of easily comparable high value products is limited, however, this method works only for a limited time and has to be succeeded by other methods.

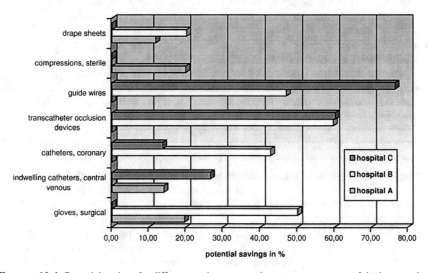

FIGURE 10-4. Potential savings for different product groups shown as a percentage of the lowest price.

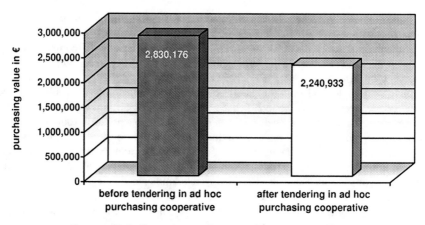

FIGURE 10-5. Change in annual purchasing value of defibrillators.

To measure the effect of an ad hoc purchasing organization, past prices for products and the prices negotiated using this method are compared. The sum of the difference equals the savings. Figure 10-5 illustrates the amount of savings possible for defibrillators due to tendering in an ad hoc purchasing cooperative. The university hospital saved about 600,000 euros per year.

If price comparisons are to be performed automatically for a large range of products, unique product identifiers and naming schemes are necessary. As the necessary harmonization efforts require time for aligning the codes and terms, ad hoc or one-off purchasing cooperatives soon reach the limits of successful cooperation.

Optimizing the Usage, Quantity and Quality of Material

To measure the quantity of materials used, a linkage between the quantity of medical processes, cases in a department, and the products used, need to be established. In an ideal situation, such as when there are clinical pathways, a medical indication is linked to a list of materials typically used for treating the patient. This information provides a cost corridor for a group of patients and is an excellent basis for performing cost analyses related to medical cases.

With or without clinical pathways, only primarily expensive or critical materials are directly charged to the patient. Materials costs that are not charged to the patient but only to the cost center, such as the department or the ward, cannot be used for calculating process costs per medical indication. Instead, an overall average of the materials costs per patient, or per case treated in this department, has to be calculated.

Changes in the number of materials used and, thus, changes in the materials costs of a medical department can therefore only roughly be correlated with the number of cases within this time period. As a result, no detailed interpretation of the findings is possible. If the costs increase, for example, this might be due to an increase in the number of cases or due to expensive drugs or other supplies needed for a certain patient. There might also be other reasons, such as wrong orders.

Sometimes high materials costs could be associated with high-class products that are not necessary for a given purpose. This is the case, for example, when chemicals with the highest degree of purity are ordered for a routine test not requiring such specification. These kinds of discrepancies and problems can only be evaluated by the clinical experts who have the knowledge about both the product and the clinical background of the product. Such problems are often related to a culture of focusing on a brand instead of looking at the product features. These deficiencies can be overcome by proper product specifications for a given purpose provided by the clinical specialists. A feature-based classification system might assist in defining these specifications.

One method of ensuring that only those products with the precise features and specifications are ordered is *evidence-based purchasing*. It requires evidence about how a material influences a medical process and its outcomes. Such evidence can be retrieved from the literature or by continuous measurements of the quality of medical processes and the impact a material has on its quality. A DRG-related report comprised of both economic and clinical parameters describing the outcome of a medical process can create such evidence. These types of analyses are emerging as hospitals are being transformed into patient-centric organizations that organize their IT infrastructure and their information management around the patient (see "DRG-related Analysis" and "COINS Case Study").

eBusiness can support the usage and quantity of material by providing additional product information. Most eBusiness applications provide the ability to link the product information within an electronic catalog or within a specialized application with detailed product specifications and with instructions for use.

Table 10-4 summarizes the methods for optimizing procurement, parameters to be measured, and the IT systems involved in these measurements.

Data Source

Most reports used to control operational materials management are created using data from the purchasing, materials management, and financial systems. The measurement of procurement process efforts also requires data from the human resources system. Data from the administration system is required for any department grouping. Electronic patient record (EPR) systems and other clinical systems need to be involved to measure any relationship to clinical processes. Table 10-4 shows the relationship between the type of business analysis and the IT systems involved.

To extract data from these various systems for the purpose of business analysis, data warehouse technology is the method of choice (see "COINS Case Study"). It requires the different systems, however, to be technically integrated (see Chapter 4). If this is not the case, the data collected are often manually extracted from the various systems mentioned previously. This is a constant source of low-quality data. In addition, manually compiling the data is tedious and requires extra time and effort.

Data Presentation

The data presentation required for the successful controlling of operational material management follows the principles of a good report—data must be unique (no redundancy) and key information needs to be easily accessible. Furthermore, a report must be tailored to the target group of that report. Clinicians, for example, demand that data is presented in connection with diagnostic and treatment information. Understanding that their focus is based on patient care rather than materials helps to present data in a clinical context to the medical staff.

Most systems creating such reports are part of an ERP system or hospital management system and are developed for use by procurement experts. The reports from such systems are asset and value oriented, listing the value, the delivery date, and the account of a

TABLE 10-4. Summary of methods in operational procurement

	Method	Parameters measured	IT systems involved
Methods for Optimizing the Procurement Process	Automating the internal eBusiness transactions, mainly the requisitioning process	Number of lines of all relevant invoices in the financial system with the number of lines in the requisitioning system	Financial system, materials management system including the requisitioning module
	Employing an electronic catalog maintained by the supplier	Number of products bought from suppliers who are responsible for maintaining their own material data	Materials management system
	Automating the external eBusiness transactions	Number of automated transactions per type of transaction (e.g. order and invoice) must be compared to the number of nonautomated transactions performed	Materials management system including the purchasing module and financial system
Methods for Product Standardization	Prioritizing suppliers: concentrating business efforts to the important suppliers	Effort per supplier categorized according to importance (suppliers of A, B and C products)	Materials management system including the purchasing module and human resources system
	Reducing the number of suppliers	Number of suppliers	Materials management system including the purchasing module
	Concentrating the purchasing value on a few suppliers	Percentage of suppliers providing given amounts of purchasing values measured over time and compared with other hospital	Materials management system including the purchasing module and financial system
	Reducing the number of materials	Number of materials purchased	Materials management system including the purchasing module
	Concentrating the purchasing value on a few products	Percentage of materials in given amounts of purchasing values measured over time and compared with other hospital	Materials management system including the purchasing module and financial system
Methods for Standardizing Product Use	Using the same materials in several clinical processes	List different products within the same product class and count frequency of use per product	Materials management system including the purchasing module, system must support a classification system
	Reducing the number of materials within the same clinical processes	List different products within the same clinical process (defined by DRG) and count frequency of use per product	Clinical system/electronic patient record system and materials management system including the purchasing module
	Optimizing the materials costs per clinical case or patient	Materials costs per clinical case or average materials costs per patient treated in the department	Clinical system/electronic patient record system and materials management and financial system

Methods for Optimizing the Results of Negotiating with Suppliers	Optimizing the purchasing price by general volume bundling	Number of products per supplier and price per product measured over time and compared with data from other hospitals	Materials management system including the purchasing module and financial system(s) of all hospitals involved
	Optimizing the purchasing price by volume bundling within ad hoc purchasing group	Product price before ad hoc group has been established and afterwards	Materials and financial management systems of all hospitals involved
	Optimizing negotiation skills by providing detailed information	Average price and lowest price paid by several hospitals for a single product or a class of similar products	Materials management including purchasing module and financial system (grouping based on classification system)
New Purchasing Methods	Evidence-based purchasing	Complication rate (clinical outcome) associated with the use of a given product	Clinical system/electronic patient record system and materials management system including purchasing module

product. Materials are described and grouped in a way that is geared towards purchasing or accounting. Reports are often very complex and it is difficult to draw conclusions from them.

As has been demonstrated above, it is important to have information about the clinical usage of a material for certain types of analyses. The conventional reports produced by ERP systems are insufficient for this purpose, and new approaches to creating reports have to be implemented.

Data warehouse technology can be extremely helpful in this aspect. It provides the ability to link material data to medical processes, gives different levels of information depth, and presents data in a graphical form, which makes it easy to focus on particular aspects of a query. They often include functions that allow them to take a look at *what-if* questions and the economic impact of different scenarios.

Strategic Procurement

Materials Management as a Strategic Component

To make materials management a component of an overall strategy, a well-defined and formulated strategy in a hospital that can be supported by the materials management department must exist. In most hospitals, purchasing managers focus on cost savings rather than on the impact a material might have on a particular medical process.

An example of a hospital's strategy in a particular medical segment would be to become recognized as a superior provider in this field, e.g. for implanting hearing devices. Within the framework of such a strategy, a supplier of hearing devices could support the hospital's marketing activities for recruiting patients, or could take over public relations activities for the hospital. Such support may be of higher importance for the hospital than reducing the price for the hearing device.

More global strategies, such as those applying to all medical departments within a hospital, are often motivated by cost containment. In countries that use DRG patient classi-fication systems, such as Germany, DRG-based remuneration has a strong impact on hospital strategies because it transfers the economic risk for providing a medical service to the hospital. Because there are variations within the medical process for each diagnostic-related group, one key strategy for many hospitals is to reduce the breadth of these variations by standardizing procedures and materials. Clinical pathways are an instrument for such standardization at the level of individual hospitals or groups of hospitals.

Curbing costs is not a strategy, per se considering side effects and medium-term impacts of a treatment, however, definitely is. In a recent study, von Eiff compared the risk associated with using one-time trocars versus that of trocars for multiple usage [3]. He also compared additional factors, including sterilization and logistical requirements of multiple-use trocars. From an economic point of view, it made sense to invest in the multiple-use trocar constructed of metal as opposed to the one-time trocars constructed of plastic. It was possible, however, to show that complication rates are much lower with one-time trocars than with multiple-use trocars. When taking the costs of potential medical complications into consideration, it made sense for a hospital to use one-time trocars, even though the costs for this material are higher. From a hospital's economic point of view, considering the side effects of a treatment is only worthwhile if they have a negative impact on costs incurred for the hospital—for example, on the costs due to an increase in the length of stay or on costs due to unplanned readmissions of patients that cannot be charged separately. Making the avoidance of negative long-term effects part of a hospital's strategy requires a close interaction between insurance companies, hospitals, and office-based physicians.

Another potential strategy for a hospital is sharing the risk of the costs incurred during treatment with suppliers. This approach requires involving the supplier deeply in the hospital's processes. Because the effort needed for the hospital staff to get suppliers involved is very great, it is only useful for a few indications with a high volume.

These suppliers have the role of a *strategic* supplier. A strategic supplier in this sense has an impact on the value of the core business. They are responsible for certain tasks within the core business, taking the risk for the fulfilment, and participating in the continuous improvement of this business. In almost any situation, they provide services (e.g., training, product customization, and maintenance) together with the product. Examples of strategic supplier relationships are companies offering capitation contracts for hospitals, such as some pharmaceutical firms do. Such contracts guarantee a fixed price for the medication of a defined group of patients, and the supplier carries the risk for the effect of the medication.

Roche Diagnostics is a good example of a pharmaceutical company executing such a strategy. Instead of selling certain diagnostics and drugs, they pursue the business model of offering fixed price bundles for given indications. Within this given indication, they provide any diagnostic item and any drug that is required for a particular patient. From the hospital's point of view, this is a reduction of economic risk. The challenge for both parties involved is to balance the economic uncertainties. By defining criteria for including and excluding patients in the agreements, the economic attractiveness of such contracts can vary a lot for a hospital.

A similar discussion is taking place within the medical product industry. Some large medical product suppliers are evaluating methods of providing packages, including all required products to support certain indications. From the supplier's point of view, this could result in the unfavorable situation of having provided more products than actually calculated. This can usually be balanced out over a period of time and by a good mix of products in the contract.

Another simpler example of a strategy for shifting responsibilities to the supplier is the consignment store. In such a case, the hospital makes suppliers responsible for having the required amount of products available at all times at the hospital's site. The hospital must define the quantity of products that it requires. As a result, it does not need to manage the storage of products and the replenishment. It can also reduce the capital tied to the value of the materials stored because the products are still owned by the supplier. The supplier is compensated for this service.

Table 10-5 summarizes the methods employed in strategic procurement. This list is not exhaustive but rather reflects strategic options being discussed at the five university hospitals. Some of these methods have been adopted already, while others are treated as long-term options and visions for the future.

The table shows that most of the strategies require a close interaction between the hospital and the supplier, referred to as collaborative business or commerce. This interaction can and should be supported by electronic media. Classic eBusiness technology provides tools for managing consignment stores, vendor-managed inventory (VMI), and other logistics services. Furthermore, electronic platforms for exchanging documents and collaborating with each other could assist in establishing the necessary flow of information required in collaborative ways of conducting business (cBusiness).

DRG-related Analysis

To measure the impact a material has on the clinical and financial outcome of a medical procedure within a group of patients in the DRG system, all factors that could have an impact on the medical process need to be included. To evaluate the financial impact, all economic factors need to be measured and weighted according to their importance. Each single process step within a procedure related to a medical category needs to be identified, and all costs including supply costs associated with this step must be captured, including common costs such as those for infrastructure and services. Often, such information cannot be derived from routine data but must be collected especially for this purpose. Because this takes extra effort, such kind of data is often not available and the costs related to that process are calculated by dividing the entire costs within a department by the number of medical cases or by the number of procedures provided in the same period. From a financial point of view, this indicates the average costs but not the real costs for a case or procedure.

Due to the effort still required for DRG-related analysis, it is recommended that consultants collect the necessary data only in those diagnosis-related groups that are of strategic importance and/or have a high volume.

TABLE 10-5. Summary of methods in strategic procurement.

Method	Impact on hospital-supplier relationship
Methods for increasing the revenue	
become center of excellence for particular medical treatment	High
Methods for increasing the clinical quality	
standardize clinical processes	Low
reduce complication rates	Medium
Methods for shifting risks and responsibilities to suppliers	
share the risks with supplier (capitation contracts)	High
outsource warehouse management (consignment stores and vendor-managed inventories)	High

Data Source

To integrate procurement and materials management into the hospital's overall strategy, controlling methods need to provide a holistic view that reflects all issues of the strategic position. At present, this often means measuring a combination of data usually kept in different unrelated systems. The technical and organizational demands that apply to data at the level of controlling the operational processes of purchasing and materials management therefore also hold true for data at the strategic level. This clearly demonstrates the strategic nature of information management. A patient-centric approach governing the strategy helps to focus on the core processes of a hospital and assists in transforming information management into *integrated* information management.

COINS [1] Case Study: Controlling Information Systems

The following example illustrates a procedure by which the clinical perspective can be included in business analysis. The example describes COINS, the controlling information system of the Medizinische Hochschule Hannover (MHH).

The MHH includes a medical school and one of the largest teaching hospitals in Germany.

More than 200 different software systems support the daily work at the MHH. About 20 systems out of the 200 are critical for integrated business analysis. With the advent of a DRG-based remuneration system for hospitals in Germany, there was a need to recognize the impact such change means for the MHH. The top management therefore defined and formalized a strategy for a balanced score card system. This balanced score card system gives detailed information about the goals for each department and timeframes in which these goals need to be reached.

Several strategic goals concern medical supplies, and therefore require the involvement of the materials management department:

- The core of the MHH strategy is to become a patient-centric organization. Among other things, this requires the technical and organizational ability to charge all direct and indirect costs to the patient
- The German DRG reimbursement allows additional revenues for certain high-price materials used within the medical treatment. It needs to be ensured that all costs generated through materials are known
- The German DRG system also allows separate negotiations with insurance companies for the reimbursement of certain very expensive drugs. As a result, the use of drugs that are potentially included in such additional reimbursements needs to be monitored, and the information about their use needs to be available for budget negotiations with the insurance companies
- Because the DRG-based reimbursement scheme is still the subject of further ongoing developments in Germany, the reimbursement per patient group, and even the groups themselves, may vary from year to year. The influence of such changes on the overall financial outcome needs to be monitored closely. In addition, the MHH has an interest in shaping the DRG-based reimbursement scheme and therefore contributes detailed information about their costs per DRG to a national pool of data that constitutes the basis for calculating the cost weights per DRG.

---

[1] COINS – Controlling Information System is a product of trinovis GmbH Hannover, Germany

- The MHH has joined a logistics initiative called NetLog Hannover. The goal is to gain more efficiency in logistics processes by benefiting from economies of scale (see Chapter 11).
- The MHH is a founding member of the purchasing cooperative COMPARATIO.

There are complex interactions between these goals and between the different departments involved—i.e., clinical departments, IT, controlling, financial, and top management. The balanced score card breaks the main strategic goals into concerted tasks and defines the responsibilities for task execution. Because the goals defined in the balanced score card also include quantitatively measurable data, one goal within the balanced score card system was to establish an integrated controlling system to measure the progress made in achieving the goals. The project was introduced to a wide audience within the MHH to increase the acceptance of the approach. Because all measurable goals defined in the balanced score card would be analyzed by the integrated controlling information system, this system became the centerpiece for enforcing the strategy and was of importance to practically anybody involved in putting the strategic goals into practice. Due to the complex issue, the following common principles for all reports produced by the system had to be agreed upon:

- Transparency strategy—every manager sees everything
- Single reporting—all reports are based on unique nonredundant data
- User orientation—handling of the system does not require technical skills

A four-level organization was established for the execution of the strategy. The four levels included:

- 1st level Master Group—this embraced the three executive managers (responsible for patient care, clinical research, and administration), the head of IT management, the head of controlling, the head of the staff council, and project management. They defined goals, gave updates of the strategies, set priorities, and had the overall responsibility for allocating resources.
- 2nd level Project Management Group—this consisted of the executive board members responsible for finance, controlling, and project management. They define resources in detail, set priorities for the execution of the tasks, and handle organizational matters and escalation processes.
- 3rd level Kernel Team—this consists of the project management specialists, controlling specialists, IT applications specialists, and other specialists of the IT department. They plan the project tasks in detail, monitor the execution of such tasks, identify conflicts in the project, and prepare escalation processes to be decided by the Project Management Group.
- 4th level Project Task Teams—these are formed from time to time to execute certain project management tasks. They consist of at least one member of the Kernel Team.

During the first project meetings of the Master Group, the Project Management Group, and the Kernel Team, the desiderata concerning information to be analyzed were defined and compiled as a long list. Because the items on this long list could not be put into practice in a short period of time, the first step was to establish a management information system reflecting the status quo and comprising information that was easily available. This system was meant to be an interim solution not aiming at the provision of perfect information but rather with the intention of getting the major players involved. The technical implementation followed the principles of constructing data warehouses (see Figure 10-6).

The Kernel Team defined the data sources for the information to be analyzed. As the data were to be derived from different systems, a task team was founded for each

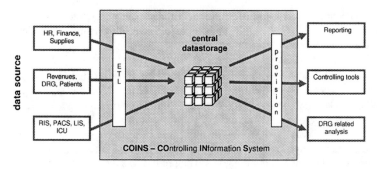

Legend: ETL - extract, transform, load

FIGURE 10-6. COINS - overview.

individual system. These task teams defined technical mechanisms to extract the required data from the various systems and the procedures that would be applied to the data on their way to the data warehouse, which included several steps.

Once the data were extracted, they would receive a timestamp and be archived together with a reference to the data source. In a next step, the data would be normalized to fit the data warehouse structure. The normalized data would then be loaded into the data warehouse database.

At this stage, intensive quality checks would be necessary to get rid of inconsistencies between the data. These consistency conflicts could be caused by organizational, technical, or logical problems.

Figure 10-7 shows a good example of such a consistency conflict between data in the three different systems: the radiology information system (RIS) operated by the central diagnostic department of the MHH, the accounting system used for billing the insurance companies (IS-H), and the financial system (FI) for transferring costs internally between cost centers.

Each service provided by the diagnostic department is entered in the RIS. Information that is required for billing is transferred to the IS-H system. If a service of the diagnostic department has been ordered by another department within the MHH, information about what service was provided to whom is passed on to the FI system. In our example, the

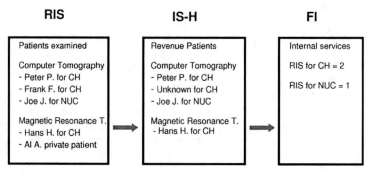

FIGURE 10-7. Different views on data from different IT systems – potentially leading to consistency conflicts.

diagnostic department provided three services for the CH department and one service for the NUC department. One patient paid for the service on his own. When transferring the data from the RIS to the IS-H, data for Frank F. obviously got lost and therefore could not be processed by the IS-H system. Data to be transferred from IS-H to the FI system are compressed and only summaries are sent to the other system. A simple query such as "How many patients were examined in a given timeframe?" results in three different answers depending on the system queried. The RIS would say five patients and is able to name them, the IS-H system would say three or four patients, and the FI system would say three patients. Basically, all of them are right if one only looks at their own data repository.

To resolve this conflict, data from all three systems are used—the patients are counted based on the RIS system, the calculation of the revenue is based on the IS-H system, and the analysis of internal charges uses both the FI system and the RIS. The reason why the data for one patient had not been accepted by the IS-H system was investigated and revealed that, in many of the cases causing problems, patient demographics data had not been entered consistently in all systems involved. Other reasons, such as wrong procedure codes or not identifying a patient as being readmitted, could be made responsible for the inconsistencies. Although in this case the data could not be made consistent by the data warehouse, analyzing data from different sources and comparing them was not possible in the past without the data warehouse.

One key issue for the materials management is charging as many supplies to patients as possible. Figure 10-8 provides an example of the flow of materials information between systems.

At the MHH, medical supplies are purchased by a central materials management department using a materials management (MM) system included in the HIS_h. This department either delivers the received products to the requesting department (surgery department, in this example) or to an internal site providing logistics services within the hospital. The logistics staff at this site bundles those products most frequently used for a given surgery into a set, and delivers the set to the department (surgery). During the surgical operation, all materials used are documented in the surgery (SUR) system. Like our sample query (How many patients were examined?), a query about "Which material was used in a given timeframe?" will be answered differently depending on

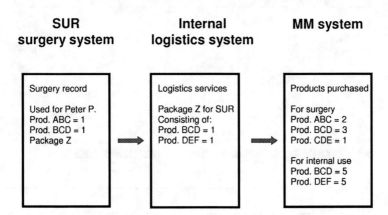

SUR surgery system

Surgery record

Used for Peter P.
Prod. ABC = 1
Prod. BCD = 1
Package Z

Internal logistics system

Logistics services

Package Z for SUR
Consisting of:
Prod. BCD = 1
Prod. DEF = 1

MM system

Products purchased

For surgery
Prod. ABC = 2
Prod. BCD = 3
Prod. CDE = 1

For internal use
Prod. BCD = 5
Prod. DEF = 5

FIGURE 10-8. Conflicts between materials data in different systems.

Timeframe   Year 2005   Cost matrix
Departments: All departments
DRG: D01 Cochlea Implantation, unilateral

	Staff cost [€]			Med. supply cost [€]					Infrastructure [€]				
	M3 [€]	N3 [€]	MT.FD [€]	MED [€]	MED.EX [€]	IMP [€]	MB [€]	MB.EX [€]	MB [€]	NMI [€]	Sum [€]	%	%
NORMAL	44,386	169,560	41,376	10,209	1,178	0	11,429	0	2,588	116,635	397,361	7.0	
ICU	1,647	4,661	368	901	0	0	910	0	241	1,486	10,214	0.2	7.0
DIALYS	0	0	0	0	0	0	0	0	0	0	0	0.0	0.0
SUR	93,678	0	178,560	2,397	0	4,250,293	32,364	9	25,803	138,786	4,721,890	83.0	
ANE	62,722	0	47,100	11,987	0	0	13,354	0	3,336	28,012	166,511	2.9	86.4
DELIV	0	0	0	0	0	0	0	0	0	0	0	0.0	0.0
CARDIO	0	0	0	0	0	0	0	0	0	0	0	0.0	
ENDO	0	0	0	0	0	0	0	0	0	0	0	0.0	
RADIOL	4,863	0	4,823	16	0	40	2,283	0	4,376	2,250	18,651	0.3	
LAB	2,085	0	6,176	4	106	0	2,066	0	657	2,308	13,402	0.2	
OTHER	148,670	471	153,911	241	0	0	875	0	1,053	57,552	362,773	6.4	6.7
Sum	358,051	174,692	432,314	25,755	1,284	4,250,333	63,281	9	38,054	347,029	5,690,802		
Sum	965,057			4,340,662					385,083		5,690,802		
%	6.29%	3.07%	7.6%	0.45%	0.02%	74.69%	1.11%	0.0%	0.63%	5.88%			
%	16.96%			76.28%					6.77%				

Cases	203		Sum days	1,498
CM	2,071		Sum ICU days	9

Report generated 9/7/2007

FIGURE 10-9. DRG report for unilateral cochlea implantation – example of hospital data.

the data that are provided by the different information systems. From the point of view of the SUR system, products ABC and BCD and set Z were used. The internal logistics system would recognize products BCD and DEF as *used* because they are contained in set Z. From the point of view of the MM system, all products delivered to the surgery department and to the internal logistics site would be listed, even though these data do not show product usage (they only show product delivery). The example also shows the importance of having unique product identifiers across the systems, or at least being able to link different materials by mapping the identifiers or descriptions used in the various systems.

Timeframe: Year 2005   Cost matrix
Department   All departments
DRG: D01 Cochlea Implantation, unilateral

	Staff cost [€]			Med. Supply cost [€]					Infrastructure [€]				
	MB [€]	N3 [€]	MT.FD [€]	MED [€]	MED.EX [€]	IMP [€]	MB [€]	MB.EX [€]	NI [€]	NMI [€]	Sum [€]	%	%
NORMAL	21,430	-21,635	-11,987	2,435	-549	0	-812	23	6,393	-4,780	-9,482	-108.6	
ICU	228	2,943	208	-227	625	2	35	0	256	1,112	5182	59.3	-55,6
DIALYS	0	0	0	0	0	0	0	0	0	0	0	0.0	0.0
SUR	-13,480	0	-85,346	1,752	961	401,233	59	1,212	-5,663	-45,941	254,787	2,917.5	
ANE	78	0	978	-3,026	1	0	2,555	0	1,447	-4,083	-2050	-23.5	2939.7
DELIV	0	0	0	0	0	0	0	0	0	0	0	0.0	0.0
CARDIO	33	0	29	0	0	0	4	0	0	8	74	0.8	
ENDO	4	0	9	0	0	0	0	0	0	0	13	0.1	
RADIOL	-1,998	0	-1,026	62	0	52	-554	132	-2,104	-204	-5640	-64.6	
LAB	-1,359	0	-3,645	22	-85	0	-117	8	-446	-1,072	-6694	-76.7	
OTHER	-111,375	58	-88,536	46	122	4	745	0	43	-28,564	-227457	-2,604.6	-2,784,0
Sum	-106,439	-18,534	-189,316	1,064	1,075	401,291	1,915	1,375	-74	-83,524			8,733
Sum	-314,389			406,720					-83,598				0
%	-1,218.81%	-213.37%	-2,167.82%	12.18%	12.31%	4,595.11%	21.93%	15.74%	-0.85%	-976.84%	Result		8,733
%	-3,600.01%			4,657.28%					-957.27%				

	hospital					national average	
Cases	203		Sum days	1,498		Sum days	1,478
CM	2,071		Sum ICU days	9		Baserate	2756

Report generated 9/7/2007

FIGURE 10-10. DRG report for unilateral cochlea implantation – example of comparison with national average.

As a result of using a data warehouse for data analysis, the MHH is now able to analyze materials usage and costs in relation to medical procedures, such as surgeries. Within the DRG-related analysis, medical supplies usage can be shown in relation to the diagnoses and clinical procedures (see Figure 10-9). Hospital-specific data can also be compared with the German average values and deviations can be graphically depicted.

In addition to the overview of the current status, deviations from the national average can be calculated that allow the management to gain an immediate picture (see Figure 10-10) of the losses and profit made per DRG. Answers to queries like "What happens to our revenue if we receive additional reimbursement for certain diagnostics in the future?" allow continuous revenue forecasts.

Conclusions

As has been demonstrated previously, business analysis relies on the availability of clean and consistent data—be it for the purpose of optimizing the operational purchasing and materials management processes or for putting a hospital's strategy into practice. These data originate from a variety of information systems, as seen in the COINS case study. This holds true, in particular, if diagnostic and treatment data are to be included. Technical means, such as a communication server, are the basic prerequisites for exchanging data (contained in messages) between systems, but are not sufficient for integrating data at a logical level. Data warehouses building upon of a coherent data model and storing data from different sources extracted at a defined time aim to generate consistent sets of data and thus perform a logical integration. As illustrated by the COINS case study, this integration can only be complete to the extent that there are consistent data. Yet a series of management reports yielding insight into the relation of materials use with diagnosis-related groups becomes possible.

The accuracy of materials data increases significantly with the adoption of eBusiness procedures. By employing an electronic product catalog, eBusiness applications impose a greater discipline on all persons involved in procurement. This discipline engenders consistent materials data to be processed, stored, and transferred. Up-to-date electronic product catalogs as used for online transactions enable structured data analysis of single products. If the products are classified according to a classification system, product data can be aggregated at various levels of granularity depending on the scope of the analysis.

The adoption of eBusiness methods often triggers materials management to change its entire approach to conducting business with suppliers. The number of products and the number of suppliers is reduced, which leads to more efficiency in managing suppliers and their products. Fewer different product types and fewer suppliers mean a concentration and bundling of the purchasing value and a more favorable position during negotiations. This effect can be accomplished at a local level within a hospital, or across hospitals within purchasing cooperatives like the COMPARATIO. If purchasing is to be harmonized within a group of hospitals, the use of electronic procedures is imperative. In the case of the five university hospitals, an electronic group purchasing information system was established. This system may not necessarily be called an eBusiness application, but it constitutes an attempt at integrating the materials data from all hospitals involved and forms the basis for joint purchasing activities.

The interaction of eBusiness and other electronic approaches in materials management, with business analysis methods supporting operational and strategic procurement, is diverse and bidirectional. As a result, eBusiness may take on the role of a generator of accurate data, as well as the role of a method for optimizing purchasing and other activities within materials management.

References

[1] Gudat, H. (2006) In der Logistik ist noch viel zu bewegen. *Krankenhaus Umschau.* **75**, 12–15.
[2] Kaczmakre, D.S. and G.R. Metcalfe. (2005) Benchmarking supply expenses the devil's in the definition: why hasn't the healthcare industry been able to fix the disconnect between the supply chain and the revenue cycle? Maybe a generally accepted definition of "supply expense" would be a start. *Healthcare Financial Management.* **59**, 94–100.
[3] Von Eiff, W. (2006) Vom Preisvergleich zum Risk Assessment. *Krankenhaus Umschau.* **75**, 24–28.

11
Logistics Services and Beyond

MICHAEL SCHÜLLER AND URSULA HÜBNER

Executive Summary

Due to high pressure on costs and limited financial resources in healthcare, hospitals – being forced to curb costs – are trying to achieve cost savings by optimizing their service departments, in particular hospital logistics. In the past, logistics processes were simply outsourced to logistics service providers (LSP) in the hope of realizing these cost savings. Today, hospitals are employing a variety of methods to keep logistics costs down while at the same time trying to obtain an optimum level of service. Some hospitals are beginning to execute their logistics tasks again by themselves, albeit using a different approach. They start up subsidiaries with suitable cooperation-partners (majority-owned) with the aim of marketing their logistics services. Other hospitals have retained classic outsourcing models through purchasing logistics services in the external market. Logistics and other service providers have also changed the spectrum of services that they offer. Regardless of how a single hospital decides to organize its own hospital logistics, cooperative structures with logistics service providers and other potential partners are essential.

This chapter shows that cooperation has to be designed in three layers. On the strategic layer, suitable partners are chosen. In this context, the decision has to be made whether to contract a multiservice provider or a multihospitals provider. Both of them pursue the objective of saving costs by using synergy effects. Multi-service providers expand their business in a qualitative way by offering services at many levels. Multihospital providers try to acquire as many hospitals as possible as customers, whereas multiservice providers attempt to offer a bundle of various services.

On the tactical layer, logistical flows and services are planned and controlled. They are executed on the operative layer. The value of information systems in supporting tasks on the two lower layers is evident, and its use has increased clearly over the last few years. Case studies illustrate examples of multiservice providers and multihospitals providers. Opportunities for future optimization, in particular the use of unified identifiers, are being discussed.

Outsourcing does not stop at nonclinical functions such as logistics (warehousing and transportation), or administrative tasks such as archive management. It also progresses into the clinical domain. Outsourcing a hospital pharmacy is not uncommon, particularly in the case of smaller hospitals for whom maintaining their own pharmacy might not be profitable. The case study of a multi-hospital/multiservice provider demonstrates the plethora of services a third party might offer on the market, ranging from logistics to pharmaceutical consultancy. Clinical know-how and experience prove to be essential to becoming successful. Unrestricted electronic information flow accompanying the business processes throughout a supply chain counteracts potential communication barriers between manufacturers and their customers in such a chain. In this sense, eBusiness has the capacity to make these barriers virtual, which are an inherent part of any supply chain.

Hospital Logistics – Which Way to Turn?

Introduction

Designing individual hospital logistics systems without connecting the various players and their IT systems is impossible today. Particularly due to the pressure to form lean structures, the cooperation model between hospitals, suppliers, and logistics service providers is becoming more and more necessary. Cooperation can generate effective contributions to cost reduction only when business processes are largely standardized and automated. Suitable systems integration between the cooperation partners in healthcare logistics, therefore, is increasingly mandatory. It is not simply a question of integrating the systems, however, but also of having systems with the appropriate features. Thus, systems are required that not only automate and optimize internal processes but that control the intercompany information flow and thereby support the materials flow.

Trends in Hospital Logistics

With the introduction of DRG-based financing in hospitals in many countries, and their fixed amount of revenue per clinical case, hospitals switched to outsourcing of nonmedical tasks to service providers. Logistic functions, in particular, were affected by these measures. Hospital logistics functions embrace procurement and production logistics functions. In contrast to other industries, distribution logistics is not included. While healthcare logistics include all logistics functions of all players in healthcare (manufacturers, wholesalers, hospitals, pharmacies, physicians), hospital logistics constitute the part that relates only to hospital-relevant activities [1]. This includes, for example, tracking and tracing ordered material, receiving material and distributing medical supplies to the clinical units, internal transport services in hospitals, and reverse logistics.

Although there is a general trend towards outsourcing logistic functions throughout all industries, different variations were observed in practice over the last twenty years. Until the 1980s, most hospitals executed logistic activities on their own with their own staff. In the 1990s, classic outsourcing to service providers became popular. A reverse trend, however, has recently been noticeable, with hospitals bringing functions back inhouse that had previously been outsourced. Unlike the practices of the 1980s, however, they do not execute the services by themselves. Instead, they establish subsidiaries, together with logistics specialists and other partners, with the goal of selling the services in the external market [2]. Not only is the development itself remarkable, but also the extent of the logistic service bundles, as well as the speed of these changes that are taking place in the market. Intercompany supply chains actually originate from the manufacturing industry and are well known in other industries as well (see Chapter 2). The implementation of such chains together with appropriate management mechanism (SCM), however, often took many years. The question, therefore, is what direction hospital logistics will take in the future. Figure 11-1 shows past developments und possible trends for the future.

Retaining classic in-house logistics does not seem to be suitable for curbing costs. It can therefore be assumed that cooperation models between hospitals and service providers will also be increasingly established in the future. In the case of cooperation models that include the establishment of a service-providing company, the logistics services are executed either for one hospital only (the majority owner of the company) or for other hospitals as well, depending on the company's strategy and market penetration. Regardless of the chosen cooperation model, hospitals face the challenge of finding the right cooperation partners. The key success factor for such cooperation is that the external service provider has a sound knowledge and understanding of the clinical processes, and the logistics processes supporting the clinical processes. Even if logistics is understood as a discipline with general concepts and methods for different industries, hospital logistics has its specific demands. For example, sterile medical and surgical products need to be treated differently from nonsterile products, and narcotics have to be distinguished from other drugs when stored. Furthermore, different procedures may exist in hospitals for similar processes. Material in the emergency department, including life-saving devices, must be organized differently than that in normal clinical units where medical products are periodically replenished. Therefore, the service provider's understanding of hospital logistics must be regarded as the major criterion for selecting potential partners or providers. In detail, hospitals should make sure that partners possess the appropriate knowledge by having them demonstrate practical experience in this field

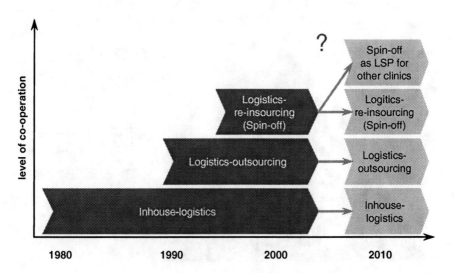

FIGURE 11-1. Past developments and future trends in hospital logistics.

before they start the cooperation. Additionally, the service provider's ability to interlink the involved partners on the operational layer and to connect and integrate their IT systems is a major decisive argument that speaks in favor of, or against, a potential partner. Such arguments are gaining more and more importance. IT systems used at different points in the supply chain definitely have to communicate with each other. In the case of external warehouse management, for example, requisitions generated by the hospital have to be transferred smoothly to the requisition management system of the logistics service provider. It is increasingly understood that standard processes supported by communication standards between the IT systems are essential to the success of such partnerships. Only an error-free information flow between the partners allows for smooth material flow. In particular, the logistical planning and control systems necessary for safeguarding the information flow rely on high-quality data being exchanged in the daily business. Only when all three factors come together—the know-how of the external partners, competitive planning and control systems, and the ability to connect processes and IT systems—can future-oriented cooperation models succeed in practice.

The success factors of cooperation exist on all three layers. From a strategic perspective, choosing the right partners, and especially a choice based on their know-how, are paramount. The optimal planning and the control of interorganizational functions take place on the tactical layer, and their implementation on the operative layer. Figure 11-2 illustrates the different layers and the questions specific to hospital logistics.

As shown in Figure 11-2, hospitals trying to find a new orientation in hospital logistics have to choose suitable partners at first (strategic perspective). Generally speaking, there are two types of service providers on the market—multiservice providers and multihospital providers. For service providers to be competitive in the hospital logistics market, it is crucial to generate cost savings for the hospitals without endangering their own margins. To this end, logistics service providers try to realize synergy effects. Synergies can be created when a critical mass of similar tasks has to be executed. This permits the efficient sharing of resources.

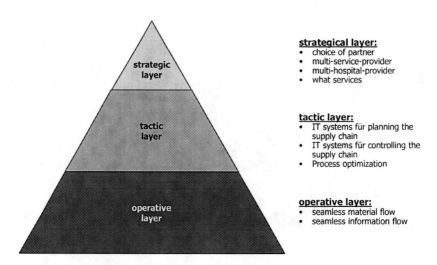

FIGURE 11-2. Different layers of cooperation in hospital logistics.

Multiservice providers achieve this goal by offering a larger range of services than the classic functions of hospital logistics usually embrace. Multihospital providers realize synergy effects by contracting with other hospitals with similar logistical tasks. While multiservice providers reach the necessary critical mass with a qualitative expansion, multihospital providers do so with a quantitative expansion. As the following examples show, both concepts have been put into practice successfully.

Case Studies

Multiservice Provider: Klinik Logistik Eppendorf

An example of a multiservice provider is the Klinik Logistik Eppendorf GmbH (KLE), a joint venture of the university hospital Hamburg-Eppendorf (UKE), the logistics service provider Hellmann Worldwide Logistics, and the facility management provider Dussmann. The joint venture now employs 250 people. Since January 2005, KLE has been UKE's provider of a variety of logistic services (see Figure 11-3). Since January 2007, it is completely owned by the university hospital.

DRG-based financing requires UKE, like all other hospitals, to monitor all patient-related costs and identify opportunities for cost savings. KLE's strategy, therefore, aims to increase the process transparency and thereby eventually reduce patient-related costs. The service bundle offered by KLE comprises patient transportation and material delivery, requisition of supplies and replenishment of the cabinets on the clinical units, mail services, archive administration, security services, reception services, call center, and management of central warehousing. It can be seen that, apart from classic logistics tasks such as transportation and warehousing, a series of other services such as archive administration, call center, security services, and reception services are executed by KLE. The advantages of such a service company are twofold. On one hand, there are qualitative benefits. The external partners bring logistical know-how and capabilities into the cooperation, which has led to significantly optimized processes. For example, the process of inbound deliveries has been completely reorganized. The items that are

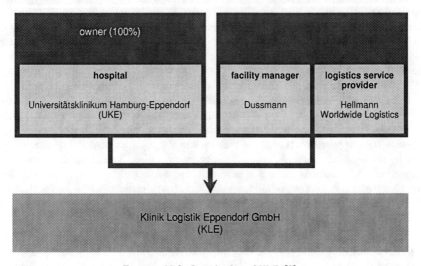

FIGURE 11-3. Organization of KLE. [3].

not included in the cabinet-based supply service of KLE, but are planned by UKE by itself (so called *bypass* items), are delivered by suppliers to a warehouse located outside the UKE premises, received by KLE employees, and delivered directly to the consignees by using the so-called *cross-docking* procedure and implementing a daily shuttle service between the warehouse and the hospital. In this case, the flow of materials managed by the cabinet-based supply service and the flow of bypass items are combined. This relieves the transportation service within the UKE premises and has led to reduced transportation costs. These effects can be also demonstrated in quantitative terms. For example, it has been possible to save hundreds of thousands of euros within a single year since KLE employees took over the responsibility for replenishing cabinets on the wards with medical consumer goods. Besides relieving clinical staff of logistic tasks, particularly stock-keeping on clinical units, it was possible to optimize the process in such a way that significantly fewer items now exceed the expiration date and have to be disposed of unused. By using barcode scanners at the point of demand, KLE staff record the type and the amount of those items that have to be replenished. The data captured are transferred to the materials management module (SAP R/3 MM) of the hospital information system, and a picking list is generated for the external warehouse. The shuttle service delivers materials 11 times in five days to the hospital, from where it is transported to the point of demand.

Transportation, staff, and routes are planned by a SyncroTESS system. This system will also be used in the future for billing the services provided by KLE for the hospital. Data exchange between the SyncroTESS system and R/3 in the hospital is planned and will permit an allocation of KLE's logistical services directly to a single clinical unit, and in the future to a single patient [4].

Multihospital Provider: Rhenus eonova

The logistics service provider, Rhenus eonova, who offers services in several regions throughout Germany, is an example of a multihospital provider. Rhenus eonova is the logistics partner in the NetLog cooperation project, which embraces five hospitals with about 5,000 beds in the Hannover area[1] and 20 suppliers of medical supplies. More than 3,000 different medical goods and consumer goods are stored on 5,300 m^2 of storage area with 4,000 shelves. Apart from warehousing, picking and transportation are also part of the service contract in NetLog—2,500 items are picked daily, prepared for shipping, and delivered at fixed time slots to fixed supply points, as negotiated with the hospitals [5].

Within the NetLog supply chain, the logistics service provider serves as a central hub between the manufacturers and the customers of the medical supplies (the hospitals). A particularly high degree of player integration is necessary for managing consignment items (see Figure 11-4). For these particular items, the suppliers themselves, not the logistics service provider, coordinate the stock in the logistics center. The requisitions sent by the hospitals, however, go to Rhenus eonova directly, and the supplies requisitioned are delivered. At the end of a month, the manufacturers receive an overview, provided by Rhenus eonova, of all items delivered to the respective hospitals and charge the hospitals on the basis of this document [6].

---

[1] Members include Klinikum Region Hannover, Kinderkrankenhaus auf der Bult, Niedersächsisches Landeskrankenhaus Wunstorf, Medizinische Hochschule Hannover (MHH), St. Bernward Krankenhaus

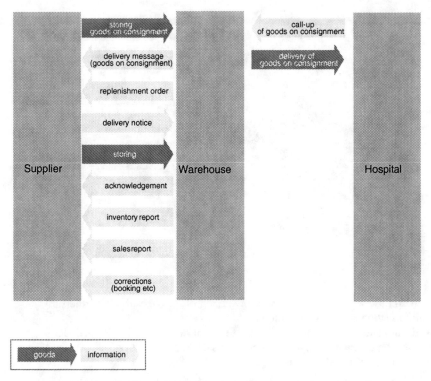

FIGURE 11-4. Flows of goods on consignment in the NetLog-Project.

There are advantages for both the suppliers and the customers. The suppliers benefit from easy order management due to the bundling of orders from different hospitals. Hospitals have a financial advantage, as they have to pay for items only at the time of use, not at the time of delivery to the warehouse [7].

The critical success factor in this cooperation model is, in fact, the use of integrated IT systems. The logistical processes on the operational layer are enabled by information exchanged automatically between suppliers, hospitals, and Rhenus eonova. All pieces of information converge on the logistics service provider's system and are prepared there for further process control. To this end, Rhenus eonova has developed its own Web-based portal, the Rhenus Logistik Cockpit. Suppliers and hospitals also retrieve all relevant logistic information from this source. For them, the Cockpit serves as a customer information portal to the Rhenus medical warehouse. Information made accessible by the portal includes, for example, stock information, materials movements, sales reports, batch stock, and expiration dates. In addition, the status of replenishment orders for those items that are automatically planned may be retrieved, and planning parameters may be edited. In the future, the information flow between the partners will be further automated by utilizing the Rhenus Business Networking Platform (BNP)—a dedicated messaging and workflow system. It is comprised of the following functions [8]:

- Technical connection of the players to the IT system
- Transformation and conversion of messages between involved partners
- Data communication via interfaces with the materials management system of the hospitals

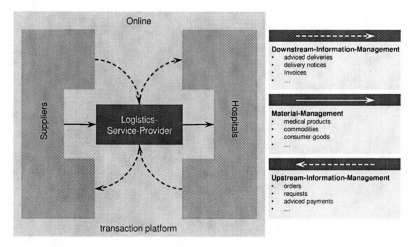

FIGURE 11-5. The logistics service provider as an information hub.

- Workflow system for systematic forwarding of messages to the partners
- Information portal via the Internet
- Event-handling system—e.g., for detection of delay in delivery
- Creation of reports—e.g., inventory and sales reports
- Archiving of transferred messages

The BNP functions reflect the importance of information logistics within the provision of overall logistics services. In particular, multihospital providers who achieve their synergy effects by high volumes, and who will thus have to rely increasingly on automatically managed information processes, have recognized their importance. More and more, the classic logistics service provider is evolving from a pure carrier or warehousing company to an integration partner who manages and integrates the flow of information (see Chapter 2). This involves the integration of a plethora of requirements stemming from hospitals, suppliers, and other partners (see Figure 11-5).

Generally speaking, a growing responsibility of the logistics service provider in the hospital logistics market can be observed. This holds true for multiservice providers as well as multihospital providers. Apart from economic advantages in the form of faster and cheaper supply systems, the primary processes in healthcare also benefit considerably from the performance of a logistics system. Besides costs and time, quality issues are also coming increasingly important. The case studies presented earlier in the chapter can therefore be interpreted only as the beginning of changes affecting hospital logistics. Better integration of all supply chain partners will be necessary in the future. First and foremost, this involves technical factors apart from thinking in terms of interorganizational processes and IT systems capable of supporting these processes. One of the most important factors is the use of a standardized article number or product code for medical supplies throughout the supply chain (see Chapter 6). Commonplace in other industries, they are also a prerequisite for cooperation structures to function properly in healthcare. Process optimization is successful only when all partners of the hospital logistics supply chain use standardized article identifiers. The activities of online trading exchanges such as GHX [9] and GSG support this process, and go hand-in-hand with activities promoted by logistics providers. The online trading exchanges that address all different players in the healthcare industry, such as the manufacturers, wholesalers, (logistics) service providers, pharmacies, and purchasing/materials management departments in hospitals have a strong interest in uniquely identifying items in the supply chain, because documents are exchanged electronically and are processed directly in the in-house system of the partners.

Multihospital Provider: NHS Supply Chain

NHS Supply Chain, the logistics provider within the British NHS, is an example of a multihospital provider on a large scale. It serves 600 hospitals and other healthcare service providers within the NHS, and provides medical supplies such as medical-surgical products and medical devices, as well as nonmedical supplies such as patients' clothing, bed linen and textiles, cleaning materials and products, office furniture and supplies, and food and beverages. A 10-year contract was awarded to DHL—a privately owned logistics company—to operate NHS Supply Chain. DHL serves as an agent of the NHS Business Service Authority [10]. NHS Supply Chain started operations in October 2006 and replaced NHS Logistics, the logistics division within the NHS. Outsourcing the logistics service to a third party was mainly motivated by the expectation of saving costs to the tune of one million pounds sterling. The contract caused a discussion about a *partial privatization* of the national health system in the United Kingdom [11].

Outlook

It was possible to demonstrate that there are different ways of optimizing hospital logistics. Regardless of the particular model chosen, all approaches have cooperative structures in common. Only with an interorganizational perspective on logistic activities can cost reduction be realized. IT systems used for supporting activities on the operational and tactical layer are therefore gaining attention. Logistics service providers have recognized these demands, interlinked their customers, and have controlled their logistical processes by using planning and management systems. Process standardization and the use of IT standards, however, are necessary prerequisites. There is a huge potential for optimization today, particularly in terms of using standard identifiers such as article numbers or product codes. Only then can hospital logistics systems unfold their capabilities and reduce costs on a large scale.

Services Beyond Logistics

Introduction

Outsourcing does not stop at nonclinical functions such as warehousing, transportation, and archive management. It also progresses into the clinical domain. For example, not all hospitals maintain a pharmacy of their own but either share one with other hospitals or contract an external pharmacy (see Chapter 2) to provide all services relating to pharmaceutical products such as procurement, delivery, making of special medicines, and the provision of pharmaceutical consultancy for clinicians. Both cases are common, particularly with smaller hospitals for whom maintaining a pharmacy of their own might not be profitable, or simply not useful. The hospital could either decide to sell its *pharmacy service* to other healthcare providers or buy the *pharmacy service* from a third party (hospital or external pharmacy). The decision to outsource the pharmacy would then be based on the consideration that maintaining a pharmacy—although it is a core business of a hospital—would not belong to the core competencies of that hospital.

Certain administrative or management functions may also be affected by outsourcing. For example, analyzing and interpreting business data for controlling or benchmarking purposes might lend themselves to taking over by an external partner as long as a contract regulates the confidential treatment of the data and the third party cooperates closely with the hospital. In some countries, other areas are also well-recognized service domains, such as human resource management, where external locum agencies offer jobs for physicians and nurses who then work temporarily in a healthcare organization. In this example, outsourcing is actually twofold—the external agency organizes external staff for the healthcare provider.

In fact, there is no limitation to what could be outsourced as long as the rules between the partners are clearly defined, the targets are measurable, and the organization buying the services controls its partners.

Case Study

Multiservice, Multihospital Provider: Sanicare Group

The subsequent case study pinpoints the plethora of services a third party may offer on the market. It should be borne in mind that this is only possible with a deep understanding of the clinical processes, their requirements, and resources.

Having started as a local pharmacy in a small town in Northwest Germany, Sanicare is now a company with about 550 employees. The Sanicare Group supplies pharmaceutical and medical-surgical products and medical devices to healthcare providers, including 45 hospitals (8,000 beds), 500 nursing homes and home care institutions (5,000 patients in long- term care institutions and 7,000 outpatients), and a large number of general practitioners. In addition, it provides

- Pharmaceutical consultancy (member of the Pharmacy and Therapeutics Committee) to its customers
- Custom-made drugs such as cytostatics
- Custom-packaged drugs (daily dosage of drugs in blister packs) for nursing home residents

In 2004, Sanicare established Germany's largest online pharmacy. Besides pharmaceutical services, it offers classic logistics functions such as warehousing (15,200 m^2) and transportation of all supplies except food and beverages. The warehouse is Sanicare-owned and managed, while transportation is performed by two carriers subcontracted by Sanicare.

In contrast to providers of pure logistics services, Sanicare also manages the procurement of the supplies—i.e., primarily the contract negotiations with the manufacturers—for those healthcare providers who have outsourced their purchasing departments. In this role, Sanicare serves as a procurement hub, pooling the purchasing volume of its customers. Purchasing data are analyzed and supplied for controlling or benchmarking purposes to each organization individually. Sanicare communicates electronically with the manufacturers either via an online trading exchange or directly via electronic messages or electronic fax.

Permitting Web-based ordering via the online pharmacy, and functioning as a procurement hub, require Sanicare to support its processes by information and communication technology (ICT). ICT management (i.e., hosting, administration, maintenance, and software customization or development) is performed by a third-party provider (arvato AG), which serves as a software consultant and a computer center. Sanicare's system is mainly SAP R/3-based, using a Web interface for communicating with its customers (healthcare providers). The online pharmacy utilizes a dedicated system (prokas 2 by promedisoft) for the online shop, which is also connected with the R/3 main system. Figure 11-6 illustrates the IT systems at Sanicare. It shows that customers and suppliers of Sanicare are connected electronically to their central system. Some manufacturers, however, can only be reached by fax, and some healthcare providers still order by

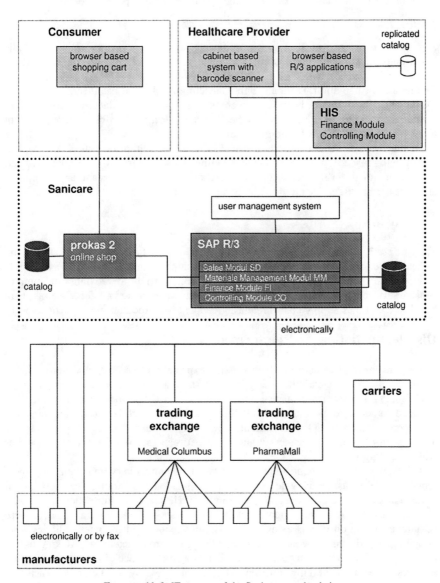

FIGURE 11-6. IT support of the Sanicare supply chain.

paper. Those healthcare providers who order electronically do so via barcode scanner or a PC workstation. In the latter case, the catalog is transmitted to the workstation and regularly updated. Both solutions are detached from the HIS_h system and do not require any integration, but at the cost of not having access to the digital order data. There is an electronic interface for sending electronic invoices and reports to the HIS_h.

The Sanicare case study is a good example of both a pragmatic IT-based solution connecting all partners (customers and suppliers) ,and an example of a third party coordinating the supply chain and providing services including, but also beyond, logistics—based on the clinical and, in particular, the pharmaceutical experience of its staff.

Outlook

A pioneer in the use of ICT in the healthcare supply chain, Sanicare had had the opportunity of gaining experience in this field from the outset. Due to technological innovation, it had to change its eCommerce software platform more than once before finding a robust solution. Difficulties in connecting small rural healthcare providers to their system have not yet been fully overcome, and some manufacturers only receive unstructured orders by electronic fax because their technical infrastructure does not allow the reception of electronic messages.

Despite the understanding that the use of IT is paramount within a supply chain, progress is only being made step-by-step and requires time. Observed from the outside, however, the changes made in the healthcare supply chain over the last decade are significant and have permitted service providers to increase their customer base tremendously.

Conclusion

The case studies presented in this chapter illustrate different mechanisms of outsourcing in healthcare, and different approaches to establishing a supply chain. It was possible to identify different types of partners ranging from carriers to providers of comprehensive services. In conclusion, it demonstrates that outsourcing is definitely an issue in healthcare and thus supply chains requiring cooperative structures are an issue as well.

Disintermediation or Reintermediation?

In the early days of eBusiness, there was the expectation that business intermediaries would be abolished, clearing the way between the manufacturer and its customers by establishing interorganizational electronic communication. Intermediaries are sometimes regarded as an intermediate layer, blocking direct contact between suppliers and customers and increasing the costs. In the worst case, they are seen as third parties trying to make profit from the business relationship between the supplier and the customer without adding value.

Although direct communication links between manufacturers and their customers remain an option and actually do exist, Zwass [12] had already argued against the myth of removal of intermediaries via eBusiness in 2003. He said that information complexity and the trust deficit in the virtual world speak in favor of intermediaries, who were beginning to take on new responsibilities. He also recognized the intermediaries' role of aggregating demand and supply and facilitating electronic exchange. Making use of intermediaries is obviously a business decision, or a consequence of a business decision, as in the case of outsourcing functions. It is dictated less by technological feasibility than by economic constraints.

Removal of intermediaries did not happen in healthcare. On the contrary, new businesses came into existence in the wake of eBusiness that either enabled electronic communication (e.g., online trading exchanges), compensated for the fragmentation of the market (e.g., procurement hubs), or facilitated outsourcing and thus saved costs (e.g., service providers), which would have been more difficult without an electronic exchange of information. In fact, establishing supply chains is, in itself, a case of reinstatement of intermediaries.

The concerns have not gone away about reduced transparency when someone act as a go-between. These concerns are expressed in the context of any third party, but particularly in the case of those who could stop the manufacturers from seeing *which product is used by whom and when*. As these are critical data for providing business intelligence, manufacturers feel that they could lose access to their customers and thus lose control over their own business.

As discussed, eBusiness does not physically abolish intermediaries in healthcare. Due to eBusiness, however, the nature of intermediaries has changed. While third parties used to block the information flow in the paper world, information can be easily passed on in the electronic world, even if somebody stands in between. It is a question of the rules negotiated between the partners about how they define cooperation or collaboration, and what information they want to share, exchange, or to pass on. And finally, it is a question of the trust among the partners. In this sense, eBusiness has the capacity to make the barriers virtual, which are an inherent part of a supply chain.

References

[1] Pieper, U., M. Michael. (2004) *Healthcare Logistik*. In Klaus, P. and W. Krieger (eds). Gabler Lexikon Logistik. Wiesbaden: Gabler.

[2] Heiny, L. (2006) Stets zu Diensten. *medbiz – Magazin für Gesundheiswirtschaft.* 08/2006: 5.

[3] Klinik-Logistik Hamburg Eppendorf. *Wer sind wir?* Available from: <www.uke.uni-hamburg.de/zentrale-dienste/kle> [Accessed 20 September 2006].

[4] Grimm, C. (2006) Operation Schnittstelle. *LogPunkt*. 03/2006, 41-42.

[5] Rhenus eonova. *NetLog*. Available from:<www.rhenus-eonova.de/content/view/46/87/> [Accessed 29 August 2006].

[6] Rhenus eonova (2004) *Health Care: Catgut Partner bei NetLog*. Available from: <http://rhenus-eonova.de/content/view/80/102/> [Accessed 29 August 2006].

[7] Rhenus eonova (2005) *Das "Rhenus Medical Warehouse" gewinnt europaweite Ausschreibung*. Available from: <http://rhenus-eonova.de/content/view/86/102/> [Accessed 29 August 2006].

[8] Pieper, U. (2006) Healthcare Logistik - Trägerübergreifende Logistikkonzepte im Gesundheitswesen am Beispiel NETLOG. Presentation Medecon, 1 September.

[9] The Global Healthcare Exchange. Available from: <www.ghxeurope.com> [Accessed 29 August 2006].

[10] Department of Health (2006) *NHS Supply Chain*. Available from: <http://www.dh.gov.uk/PublicationsAndStatistics/ > [Accessed 31 October 2006].

[11] Logistik-inside online (2006). *Post erhält Milliardenauftrag von Gesundheitsbehörde*. München: Springer. Available from: < http://www.logistik-inside.de/sixcms/detail.php?id=426039> [Accessed 12 September 2006].

[12] Zwass, V. (2003) Electronic Commerce and Organizational Innovation: Aspects and Opportunities. *International Journal of Electronic Commerce*. **7**, 7-37.

12
The Expert's Opinion:
Part I – The Healthcare Providers

URSULA HÜBNER

Executive Summary

The following two chapters form a single unit summarizing the results of interviews conducted with experts from centers of excellence in eBusiness. While this chapter concentrates on the healthcare providers' view, the next one focuses on the suppliers' perspective and provides a conclusion drawn from all findings. The goal of the interviews was to get a coherent picture of the eBusiness arena by reflecting the experts' opinions on

- What is to be gained for an individual organization by adopting eBusiness procedures
- What needs to be considered when changing an organization and its processes
- What type of barriers still exist in the eBusiness environment
- What are the driving forces for moving the providers and suppliers towards the critical mass of users in the eBusiness community
- What kind of new opportunities arise from eBusiness besides optimizing the order-to-payment cycle
- What the future of eBusiness in healthcare will be

Besides general facts about the organization the experts come from and its eBusiness activities, we were mainly interested in an appraisal of the status quo, the expectations, and opinions about new options to better understand the underlying mechanics and dynamics of electronic trading activities in healthcare. Experts from 16 organizations were interviewed: 15 representatives from the healthcare industry (seven providers and eight suppliers) plus one expert from the paper industry serving as a contrast to the healthcare sector. In contrast to initial assumptions that the hospitals were mainly guided by the idea of process automation and the reduction of process costs, the interviews revealed a multitude of reasons to motivate eBusiness. The primary reason for hospitals to adopt eBusiness were 1) process optimization in terms of greater efficiency and less errors, 2) standardization of procurement procedures coupled with a greater discipline in ordering products imposed by the system, and 3) the aggregation and standardization of the range of products purchased constitute the primary reasons for hospitals to adopt eBusiness. Decreased process costs played a less important role because it was unclear whether or not there would be any true savings without making staff redundant. The option of getting clean data and insight into the supply chain was considered to be of increasing importance for hospitals.

When transforming the organization towards eBusiness procedures, hospital experts had the experience that backing from the executive level together with assembling a team of individuals dedicated to the ideas of eBusiness were the keys to becoming successful. Although barriers still existed, they did not hamper the adoption of eBusiness today as they did in the past. The technology was available and the technical infrastructure was implemented in many hospitals. Problems were found, instead, at the organizational level. Barriers and deficiencies could be overcome if all the different stakeholders made their contribution—the healthcare providers exerting pressure on the suppliers, the manufacturers providing concepts, and both cooperating in their efforts. Third parties, such as major online trading exchanges, group purchasing organizations, and purchasing cooperatives were also considered to be in a good position for fostering eBusiness procedures.

eBusiness was acknowledged to be more than a tool for optimizing the business transactions, as had been clear when asking about the main reasons for adopting electronic procedures. Those hospitals that had gained experience in, or had focused on, new logistics concepts saw a close connection between logistics services and eBusiness, both of them mutually influencing each other. Supply chain principles require processes to become electronic-based, at the same time eBusiness-enabled information flow makes the users aware of events and errors down in the supply chain. Similarly, group purchasing is closely related to eBusiness. Group purchasing was viewed differently depending on the country the experts came from— however, all agreed that group purchasing depended on the data generated by electronic procurement procedures. The experts regarded eBusiness as an enabler for new services but referred to improved transactions rather than to totally new services—with the exception of one expert who strongly promoted the concept of an extended supply chain including insurance companies. In contrast to findings in the literature that tend to support the assumption that eBusiness improves the customer-supplier relationship, the results of this study show a mixed picture with opinions ranging from "yes, it helped to build a trustful relationship" to "it remained unaffected."

According to the hospital experts, there will be a significant increase in users in the next five years and eBusiness will further gain momentum. The discussion will also be dominated by cost issues in the future. Whether or not eBusiness influences the market to move towards greater competition among the companies was discussed controversially, but globalization will definitely play no role in conducting business between healthcare providers and suppliers— according the hospital experts.

Introduction

Interviews with Experts from the Healthcare Industry

In addition to the individual case studies presented so far, the next two chapters will try and round up the picture of eBusiness in healthcare by presenting the experts' opinion on key questions such as, "What is to be gained by these methods?", "What needs to be considered when moving an organization towards online procedures?", "What are the driving forces?", "What type of barriers still exist?", and "What will the future of eBusiness in healthcare be?" Interviews were carried out with representatives from centers of excellence in eBusiness who had been gaining experience in this field over many years. Due to the duality in eBusiness, with its buying and selling sides, both the supplier's and the healthcare provider's point of view are covered. This chapter focuses on the healthcare providers and the following chapter concentrates on the suppliers. This double perspective should not only provide a more comprehensive picture but should also permit the mutual understanding necessary for developing a common culture of electronic business.

The goal of the following two chapters is twofold. First, we aim to provide an overview of factors concerning the individual organizations that should help managers, in terms of developing realistic expectations, preparing the organization for the change, and exploiting new opportunities.

Second, we aim to gain a better understanding of the current situation and consider themes presented in Chapter 7 for further analysis. In addition, our approach was guided by proposals derived from the literature about barriers and new opportunities for B2B between business partners.

Besides general facts about the organization and its eProcurement/eCommerce activities, we were mainly interested in an appraisal of the status quo, in the expectations and opinions about new options, to better understand the underlying mechanics and dynamics of electronic trading activities in healthcare. We wanted to know what kept things going and in what direction were things moving. By interviewing experts from different countries, we were able to arrive at more generally valid conclusions spanning several types of national healthcare systems.

Assumptions Guiding the Interviews

In the days of the Internet hype, all sorts of different promises and assumptions on the (positive) effects of eBusiness were circulating. Only a fraction of those promises materialized over the following years as electronic trading matured. We therefore base our assumptions mainly on those topics with backing from general eBusiness literature.

1) Main Motivation: Process Automation and Cost Reduction?

Our central assumption was that eBusiness was all about reducing costs, so the main reasons for doing eBusiness were **process automation** and reduced process costs. The promise to take costs out of the supply chain are well reflected in Chapter 7. There is also support from the literature. Eakin, for example, speaks about "hard, money wise, benefits that are directly measurable and yield immediate gains." [1] These are lower process costs engendered by automation and price reductions arising from strategic sourcing and caused by bundling buying volume through better contract compliance [1]. Eakin also argues, however, that there is a series of soft benefits accompanying the hard benefits. One of these is increased data accuracy that leads to trustworthy data and thus to enhanced analytical capabilities.

2) Major Barriers: Inappropriate Technology and the Lack of Standards?

In the early days of eBusiness, there were often complaints that technology was not able to support eBusiness functionality and that the systems were primarily proprietary. These functional, as well as structural, deficits hampered the adoption of eBusiness methods. In a more recent study, the assumption that the lack of appropriate IT systems impeded eBusiness was no longer regarded as valid, although some of the study participants mentioned technical problems at the level of some hospitals. [2] With improved IT systems, many technical incompatibilities due to proprietary approaches were solved.

The problems due to a lack of standardized identification numbers for medical-surgical supplies and devices addressed in 2002 [3], however, persisted in 2005 and were clearly regarded as an important deficit, together with the lack of a generally agreed nomenclature [2].

3) Managing the Change: Only Possible with Backing from Executives?

There is evidence from the literature that the interest and involvement of executives in supply chain matters needed to be strengthened. [2] In terms of change management, the role of executives as a major facilitator is indisputable. What this means for supply chain management and for eBusiness seems less clear and needs to be looked at more thoroughly.

4) New Opportunities: Management Information at your Finger Tips?

In 2002, analytical capabilities created by access to accurate data, and their impact on managing the supply chain, had been identified as an important by-product [1]. In 2005, it had already become the focus of eCommerce for some healthcare systems [4]. These hospitals had obviously understood the power of data. Only if management decisions were data-driven could the supply chain be optimized and behavior (of clinicians and materials managers) be changed [2]. Due to the limitations of semantic standards applied to the data, however, the spectrum for analyzing the data is limited, as is shown in Chapter 10. Therefore, a second look at this question is definitely required.

5) New Opportunities: Collaboration Within the Supply Chain and Beyond?

Outside the healthcare industry, eBusiness has been well recognized as a driver for moving the focus from transactions to collaboration [5]. Collaborative commerce (cCommerce) describes an approach to using electronic means for coping with uncertainty, and for enhancing knowledge in a critical area of functioning, such as when there is a high need for innovation [6]. cCommerce explicitly requires the use of dedicated electronic platforms supporting collaboration in research and development (R&D) or in product testing and evaluation.

Furthermore, collaboration is not a new concept. Already within classic supply chain management, collaboration constitutes a major component and embraces collaborative planning, forecasting, and replenishment (CPFR) and VMIs. As opposed to cooperation and coordination, collaboration builds on a high level of trust [7]. As there is effectively no literature on cCommerce in healthcare, it would be interesting to know whether the healthcare industry is ready for electronically enabled collaboration.

6) eBusiness Beyond Technology: Improved Customer-Supplier Relationships?

Collaboration is one special type of the more general concept of "intercompany connectedness." Analyzing different supply chain management frameworks revealed *intercompany connectedness* as the key factor [8]. According to one of these frameworks (GSCF), customer and supplier relationship management are the critical links within the supply chain, and intercompany connectedness is a concept that may lead the partners from arm's length relationships focusing on transactions, to more close-knit relationships creating value. We were therefore interested in whether eBusiness, as a practical, technical approach to supply chain management, has an effect on the customer-supplier relationship and what kind of impact that would be.

7) eBusiness in a Global World

Competition

Whether eBusiness capabilities are a competitive advantage is a debated subject [9], and has to be gauged for each specific marketplace. It depends on two factors—how widespread the technology is and whether the customers expect the suppliers to be electronic. The more commonplace a technology is, the smaller the chance is for a company to distinguish itself from the competitors in this field. On the other hand, early adopters of a certain technology may find it hard to *sell* their new capabilities to the customers if the customers are not yet ready to appreciate them.

The Internet—notably through electronic marketplaces—has a proven record as an instrument for opening up markets, for making demand transparent, and for allowing customers to better compare bids. In other words, it increases the competition. Although electronic marketplaces in healthcare moved in a quite different direction than in other sectors, acting as technical exchanges rather than as marketplaces, the question of whether there will be greater competition among firms in a digital world also applies to healthcare. Greater competition may be achieved by more firms from foreign countries also offering similar products, or by the present number of firms offering their products in a more transparent way. We wanted to know whether this applies to healthcare as it does to other industries.

Global Sourcing

Sourcing without geographical restrictions in an international business environment is common practice in other industries, and represents one of the most powerful impacts of eCommerce on procurement. [10] As national boundaries are melting with the Internet, global sourcing is therefore certainly a question to be raised in healthcare.

Background

The proposals found in the literature constituted the cornerstone of the interview questions. In addition, further questions derived from informal sources were included. This led to a collection of 26 questions addressing 10 topics (see Table 12-1). Some of the topics related to the expert's organization, while others were detached from the specific organization and aimed at the expert's opinion about general themes in eBusiness.

We conducted interviews with eBusiness experts from 16 organizations: 15 from the healthcare industry and one from another type of industry serving as a contrast. Among the 15 organizations, there were six healthcare providers and one organization representing a group of healthcare providers, and eight manufacturers of medical devices,

TABLE 12-1. Topics addressed by the interview.

No.	Focus	Topic
1	Expert's organization	Beginning of eCommerce and current trends within organisation
2		General motivation for eCommerce
3		Practical reasons for online trading
4		Management of change within organisation
5	Entire	General barriers for online trading
6	healthcare industry respectively	Barriers concerning hospitals and suppliers
7	the national healthcare system	Driving forces for eCommerce: hospitals, GPO, suppliers, others?
8		Incentives for eCommerce?
9		New functions enabled or supported by eCommerce
		Logistics
		Purchasing
		Customer-supplier relationship
		Controlling and business intelligence
10		Future
		Time frame for achieving the break through
		Costs vs. quality: which of the two will dominate the discussion
		Market orientation and competition
		Globalization of trade

TABLE 12-2. The experts and their organisations.

Type	Code	Organization	Country/Market
Healthcare	H1	single hospital	Germany
Providers	H2	healthcare system	USA
	H3	trust	UK
	H4	healthcare system	Germany
	H5	healthcare system	USA
	H6	single hospital	Germany
	H7	pharmacy	Germany
Manufacturers	M1	multinational firm	Germany
	M2	multinational firm	USA
	M3	multinational firm	Germany
	M4	multinational firm	Europe Middle East Africa
	M5	multinational firm	Germany
	M6	multinational firm	Europe
	M7	multinational firm	Germany
	M8	multinational firm	USA
Contrast	C1	multinational firm	global

medical-surgical supplies, and pharmaceutical and biochemical products. Table 12-2 shows the details of the study participants.

All healthcare providers (except one) were large nonprofit organizations either combining several types of healthcare providers or acting as a large single hospital (German university hospitals). In the United States, a group of healthcare providers belonging to the same organization is referred to as a *healthcare system*[1], and in the UK it is referred to as a *trust*. Due to the lack of a standardized term for this concept in Germany, we have adopted the U.S. term to denote a group of healthcare providers organized under the roof of one organization.

HP7 is a for-profit organization (pharmacy) that contracts with 45 hospitals, 25 nursing homes, and 500 nurse-led organizations in northwest Germany (see also Chapter 11). We have deliberately not included group purchasing organizations in either country as this would be a topic of its own [3]. We asked all study participants, however, about their opinion on the role of group purchasing organizations in eBusiness. In fact, some of the interviewed healthcare providers are members of a group purchasing organization, while others are not.

All experts from the suppliers' side were working for large multinational companies. Due to their working environment, they provide a focused view on a particular market.

The views from healthcare industry experts were contrasted with the view from a paper industry expert. The paper industry was chosen as an example of a manufacturing industry outside healthcare that is different enough from healthcare. The company[2] we included in this study is well known for its eBusiness capabilities.

---

[1] The term *healthcare system* denotes an organization that combines several types of healthcare providers including hospitals, nursing homes, clinics, rehabilitation centers and others. It is to be distinguished from the national healthcare system in each country.

[2] It provides commodities as well as highly specialized and innovative products. By its own account it conducts business in a rather „conservative" environment. In this respect it is much better suited for a comparison with manufacturers in healthcare than the automotive industry, which is regarded as an opinion leader in eBusiness.

To be able to clearly describe the organizations' eBusiness background, we asked all study participants to give a brief account of the experience their organization has gained in this field, to rate its motivation for practising eBusiness, and to rate its success achieved so far. With only a few exceptions, all organizations started eBusiness activities around 2000 or earlier, and may well be characterized as *early adopters*. The year 2000 roughly marked a milestone in eBusiness as the Internet became an interactive instrument permitting business transactions as opposed to the years before when a more or less static display of Web pages used to be the main Web application. While, at that point, the first IT solutions had been on the market for some time, it was still the heyday of Internet promises. Organizations embarking on eBusiness then took, in fact, the considerable amount of risk that characterizes the *early adopters*. Those that have been involved in eBusiness for an even longer period reported on an extensive phase for restructuring their internal processes—*doing our homework*, as one hospital put it, to get ready for using electronic means in transactions with the outside world. Others gained their first experience before 2000 in a research project, or pursued some experimental approaches with rudimentary technology. Homework, research, and experiments were all strategies to cope with the risk associated with eBusiness at that time. Knowledge in how to communicate electronically with wholesalers proved to be of value for some manufacturers, while others explicitly expressed doubts about being able to compare B2B with wholesaler transactions due to the greater complexity of the data transmitted in B2B. The organization with a least experience (H3) was established only a few years ago but started doing eBusiness right from the start.

Despite having gone through the ups and downs of eBusiness—changing the technical approaches at least once, and in some cases several times—the overwhelming majority of the organizations still rated their motivation as very high. Some regarded themselves as absolute eBusiness drivers, others as *almost* eBusiness drivers, and one expert characterized his organization as a *fast follower*. Among the group of manufacturers, some felt a strong obligation to promote eBusiness to underline their market leadership or their corporate strategy, which explicitly stipulated the use of innovative electronic media.

A good amount of experience and a high level of motivation are excellent facilitators, but cannot entirely determine the success one achieves. Too much influence originates from external factors that cannot be controlled, yet have a significant contribution on the overall success. Therefore, we wanted to know how the experts rated the organization's success. Because success is no absolute parameter, but rather measured in comparison with something, many study participants distinguished the degree of their success compared with *what is possible right now in the market* from the degree of success measured against their own aspirations. Judged by the amount of success the others have had and measured against *what is possible right now*, many hospitals and manufacturers rated their own success as quite high. Measured against their own ambition, they felt it was definitely lower. This discrepancy in their judgments reflects the gap between their own standards and the reality of eBusiness. Other study participants tried to summarize this experience, stressing the dependency on the other side or commenting that *nobody is higher than a medium score*. These statements clearly revealed the reciprocity of success in eBusiness as an inherent feature of this method. Most of the experts felt that they had not achieved their goal. Only two (one manufacturer and one hospital) found that they had reached the degree of connectedness with the customers or with the suppliers they initially had in mind.

The extent of their experience, the degree of their motivation, and the qualified judgements on their success hallmark the organizations included in this study as members of the healthcare industry with a distinct dedication to eBusiness. Their opinion therefore reflects the eBusiness world from the viewpoint of its advocates, giving an insight into what is achievable right now, what needs to be changed, what opportunities exist, and where the future might lead.

Results–The Hospitals' Perspective

Reasons for eBusiness: Optimization, not Automation

Our primary assumption was that the main reason for embarking on eBusiness was process automation and the reduction of process costs. Four of the seven healthcare providers, however, answered the question with a clear *no* and the other three gave a qualified *yes*. Obviously the term process automation did not describe exactly what they really meant. Instead *process optimization* was either given verbatim as the main reason or was circumscribed in one way or the other. Targets for optimizing the processes were speed, efficiency, error rate, and error detection. On all these parameters, online trading was regarded as superior to paper-based methods. Working in an optimized environment leads to the early detection of errors and the identification of cost drivers. In one case, the integration of nine different hospitals into one organization had forced the new organization to streamline its procurement processes and utilize electronic means to achieve the integration of the different purchasing methods. In another case, process optimization and process standardization were seen as an integral part of a highly professional materials management department. eBusiness was an instrument to support these new processes.

In addition to process optimization, *avoiding errors through clean data* was explicitly mentioned as a major motivation for eBusiness. Better processes obviously do not do the job alone but must be combined with error-free and consistent data.

Whether eBusiness per se actually reduced process costs remained a point at issue. One expert agreed with the statement that eBusiness lowered process costs, five others thought this was not the case, and one did not respond to the issue of process costs. One of the skeptics argued that unless you make people redundant, no significant costs are taken out of the process. Another had achieved only marginal savings as a result of the employment of electronic media. What looks like a marked contrast to other findings, at first glance is not the case, because the response one receives very much depends on the way the question is phrased. When referring to process costs, very little to no cost reduction is found unless staff costs—the major source of costs—can be truly curbed. When looking at eBusiness-mediated effects such as standardization and contract compliance, however, real savings can be achieved. This was obviously the reason the hospital experts were keen to explain what other motivations they had for adopting eBusiness.

When asked what other reasons existed for considering eBusiness as the preferred procurement method, the experts listed a great number of quite divergent reasons. The need to standardize procedures and data in combination with reducing the number of articles and vendors appeared to be a central issue (see also Chapter 10). The expectation of introducing more discipline through eBusiness was of similar importance for adopting eBusiness as standardization. The organizations expected a greater amount of discipline—in terms of what is ordered, when is it ordered, and by whom is it ordered—that eBusiness would impose on them and that would decrease the incidents of maverick buying. One expert spoke about a *change in the culture* in this context and another called it a *governance issue*. But it was not simply the wish for greater restriction that drove the healthcare providers. Quite in contrast to standardization and discipline, the experts also expressed the hope of gaining new freedom through eBusiness, "to have free time for doing other important things." These other important things embraced:

- Reorganization of internal structures and processes, such as the introduction of cabinet-based requisitioning systems
- Better services for the internal customers (the clinicians)
- Restructuring of the organization, such as the integration of new hospitals into the healthcare system

Other reasons for adopting eBusiness were clearly motivated by strategy. One healthcare system wanted to implement its vision of setting up a supply chain together with an alpha vendor. This could only be achieved by installing an information system capable of producing, transmitting, and showing all relevant information. The expert from another healthcare system spoke about their general strategy to foster innovation in all areas, as well as in purchasing and materials management. He said that he could not understand why healthcare providers should limp behind the general trends of conducting business online.

In conclusion, the suggestion that process automation and reduced process costs are the main motivator for eBusiness in organizations providing healthcare cannot be supported by our interviews. At first glance, one might suspect that the term *automation*, with its connotation of *manufacturing* and *mass data processing* was felt to be incongruent with providing healthcare. Our findings, however, might also be explained by the subtle difference between the two terms *automation* and *optimization*. In contrast to process automation, process optimization definitely refers to an improvement and the need for such an improvement. Automation is not necessarily an improvement in itself, as seen in cases when inefficient processes are made electronic. Furthermore, optimization describes the way or the method, and not explicitly the goal. In the context of eBusiness, online methods may be linked to several positive effects such as standardization and discipline, or may give rise to a series of benefits such as free time or access to information at the downstream part of the supply chain. In fact, the interviews revealed not just one reason why an institution adopted online trading, but a wealth of good reasons and explanations. In this sense, the expected outcome was multidimensional, not one-dimensional as process automation would suggest (see Figure 12-1).

Among these different reasons, standardization and discipline played a central role. Interestingly, both are two sides of the same coin. Standardization is the prerequisite for disciplined behavior and discipline enforces the outcomes of the standardization process.

Management of Change: People's Issues Matter

Good reasons and strong arguments in favour of eBusiness help to initiate the necessary steps but alone they are not able to change a whole organization. We wanted to know, therefore, what the internal key factors of success were and how the change was managed.

The interviews revealed a series of individual factors contributing to the management of change that could be clustered around the three main themes: people's issues, management issues, and being prepared. Judging by the number of people's issues provided by the hospital experts, this factor obviously seemed to have the greatest influence, followed by management issues and being prepared. A "good team" and

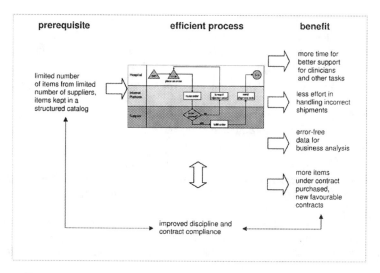

prerequisite   efficient process   benefit

limited number
of items from limited
number of suppliers,
items kept in a
structured catalog

more time for
better support
for clinicians
and other tasks

less effort in
handling incorrect
shipments

error-free
data for
business analysis

more items
under contract
purchased,
new favourable
contracts

improved discipline and
contract compliance

FIGURE 12-1. Multi-dimensional effects of eBusiness – healthcare providers.

"motivated staff" "supported by the executive level" which "gives them a free hand" were the most important elements for achieving the change associated with eBusiness. They were either mentioned as single elements or in combinations by the majority of the hospital experts. These characteristics apply to the experts in materials management or the supply chain who become the principal change agents. They believed in eBusiness, had the competence to make the right decisions, and they were given the freedom to pursue their plans and visions. They did not act completely autonomously, however, but received backing from the executives who were open-minded towards eBusiness. Generally speaking, managers with a vision combined with the willingness to take the risks of innovation were regarded as a decisive factor in enabling change throughout the organization. In the case where the top level managers were not yet ready to support eBusiness, one expert reported that providing them with comprehensive information on a regular basis proved helpful. The role of informing others in triggering change must not be underestimated. Clinicians and other users also needed to be informed about what eBusiness was and what kind of practical positive effects it created, continued the expert. Only then could it be expected that the users supported the changes necessary to implement and make use of eBusiness. Besides the top managers and the end users, the IT department had an extremely positive influence on moving from paper to computers. Without a good working relationship with the IT department, this change would not have been possible, said one expert. He stressed that it was the nonbureaucratic way of communicating between his department and the IT department that made things happen. No long official contracts were needed in order to receive the necessary support.

In addition to what has been already been said about the role of the managers, other management issues strongly influence the speed and the success of adopting online trading procedures. According to the experts, change within the organization was only possible if there was an overall strategy to which eBusiness contributed, followed by the necessary investments of money and human resources.

Still, the ultimate success in making an entire organization change its working habits needed thorough preparation, and homework had to be done. Practically speaking, this meant changing the processes step-by-step, starting with internal processes before tackling the external ones. The expert who had pointed out this fact reported on introducing electronic requisitioning and the use of cabinets on the clinical units first before actually establishing the electronic order completely.

Last, but not least, there was the conclusion that "success sells," as one expert expressed it. If the ice was broken and first signs of positive effects appeared, the spreading of the new technology and its use throughout the organization came almost automatically.

A compilation of our results eventually leads us to the finding that change needed two main ingredients: first, a good team with innovative ideas and a feeling for a step-by-step approach, and second, open-minded executives with a vision and the courage to take risks. This is neither a top-down nor a bottom-up approach, but rather a mutually encouraging process with contributions from each party. Figure 12-2 summarizes the elements of a successful transformation and their interaction.

Barriers on the Road to eBusiness

All experts from the healthcare providers' side shared the opinion that there were still obstacles impeding the adoption process of eBusiness in the healthcare arena. Their answers to the following three questions helped to identify barriers within the entire system—i.e., concerning all players in the healthcare industry or in the national healthcare system. The first question addressed the lack of appropriate technology, the second addressed organizational problems, and the third involved the absence of standards.

In contrast to earlier assumptions, the large majority of the hospital experts did not think that technical deficiencies still pose the main problem in eBusiness today. "The technology is there and it is not extremely expensive," said one of them. Still, two experts admitted that there were still technology problems in small hospitals. One of the experts explicitly referred to the infrastructure problems of hospitals with no broadband internet access and limited LAN resources, which made the implementation of eBusiness impossible. From a technological point of view, however, these barriers were not regarded as insurmountable. All hospital experts agreed that the technological difficulties, if there were any, were rooted in organizational problems and other nontechnical constraints. These hospitals had other things to worry about, were struggling for survival, and either

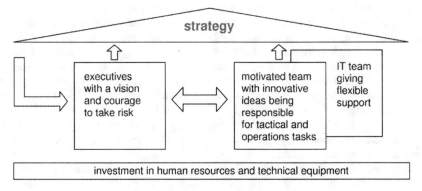

FIGURE 12-2. Elements of successful change management.

had no budget for eBusiness or simply had no time to deal with it. The time problem, in turn, goes back to a lack of human resources, or, as one expert put it, "the hospitals are so tightly managed in terms of staffing" that there is effectively nobody to take care of eBusiness. But apart from these external constraints, there were also homemade barriers the hospital experts were frank enough to admit. Some hospitals, they said, were just badly organized, the roles of the employees were not well enough defined, or the people were not trained for eBusiness. One expert complained that some hospital managers had not recognized "the importance of clean data and the power coming from them, such as consolidating data and reporting." These external and internal problems impeded the adoption of eBusiness procedures and were held responsible for a hesitant attitude towards eBusiness on the part of the hospitals.

Although the hospital experts were self-critical enough to identify the hospitals as a source of the problems, they stressed that there were major barriers on the side of the suppliers as well. Sometimes, one expert reported, there were communication problems between the sales force and customer service, leading to an unclear situation about the firm's eBusiness strategy towards the customer. Some hospital experts suspected that it was the fear of losing their jobs that made people work against, or at least not support, their company's eBusiness activities. Two experts clearly expressed the lack of classified product data as the principal barrier to eBusiness, because without them the added value of online trading was limited for healthcare providers. Aggregating data for reporting purposes was simply not possible, and therefore made eBusiness less attractive for them. Along the same lines, they complained that no identification systems (universal product numbers) were used that allowed them to automatically identify the goods being delivered. They demanded that the use of classification and identification systems should be promoted by the manufacturers.

When asked directly about the absence of standards as a potential source of problems, more hospital experts shared the opinion of their colleagues. The problem, however, was not an actual lack of standards but a matter of compliance, they said. They found it was the manufacturers' duty to comply with the already existing standards to get more healthcare providers to implement eBusiness procedures and to help providers who were already online make better use of their eBusiness applications. This, as stated above, concerned mainly classification and identification standards and, to a lesser extent, technical standards, which were either regarded as causing no problems or were outside the perspective of the study participants with their business background.

Generally speaking, most of the experts admitted that all players were moving more or less towards eBusiness ,and none of them was deliberately acting against it. There were fears associated with eBusiness, however, that impeded the speed of adoption. Among these was the fear of losing one's job, which was the one referred to by several experts and appeared as a recurrent concern expressed during the interviews. It actually existed on both sides, they said—not just on the side of the manufacturers. Another expert suspected that eBusiness aroused a fear on the side of the manufacturers that eBusiness might "convert their product into a commodity" because products can be compared more easily in the electronic world and products could be substituted with less difficulty. Despite these concerns, nobody really wanted to return to the paper world (as one expert said) once they had decided to adopt eBusiness procedures and once they were actually practicing them.

In conclusion, the hospital experts' believe that technology is no longer an important barrier for eBusiness, nor are technical standards for transmitting the messages. It is not the external factors over which the parties involved have no control, therefore, that hinder them from doing eBusiness. Barriers rather come from inside the organizations, in aspects of the management strategy, the staff, and the general organization (see Table 12-3), and can be eventually overcome by the organizations themselves. Although these individual barriers had been reported by different experts separately, each barrier contributed to the overall picture of what hinders hospitals from becoming active in eBusiness. Strategic issues such as a general understanding of the potential of eBusiness for the management, and the degree of priority given by the healthcare providers to this topic, are decisive in terms of whether the organization embarks on eBusiness or not. Furthermore, an unclear strategy goes hand-in-hand with an ambiguous situation for the staff and generally bad internal organization. Neither facilitates eBusiness—on the contrary, they block it.

From the healthcare providers' perspective, the suppliers also have a strong influence on how well eBusiness works in healthcare organizations. The suppliers must realize that without the use of standards (classification and identification systems), the added value of eBusiness for the healthcare providers is limited. Decisions to change this situation must be made at the management level and are strategic in nature. At the operational level, an unclear message from the suppliers to their customers about how to proceed in practical terms complicates things and effectively works as a barrier. Inconsistent messages can be caused by bad internal communication or by staff who fear eBusiness rather than support it.

About Drivers and Incentives: Together We Are Strong

Having agreed that there were barriers to overcome, the experts were asked who should take the initiative to clear the way for eBusiness: should it be the healthcare providers, or the manufacturers, or somebody else? This used to be a major issue of discussion in the past, so we were interested to see if it still held true. In the opinion of the hospital experts, there was no golden rule for solving this problem. There was the full breadth of possible answers with the exception that all hospital experts agreed that it should not, nor could not, be a single hospital alone. Only by acting together, either as ad hoc groups of hospitals, as large healthcare systems, as purchasing cooperatives, or with the support of GPO's did they have a chance to turn the wheel. Some experts suggested instead it should be both—the manufacturers and the hospitals. Others said it should be the online trading exchanges, and yet another thought it should be all three together. Interestingly, one expert denied that there was a need for extra efforts from anybody.

TABLE 12-3. Organisational barriers – healthcare providers' perspective.

Source of the Barrier	Focus	Barrier
	Management strategy	lack of understanding
		low priority
Healthcare Providers	Staff	no human resources
		roles not defined
		staff not trained well enough
		fear of losing one's job
	General organization	badly organized
Suppliers	Management strategy	use of standards
	Staff	fear of losing one's job
	General organization	poor internal communication

He was convinced that eBusiness would come in any case because external forces such as cost containment measures in healthcare did not leave the healthcare industry any other choice than to move towards eBusiness.

Along the same lines, we wanted to hear the hospital experts' opinion on incentives—in particular, financial incentives for using eBusiness methods. The answers to this question were more unequivocal than were expected. There was only one expert who explicitly demanded that financial incentives should be given—specifically to help small hospitals take the hurdle. The rest of the experts were either quite skeptical about the effect of luring hospitals into eBusiness using money, or found that the incentives (i.e., the benefits) were already there and hospitals only needed to understand them. In fact, two experts explained that financial incentives already existed to some extent. In Germany, manufacturers already gave indirect incentives to the hospitals by paying the fee of the Internet trading exchanges, and in the United States, GPO's supported hospitals to implement eBusiness technology.

Getting incentives was not only a one-way issue—the manufacturers also needed incentives, albeit incentives of a different nature. Hospitals could reward those manufacturers who have electronic trading capabilities by explicitly demanding electronic capabilities in the tenders, and by preferring those manufacturers with the required capabilities. Referring to the situation in Germany, one expert suggested that the pricing scheme of the online trading exchanges also had to be changed to motivate manufacturers to support the electronic invoice. The price the manufacturers pay for receiving an order, he continued, should be reduced if they send back electronic documents.

All the answers have one thing in common: they support the idea of online trading as a reciprocal business yielding benefits for both parties. The old misconception of eBusiness creating only positive effects for manufacturers did not seem to be supported by the hospital experts.

New Opportunities

The identification of existing barriers is one way—and certainly a very important one—of overcoming them. Another approach to facilitating eBusiness is exploring the emerging opportunities that are either caused by eBusiness, or accompany the daily practice of online trading.

Logistics

All hospitals experts agreed that there was a strong coupling of different logistics services with eBusiness, yet they differed in terms of what it meant to their own organization. In general, they appreciated the efficiency and speed of those services enabled through electronic methods. Only those experts with an outspoken affinity to supply chain management principles, however, saw a direct and strategy-motivated line from eBusiness to logistics. These were the people who had gained experience in just-in-time (JIT) delivery and outsourcing of inventory management, or who explicitly wished to get more transparency in the supply chain through tracking and tracing methods. Some of the experts who were more reserved about an automatic linkage between online trading and new logistics services mentioned problems that still existed with connecting consignment warehouses to the online trading exchange and eBusiness technology in general. They also saw the potential, however, once the technology was mature enough.

It appears that more practical experience and empirical evidence are needed to recognize the full potential of eBusiness for new logistics services and vice versa.

Group Purchasing

Those experts (five out of the seven) whose organization was either a member of a group purchasing organization, a purchasing cooperative, or otherwise had experience of pooling the procurement power, unanimously agreed that there was a strong dependency between bundling purchasing volume and conducting electronic business. They argued that only through eBusiness mechanisms did structured data become available, which entails the opportunity of analyzing buying patterns and monitoring contract compliance. Now they could, for the first time, negotiate with the suppliers on the basis of real-time and accurate data. This made eBusiness so attractive for GPO's and purchasing cooperatives, and was the reason why the most advanced of these organizations promoted eBusiness.

In the United States, most of the big GPO's possess an eBusiness branch through which their members can order electronically (see Chapter 7). In Germany, where the role of the traditional purchasing cooperatives in negotiating common contracts used to be less pronounced, new initiatives are emerging. These initiatives realized the strong demand for data to streamline activities and engage in eBusiness, either by setting up an electronic purchasing platform of their own, or by aligning with an existing online trading exchange. Two of the experts interviewed played an extremely active role in this field. One of them owns a large pharmacy which serves, among others, 5,000 hospital beds. The other had established the purchasing cooperatives of North German University Hospitals, together with his colleagues from the other university hospitals. Both have been promoting online purchasing for many years and strongly support the notion of mutual benefit between group purchasing and electronic procurement.

The English expert fully agreed with this view. In England, purchasing had been handled by an NHS agency that used to negotiate country-wide contracts with suppliers for all NHS trusts. Only recently was this strategy given up in favor of regional procurement organizations called Collaborative Procurement Hubs (CPH). Among the problems the national contracts suffered from, he reported, was the difficulty of collecting relevant information on actual purchasing volumes. The conditions offered by these contracts were therefore less favorable than they could have been. He hoped the new strategy focusing on the regional CPHs would improve the situation—in particular, once the CPHs had electronic access to all relevant information.

Despite the quite big differences in procurement strategies in the three countries, the underlying principles of volume bundling and contract negotiating on the basis of real-time facts are identical. It therefore seems that in the context of eBusiness, the organizational differences can be neglected and the problem actually boils down to the simple fact of better availability of the data through electronic means.

eBusiness, however, does not solve all the problems of group purchasing. In particular, one of the experts pointed out that enforcing contract compliance was a totally different matter. This could not be solved at the electronic level. eBusiness is no panacea for group purchasing, nor is group purchasing itself entirely undisputed—particularly in the country with the longest history of GPOs, but also in others, as the contributions of some of the experts reflected.

Business Analysis

In the hospital experts' opinion, the GPOs' motivation for eBusiness originated from the electronic access to purchasing data. According to our interviews, the hospitals also knew about the power of the data. eBusiness-enabled data analysis was regarded as one of the major achievements of electronic procurement. It was an absolute must for each organization, said all experts, and the advantage of eBusiness was that it made these data available. Some qualified their judgment, however, saying that the eBusiness systems did not provide any means for carrying out these analyses, but that it was the ERP system or the HIS_h that provided the necessary tools. This view underlines the absolute necessity for integrated information systems that allow a seamless flow of information between different subsystems. Just collecting data without having any means for further analysis bereaves eBusiness of its power.

Chapter 10 investigates the types of business analysis that are possible with certain kinds of data, for certain purposes and using certain tools by providing examples that illustrate the analysis and interpretation of materials data for management purposes.

eBusiness as an Enabler of New Services

Looking into the interdependencies between eBusiness on the one side, and logistics, group purchasing and business analysis on the other side, yielded insight into how electronic media interact with, support, and promote existing services. When asked what new services eBusiness has in store, the experts did not come up with entirely new ideas but instead underlined that the potential of conducting electronic business had not yet been fully exploited from a practical point of view. By this they meant that, for example, electronic invoices, tracing products with smart technology, electronic contracts, electronic support for consignment warehouses, and other types of vendor-managed inventories were not yet fully in place. Although the concepts themselves were not new at all, they were still new for the organization.

This hints at the fact that there is still some way to go to actually see them working in reality, even at sites of eBusiness excellence. The experts did also mention new services, however, such as enhanced catalogs and electronic transfer of funds. Right now, electronic catalogs contain information on basic business characteristics of a product. In principle, the spectrum of information included could be widened and clinically relevant features of a product could also be included in the catalogs. This does not necessarily mean that these features have to be presented in multimedia and 3D, but that the enhanced catalog should convey information required by the person who has to answer a specific clinical question and has to eventually make a purchasing decision. What specific type of information this would be has to be investigated product by product, and the experts did not expand on it.

One of the experts raised the question of whether or not eBusiness could help hospitals to retract from their role as sellers of products. Right now, he argued, hospitals were acting as middlemen between the insurance companies who paid for a product needed by the patient and the manufacturers who provided the product. It was not the business of hospitals to sell products, but to provide professional (clinical) services. Given an uninterrupted flow of information between all parties involved, the electronic transfer of funds could be managed from the insurance company to the suppliers. This would allow the insurance companies to negotiate directly with the suppliers on significantly larger volumes than with a healthcare system. He concluded that including the payers in the supply chain would be the consistent extension of the vision behind supply chain management in healthcare (see Figure 12-3).

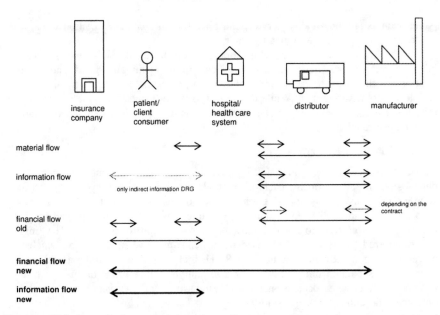

FIGURE 12-3. New eBusiness enabled service – direct payment between insurance company and manufacturer.

New Customer–Supplier Relationship

In contrast to the literature, which emphasizes the more trusting relationship between the partners in a supply chain, the hospital experts did not unanimously support the theory of an improved relationship. In fact, the experts fell into two camps of nearly equal numbers: the supporters of more trust, and the skeptics. The supporters argued that due to the reduced number of errors in eBusiness, customers and suppliers did not have to deal with order fulfilment problems and could instead spend the time discussing new products and services. "We focus on products, not on errors" one expert summarized the new relationship. Another expert stressed the fact that due to the greater transparency ("we know more about them and they know more about us"), there was less suspicion on both sides. On the other hand, the skeptics either denied any change or concluded that it became more "matter of fact." Because there was more transparency in the supply chain, the attitude on the side of the hospital was more fact-based and solution-oriented. "Where did it break down and how can we fix it?" reported one expert. He, however, refused to call it *greater trust*.

The different opinions were probably brought about by a different understanding of what the relationship means. There are various layers of a relationship between a customer and a supplier, one of which is the transactional level. By employing eBusiness technology, this type of relationship becomes less dominated by errors. If errors occur, they are handled in a less emotional, more relaxed manner ("we tend to be more tolerant towards the supplier") because they can be located sooner and more accurately. As a consequence, a good transactional relationship develops. Whether, and to what degree, this single aspect impacts the overall relationship with the supplier is less clear and obviously depends on the hospital because there are other factors beyond transactional issues such as product quality, service, and price that influence the relationship at least as strongly, and perhaps to a much greater extent.

A good relationship that develops out of well-managed, electronically enabled business transactions must be distinguished from an initially good and trusting relationship that leads to establishing interwoven processes, deep technical integration, and access to sensitive data. While the latter type of eBusiness is common practice in other industries, healthcare is much more cautious and thus less inclined to establish such a close relationship.

R&D and Product Evaluation

Cooperation and collaboration in developing new products and conducting clinical trials depends on all parties trusting each other. It addresses yet another layer of a customer-supplier relationship. By focusing on product issues and patient care, it primarily involves clinicians. All supply chain experts interviewed felt that they had too little experience in this field to make a substantial contribution to this topic. The English expert referred to the evidenced-based purchasing initiative of the NHS, which was currently evolving. Business issues and R&D, including clinical trials, are obviously kept entirely separate from each other. This certainly requires further discussion as there is a need for fact-based decision-making in purchasing, with the facts related to clinical outcomes and clinical process quality.

The Future

The positive experience of the early adopters, the waning influence of barriers, and new opportunities being facilitated by eBusiness,all contribute to paving the way towards recruiting a broad range of healthcare providers with differing motivations to embark on the path to eBusiness. A question often raised in this context is "How long will it take to get the critical mass of users to benefit from networking effects in eBusiness?" Five years is a time frame most hospital experts felt was realistic to achieve this goal. A minority estimated it would still take about 10 years. As all experts felt it was very difficult to make exact forecasts, these figures must be regarded as rough estimates and express the general feeling that it will still take some time before networking effects will materialize—but this process will happen within a reasonable time frame.

When asked what arguments will drive the process in the future, the majority of experts predicted that cost issues would prevail, and would dominate the discussion in the future. One hospital manager continued "that quality issues would come in when a plateau was reached where no further costs could be taken out." This is interesting against the backdrop that most hospital managers thought the main benefits of eBusiness were better processes, error-free data, improved discipline, and free time for solving other problems. Only when staff are made redundant can process costs be decreased, they argued. Cost savings seem to be no direct consequence of eBusiness, but are rather mediated by eBusiness-supported purchasing behaviors and contract compliance. Nevertheless, the experts stated that eBusiness was expected to create cost savings. There is obviously a discrepancy between what could be called the front-end argument (cost issues) and the back-end body of many good reasons for practicing eBusiness (quality issues) that positively influence the cost situation. Pushing cost issues to the front in the future also may be explained by the fact that new investments in eBusiness technology can often only be justified with cost reductions.

Cost reduction can be achieved by cutting process costs, but also by negotiating more favorable conditions and prices. Greater competition among suppliers helps customers have a greater choice and be less dependent on one single supplier. We therefore asked the hospital experts whether or not they believed that more competition in the market could be possible as a result of eBusiness. The opinions varied quite a bit. Two experts fully agreed, arguing that the Internet caused greater product transparency which, in turn, opened up the market and fostered competition. Others predicted that there would eventually be fewer players in the market, which reduces the choice for the customers. Still others argued that eBusiness was a competitive advantage for companies, giving those who had adopted the technology early a head start and enabling them to better meet the customer requirements for electronic capabilities. Whether eBusiness is a real competitive advantage had been doubted by several sources, as mentioned in our assumptions guiding these interviews. So it was all the more interesting to hear experts vindicating this point of view. It is also remarkable to find no unanimous support for the proposition that eBusiness also opens up markets in healthcare. This may have two reasons. First, it may not be true for healthcare because it is a special market. Second, eBusiness may not have unfolded its real potential as a market opener.

The last question about global sourcing deepens the issue of open markets. Three of the seven healthcare organizations had already gained experience in cross-border ordering, mainly in one of the neighbouring countries. Most of them had encountered difficulties such as problems with customs or with companies that protected the national market by stopping foreign customers from ordering products. Other problems mentioned, in addition, were language problems, not enough volume to make the effort worthwhile, legal restrictions, and no local after-sales support. Two hospital experts explicitly said that globalization was an issue for vendor-to-vendor business, but not for hospitals. All the same, some hospital experts thought it made sense for commodities to be ordered where they could offer the best price-performance ratio.

Like the issue of competition, global sourcing also seems not to have reached the healthcare market completely. It remains to be seen whether this is simply due to a time lag between the healthcare and other markets, or whether the healthcare market follows its own rules and habits.

The future of the digital healthcare market is hard to predict, according to the opinions voiced by the hospital experts. For one thing, eBusiness has not yet unfolded all its powers, and for another thing, it is still unclear if the healthcare market will follow general business trends or if it will remain a special market. In any case, eBusiness in healthcare is about to become a fact and electronic capabilities will become a must for companies to meet customer demands.

Conclusions

The main conclusions from these findings will be drawn at the end of the next chapter, after the suppliers' point of view has been presented.

References

[1] Eakin, D. (2002) Measuring e-Procurement benefits. *Government procurement.* **10**, 6–12.
[2] McKone-Sweet, K. E., P. Hamilton, and S. Willis. (2005) The Ailing Healthcare Supply Chain: A Prescription for Change. *Journal of Supply Chain Management.* **41**, 4–17.
[3] Burns, L. R. and Wharton School Colleagues (2002) *The Health Care Value Chain: Producers, Purchasers, and Providers.* San Francisco: Jossey-Bass.

[4]   Perrin, R. A. and K. Conway. (2005) How to achieve the promise of eCommerce. *Healthcare Purchasing News.* **74**, 68–69.
[5]   Markus, M.L. and E. Christiaanse. (2003) Adoption and impact of collaboration electronic marketplaces. *Information Systems and e-Business Management.* **1**, 139–155.
[6]   Hartono, E. and C. Holsapple. (2004) Theoretical foundations for collaborative commerce research and practice. *Information Systems and e-Business Management.* **2**, 1–30.
[7]   Wang, S. and N. Archer. (2004) Supporting collaboration in business-to-business electronic marketplaces. *Information Systems and e-Business Management.* **2**, 269–286.
[8]   Lambert, D. M., S. J. Garcia-Dastugue, and K. L. Craxton. (2005) An Evaluation Of Process-Oriented Supply Chain Management Frameworks. *Journal of Business Logistics.* **26**, 25–51.
[9]   European Commission, Directorate General for Enterprise (2004) *The European e-Business Report 2004 edition.* Bonn: empirica. Available from: <http://www.ebusiness-watch.org/resources/documents/eBusiness-Report-2004.pdf> [Accessed 01 September 2006].
[10] Yen, B. P.-C. and E. O. S. Ng. (2003) The Impact of Electronic Commerce on Procurement. *Journal of organizational computing and electronic commerce.* **13**, 167–189

Appendix

List of Interview Partners

Hospital Experts

I wish to thank the hospital experts who participated in this study. Their names and institutions are listed in the following table.

Hospital	City	Contact
University Hospital Freiburg	Freiburg, Germany	Frank Reichenbach
Virginia Mason Medical Center	Seattle, US	Daniel Borunda
Pennine Acute Trust - The Royal Oldham Hospital	Manchester, UK	Peter Mallon
Katholische Johannes Gesellschaft Dortmund	Dortmund, Germany	Michael Bremshey
Resurrection Healthcare	Chicago, US	Edward Friese
University Hospital Göttingen	Göttingen, Germany	Detlef Bruer
Hospital Pharmacy	**City**	**Contact**
Sanicare	Bad Laer, Germany	Johannes Mönter

I also thank Kevin Pritchard, Director of Procurement at the Greater Manchester Collaborative Procurement Hub, for providing valuable background information on new developments in procurement within the NHS.

13
The Expert's Opinion:
Part II – The Suppliers

Ursula Hübner

Executive Summary

This chapter continues to summarize the results of the interviews, with a special focus on the suppliers' perspective. In the conclusion, the main results from both points of view are compiled, compared, and discussed in an attempt to arrive at answers to the questions of whether the initial assumptions still hold true, whether there are real differences between the healthcare providers and the suppliers, and if the healthcare market is to be regarded as a special market.

The suppliers reported that the main reasons for adopting eBusiness procedures in their organizations were a combination of *process automation*, *process optimization* and *error-free data*. Many of the experts additionally stated that they wanted to share their expertise in process management with their customers. This serves the hospitals, but also the suppliers, who know that only if the processes in the hospitals are well-managed will process automation and optimization work on their side as well.

Changing an organization and its processes was not easy, according to what the industry stated. It needed measures at all levels—in particular, training and informing people so that the changes associated with eBusiness were not a source of fear but rather an opportunity for their professional career. Training measures should concern the account managers and the sales force, as well as the staff working in the customer canvassing department who could now be promoted to better positions in customer service.

Despite the achievements within one's own organization, however, there were still barriers that impeded the general utilization of eBusiness methods. The industry experts said that most of the problems originating from hospitals were caused by a "lack of understanding of the importance of eBusiness," which was followed by a reluctance to make the necessary investments in eBusiness in combination with a "lack of support from the management level."

Although there is still the suppliers' demand for hospitals to become more active in eBusiness today, there is an understanding that both parties are needed to establish electronic business communication. The industry experts, however, insisted they needed input from the customers in the form of a clear demand for eBusiness because the industry had no means of forcing the hospitals into electronic purchasing.

In accordance with the hospitals, the manufacturers saw eBusiness not only as an enabler for online procurement but also as a technical facilitator for other services, such as logistics. The industry experts agreed that the most important innovative service promoted by eBusiness was the electronic catalog. With its additional product information and linking to scientific resources, the enhanced catalog was a service for the customers to inform themselves better and faster about recent developments and new products.

Not only is the catalog an advanced new service, it also constitutes the core element of conducting electronic business. It is, in fact, the basic prerequisite for getting *clean data* and for allowing both sides to analyze their business data properly. The interviews showed that the industry experts appreciated the value of *clear data* very much and explicitly expressed this.

There was less agreement on other issues of eBusiness among the industry experts. Some assumed that eBusiness creates a more trusting, and potentially closer relationship between suppliers and their customers. While some industry experts fully agreed, others stated it was only the product that defined the quality of the relationship.

Another controversial issue among the experts was the link between R&D and eBusiness. The first group of experts stated that R&D and clinical trials were beyond the scope of the supply chain and eBusiness. The other group doubted that communicating with customers via electronic channels was the right approach in a field requiring creativity, such as in R&D. On the bottom line, it seems that product development and evaluation have very little in common with how eBusiness is currently understood.

Hospital and industry experts very much agree on how they envisage the future of eBusiness in healthcare. Five years was a realistic timeframe to get a critical mass of eBusiness users, and cost issues would continue to dominate the discussion in the future. Practicing eBusiness was not a competitive advantage (for most experts), but not having it would be a competitive disadvantage. Globalization played no role in the customer-supplier relationship.

In conclusion, the results from both groups of interview partners show that hospitals, as well as manufacturers, assume a pragmatic attitude towards eBusiness characterized by the success already achieved, as well as by the understanding of what comes next on the agenda. The second wave of eBusiness is no longer dominated by unrealistic promises, but by the certainty that eBusiness is on its way towards achieving value in several areas. The initial assumptions about eBusiness, its benefits, impacts, and barriers can only be partly supported by this study. eBusiness is definitely more than process automation—its power is established by high-quality data and opportunities derived from accessing them with the catalog being the keystone. Technical barriers are waning, but standards remain an issue to be solved, many experts said. Healthcare providers and suppliers largely agree in their appraisal of the status quo of eBusiness and also in their predictions about future developments. Many arguments put forward support the assumption that the healthcare market is special.

Evolving from a *nice to have* to a *must have*, eBusiness will contribute to distinguishing between those who will stay in business versus those who will be out of business—and this holds true for hospitals and suppliers alike.

Results – The Suppliers' Perspective

Reasons for eBusiness: Process Automation Plus Customer Support

The main reasons for moving to eBusiness given by the manufacturers were process automation, process optimization, and error free data, albeit often stated in combination with the argument "to help the customer" either to reduce the costs, to share expertise, or to pass on their experience. Two manufacturers mentioned they were driven by their customers to adopt eBusiness technology after having been skeptical about its use at the beginning. Other reasons provided by individual manufacturers included

- Reduced cycle time or payment period
- Implementation of logistics concepts, such as just-in-time delivery enabled by eBusiness
- Time for taking over responsibilities in customer service instead of retyping paper-based orders

The issue of whether eBusiness actually increased sales was a controversial discussion. While one manufacturer admitted that they had initially thought that eBusiness would boost sales (hence a competitive advantage), which later proved wrong, another manufacturer believed eBusiness would contribute significantly to the growth of the company. This discrepancy might be explained by differences in the customer base because the first manufacturer provided supplies to hospitals that were ordering electronically via their purchasing department, and the latter provided chemicals to researchers ordering online by themselves.

In contrast to the hospital experts, the manufacturers were less hesitant to speak of process automation, mainly referring to automating the retyping work once the orders had arrived. Most of the experts, however, preferred the term *process optimization*, which included increased efficiency coupled with a decreased error rate. Process automation pays off when mass data of similar structure are processed, as is the case with large manufacturers. This explains why simple automation already leads to a tangible benefit for them.

It seems that the manufacturers are somewhat better aware of the advantages of having error-free data than the hospitals, because correct input data are an immediate requirement for process automation to be effective. For hospitals, accurate data pay off at a later stage when the right goods arrive at the right time and at the right place, and when it comes to analyzing the data for decision-making.

The manufacturers' involvement with the customers to help them optimize their processes may sound surprising initially, but it actually originates from the understanding that suppliers depend on their customers. Due to the reciprocal nature of eBusiness, manufacturers can only implement electronic transactions successfully if there are also well-managed processes utilizing error-free data on the other side. This is a crucial issue because "if errors occur in the electronic process, it takes more time to fix the problem than if errors occur in the conventional process," as one expert expressed it clearly. Figure 13-1 summarizes the multidimensional effect of eBusiness from the suppliers' perspective.

Reasons for moving to eBusiness provided by the healthcare manufacturers resemble those of other industries at first glance, as the comparison with the expert from the paper manufacturer reveals. The latter also mentioned increased efficiency through

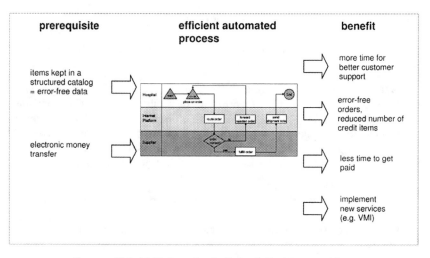

FIGURE 13-1. Multi-dimensional effects of eBusiness – suppliers.

standardization and automation, improved data quality, and achieving greater productivity with the same staff. In addition to that, however, he also reported that the company had expected to be able to provide new services based on eBusiness, to distinguish themselves from other competitors (competitive advantage) and to achieve a greater binding of customers by interleaving the processes of both organizations.

Management of Change: The Key is Information and Training

Looking at how the companies coped with the internal challenges of moving from conventional to electronic business showed again the importance of good support from the executives. The most urgent issue for companies, however, was to "train and inform the people" at all levels—the ones who used to receive the paper, fax, or phone orders, the sales force, and the account managers. For all of them, doing business electronically could pose a threat, therefore the company experts stressed the measures undertaken to make people understand what eBusiness meant to them. This was exactly mirrored by what the paper industry expert expressed.

Similarly to the hospital experts, the manufacturers also mentioned "a good relationship with and support from the IT department," "existence of a strategy," and "the importance of individuals dedicated to eBusiness, particularly at the beginning." These issues seem to play a minor role as compared to "support from executives" and "information and training," but they reflect that changing an organization requires a multitude of measures to become successful.

Barriers on the Road to eBusiness

Most industry experts answered the question of whether a lack of appropriate technology hampered the adoption of eBusiness with "No." The technology was mainly there, they said, but most of them had experienced that the necessary technology was not available in (some) hospitals and that this certainly had had an influence on the adoption process. One expert also complained about a lack of good solutions for consignment warehouses, and another expert expressed the wish for more semantic interoperability among the systems in use. All of the experts believed that there were other barriers than technology, and they provided a long list of potential factors impeding the breakthrough of eBusiness. According to their opinion, most of these factors by far originated from hospitals with "lack of understanding the importance of eBusiness" on top of the list, followed by "no budget/reluctance to invest," and a "lack of support from the management level." The structures and procedure in hospital decision-making also were inappropriate for finding solutions in a reasonable time, one expert criticized, and two other experts said the hospitals were responsible for not wanting to change old processes, including the problem of maverick buying. Despite this criticism, the manufacturers expressed understanding for the situation of the hospitals, who often had to concentrate on other priorities to survive. They also conceded that the situation was improving. Interestingly, only two of the experts thought there were any organizational barriers to be identified on the side of the manufacturers. One argument was that the costs of conducting eBusiness were much higher than those of paper-based business. The other argument concerned the training of the employees—i.e., if there was not enough training, this definitely caused a disruption when implementing electronic processes. Interpreting these results is not easy—in particular, because the manufacturers mainly blamed the hospitals without mentioning the problems in their own organizations. All the same, their perspective might indeed reflect the truth, or at least part of the truth, because the hospitals had also felt that there were deficiencies on their side. The deficiencies perceived by the hospitals, however, differed from those perceived by the manufacturers. They only agreed on the problem of high costs for the hospitals combined with a reluctance to make investments.

The manufacturers should be advised to analyze their difficulties in more detail, and pay attention to what the hospitals said about the manufacturers' problems, because the game is not about pointing one's finger at the other but rather about overcoming the barriers together. The manufacturers' offer to the hospitals to help them optimize their processes is a step in the right direction, indeed.

In terms of costs, the manufacturers also felt themselves under pressure as obviously eBusiness procedures are not cheaper in every case than paper-based methods—on the contrary, they are even more expensive. This concern was expressed explicitly by only one of the experts from Germany in the interviews, but is heard in informal discussions also. The expert had not detailed from where these costs actually stem, but she was also concerned that the fees of the Internet trading exchanges might be too high. The cost discussion obviously demonstrates that costs can only be saved when a critical mass of hospitals and manufacturers employ electronic methods and shows that costs can even rise or stay the same during a transition period.

Although major technical difficulties do not seem to exist because there were sufficient solutions on the market, the lack or abundance of technical standards might still be a problem. The reaction to this question was very mixed, ranging from "there are enough standards," and the problem rather being "a lack of compliance" and "a lack of understanding of the importance of standards," to "there are too many." One expert clearly expressed the need for an identification standard (universal product numbers). The issue of classification systems was debated. In a regulated market, such as the one in the United Kingdom, the industry expert expected the NHS to give clear supraregional directives in terms of the standards with which they must comply. In countries where Internet trading exchanges play a major role, as they certainly do in the United States, Germany, and the United Kingdom, these trading exchanges could become the most important driving force for promoting standards, as one expert suggested.

Standards are a concern of the experts both from industry and from the hospitals. A coherent approach that puts standards on the agenda and bundles various initiatives still seems to be missing, however. Today, most manufacturers have to pragmatically handle connectivity on an individual project basis to link up with as many customers as possible. Internet-based trading exchanges and the prevalence of a limited number of technical systems (e.g., SAP R/3 in Germany) have contributed to harmonizing connectivity issues, and yet they are far from being entirely solved.

The paper industry is no different from the healthcare industry in terms of standards and the availability of technical systems for eBusiness. When asked whether there were any barriers, the expert replied "no"—just the usual ones of "money and time."

Similar to the hospital experts, the industry specialists felt that eBusiness had reached a level of acceptance where none of the major groups were actively sabotaging or working against it. This used to be different, one U.S. expert stated, when manufacturers acted very hesitantly in the electronic market due to fears about the misuse of data and the interference from third parties with an unsound background. As these issues had been definitely resolved, there were no worries any longer on the side of the manufacturers.

Summarizing the question about barriers, business partners today agree that many of the problems have been solved and that there is no discussion about whether eBusiness is acceptable and feasible or not. From their statements, it can be concluded that eBusiness matters, including the barriers, must be dealt with in a matter-of-fact style—the problems must be analyzed and solutions provided.

Drivers and Incentives: The Chicken and the Egg

While the hospital experts said that a single hospital was too small to drive eBusiness and had voted for a mixed approach, nearly all experts from industry stated that the companies, driven by their customers, only required the hospitals to express a clear wish to purchase electronically. Some of them reported that they had initially thought they could drive the process by convincing the customers, but instead were driven to the conclusion that they were banging their head against a brick wall.

What seems a contradiction at first glance, is actually not one because both are right. Manufacturers would not change to eBusiness because one single hospital wishes them to do so, nor would they turn down a significant number of hospitals or healthcare systems if the latter approached them with their demand to implement electronic processes. Manufacturers, particularly with no eBusiness capabilities, can therefore only be forced by the power of the market with strict requirements for electronic transaction methods— already at the stage of tendering.

Many of the problems in procurement can generally be traced back to the asymmetry in size between the healthcare providers and the suppliers. Healthcare providers must learn to speak with one voice and are, in fact, on the way to doing so. In the paper industry, retailers acting together and appearing as eBusiness leaders drove the paper manufacturers into electronic trading, dictating the methods employed. At the same time, the paper manufacturers had shaped the electronic transaction processes at an early stage with their large customers, setting standards for others. Is there anything to be learned from this example? It certainly shows that aggregating the purchasing power puts organizations in a position to better drive things, given the fact they exert pressure and express their demands. It also shows that dealing with single large accounts can be quite favorable for a manufacturer, and in terms of defining technological standards provided the manufacturer is agile enough to be the first in the field.

The industry experts all denied that giving hospitals financial incentives would drive eBusiness. They were very skeptical about the effect of such incentives, and added that the incentives were already there once a hospital practiced online purchasing. In this context, they particularly referred to clean data becoming available through eBusiness and referred to documents being returned to the hospitals by the manufacturers (i.e., the electronic advance shipping notice and the eInvoice). One expert explained that you must "make sure" the hospitals "are embracing change for the right reasons." Another expert added that eBusiness could only unfold its power for a hospital if it had been integrated into the hospital's overall strategy.

The general skepticism about financial incentives working as drivers, however, did not preclude experts from stating that financial savings, once they were actually achieved, could be passed on to the customers.

Looking at the types of incentives that work for manufacturers, one of the experts summarized that "pressure from the customers" would be the best vehicle to motivate change in eBusiness. In doing so, she repeated the general demand expressed by the manufacturers that hospitals and healthcare systems should commit themselves to eBusiness procedures and should explicitly require online trading from the manufacturers.

Comparing the answers of the hospital and the industry experts revealed, surprisingly, many similarities and a common understanding that both parties must say "Yes" for eBusiness to work. The old question of "Who should be the driver?" does not apply any more. As one industry expert phrased it, it would be as useless as asking "Who is first, the chicken or the egg?"

New Opportunities

Logistics

Asking whether or not eBusiness would stimulate logistics and vice versa tended to yield the answer "Yes, but ...." All experts agreed that both are closely linked, with eBusiness acting as a "facilitator" and "a technical enabler" for new logistics concepts. But in the end, it was a business decision to change to new logistics services, one expert explained. Other experts who defined eCommerce in a more restricted way thought that logistics was not a central issue of eCommerce, but rather an issue of its own.

On the other hand, there were experts who definitely expressed the view that the combination of both could create added value for the suppliers and the customers. One of them explained that it was too short-sighted to concentrate on consignment warehouses. He suggested one should rather discuss vendor-managed inventories (VMIs) that also include facilities such as self-billing. In addition to VMIs, he mentioned just-in-time delivery, or "on time in full," as he called it. It was a particular logistics service the company could offer only because of the electronic capabilities that eBusiness had offered the company. Another expert reported that his company very much fostered the idea of multivendor supply centers in the context of eBusiness. This expert continued that electronic means had made it possible for customers to define their own unique product bundle (set) that could be treated as a single product and could be delivered to the customer as such. One expert who also believed in a strong linkage between the two topics conceded that the real benefits arising from mutual stimulation would only unfold once a critical mass existed.

The consignment warehouses and VMIs were also not a new topic for the expert from the paper industry. He strongly supported the theory that eBusiness and logistics were cross-influencing each other. He also expressed in a plain-spoken manner that consignment warehouses and VMIs were controversial concepts—the first was favored by the customers, and the latter by the manufacturers, and it depended on the business context which one was implemented.

This may have been a reason why some healthcare experts reacted rather cautiously when asked about the connection between eBusiness and logistics, knowing that it only made things worse when combining two critical issues at the same time. In addition, not all hospitals favor new logistics concepts such as JIT and warehouse outsourcing, as has been shown by the interviews with the hospital experts.

Group Purchasing

The answers to the question about whether group purchasing and eBusiness influence each other mutually reflect the different history of, and experience with, group purchasing in the three countries. While the experts investigating the German market responded in a positive manner, the other experts were a bit more skeptical. In Germany, where group purchasing had not taken place effectively before, those purchasing cooperatives that strictly bound their members were regarded as highly eBusiness-motivated and just as capable of actually stimulating eBusiness. Provided that the hospitals purchased online and agreed on the use of standards, they were in a position to analyze their purchasing data and pool them with the data from the other members of the cooperative. In the United States it was different, according to the results of the interview. Although the GPOs had thought that they would be able to drive eBusiness in hospitals, they were "more of an encourager" than a real driver, it was said.

Business Analysis

The industry experts all agreed that access to clean data enabled by online transactions was the key to gaining more insight into what really happened—on the side of the healthcare providers as well as on the side of the manufacturers. Most of them had already raised this issue by themselves during the interview when responding to the question about their reasons for adopting eBusiness procedures. This again demonstrates that the manufacturers definitely appreciate the existence of clean data and the access to it. Because there is a growing understanding about the importance of data in hospitals, too, they might become better aware of the early benefits of eBusiness.

Industry has had a longer culture of basing management decisions on empirical facts than hospitals (in general), and in regulated or highly regulated healthcare markets in particular. With cost containment measures becoming a real threat to the survival of healthcare providers, managers much more eagerly adopt business management methods from industry. Against this backdrop, the statement that hospitals had other priorities than eBusiness, due to their struggle for survival, had to be given a second thought. Interestingly, both hospital and manufacturer experts had provided these arguments when asked about potential barriers to eBusiness.

eBusiness as an Enabler of New Services

The idea of data as the key prerequisite and benefit of eBusiness runs like a red line through the interviews with the industry experts. Most of the experts also mentioned enhanced catalogs as the primary new service they offered, or would offer, to their customers. This new type of catalog would include "classified items," supplier-specific "information about the full capabilities of the products" tailored to the physicians' needs, and "intelligent user manuals". It would be linked with an independent scientific database. The only expert who did not specifically mention catalogs did so indirectly, saying that access to research findings and the provision of continued medical education were services he could imagine enhancing electronic transactions. These results confirm that the catalog is the focal point of eBusiness. Today, the potential has not yet been fully exhausted and there is still room for further developments, particularly in terms of enriching the catalog with product-specific and scientific information for the clinicians and the clinical researchers (see Figure 13-2).

In addition, other services enumerated were "cleansing materials data in the hospital's master database," "better equipped consignment warehouses, and improved replenishment methods."

In contrast to the industry experts, the hospital experts stated other preferences, mainly referring to transactions promised by eBusiness but not yet always fully implemented, such as information about the delivery status, the electronic invoice, the electronic contract, and electronic inventory support (so-called *managed services*). Only one hospital expert explicitly mentioned "better information about the product for our internal customers, the clinicians." These findings reflect different perspectives among the experts, depending on whether they come from a healthcare provider or the manufacturing industry. While the hospitals experts who were responsible for materials and supply chain management focused on operational issues, the industry experts primarily had the clinical decision-makers in mind.

In conclusion, these two perspectives actually supplement each other rather than contradict each other, and much is to be learned from them. The lesson for the manufacturers seems to be that down-to-earth transaction problems still need to be resolved, and the lesson for the hospitals is that eBusiness not only refers to transactions but may prepare decision-making based on supplier-specific and independent scientific information.

New Customer–Supplier Relationship

The issue of eBusiness causing a more trusting and potentially closer relationship between suppliers and their customers that is raised by the literature cannot be entirely

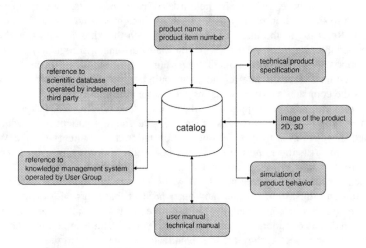

FIGURE 13-2. Catalog linking to related information.

supported by our findings. Just like the group of hospital experts, the industry experts were split into two camps, and the only difference was that none of the industry experts completely denied that eBusiness changed the relationship. But there were strong supporters who believed that eBusiness was a means to forge better relationships, and those who wanted to qualify this assumption, saying "Yes, but" what really counted was the product. The supporters spoke about

- Greater transparency that led also to greater intimacy and trust
- Greater potential for reaching customers 24 hours a day and for providing information in a much more unobtrusive manner than before
- Opportunity to address not only the clinicians but the purchasing managers, talking about processes with them and not only about the product price
- Technical ability to reach a wide audience, including students, who are the prospects of the future

Two experts stated that the transparency that eBusiness methods entailed may not always be regarded as a positive effect. They reported on their experiences with customers that had not wanted the manufacturers to know too many details about their purchasing behavior. The experts concluded that, despite the capability of reaching many institutions electronically, eBusiness (in particular, information distributed over the Web) was not to be seen as a marketing tool in healthcare for attracting more customers—at least not in areas with a high coverage of sales representatives. Products requiring explanations could not be marketed virtually, but needed sales representatives to come to the hospitals personally, they said. Of course, the sales force could be supported by electronically available information, which would certainly strengthen existing relationships, they continued. The same experts were the ones who saw the product in the center of shaping a customer-supplier relationship.

This might not hold true for commodities which need factors other than product features to make them attractive, such as price and maybe also the electronic capabilities of the supplier. None of the experts from companies that, among other things, also provide commodities suggested an entirely virtual way of selling their products, however.

The expert from the paper industry agreed with the statement that "you do not attract customers in cyberspace," which also held true for paper products. He contradicted this with regard to the trusting relationship, which he thought was an essential outcome of eBusiness. Referring to the interwoven processes with their key accounts, and to new eBusiness-enabled services such as allowing their customers to regularly retrieve up-to-date reports about the product quality (e.g., humidity of the paper) from the website, he illustrated how close the interrelationship could become. "You can see what we can see." was the company's motto in dealing with large customers.

Apart from the traditional supplier-healthcare provider connection, one expert reported that a new type of relationship was emerging—the supplier-patient axis, which also motivated manufacturers to provide information tailored for patients via the Web. In the light of the growing importance of health consumer informatics, this statement is not surprising at all. With patients becoming more interested in why and how they are treated by healthcare professionals, they are increasingly demanding background information on drugs, implants, and any other product that stays with the patient. Not only are manufacturers concerned, but those businesses that actually deal electronically with the consumers or patients are also involved. Typically, these are online pharmacies. In the primary care sector, they are the manufacturers' interface to the consumer, and because this interface is Web-bound, all product information has to go through electronic channels. It is expected that the supplier-patient axis, including online pharmacies and other online businesses, will gain more and more importance in the future.

R&D and Product Evaluation

The supplier-customer relationship is influenced by a number of factors, as has been discussed previously—by the product, by the processes between the supplier and the customer, and by the electronic capabilities that streamline these processes and allow more transparency throughout the supply chain. These processes pertain to traditional business transactions. They may also refer to supplier-customer collaboration, however, for product development and product evaluation, as has been discussed in the literature. When we asked if such collaboration existed, if it was supported electronically, and if it had any influence on the supplier-customer relationship in the context of eBusiness, we received "Yes, but..." answers from most of the industry experts. The "Yes" part of the answers embraced the fact that they were cooperating with clinicians for these purposes, and also reflected the general attitude that electronic systems were very suitable in this context. Some experts reported that their companies were using such systems in clinical trials for testing drugs and medical devices. The "but" part of the answers referred to two distinct issues. The first group of experts stated that R&D and clinical trials were beyond the scope of the supply chain and eBusiness. The other group doubted that communicating with customers exclusively via electronic channels was the right approach. Product development needed "creativity," and understanding the clinical requirements needed "face-to-face meetings." The "personal communication" could not simply be replaced by computers, they argued.

These findings fit strongly with earlier statements about the sales force being an essential link to the customer and maintaining a two-way communication channel between the customer and the supplier. These results obviously pointed less in the direction of R&D, but rather in the direction of marketing. On the bottom line, it seems that product development and evaluation have very little in common with how eBusiness is understood today.

This stands in marked contrast, however, to what is reported by the literature. Maybe whether or not electronic communication can be of any help in product development depends on the nature of the product and what is understood by product development. Support for this interpretation came from the answers of two other experts. The expert from the paper industry very much endorsed the statement that products could be developed online, which referred to their eCommerce system and allowed customers to configure a product according to their own specifications. A similar point was made by the representative of the biochemical company. The company provides products to research labs and hospitals that can be customized by the end user on demand. Both examples show that it depends on the nature of the product (i.e., if it is configurable or not) whether or not there is an option for products to be developed online. This raises the question of why some products are configurable and others are not. This question cannot be answered fully by our findings. Maybe some products, such as chemicals, lend themselves to customization, and products used as some sort of raw material for further processing, such as the chemical substances in research labs and certain paper products, must be configured to meet the customer's requirements. Maybe the manufacturer's decision to allow the customers to define their product also depends on the size of the customer, which would make it a business decision.

The paper industry example provides evidence that a mixture of customer require-ments and the size of the customers (large accounts) are the decisive factors. The biochemical industry example, however, points in the opposite direction in terms of the size of the customer account (they enable all customers to configure their products), but also supports the "customer requirements" hypothesis and the "product nature" hypothesis. In any case, further research is needed, which means further investigations for academics. For the manufacturers, it means rethinking whether or not their products could be made configurable and whether the market would accept such an approach.

In case configurable products make no sense for either the manufacturer or for the customer, it still seems worthwhile to give electronically supported product development and evaluation a thought. With manufacturers referring to enhanced catalogs containing (or linking to) scientific findings, additional electronic resources reflecting the clinical experience might indeed bridge the gap between a business-oriented perspective and an R&D perspective. With electronic media becoming progressively commonplace and ubiquitous in daily life, and with a new computer-trained generation of people moving into decision-making positions, electronic resources will play a more pronounced role than they had in the past.

Independent or manufacturer-moderated electronic discussion forums for clinical users, or reports summarizing the daily experience of clinicians with a product that are compiled in a clinical knowledge management system are both new methods for giving customers a say. Figure 13-3 summarizes and integrates the interview results with regard to the influence electronic communication and collaboration may exert on the customer-supplier relationship.

The Future

Returning to the transaction level of eBusiness, we wanted to know how soon electronic purchasing could become a reality for a critical mass of hospitals. Just like the hospital experts, the majority of the industry experts also said that five years was a realistic and reasonable timeframe to achieve the goal.

With regard to the question of whether or not costs will continue to dominate the discussion about eBusiness, the industry experts shared the opinion of the hospital

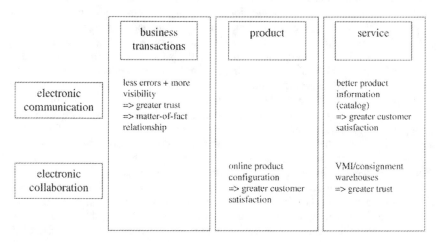

FIGURE 13-3. Summary of the potential impact of electronic communication and collaboration on the customer-supplier relationship in the areas of business transactions, the product and the services – as reported by the interview partners.

experts, who had said that cost reduction would remain the primary argument. One expert, in fact, pointed out that the quality issues—mainly data quality—came first. This entailed the reduction of transaction costs. Other experts shared this position, stating that quality issues (i.e., eBusiness positively influencing process and data quality) should be more emphasized, but conceded that they were more difficult to measure than costs. Cost reduction will still be the main focus in healthcare as well as in the paper industry—according to the experts.

eBusiness will obviously continue to be discussed as one means among many to cope with difficult conditions (e.g., cost containment measures in national healthcare systems), due to its potential to contribute to decreased costs. Could eBusiness also make business environments tougher by, for example, increasing the competition among companies? Three industry experts said "Yes.". Information retrieval would become easier for the customers because of the Web allowing purchasers to better compare products. Visibility and transparency would also increase in the future due to the greater potential of making data available for further analysis. At the same time, eBusiness was not a competitive advantage for the companies, argued other experts. Some of them clearly stated that solely the product—be it a high-quality medical device or a newly developed drug—differentiated the companies.

On the other hand, it would be rather a "competitive disadvantage not having it," as one expert phrased it, particularly in the years to come. The manufacturers thus had no choice other than to offer customers the opportunity to purchase electronically, regardless of whether or not it made business more difficult.

Competition, however, does not only affect companies. eBusiness would become a competitive advantage for those hospitals that transformed their organization into a lean structure, one industry expert predicted. This shows that hospitals have to think in business terms as well. A company's eBusiness capabilities, however, are only a competitive advantage as long as the others do not possess that same characteristic.

Another potential way for Internet-based trading to influence the market comes from its technical ability to connect suppliers and customers worldwide. Outside the healthcare industry, this had engendered global sourcing as well as serving customers 24 hours a day. Being able to serve customers in different time zones, and in areas with little sales force coverage, was a major advantage for the paper manufacturer, the expert reported. Although they would not win new customers over the Web, being able to better manage existing large customers electronically was also regarded as a great benefit by the executives, he said. In contrast to his experience, the representatives of the healthcare industry were far more reserved with regard to globalization. Legal restrictions, language problems, and the lack of local customer service were barriers the hospitals had already mentioned and were now repeated by the manufacturers. In addition, the shipping costs were too high in comparison to the purchase volume. One hospital expert had also made a similar point, saying that global sourcing made sense if you were ordering in the magnitude of shiploads.

Like so often with other issues in healthcare, the relatively small size of the healthcare-providing organizations, in combination with national health laws and regulations, make global sourcing less attractive for healthcare providers. Still, there seems to be some potential for a transnational market. One of the industry experts explained that the manufacturers must learn to think European—i.e., to address the European market as a single market despite the different national healthcare systems. An additional option would be to address regional transnational markets and establish sales organizations for certain regions. This would not solve the problem of different regulations in different countries, but could make logistics and after-sales services more convenient. Some hospitals had some experience in purchasing across borders. For example, one of the hospitals located in southwest Germany had purchased medical supplies in France, and one of the U.S. hospitals located near the Great Lakes had obtained goods from Canada.

Generally speaking, language might be a problem. It is definitely not a problem in the medical scientific community, which makes it easy for companies to distribute scientific product information globally. This is common practice, as two industry experts explained: attracting and contacting customers worldwide, but conducting business, via the sales organization of the country in which the customer is located conducting the business.

Cross-border electronic business only makes sense for those companies with no sales representatives in the other country, as was the case for the paper manufacturer in some countries. Big multinational companies, such as the ones included in this study, have subsidiaries or branches in all major industrialized countries, which makes this aspect of eBusiness less relevant for them. Things might be different for small and medium-sized enterprises striving to gain market share and targeting the international market without having the resources to establish a large sales force in each country in which the company is operating.

Table 13-1 summarizes the potential impact of eBusiness on the market, as seen from the suppliers' and the providers' point of view. In their anticipation of the future, both partners do not differ largely. Not only do they share the same predictions about the time frame, they also envisage a similar picture of the future.

The statements provided by the manufacturers also pinpoint the risks for them that are associated with eBusiness: greater visibility in the market, possibly resulting in greater competition, and erosion of prices due to customers being able to pool and analyze their data electronically. The opportunities—including increased efficiency and service orientation ("helping our customers"), coupled with a desire to demonstrate their leadership in technological innovation—are motivation enough to further drive eBusiness and shape the market.

Is There any Difference Between the Countries?

Because this is a complex issue, this question was not posed directly. The answer, therefore, has to be found in the individual statements of the experts. Due to the large spectrum of their answers, no clear country-specific patterns could be discerned. They

TABLE 13-1. The future of eBusiness in healthcare – summary of the manufacturers' and providers' perspective.

general effect	potentials factors influencing the market	Manufacturers	healthcare providers
increased	greater opportunity to compare products	yes	yes
competition	better provision of information	yes	-
competitive	eBusiness capabilities are decisive for a customer	no	potentially
advantage	eBusiness increases sales	no	-
globalisation	hospitals source globally	-	no
	serving customers in other countries	no	-
	attracting customers from abroad	yes	-
regional market	serving customers in regions	yes	-
	sourcing regionally	yes	yes

often mentioned the same achievements, concerns, and hopes. One of the areas where country-specific differences became obvious was group purchasing, as has been shown previously. To come to a final conclusion, more data need to be collected, preferably in comparative surveys.

Conclusions

The Second Wave

The days of the great promises are definitely over, and today healthcare providers and suppliers assume a down-to-earth pragmatic attitude towards eBusiness. They look back at a good amount of work and considerable success and they know what needs to be done next—with the understanding that eBusiness is the key for a number of solutions. Having started primarily as a means for process automation, eBusiness today is spawning a series of opportunities for both parties. Standardization of procurement in terms of processes and goods, greater contract compliance, and finally business analysis based on recent accurate data, spotlight the opportunities for healthcare providers. They are aware that the incentives for doing eBusiness are already there. Beyond benefiting from all steps of an electronic transaction (from order to invoice), eBusiness allows the suppliers to get into a position where they can provide more comprehensive services ("helping our customers"). These services may affect all processes within the organization, including procurement and logistics in addition to patient care, depending on the scope of the company.

Most of the experts were cautious about formulating a vision for eBusiness, and instead demonstrated a matter-of-fact pragmatism. "Let's do our homework first before we come to the future," seemed to be a motto that characterized the second wave in eBusiness.

There are also visions inspired by the achievements. For the first time, the business partners in healthcare are able to think about implementing a supply chain due to the information flow enabled by eBusiness. The enhanced catalog containing clinical and business information will become a turntable for distributing information to clinicians and purchasers at the same time.

Initial Assumptions Revisited

We wanted to know whether process automation and cost reduction are the primary motivators for eBusiness. Today, the experts have a more differentiated view when speaking about process optimization and about the number of effects accompanying and preceding cost reduction—first and foremost were accurate data and standardization of processes—which are both well understood.

Inappropriate technology does not hamper eBusiness any longer, and both parties have learned to live without technical and semantic standards. There is, however, a growing concern that eBusiness cannot do without them in the long run.

Executives supporting eBusiness are essential for managing the change within the organization, but they are not the only fathers of the success. Individuals dedicated to eBusiness and a motivated team are as much responsible for transforming the organization.

The opportunity and importance of getting access to accurate data are well understood by the suppliers. Because there is a growing demand for management information in hospitals, access to recent data is increasingly appreciated. The hospitals have only started exploiting their own data, and there are many more options for utilizing the data such as improving the supply chain and changing existing behaviors.

Electronically enabled collaboration seems to still be beyond the scope of eBusiness in healthcare. The electronic order-to-payment cycle needs to be implemented completely before other types of collaboration seem realistic. Furthermore, they definitely require the involvement of clinicians in eBusiness processes, which is an approach to be pursued more rigorously in the future.

Whether or not eBusiness actually improves the customer-supplier relationship cannot be completely clarified. It definitely does no harm. There are many good arguments for why the relationship gets better—in particular, the fact that suppliers and customers need not bicker about errors but spend time focusing on important issues, such as the product. If errors occur, they can be dealt with in a much more matter-of-fact style.

Has healthcare *arrived* in a global world? On the basis of our findings, eBusiness has not (yet) been able to globalize procurement in hospitals and will not do so unless the national regulations are harmonized—at least to some extent—and unless healthcare providers can bundle their purchase volume to a significant magnitude. In contrast with other industries, global sourcing and global competition[1] are not an issue in healthcare.

Increased competition due to eBusiness has not yet materialized, but could do so due to the greater visibility enabled by eBusiness. Our results also leaned in the direction that electronic trading capabilities are not a competitive advantage in healthcare. They will, however, become an essential for every company wishing to stay in this market.

Are There any Differences Between Healthcare Providers and Suppliers?

Healthcare providers and suppliers largely agree in their appraisal of the status quo of eBusiness and also in their predictions about future developments. This holds true particularly for the estimated time frame that eBusiness will reach a majority of users, and their prediction that cost issues will also prevail in the future. Interestingly, they also agree on the concept of financial incentives, with the majority of experts on both sides being skeptical. Despite the many reasons they give for adopting eBusiness methods, some of which are very varied, they share the opinion that eBusiness is a vehicle for transforming and optimizing processes. All the same, some issues arise regarding the marked differences between the healthcare providers' and the suppliers' view of the eBusiness arena when it comes to who should become more active, and where the barriers are.

Is the Healthcare Market Special?

Summarizing our findings, we can conclude that the healthcare market is special. The main reasons for this difference are

- Asymmetry of business partners in terms of size and IT infrastructure
- National laws and regulations
- Differences in decision-making structures and processes between healthcare providers and suppliers
- Fewer interwoven processes between the business partners than in other industries
- Customer-configured products that are discussed in the literature as one of the major opportunities of eBusiness [1] are (still) the exception rather than the rule in healthcare

These features of the healthcare market might be subject to change in the years to come, with the changes also being potentially triggered by eBusiness, among other things. How the market for medical suppliers will actually evolve needs to be monitored regularly.

---

[1] This does not mean that multinational companies are not operating globally. It instead refers to the fact that they prefer to establish branches in those countries in which they would like to do business rather than to do business globally.

From "Nice to Have" to "Must Have"

The experts made it clear that eBusiness would move from a "nice to have" to a "must have" situation, with the consequence that those who don't have it will be out of the game. This was said to be true not only for the suppliers but for the healthcare providers as well. Those still hesitating with regard to eBusiness should keep in mind that eBusiness is not only about buying some pieces of new hardware and software, but is about changing the organization and its processes. This definitely takes time—maybe even years—as it became clear in the interviews. The idea of jumping on the bandwagon once the eBusiness train has gained enough speed might sound clever at first glance, but it is short-sighted with regard to the point in time when the benefits of eBusiness methods can materialize. Only after internal processes are optimized can the new system unfold its effects—and this might be too late for those who have not yet adopted eBusiness.

References

[1] Zwass, V. (2003) Electronic Commerce and Organizational Innovation: Aspects and Opportunities. *International journal of Electronic Commerce.* **7**, 7–37.

Appendix

List of Interview Partners

Industry Experts

I also wish to thank the industry experts who participated in this study. Their names and institutions are listed in the following table:

Company Name	City	Contact
Boston Scientific Medizintechnik GmbH	Ratingen, Germany	Elke Slavik
Boston Scientific Corporate Headquarters	Natick, MA, USA	Dan Stevens
Johnson & Johnson Ethicon GmbH	Norderstedt, Germany	Karin Möller
Johnson & Johnson Europe, Middle East, Africa (EMEA)	Ascot, UK	Craig McLaren
B. Braun Melsungen AG	Melsungen, Germany	Holger Clobes
3M Deutschland GmbH	Neuss, Germany	Alfons Rathmer
Hoffmann La Roche AG	Grenzach-Wyhlen, Germany	Klaus Giokalas
Invitrogen Corporation	Carlsbad, CA, USA	Edward Pisarcheck
Felix Schoeller	Osnabrück, Germany	Frank Meyer-Niehoff

Part IV
Outlook

14
The Supply Chain Model of eBusiness in Healthcare

Ursula Hübner

Executive Summary

This chapter aims at synthesizing a model of supply chain activities within the context of eBusiness. It builds on the practical experience and incorporates visions of how eBusiness in healthcare might look in the future. It is motivated by the understanding —expressed by all experts interviewed and highlighted by the case studies—that the essence of eBusiness lies in its ability to provide structured error-free data for business analysis, and ultimately for decision-making. It further recognizes that these data result from optimized processes, and at the same time that these data allow the processes to function smoothly.

The model is developed taking the four behavioral components of eBusiness into consideration: information distribution and search, transactions, collaboration, and decision-making.

Before formulating the model, two major process-oriented supply chain management models are presented and discussed in terms of their use in healthcare. It is concluded that they may provide a suitable framework, but focus too much on manufacturing and the classical supply chain perspective of a major manufacturer with its suppliers and customers. Instead, it is proposed to describe the supply chain in healthcare from the customer's point of view, as it is the customer (namely the healthcare provider) who makes this supply chain specific to healthcare.

The supply chain model of eBusiness in healthcare that we present here integrates a process, a document, and a functional model that are all geared to the combined view of clinical and economic issues related to the procurement, provision, and use of medical supplies. To this end, the model description begins with a presentation of the healthcare value chain, supplemented by the information track that is associated with the delivery of patient care, and that finally results in a clinical outcome analysis. The first of the three submodels, the supply chain process model, is split into two parts—the strategic model and the operations model—that both distinguish between healthcare-provider and supplier-specific processes. The second model, the document model, concentrates on data related to the product and shows the various data sources, namely the documents, that become relevant in the product life cycle. Again, these documents embrace clinical as well as economic, cases of use. The document model is structured according to the product life cycle, which starts with product development and clinical trials, continues with products being purchased and used, and finally ends with the decision to replace a product. During this cycle, the main questions to be answered by the data in the various documents pertain to the quality, the costs, and the degree of innovation of the product.

The third model, the function model, integrates the process and the document models. Similar functions are grouped into layers. The function model describes the following layers: Content, Contract, Order-to-Payment, Service, Clinical Process, Clinical Outcome, and Knowledge. These layers are arranged as a stack that roughly follows the product's path from the manufacturer to the healthcare providers, where the product is used and where knowledge is accumulated about the product's clinical usefulness and the cost-to-benefit ratio.

The supply chain model of eBusiness in healthcare is meant to support practitioners in assessing how supply chain concepts and eBusiness can strengthen their organization and help them develop an appropriate strategy to achieve this goal. In applied sciences, the model is intended to stimulate further questions about what direction supply chain and eBusiness will take in the future.

So What is eBusiness About?

It may seem odd to ask this question at the end of the book rather than at the beginning. We do not think so, because we initially came up with a definition that was as generic as possible and then illuminated diverse aspects of eBusiness in healthcare during the course of the book. In the first chapter, we defined electronically supported processes originating from the business management domain as "eBusiness in healthcare," and referred to the customer/provider matrix of B2B for salient examples focusing on the supply chain and its relation to eProcurement (healthcare providers) and eCommerce (suppliers).

To date, the automation/optimization of the order-to-payment cycle dominates the understanding of what eProcurement and eCommerce mean. In contrast to earlier interpretations, experts in this field have learned to recognize eBusiness as an instrument for generating structured error-free data, and thus for reducing process errors significantly, enabling them for the first time to perform business analysis on a large scale. Against this background, eCommerce and eProcurement are not simply electronic means for automation, but are a general enabler of many other services and functionalities. This may sometimes lead to a considerable overlap of concepts and ideas. eProcurement and eCommerce, for example, are both entangled with logistics and group purchasing, and the perceived benefits of eProcurement and eCommerce are often closely associated with these functionalities.

Despite today's almost exclusive focus on transactions, one should not forget the roots of eBusiness in the 1990s, and at the same time one should not mask future developments. The first applications of eCommerce are rooted in the Web's potential to display and distribute static contents, mainly for marketing purposes. This functionality has pervaded our daily life to such a great extent that today it is rarely mentioned any longer in the context of eBusiness. Transaction issues will also disappear from the public and scientific mind as they become omnipresent.

"eBusiness beyond transactions" may embrace several dimensions, including collaboration, which is one of the most discussed issues in the literature (e.g., [1–7]). Electronically supported collaboration is not a new concept in computer science but is only emerging within eBusiness as collaborative commerce (cCommerce). It is a consequent continuation of transactions at a higher level, deliberately including human experts in their roles as researchers, analysts, developers, and decision-makers. Collaboration is the foundation of supply chain management, and the counterpart of eBusiness from the angle of forecasting and advanced planning. Both methods seek to optimize the information flow in the logistics chain, require recent and sensitive data from supply chain partners, and heavily depend on a culture of collaboration within the chain. There is more to collaboration than optimizing logistics, however—it also includes other business-critical areas such as research and development of new products. We have seen in previous chapters that these ideas are currently not yet regarded as the current focal point of eBusiness in the healthcare industry. On the other hand, many big companies maintain knowledge management systems, including document centers and communication tools for internal usage, and have acquired internal experience in electronic collaboration. This approach could be adopted without effort for the purpose of supplier-customer communication—not replacing, but rather enhancing the work of the sales force. As a result, many companies could benefit from eBusiness-enabled collaboration by knowing their customers' requirements better.

Yet another dimension emerges from "eBusiness beyond transactions." As human beings are freed from repetitive work (transactions) by eBusiness, and clinical and business data become accessible for analysis, the experts are more and more in a position to make fact-based product decisions (see Chapter 10). The electronic patient or health record (EPR and EHR) combines information about the clinical outcome with the procedures and related resources leading to that particular outcome. By employing an EPR or an EHR system, a healthcare-providing organization gathers sufficient data over time to arrive at meaningful interpretations of these data about the clinical usefulness of a product. In combination with economic data, this allows an estimation of the cost-benefit ratio for a product and gives rise to fact-based purchasing decisions. These data very much reflect the local context und usage of a product, and thus lend themselves to decisions specific for that organisation. If necessary, they can be combined with scientific findings from the world literature.

In summary, the field we simply denoted as *supply chain* in the introductory chapter (see Table 1-2) to combine eProcurement with eCommerce actually consists of the four core following behaviors:

• Information distribution and search
• Transactions
• Collaboration
• Decision-making

Describing eBusiness in such abstract components helps to develop a strategic understanding of what eBusiness may ultimately mean for an organization, and how eBusiness can contribute to the organization's overall strategy. These components will be referred to later when developing a model to describe the supply chain of eBusiness in healthcare.

Nevertheless, there are dimensions of eBusiness not yet discovered, as one of the hospital experts predicted. eBusiness will develop its own dynamics once process automation/optimization and unrestricted access to clinical and business data have unfolded to their full potential, he said.

Is There Anything to be Learned from Supply Chain Management?

Supply Chain Management in Healthcare

Although originating in the manufacturing industry, supply chain management (SCM) is a concept that is easily applicable in healthcare. It is suitable for describing the primary processes (i.e., the provision of patient care, as well as modelling procurement and order fulfilment), as was demonstrated in Chapter 2. Adopting SCM in healthcare, however, changes the perspective from manufacturing to delivery of care, and thus from the manufacturer's point of view to the customer's point of view, shifting the focus onto utilization of a product. Although many definitions of SCM emphasize the customers and their demand to be the drivers of the chain, the primary attention is given to the manufacturers' interests in managing this demand and utilizing the information for production planning. Changing the perspective to the customer, therefore, is not simply a formal act, but brings about a series of important modifications. First and foremost, the value added along the chain is not economic but patient-related and health outcome-related. Economic issues may need to be considered here, but the ultimate reason why a certain product is used for a patient is to cure the patient or improve the patient's health status. Clinical outcome—though complex in nature—is just as measurable as economic values.

While supply chains in manufacturing are often dominated by a large manufacturer contracting with smaller suppliers and dictating the terms and conditions of the cooperation, the healthcare supply chain is characterized by a reverse asymmetry of size. Even large healthcare systems in the United States, big trusts in the United Kingdom, and hospital chains in Germany are smaller than the multinational global manufacturers of medical supplies. This asymmetry is less pronounced at the level of GPOs negotiating with manufacturers, but it still exists there as well. The difference in size holds true, in particular, for the pharmaceutical industry. It concerns other suppliers of medical products to a lesser extent because there are many small and medium-sized companies in the medical devices and medical-surgical products market segments. Depending on the product, the partners, and the type of relationship, contracts at eye-level are possible.

For supply chain management to work as a complex network, the organizations involved have to be differentiated enough, which means that they have either outsourced various (noncore business) functions to external firms, or that they have defined self-contained functional units (e.g., cost centers) operating under the roof of the entire organization. If this is not the case, the supply chain is rather rudimentary and focuses on two partners only—the supplier and the healthcare provider. We have seen several examples of different types of functions outsourced, such as warehouse management and internal delivery of goods, procurement of medical supplies, and clinical consulting for pharmaceutical and other medical products. In all these cases, outsourcing had been recognized as a means to cut costs in a similar way to other industries. Chapter 2, however, also reflected the discussion that outsourcing is not a panacea and that the risks of outsourcing are also increasingly being discussed. Insourcing certain functions would turn the external supply chain into an internal one, with similar rules governing the chain but depending less on third parties.

While planning and forecasting are big motivators for companies to manage the supply chain in manufacturing, predicting the demand in healthcare is more fuzzy and therefore seems to play a more inferior role in the healthcare supply chain. With more and more hospitals introducing controlling principles, planning becomes both necessary and possible and relates to many parameters, including the number of patients in a given patient group (e.g. DRG's) and the resource consumption per group. Clinical pathways are powerful instruments for steering the materials consumption, provided they are detailed enough to contain information on the materials use with this particular type of patient. If good estimates of the number of patients per pathway exist, the overall demand is predictable. These figures must still be broken down by months, or even smaller time periods, for the purpose of demand management. These estimates are less precise by nature than forecasts in production planning due to the different types of patients to be treated.

As an alternative to predicting the demand, consumption data can be measured and the demand can be deduced retrospectively. If captured electronically at the point of care, they could be transferred directly to the supplier or to the warehouse for immediate, or nearly immediate, replenishment. Both approaches are technically feasible at present and could be employed for coping with demand management in healthcare supply chains, both externally and internally.

Supply Chain Models

Depending on one's point of view, various definitions of what a supply chain comprises are provided in the literature. In the following section we will refer to two well-known supply chain models—the Supply Chain Operations Reference-model (SCOR) and the Global Supply Chain Forum (GSCF) model—and will discuss their strengths and weaknesses with regard to healthcare prior to describing a healthcare-specific model in the final part of this chapter.

The SCOR and the GSCF model are both well recognized frameworks for process-oriented supply chain management [8] which, however, differ in their understanding of the purpose and the breadth of the model. The SCOR approach assumes a trans-action perspective and defines five major business processes as relevant to supply chain management from the transaction perspective, thereby addressing transaction efficiency, cost reduction, and asset utilisation. The five processes [9,10] are

1. Plan (demand and supply planning and management)
2. Source (the raw materials)
3. Make (plan production and produce)
4. Deliver (all steps in the order to payment cycle)
5. Return (the raw materials to the supplier or receive returned goods from the customer)

and primarily refer to manufacturing, as becomes evident by the process titles. These five processes are further detailed by SCOR, making reference to the operations strategy of a company. Applied to healthcare, the number of relevant processes would be reduced to three to four out of the five, namely Plan (if possible), Source (medical supplies), Deliver patient care (which would be a mixture of Make and Deliver in the original model) and Return (defect materials). Returns management would be simpler because it would cover only the defect items returned to the supplier. In a wider sense, however, unplanned readmission of patients could be also subsumed by this process or would become a process of its own. Due to its background in manufacturing, the entire SCOR strongly builds upon a proper planning process. As a result, SCOR processes can only be partly translated into healthcare.

In contrast to SCOR, the GSCF framework first and foremost addresses relationship management and the economic added value, and puts less emphasis on transactional efficiency. It thus emphasises the overall corporate strategy rather than the operations strategy, as does SCOR. GSCF [11] defines eight processes that partly overlap with SCOR. Each of the processes is composed of strategic and operational subprocesses. They are

1. Customer relationship management
2. Customer service management
3. Demand management
4. Order fulfilment
5. Manufacturing flow management
6. Product development and commercialization
7. Supplier relationship management
8. Returns management

The main differences with SCOR are "supplier and customer relationship" and "product development and commercialization." As with SCOR, the GSCF framework originates in manufacturing and therefore similar problems occur when transferring the approach to healthcare without modification. In the following section, we will therefore suggest a supply chain model that takes the constraints of healthcare into account—i.e., the customer's perspective, a prediction of the demand based on fuzzy data, and less complex supply chains than in other industries.

The Supply Chain Model of eBusiness in Healthcare

Introduction

Modelling eBusiness in healthcare naturally has to consider the primary processes in healthcare, namely the provision of patient care. This is the reason for repeating the healthcare value chain as presented in Chapter 2. For a hospital, the internal value chain covers admission, diagnostic procedures, therapeutic procedures and nursing care, and discharge management (see Figure 14-1). In addition to the original model, we now add a second track that explicitly specifies the data and information value chain. Typically, this track is hidden in the original value chain because it is an integral part of it.

To achieve the best possible outcome for a patient, and to avoid harm, more and more hospitals are formalizing the way data are gathered and how information is exploited by utilizing quality assurance instruments such as clinical pathways, multidisciplinary electronic documentation (EPR/EHR), and measurable outcomes. They are all closely linked with regard to their goal of enabling transparency and accountability by building upon standards and allowing data analysis.

Proper clinical documentation, using critical clinical outcome parameters, is a means of steering the clinical process and ultimately accruing clinical knowledge. This knowledge embraces knowledge about utilizing resources in the process and therefore also includes products, their usage, and evidence about their effectiveness and usefulness. In particular, analyzing the variance of a clinical pathway yields good evidence about the performance of a product (e.g., medicine, medical devices) and its potential contribution to the deviation from the path. As one of the industry experts stated in the interviews,

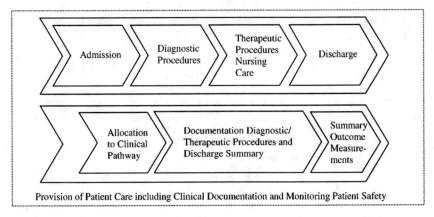

FIGURE 14-1. The health care value chain – the purview of a single health care provider.

the EPR and the EHR will play a central role in eBusiness due to their capacity for relating product information to clinical information.

Support or auxiliary processes are distinguished from primary processes in healthcare because they do not focus on patient care but rather support its provision, as was shown in Chapter 2. From the hospital's perspective, procurement definitely belongs to the support processes but is closely interwoven with the primary processes (clinical processes), as far as medical supplies are concerned (see Chapter 10).

While the value chain concept allows the sketching of a grand picture and, at the same time, scrutiny of those parts of the chain where value is added, the supply chain concept focuses on the supply. We have discussed the strengths and weaknesses of the SCOR and GSCF models as applied to healthcare, and have arrived at the conclusion that both approaches may stimulate the creation of a healthcare model but are too much geared to highly predictable processes to be adopted in healthcare exactly as they are. In accordance with the intention of the book, we focus on eProcurement and eCommerce and propose a supply chain model of eBusiness in healthcare that expands on eProcurement and eCommerce issues and incorporates healthcare-specific issues derived from the healthcare value chain.

In contrast to pure economic models of supply chain management, which often describe the activities (including those taking place further up or down the supply chain) from the perspective of a central partner of the supply chain with his suppliers and customers, we seek to describe the supply chain from the customer's point of view— namely, the one of the healthcare provider. It is our aim to embrace all issues that affect the customer and the supplier, but first and foremost we address the product and its contribution to the clinical process and the clinical outcome. This widens the perspective from making and providing a product to issues of using it to generate clinical value added (CVA). In fact, it is the customer perspective that makes our supply chain model specific to healthcare. Based on these assumptions, we propose the supply chain model of eBusiness in healthcare

a) to demonstrate that supply chain activities in healthcare extend into the clinical realm and that there is no friction between purchasing/materials management and patient care, and

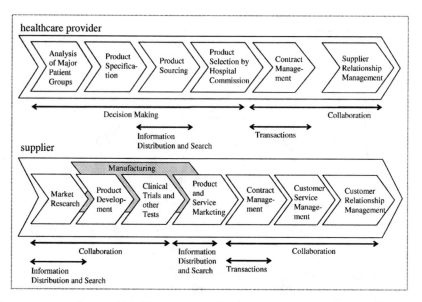

FIGURE **14-2.** The supply chain from the strategic perspective.

b) to explain the full range of the supply chain of medical-surgical and pharmaceutical products, from attracting the customers and raising their interest about a product, to evaluating, using, and reevaluating the product and preparing the ground for decisions about purchasing the product in the future.

The model is comprised of processes, documents, and functions. All models are validated against the four behavioral components of eBusiness, which serve as an overarching structure for the models.

The Processes

Based on the understanding that supply chain management possesses a corporate strategy dimension and an operations dimension, we divide the process model into two parts. The first one describes strategic/tactical issues that cover a long-term and medium-term period (see Figure 14-2), while the second one describes operational and short-term issues directly related to ordering and order fulfilment (see Figure 14-3). Both figures also show the correlation of the different subprocesses with the four behavioral components of eBusiness (see Figures 14-2 and 14-3).

Any supply chain is triggered by demand. In healthcare, forecasting the precise demand in a certain period is more difficult than in other industries, and very often demand management is done on an ad hoc basis. More and more healthcare providers, however, recognize the benefit of planning and therefore retrospectively analyze the major patient groups they have treated, together with the resource consumption per group. As a result of this analysis, the healthcare provider might specialize in treating particular patient groups, or at least define those groups that will not be treated any longer by this particular institution. This has implications on the products to be used and, among other things, defines what products will be used and, in the best case, what specifications these products have. If the process is performed systematically, a

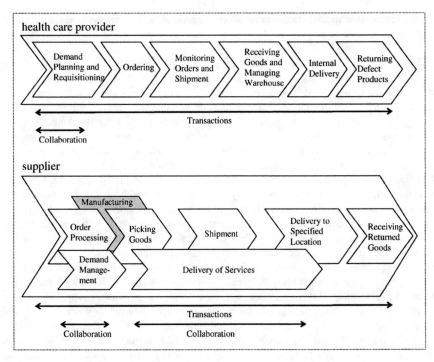

FIGURE 14-3. The supply chain from the operations perspective.

series of products is sourced and tested, with the test results influencing the decisions made by the hospital commission on what items will be put on the list of preferred products. Depending on the product, contracts covering the terms and conditions of order fulfilment, the services including support, and other issues such as collaboration and information exchange, are negotiated with suppliers and/or with GPOs. In this sense, contracts are necessary prerequisites for transactions and collaboration.

If the contract has been negotiated with a strategic supplier, both parties are often bound beyond mere order fulfilment. This situation requires systematic supplier relationship management.

The suppliers, on the other hand, try to keep in close contact with their customer base and the market in general. If they do this systematically, they perform a market analysis that shows what products are needed. Products are developed accordingly and must undergo a formal regime of clinical trials and testing before they are officially approved. Only then are they marketed. This holds true primarily for drugs and medical devices. Keeping in close contact with customers for a better understanding of market needs, product development, and product evaluation (clinical trials) may all be done in a collaborative manner, involving customers and other companies and utilizing electronic means.

At a strategic level, framework contracts with customers are negotiated. As more and more suppliers enhance their products through services, customer service management becomes vital for a company and is therefore included in the model. Parallel to the healthcare providers, the suppliers also seek to stay in contact with the other side and therefore maintain special customer relationship programs. This not only aims at binding customers but also at staying in close touch with the market and its need for new and improved products.

The descriptions show that several of the GSCF processes were adopted in our healthcare-specific strategic supply chain model because the GSCF approach emphasizes the corporate strategy and long-term aspects.[1] *Product development and commercialization, customer service management,* and *customer/supplier relationship management* were directly included because they reflect long-term issues of a supply chain. *Demand management, order fulfilment,* and *returns management* are covered by the operations model. New and healthcare-specific processes mainly concern the healthcare provider side, and relate to those strategic processes of outlining the demand for a product and finally selecting one to be put on the hospital list of preferred products. *Contract management* is an essential in any supply chain, and was therefore added on both sides. The closer the supply chain partners are, and the greater the intimacy in sharing critical information, the more sophisticated the contract must be as well as the monitoring of contract compliance. *Market research* and *clinical trials and other tests* were added to our model on the supplier side. *Market research,* in fact, corresponds to *customer relationship management* in terms of its capacity to systematically prepare *product development. Clinical trials and other tests* is a healthcare-specific feature of the model. *Product [...] commercialization* became *product marketing* and was supplemented by *service.* Strategic issues of *manufacturing* are included because they are part of any supply chain. However, if the manufacturer and processes relevant to manufacturing are to be analyzed utilizing the classical supply chain, management models (such as developed by the GSCF) might be more appropriate. Thus *manufacturing* appears in the models but is not expanded on further.

The strategy model is supplemented by the operations model (see Figure 14-3), which primarily reflects the order-to-payment cycle (thus mirroring the *transactions* component), including demand management and the delivery of services associated with the product (both referring to the *collaboration* component). It is this model that describes all transactions associated with order fulfilment, and relates to both the physical flow of goods and the physical and virtual flow of information. Because these processes have been presented and discussed in great detail in the previous chapters, we will not describe them further. In parallel with the strategy model, we also added *manufacturing* in the operations model for reasons of completeness, but without providing any details. The processes in our model largely match the demand management, order fulfilment, and returns management processes in the GSCF model, and the deliver and return processes in the SCOR model.

The Documents

As has been demonstrated in the previous chapters over and over again, eBusiness is an enabler for generating, accessing, and analyzing data. Product data may appear in quite different documents needed for different purposes. Nevertheless, the documents

---

[1] The GSCF framework also includes operational subprocesses related to the strategic subprocesses. It would therefore be wrong to assume that GSCF neglects the operational side. Its general approach, however, aims at long-term relationships between customers and suppliers and looks at processes that support this type of relationship [8].

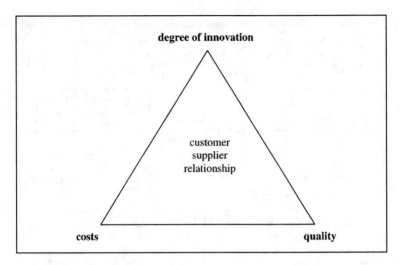

FIGURE 14-4. Product characteristics defining the customer-supplier relationship.

refer to the same product. Information derived from documents that accompany the product along the supply chain on its way from the manufacturer to the patient is the key element of the document model.

In fact, information about a product must answer the basic questions about the quality, costs, and degree of innovation of the product. This is described as the quality-cost-innovation triangle that defines the field of forces in which eBusiness is operating (see Figure 14-4 and Figure 1-6).

The pieces of information reflected in each corner of the triangle have been kept separately and used by different professions. As patient care is forced to meet the demand for high quality combined with cost efficiency, information about all aspects of a product has to be made accessible for clinical and management decision-making. Against the background of the rapid changes in the medical world, new results from clinical and technical research, and new products coming into the marketplace, there is a constant demand to cope with innovation again at the level of both clinical and management decision-making. Information about the performance of a product during the clinical process, and about the outcome of a treatment and its costs, is the only way of coming to practical conclusions about how to deal with new innovative products and procedures in the clinical day-to-day routine.

The documents constituting the data sources (see Figure 14-5) are grouped around the product in a circle, with the entry point at the upper right corner describing the beginning of the product life cycle when clinical trials have been finished successfully, the product is approved, and it is being marketed. Product data are published on the Web and in catalogs. Suppliers and healthcare providers negotiate a contract. Once customers actually order the product, its data are passed on during the various stages of order fulfilment. When used in the treatment of an individual patient, the product data are documented in the medical record if clinically useful and/or required by health regulations. Because measuring the clinical outcome is gaining importance, various statistics can be computed from data in the medical records, including outcomes grouped according to different criteria such as DRG, treatment type, and age. These results feed

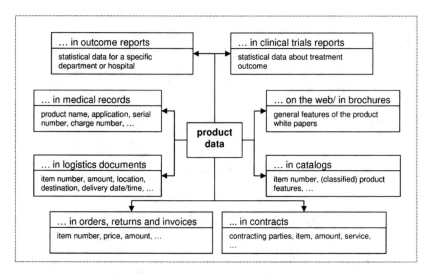

FIGURE 14-5. Sources containing references to product data.

the hospital's personal knowledge base and can be used for quality reports, refining clinical pathways, and defining the hospital catalog of preferred products. The product is used unless the clinical knowledge base provides evidence of problems indicating the need to look for alternative products.

As with the process model, there is a strong linkage to the four behavioral components of eBusiness. *Information distribution and search* is the underlying idea of putting product information on the Web or in brochures, as well as in catalogs. Likewise, catalogs, contracts, orders, return documents, invoices, and logistics documents (basic logistics) constitute the major documents of *transactions*. Contracts and logistics documents (for advanced logistics services) are further subsumed by the *collaboration* component, as is the *medical record*. Outcome reports and summary reports of product evaluations (e.g., clinical trials) are essential for *decision-making*. Evaluation reports may result from *collaborative* work between manufacturers and healthcare providers.

Among the four components, *decision-making* is the key to any other activities. Product data contained in the various documents (see Figure 14-5) become information to be used in decision-making when they are employed to reduce uncertainty and to come to conclusions. Decisions about a product are made at various levels: 1) whether it is found generally suitable in treating a certain type of disease and thus included in clinical pathways, 2) whether it is included in the hospital's catalog of preferred products and used in contracts with the suppliers, and 3) whether it is actually used with a specific patient.

The documents containing these data need not be electronic—they can still be paper-based or can even exist only in the expert's mind. The amount of data and the depth of information derived from these data, and thus the complexity of the possible data analyses, grow exponentially with each step. Consequently, the use of computerized systems to manage the data and analyze them is unavoidable. This is where eBusiness comes in.

The document model is a high-level model. If necessary, it can be combined with a data model or an information model. Among the information models discussed in healthcare and in business, only a few allow for a coherent combination of clinical and commercial aspects. HL7's reference information model (see Chapter 4) is an approach that aims at providing a comprehensive description of the field as a basis for exchanging messages, and also covers business transactions and related items. It includes *invoice elements*, *financial transactions*, *financial contracts*, and *supplies* in its Act model and incorporates *materials* (-> Manufactured Material -> Device and Container) in its Entity model. It is less strong with regard to logistics and the product catalog (see Chapter 6) and, compared to the elaborate list of data items included in the various eBusiness standards, it is less explicit. HL7's intention for combining clinical and business elements, however, is clear. The model is therefore suitable (in principle) for describing eBusiness-related information, and may supplement the document model.

The Functions

When looking at eBusiness more thoroughly at the beginning of this chapter, we identified the four behavioral components: information distribution and search, transactions, collaboration, and decision-making. So far, practical applications of eBusiness have integrated certain of the components while ignoring others. Contents on the Web, order and invoice management are examples of well recognized functions in eBusiness, while the use of medical records and outcome analyses are regarded as future applications.

In the following sections, we will use the terms *application* and *function* as synonyms to denote realizations of the four behavioral components. A component may generate several functions, and a function may refer to several components. Groups of functions form a layer. They are self-contained entities pertaining to the focus of interest, and eventually to the electronic system for managing the data, with interdependencies among each other.

The layer model of eBusiness functions (see Figure 14-6) consists of seven non-hierarchical layers that are arranged in a stack. The sequence of the layers roughly follows the product path from attracting customers to gathering knowledge about a product through usage and evaluation. The seven layers are called Contents, Contract, Order-to-Payment, Service, Clinical Process, Clinical Outcome, and Knowledge.

In addition to the document model, the layer model explicitly describes the context in which the data are used, and what components characterize the context of their usage (see Table 14-1). The data of the product life cycle (document model) translate directly into the layers as shown in Figure 14-6. Similarly, the process model can be mapped to the function model (see Figure 14-6). For this purpose, the processes were broken up to be able to match the subprocesses to the functions. Subprocesses from the healthcare value chain (information value chain), from the strategic and operational supply chain models, were combined depending on the focus of the layer. Likewise, healthcare provider and supplier subprocesses were brought together on those layers where appropriate. Supplier and customer relationship management may affect all layers and therefore not shown specifically in the diagram (Figure 14-6). In the best case, all functions benefit from sustainable trusting relationships that are directed towards maximizing the CVA.

The *contents* layer comprises all applications that inform a potential customer and the public about the product. The applications are derived from the *information distribution and search* component. Its preferred technical mode for conveying the information are Web pages, which allow for easy updates of the contents, wide distribution information,

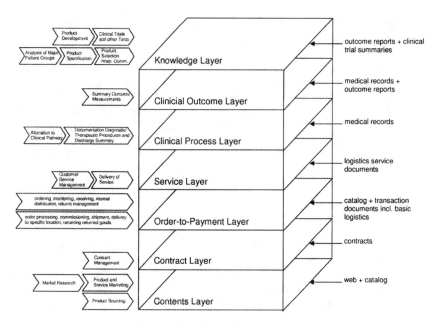

FIGURE 14-6. Stack of function layers.

and good search capabilities. Applications in the contents layer can be evaluated by how well they achieve information distribution, in terms of visitors per page or links to this site, and how well the information is presented and can be navigated. Technologies for providing contents on the Web are broadly available, and there is a huge amount of experience with these technologies. In fact, eBusiness started with this type of application, and the first wave of eBusiness very much focused on attracting customers through easily accessible information.

The *contract* layer is an interim layer between the contents layer and the order-to-payment layer that embraces all contract issues related to transactions and collaboration—in particular, those that concern financial issues. The contract is usually the result of the negotiation process, which may include tendering and bidding activities. Questions about who is going to pay for what product, and what service is provided under what terms and conditions, are dealt with on this layer. These activities cover more than just the product price and discount rates on orders of certain amounts. In a mature supply chain relationship, these contracts are needed to describe the business interaction between the healthcare provider and the supplier, and the guarantees given by both sides. In fact, there are no limits as to what may be covered by such contracts, including, for example, guaranteed minimum amounts (customer), time of payment (customer) and margins (customer) or price and delivery times (supplier), low error rates during the transaction process (supplier), and even clinical performance of a product (supplier) These were covered in Chapter 10. Common goals such as joint endeavors to curb costs on both sides can be shared, including sharing the savings. Contracts may regulate the provision of mutual access to internal information. This may help suppliers better manage production resources by getting real-time data on demand, and may also help healthcare providers monitor the product quality and delivery capacity of the

TABLE 14-1. Characteristics of the seven layers.

| Layer | Characteristics | | | |
	Focus of Interest	Performance Metrics (examples)	Technology	Impact
Contents	Availability of up to date product information	Number of visitors, number of links to page, user satisfaction	Web pages/ Content Management Systems	The informed customer and consumer
Contract	Contract (price, margins, clinical performance of product)	Time lag between billing and paying, degree of contract fulfilment	ERP Systems	Risk sharing, customer- supplier relationship
Order-to-Payment	Process automation	Number of errors, transaction time, process costs, customer satisfaction	Exchanges	Increased productivity and efficiency
Service	Inventory management and delivery, user training, product services	Number and volume of stock items, delivery time, customer satisfaction	Mobile clients, specific systems	Outsourcing, focusing on core business areas, enhancing product use
Clinical process	Process support	Process time and costs, staff satisfaction, patient satisfaction	EPR/EHR Systems	Patient safety, patient costing, cost effective delivery of care
Clinical outcome	Improvement of the patient's health status	Number of complications and unplanned re-admissions, patient satisfaction, degree of reaching clinical goals	EPR/EHR Systems	Patient safety, quality of life
Knowledge	Clinical decision making, product decision-making	Number of studies, degree of evidence	Knowledge Management Systems	Evidence-based purchasing, personalized evidence

supplier—as is very common in other industries. It is vital, however, that the attainment of these goals is measurable, that eBusiness is capable of providing the necessary data and, finally, that there is enough trust between the parties to exchange these data. It also ultimately touches on issues about who is the actual customer and who should therefore be included in the contract—is it the healthcare provider, the health insurance company, or the patient? Admittedly, activities on this layer are rather rudimentary so far, but with the increasing availability of data on all layers of the supply chain, contract issues will become more sophisticated in the future.

Because contracts are the prerequisite of any kind of transaction and collaboration, functions on this layer are derived from the *transaction* and *collaboration* components.

The *order-to-payment* layer describes the next step of eBusiness, meaning electronic approaches for automating the order-to-payment process using Internet-based technologies. It combines functions related to the *transaction* component. The Internet and its TCP/IP protocol are the common denominator for a vast variety of technical solutions necessary for connecting customers to their suppliers. Although there are all sorts of direct links between the business partners, the preferred route of communication is through an exchange or a hub that connects the systems and guarantees clean data that can be automatically interpreted at both ends. Process automation leads to a reduction of the process costs and the process time, and it enhances the quality of the process in terms of producing less errors and requiring less time for error handling. These features of process automation are directly measurable. In addition, error-free transactions can translate into a good customer-supplier relationship. Although more difficult to measure than other benefits of automated transactions, customer satisfaction is an indicator for the quality of the customer-supplier relationship. As the previous chapters have reflected, eBusiness in healthcare is currently very much concerned with transaction management, and this will continue in the years to come.

The *service* layer is separated from the transaction layer, although there is some overlap with regard to logistics. While basic logistics are subsumed by the order-to-payment layer, dedicated logistics services are part of the service layer—in particular, those require an intensive exchange of information and build on collaborative structures. The *collaboration* component thus influences functions provided in this context.

By logistics services, we mean specific services enabled by eBusiness, which include different types of inventory management (i.e., VMI, consignment warehouses, automatic replenishment, distribution centers) and goods delivery (i.e., JIT). The main goal is to reduce the number of stock items without compromising the availability of the goods. The performance of applications and services on this layer are measured, among others, by the number and volume of stock items, by the delivery time, and also by scales of customer satisfaction. The strategy behind contracting logistics services aims to outsource support processes and concentrate on core business areas, which in healthcare means focusing on the delivery of patient care. Apart from logistics, any other type of service is included in this function layer as well. Manufacturers often offer dedicated user training on the product, or direct services for customizing and maintaining the product, if it requires such support. In fact, there is no limit as to what services might be offered to enhance the product and its use.

The *clinical process* layer describes applications supporting the quality of the clinical process, particularly the EPR and EHR in conjunction with a workflow management system. We explicitly refer to clinical documentation as a means to enhance the process quality by supporting communication and collaboration. In the context of eBusiness, we focus on those issues of documentation in which medical-surgical and pharmaceutical products are involved. This effectively starts with a physician ordering a diagnostic or therapeutic procedure. Physician order entry systems (POES) are increasingly employed to support this activity electronically. These systems feed directly into the EPR/EHR. In fully integrated hospital information systems (HIS_h), ordering a procedure can trigger a requisition for the drugs and material used in this procedure, and put it through to the materials management or pharmacy system. This works in a straightforward way in the case of ordering drugs, implants, devices, and procedures with defined sets and procedure kits. It is not applicable to single commodities that are not related to a patient, and which are subsumed in a lump sum for patient costing methods.

Once the communication route between EPR/EHR and the materials management and pharmacy system has been established, and physician orders have been routed through, information on the products, such as serial number and charge number, can be directly returned. This adds to the safety of the clinical process and to improving accountability.

There is yet another aspect to the clinical process. Not only do electronic systems support the handling of materials during the clinical process, but also the materials

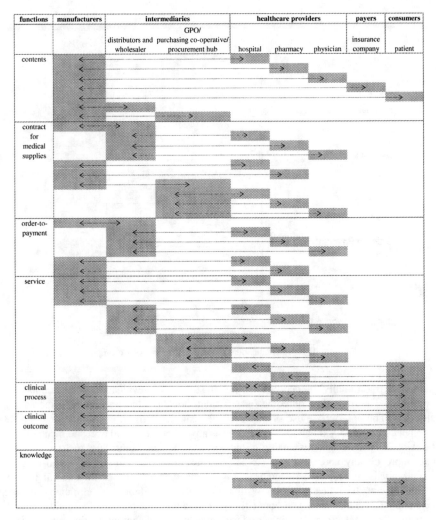

FIGURE 14-7. Function layers and typical stakeholders involved – examples .

themselves contribute to the efficacy and time of the process. These are, in fact, clinical parameters with a high economic impact and should influence the choice of a product as much as the price does. The problem, however, arises when measuring the effect of the product on the clinical process. Clinical trials should, therefore, not just look at outcome but also look at the process variables.

Due to the dual nature of the clinical process layer, applications may be derived both from the *collaboration* component (materials requisitioned/ordered via the EPR), as well as from the *decision-making* component (How well does a product support the clinical process?).

These considerations directly lead to the *clinical outcome* layer, which is strongly influenced by the *decision-making* component. Clinical outcomes of a treatment are

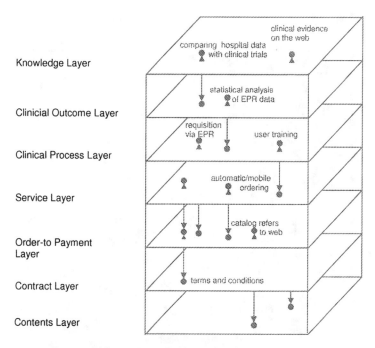

Knowledge Layer

Clinicial Outcome Layer

Clinical Process Layer

Service Layer

Order-to Payment
Layer

Contract Layer

Contents Layer

FIGURE 14-8. Interdependencies between the layers – examples.

measured traditionally in dedicated clinical studies for evaluation of a product or procedure. The individual outcome for a patient, however, has been gaining increasing attention. The appropriate use of the right medication, of the right device, or the right implant contributes as much to the outcome as any other factor and needs to be analyzed. Modern EPR/EHR systems enable clinicians and medical controllers to look at these data more closely and on a regular basis. Thus, not only short-term but also long-term analysis of the clinical outcome, taking into account the entire clinical history of the patient, becomes possible. With these results available, the clinicians get the necessary fact-based evidence about the performance of a product for making better decisions when selecting a product, and for vindicating and communicating this decision throughout the organization. In addition to clinical studies, which provide general evidence about the clinical effectiveness of a product, information derived from clinical routine data constitutes a type of evidence that is personalized for the organization and helps individuals make the right clinical and business decision. Not only can outcomes be made explicit, but also any piece of clinical knowledge about a product. This can be stored and provided electronically. Knowledge management systems (KMS) serve to manage documents, personal notes, and discussion forums around dedicated topics and may well be employed for this purpose in healthcare enterprises. Using this technology, they can build upon the large body of experience with these systems in other industries. Systems and methods supporting the generation of evidence and collection of knowledge are subsumed under the *knowledge* layer of this model. It is the most advanced and challenging of all seven layers, with a bearing on the clinical and economic decision-making of an organization. Dedicated decision support systems will emerge and assist in these efforts. Applications on the knowledge layer will generate the appropriate input for product decisions, taking economic as well as clinical facts into consideration. This clearly associates these functions with the *decision-making* component.

We distinguish between different stakeholders associated with each layer, and follow the scheme proposed in Chapter 2 (Figure 2-16) for illustrating the interaction between them. In contrast to the interaction scheme of Chapter 2, which depicts the information exchange, we show the collaboration (see Figure 14-7) between the stakeholders with regard to the functions.

Though distinct in nature, the seven layers communicate with each other (see Figure 14-8) and form an entirety that describes both the current status of eBusiness in healthcare and outlines a vision of how data used and provided on each layer can steer decision-making and organizational behavior towards a rational approach.

Conclusions

Summary

In summary, the supply chain model of eBusiness in healthcare aims

a) to pinpoint the importance of data, their availability and role in delivering the information base for decision-making
b) to address quality, cost and innovation issues
c) to maintain a focus on the CVA generated during patient care

The model integrates aspects of procuring and delivering medical supplies into the overall healthcare value chain and formalizes the request for delivering "the right product at the right time at the right price to the right patient."

The supply chain model of eBusiness in healthcare is meant to support practitioners in assessing how supply chain concepts and eBusiness can strengthen their organization and help them develop an appropriate strategy to achieve this goal. In applied sciences, the model is intended to stimulate further questions about what direction supply chain and eBusiness will take in the future.

References

[1] Wang, S. and N. Archer. (2004) Supporting collaboration in business-to-business electronic marketplaces. *Information Systems and e-Business Management.* 2, 269–286.
[2] Hartono, E. and C. Holsapple. (2004) Theoretical foundations for collaborative commerce research and practice. *Information Systems and e-Business Management.* 2, 1–30.
[3] Markus, M. L. and E. Christiaanse. (2003) Adoption and impact of collaboration electronic marketplaces. *Information Systems and e-Business Management.*1,139–155.
[4] Spekman, R. and A. Harahsheh. (2006) *Collaborative E-Commerce: Shaping The Future Of Partnerships In The Heathcare Industry.* University of Virginia: Charlottesville. Available from Social Science Research Network: <http://ssrn.com/abstract=910093> [Accessed 30 October 2006].
[5] Chu, C.-H., C.-J. Chang, and H.-C. Cheng. (2006) Empirical Studies on Inter-Organizational Collaborative Product Development. *Journal of Computing and Information Science in Engineering.* 6, 179–187.
[6] Yoon, H. S. and I.-W. G. Kwon. (2006) The roles of electronic marketplace for buyer-supplier relationship: collaborative system architecture. *International Journal of Services and Operations Management.* 2, 335–351.

[7] Catalán, J. (2005) Collaborative commerce: A possible route to a new market harmony. *Journal of Medical Marketing*. **5**, 66–73.

[8] Lambert, D. M., S. J. García-Dastugue, and K. L. Croxton. (2005) An evaluation of process-oriented supply chain management frameworks. *Journal of Business Logistics*. **26**, 25–51.

[9] Supply Chain Council (2006) *SCOR V 8.0 Overview Booklet*. Washington. Available from: <http://www.supply-chain.org/page.ww?name=SCOR+8.0+Download+Thank+You&section=SCOR+Model> [Accessed 30 October 2006].

[10] Supply Chain Council (2006) *SCOR V 8.0 Quick Reference*. Washington. Available from: <http://www.supply-chain.org/page.ww?name=SCOR+8.0+Download+Thank+You&section=SCOR+Model> [Accessed 30 October 2006].

[11] Lambert, D. M. (2006) *Supply Chain Management: Processes, Partnerships, Performance*. Sarasota: Supply Chain Management Institute.

Subject Index

Health Informatics Series
(formerly Computers in Health Care)

(continued from page ii)

Health Informatics Series
(formerly Computers in Health Care)

Consumer Informatics
Applications and Strategies in Cyber Health Care
R. Nelson and M.J. Ball

Public Health Informatics and Information Systems
P.W. O'Carroll, W.A. Yasnoff, M.E. Ward, L.H. Ripp,
and E.L. Martin

Advancing Federal Sector Health Care
A Model for Technology Transfer
P. Ramsaroop, M.J. Ball, D. Beaulieu, and J.V. Douglas

Medical Informatics
Computer Applications in Health Care and Biomedicine, Second Edition
E.H. Shortliffe and L.E. Perreault

Filmless Radiology
E.L. Siegel and R.M. Kolodner

Cancer Informatics
Essential Technologies for Clinical Trials
J.S. Silva, M.J. Ball, C.G. Chute, J.V. Douglas, C.P. Langlotz, J.C. Niland,
and W.L. Scherlis

Clinical Information Systems
A Component-Based Approach
R. Van de Velde and P. Degoulet

Implementing an Electronic Health Record System
J.M. Walker, E.J. Bieber, and F. Richards

Knowledge Coupling
New Premises and New Tools for Medical Care and Education
L.L. Weed

Healthcare Information Management Systems
Cases, Strategies, and Solutions, Third Edition
M.J. Ball, C.A. Weaver, and J.M. Kiel

Organizational Aspects of Health Informatics, Second Edition
Managing Technological Change
N.M. Lorenzi and R.T. Riley

Information Technology Solutions for Healthcare
K. Zieliński, M. Duplaga, and D. Ingram

Healthcare Knowledge Management
Issues, Advances, and Successes
R.K. Bali and A.N. Dwivedi

e-Business in Health care
U. Hübner and M.A. Elmhorst

Printed in the United States
91678LV00001B/142-195/A